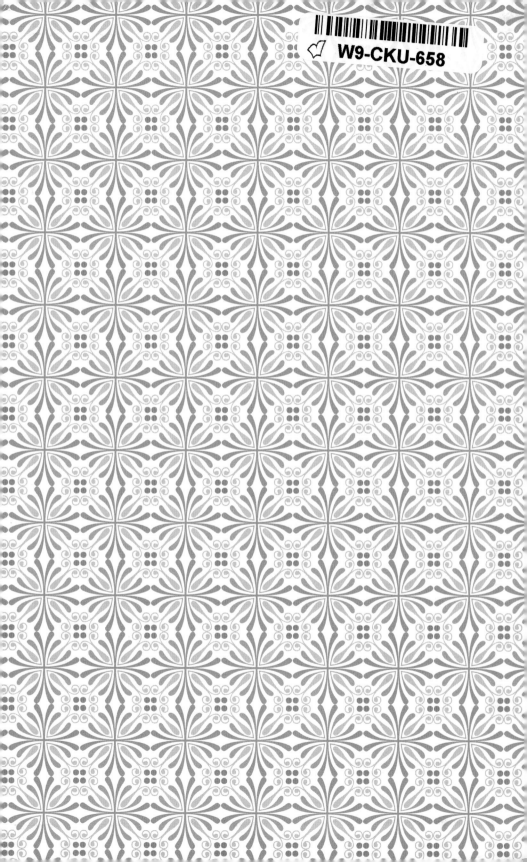

The Book of

Mis-
information

Publications International, Ltd.

Contributing writer: Caroline Delbert

Cover and interior art: Images from Alamy, ClipArt, Jupiterimages Unlimited, ThinkStock and Shutterstock.com

Louis Weber, CEO
Publications International, Ltd.
8140 Lehigh Avenue
Morton Grove, IL 60053

Permission is never granted for commercial purposes.

ISBN: 978-1-64030-155-9

Manufactured in China.

8 7 6 5 4 3 2 1

This publication is only intended to provide general information. The information is specifically not intended to be substitute for medical diagnosis or treatment by your physician or other healthcare professional. You should always consult your own physician or other healthcare professionals about any medical questions, diagnosis, or treatment. (Products vary among manufacturers. Please check labels carefully to confirm that the products you use are appropriate for your condition.)

Contents

✳ ✳ ✳ ✳

A Real Head-Scratcher ✦ History's Lady Pirates ✦ Unlucky Friday the 13th ✦ Don't Mess With Her! ✦ Scarlet Woman ✦ It's Over There–The Real Battle of Bunker Hill ✦ Culture and History of the Cherokee ✦ Famous Figures in Ghost Research ✦ Who Cracked the Liberty Bell? ✦ Will the Real Buccaneers Please Stand Up? ✦ The Democratic-Republic Party ✦ Early Settlers Use First Nation Tribes as Scapegoat ✦ Exposing the Sundance Kid ✦ Remember the Alamo, Correctly ✦ With a Whistle in His Hand ✦ A Real Bag Lady ✦ The Genuine Cowgirl Lifestyle ✦ King Henry VIII's Children ✦ We Know Them . . . Or Do We? ✦ "Lady" Loch Ness ✦ Revolutionary Leader Loses His Head ✦ King Henry VIII's Wives ✦ Maiden Voyage ✦ The Men Behind the Beheadings ✦ Pride and . . . Ööps! ✦ Hip, Happening Florence ✦ Peace Churches: Anabaptists and Quakers ✦ Working For The Man In Olde England ✦ Julius Caeser: Rome's Greatest Emperor? ✦ Ghost Towns of The Ancients ✦ Were Roman Gladiators Condemned by Their Audiences? ✦ Neanderthal Man ✦ I, Claudia, Trophy Wife ✦ Lords of the Rising Sun ✦ Brains and Brawn ✦ Wisconsin's Federal Fearmonger ✦ Rural 1920s America

Chapter 1

Movie Magic

Anything but Splendor: Natalie Wood

The official account of Natalie Wood's tragic death is riddled with holes. For this reason, cover-up theorists continue to run hog-wild with conjecture. Here's a sampling of the questions, facts, and assertions surrounding the case.

※　※　※　※

A Life in Pictures

THERE ARE THOSE who will forever recall Natalie Wood as the adorable child actress from *Miracle on 34th Street* (1947) and those who remember her as the sexy but wholesome grown-up star of movies such as *West Side Story* (1961), *Splendor in the Grass* (1961), and *Bob & Carol & Ted & Alice* (1969). Both groups generally agree that Wood had uncommon beauty and talent.

Wood appeared in her first film, *Happy Land* (1943), in a bit part alongside other people from her hometown of Santa Rosa, California, where the film was shot. She stood out to the director, who remembered her later when he needed to cast a child in another film. Wood was uncommonly mature and professional for a child actress, which helped her make a relatively smooth transition to ingenue roles.

Although Wood befriended James Dean and Sal Mineo—her troubled young costars from *Rebel Without a Cause* (1955)—

and she briefly dated Elvis Presley, she preferred to move in established Hollywood circles. By the time she was 20, she was married to Robert Wagner and was costarring with Frank Sinatra in *Kings Go Forth* (1958), which firmly ensconced her in the Hollywood establishment.

The early 1960s represent the high point of Wood's career, and she specialized in playing high-spirited characters with determination and spunk. She added two more Oscar nominations to the one she received for *Rebel* and racked up five Golden Globe nominations for Best Actress.

This period also proved to be personally turbulent for Wood, as she suffered through a failed marriage to Wagner and another to Richard Gregson. After taking time off to raise her children, she remarried Wagner and returned to her acting career with gusto.

Shocking News

And so, on November 29, 1981, the headline hit the news-wires much like an out-of-control car hits a brick wall. Natalie Wood, the beautiful, vivacious 43-year-old star of stage and screen, had drowned after falling from her yacht the *Splendour*, which was anchored off California's Santa Catalina Island. Wood had been on the boat during a break from her latest film, *Brainstorm*, and was accompanied by Wagner and *Brainstorm* costar Christopher Walken. Skipper Dennis Davern was at the helm. Foul play was not suspected.

In My Esteemed Opinion

After a short investigation, Chief Medical Examiner Dr. Thomas Noguchi listed Wood's death as an accidental drowning. Tests revealed that she had consumed "seven or eight" glasses of wine, and the coroner contended that in her intoxicated state Wood had probably stumbled and fallen overboard while attempting to untie the yacht's rubber dinghy. He also stated that cuts and bruises on her body could have occurred when she fell from the boat.

Doubting Thomases

To this day, many question Wood's mysterious demise and believe that the accidental drowning theory sounds a bit too convenient. Pointed questions have led to many rumors: Does someone know more about Wood's final moments than they're letting on? Was her drowning really an accident, or did someone intentionally or accidentally *help* her overboard? Could this be why she sustained substantial bruising on her face and the back of her legs? Why was Wagner so reluctant to publicly discuss the incident? Were Christopher Walken and Wood an item as had been rumored? With this possibility in mind, could a booze-fueled fight have erupted between the two men? Could Wood have then tried to intervene, only to be knocked overboard for her efforts? And why did authorities declare Wood's death accidental so quickly? Would such a hasty ruling have been issued had the principals not been famous, wealthy, and influential? We'll never know.

Ripples

At the time of Wood's death, she and Wagner were seven years into their second marriage to each other. Whether Wood was carrying on an affair with Walken, as was alleged, may be immaterial, even if it made for interesting tabloid fodder. But Wagner's perception of their relationship could certainly be a factor. If nothing else, it might better explain the argument that ensued between Wagner and Walken that fateful night.

Case Closed?

Further information about Wood's death is sparse because no eyewitnesses have come forward. However, a businesswoman whose boat was anchored nearby testified that she heard a woman shouting for help, and then a voice responding, "We'll be over to get you," so the woman went back to bed. Just after dawn, Wood's body was found floating a mile away from the *Splendour*, approximately 200 yards offshore. The dinghy was found nearby; its only cargo was a stack of lifejackets.

In 2008, after 27 years of silence, Robert Wagner recalled in his autobiography, *Pieces of My Heart: A Life*, that he and Walken had engaged in a heated argument during supper after Walken had suggested that Wood star in more films, effectively keeping her away from their children. Wagner and Walken then headed topside to cool down. Sometime around midnight, Wagner said he returned to his cabin and discovered that his wife was missing. He soon realized that the yacht's dinghy was gone as well. In his book, he surmised that Wood may have gone to secure the dinghy that had been noisily slapping against the boat. Then, tipsy from the wine, she probably fell into the ocean and drowned. Walken notified the authorities.

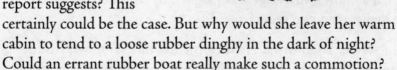

Was Natalie Wood's demise the result of a deadly mix of wine and saltwater as the coroner's report suggests? This certainly could be the case. But why would she leave her warm cabin to tend to a loose rubber dinghy in the dark of night? Could an errant rubber boat really make such a commotion?

Perhaps we'll never know what happened that fateful night, but an interview conducted shortly before Wood's death proved prophetic: "I'm frightened to death of the water," said Wood about a long-held fear. "I can swim a little bit, but I'm afraid of water that is dark."

Thelma Todd: Suicide or Murder?

During her nine-year film career, Thelma Todd costarred in dozens of comedies with the likes of Harry Langdon, Laurel and Hardy, and the Marx Brothers. Today, however, the "Ice Cream Blonde," as she was known, is best remembered for her bizarre death, which remains one of Hollywood's most enduring mysteries. Let's explore what could have happened.

✳   ✳   ✳   ✳

Sins Indulged

TODD WAS BORN in Lawrence, Massachusetts, in 1906 and arrived in Hollywood at age 20 via the beauty pageant circuit. Pretty and vivacious, she quickly became a hot commodity and fell headlong into Tinseltown's anything-goes party scene. In 1932, she married Pasquale "Pat" DiCicco, an agent of sorts who was also associated with gangster Charles "Lucky" Luciano. Their marriage was plagued by drunken fights, and they divorced two years later.

For solace, Todd turned to director Roland West, who didn't approve of her drinking and drug use, though he could not stop her. With his help, Todd opened a roadhouse called Thelma Todd's Sidewalk Café, located on the Pacific Coast Highway, and the actress moved into a spacious apartment above the restaurant. Shortly after, Todd began a relationship with gangster "Lucky" Luciano, who badgered her to use a room at the Sidewalk Café for illegal gambling. Todd repeatedly refused.

On the morning of December 16, 1935, Todd was found dead in the front seat of her 1934 Lincoln Phaeton convertible, which was parked in the two-car garage she shared with West. The apparent cause of death was carbon monoxide poisoning, though whether Todd was the victim of an accident, suicide, or murder remains a mystery.

Little evidence supports the suicide theory, outside the mode of death and the fact that Todd led a fast-paced lifestyle that sometimes got the better of her. Indeed, her career was going remarkably well, and she had purchased Christmas presents and was looking forward to a New Year's Eve party. So suicide does not seem a viable cause, though it is still mentioned as a probable one in many accounts.

The Accident Theory

However, an accidental death is also a possibility. The key to her car was in the "on" position, and the motor was dead when Todd was discovered by her maid. West suggested to investigators that the actress turned on the car to get warm, passed out because she was drunk, and then succumbed to carbon monoxide poisoning. Todd also had a heart condition, according to West, and this may have contributed to her death.

Nonetheless, the notion of foul play is suggested by several incongruities found at the scene. Spots of blood were discovered on and in Todd's car and on her mouth, and her nose was broken, leading some to believe she was knocked out then placed in the car to make it look like a suicide. (Police attributed the injuries to Todd falling unconscious and striking her head on the steering wheel.) In addition, Todd's blood-alcohol level was extremely high—high enough to stupefy her so that someone could carry her without her fighting back—and her high-heeled shoes were clean and unscuffed, even though she would have had to ascend a flight of outdoor, concrete stairs to reach the garage, which was a 271-step climb behind the restaurant. Investigators also found an unidentified smudged handprint on the left side of the vehicle.

Two with Motive

If Todd was murdered, as some have suggested, who had motive? Because of her wild lifestyle, there are several potential suspects, most notably Pasquale DiCicco, who was known to have a violent temper, and "Lucky" Luciano, who was angry at Todd for refusing to let him use her restaurant for illegal activities.

Despite the many questions raised by the evidence found at the scene, a grand jury ruled Todd's death accidental. The investigation had been hampered by altered and destroyed evidence, threats to witnesses, and cover-ups, making it impossible to ever learn what really happened. An open-casket service was held at Forest Lawn Memorial Park, where the public viewed the actress bedecked in yellow roses. After the service, Todd was cremated, eliminating the possibility of a second autopsy. Later, when her mother Alice Todd died, the actress's ashes were placed in her mother's casket so they could be buried together in Massachusetts.

Rudolph Valentino

Hollywood is chock-full of male sex symbols. However, none of today's pretty boys holds a candle to the great Rudolph Valentino. When the iconic Italian actor died unexpectedly in 1926 at age 31, many of his female fans were despondent to the point of suicide.

✳ ✳ ✳ ✳

IN 1895, RODOLFO Pietro Filiberto Raffaele Guglielmi di Valentina d'Antonguolla was born in Castellaneta, Italy, to Marie Berthe Gabrielle Barbin and Giovanni Antonio Giuseppe Fidele Guglielmi, a veterinarian who died of malaria when Rodolfo was 11. According to news reports at the time of Valentino's death, as a child, he was spoiled by his mother and was somewhat of a delinquent. Eager to leave his village, he set sail for America in 1913, where he worked odd jobs until landing a gig dancing at Maxim's, a nightclub for the wealthy in New York City, where he specialized in the tango. That led to a national dance tour, which eventually took him to Hollywood, where his dashing good looks and exotic persona propelled him to superstardom.

Hitting the Big Time

Indeed, Valentino quickly became one of the most popular actors of Hollywood's silent era, appearing in classics such as *The Sheik* (1921), *Blood and Sand* (1922), and *The Son of the Sheik* (1926), which turned out to be his last film. At the height of his success and popularity, Valentino was pulling in a whopping $7,500 per week!

Valentino's tragic end came while he was promoting *The Son of the Sheik*. He took ill on August 15, 1926, and was rushed to Polyclinic Hospital in New York City, where he was diagnosed with a ruptured appendix and gastric ulcers. Doctors performed surgery, but the actor's condition only worsened. He died on August 23 of peritonitis and a ruptured ulcer, complicated by septic pneumonia and septic endocarditis.

The public's outpouring of grief over Valentino's death was unlike anything seen before. Police had to cordon off the hospital to keep the growing throngs of female fans at bay. Legend has it that two women attempted suicide outside the hospital, while in London, actress Peggy Scott actually drank poison while gazing at photographs of the actor. An estimated 80,000 to 100,000 people passed through his open-casket viewing in New York City. Actress Pola Negri, who claimed she was engaged to Valentino, sent a floral arrangement that included 4,000 roses.

An Outpouring of Grief

When Valentino's body was transported to Hollywood, thousands of people watched the funeral train pass by. An invitation-only service was held at the Church of the Good Shepherd in Los Angeles, while a crowd estimated at 7,000 showed up at Hollywood Memorial Park, where the actor was entombed. Charlie Chaplin was a pallbearer, Lon Chaney and John Gilbert were ushers, and Cecil B. DeMille, Douglas Fairbanks, and Samuel Goldwyn were honorary pallbearers. Bushels of flowers were dropped from an airplane as Valentino's casket was carried to the vault in the Cathedral Mausoleum.

Valentino's burial there was supposed to be temporary while an elaborate mausoleum was constructed, complete with life-size statues of the actor in his most famous movie roles. But the Valentino estate didn't have the funds for such a memorial, and his resting place in the Cathedral Mausoleum looked like the actor's permanent resting place.

Valentino's plot was owned by June Mathis, who is often credited with discovering the actor. Mathis died of a heart attack a year after Valentino, and his body was transferred to the vault intended for Mathis's husband, where it remains.

The Lady in Black

The bizarre theatrics surrounding Valentino's death didn't
end after he was laid to rest. Since 1927, an annual memorial
service has been held on the anniversary of his death. Over the
years, the service has often been attended by the Lady in Black.
Around 1930, a woman dressed all in black, her face hidden
behind a veil, brought flowers to the actor's crypt; she continued the tradition for decades. Several rumors arose regarding
the mystery woman's identity, including one that suggested
she had been a gravely ill girl who had once been visited by
Valentino.

Alas, the truth is a lot more complicated and cynical. In fact,
there have been multiple ladies in black, some of them planted
by Paramount Pictures to continue Valentino's legend long
after his death. The first was probably Ditra Helena Medford,
also known as Ditra Flame, a former vaudeville performer who,
in 1940, came forward as the Lady in Black. Flame was the
head of the Valentino Memorial Guild, a fan organization, and
she claimed she had been coming to Valentino's crypt incognito
as the Lady in Black for years. She stepped up in 1940 in order
to stake her claim as the original because she felt imposters
were invading her territory. In the early 1950s, her appearances
at the crypt irked the Valentino family, and there was much
controversy over whether such theatrics were proper. In 1954,
when the newspapers were much less respectful of Flame's
devotion than they had been, she stopped going to the crypt on
the anniversary of Valentino's death. She returned in the mid-
1960s dressed in street clothes like the other memorial attend-
ees. In 1977, she changed her mind and began attending the
memorial services as the Lady in Black once again.

In 1938, Paramount Pictures hired a woman to be a Lady in
Black to coincide with the rerelease of *The Sheik* that year.
Sometimes more than one Lady in Black showed up in the
same year on the anniversary of Valentino's death, exploiting
the theatricality of the whole phenomenon.

Other Ladies in Black included Marion Benda, a chorus girl who had been Valentino's date on the night he fell ill. Emotionally unstable, she actually believed Valentino had married and impregnated her. For a while, Benda and Ditra Flame fought it out in the press over who was the real deal, but Benda's outrageous lies and deteriorating mental condition gave Ditra's story the edge. Then there was Estrellita del Regil, a peculiar fan who claimed her mother had been the original Lady in Black and that she had become one to honor a family tradition. Other family members disputed this, but del Regil kept her vigil from 1976 to 1993. And in 2002, 76 years after Valentino's death, a new Lady in Black emerged; Karie Bible has "taken the veil," so to speak, as a way to preserve a piece of Hollywood history.

Rudolph Valentino was the original Latin Lover, a role he played on-screen and off. And though his films are seldom shown today, dedicated fans continue to pay their respects and visit his final resting place.

What's in a Name?

During the studio era, actors commonly changed their names to something more glamorous at the urging of their controlling studio bosses. Sometimes, the change was as simple as altering a single letter, such as Warren Beatty (born Warren Beaty). In other cases, the story is much more interesting.

Doris Day

Born Doris von Kappeloff, the singer and actress was renamed Doris Day by bandleader Barney Rapp, for whom she sang "Day After Day." Her biggest movies include *The Pajama Game* (1957), *Teacher's Pet* (1958), and *Pillow Talk* (1959). She was nominated for an Academy Award for her role in the latter.

Judy Garland

A popular child actress, Garland entered this world as Frances Ethel Gumm. Her stage name, which was reportedly suggested by entertainer George Jessel, came from the Hoagy Carmichael song "Judy" and the last name of Chicago theater critic Robert Garland. Best remembered as Dorothy in *The Wizard of Oz* (1939), Garland also starred in *Meet Me in St. Louis* (1944), *The Harvey Girls* (1946), *Easter Parade* (1948), and *A Star Is Born* (1954), the latter of which earned her an Oscar nod.

Judy Holliday

No one played ditzy blondes better than Judy Holliday, who was born Judy Tuvim—*tuvim* being the Hebrew word for holiday. Her film career began in 1938, with an unbilled bit in Orson Welles's comedy short *Too Much Johnson*, and ended in 1960 with *Bells Are Ringing*. In between, Holliday starred in several rollicking comedies, including *Born Yesterday* (1950) (for which she won an Academy Award), *The Marrying Kind* (1952), and *It Should Happen to You* (1954).

Rock Hudson

The epitome of rugged, Hudson was born Roy Scherer Jr. He received his screen name from his agent, Henry Willson, who, according to Hollywood legend, combined the Rock of Gibraltar and the Hudson River. Hudson was in his first movie in 1948 (an uncredited role in *Fighter Squadron*) and was soon in high demand. His best-known movies include *Giant* (1956), which earned him an Academy Award nomination; *A Farewell to Arms* (1957); *Pillow Talk* (1959); and the cult favorite *Seconds* (1966).

Buster Keaton

One of the greatest comedic actors and directors in movie history, Keaton was known to his family as Joseph until he tumbled down some stairs as a baby. Family friend Harry Houdini reportedly remarked to Keaton's dad, "That was some buster your boy took!" Keaton starred in and directed or codirected dozens of comedies over the years, including *The Boat* (1921), *Cops* (1922), *Sherlock Jr.* (1924), and *The General* (1927).

Carole Lombard

Best remembered for her beauty, her acting, and her marriage to Clark Gable, Lombard was known simply as Jane Alice Peters before she hit the big time. When it came time to choose a more glamorous moniker, her studio, Fox Films, named her Carol Lombard. Later, she added the *e* for luck. Her films include *My Man Godfrey* (1936), *Nothing Sacred* (1937), *Mr. & Mrs. Smith* (1941), and *To Be or Not to Be* (1942).

Groucho Marx

Groucho, a comedy legend whose films still make audiences laugh, was born Julius Marx. His stage name and those of his brothers, Chico, Harpo, Zeppo, and Gummo, were inspired by the names in a popular comic strip called *Mager's Monks*, in which all the characters' monikers ended in *o*. The Marx Brothers' most beloved movies include *Animal Crackers* (1930), *Monkey Business* (1931), *Horse Feathers* (1932), *Duck Soup* (1933), and *A Night at the Opera* (1935). Groucho also hosted the popular television game show *You Bet Your Life* from 1950 to 1961.

Marilyn Monroe

Still an icon more than 45 years after her death, Marilyn Monroe was simply known as Norma Jean Baker (or, by her married name, Norma Jean Dougherty) before the 20th Century Fox talent director renamed her after one of his favorite performers, Marilyn Miller. Monroe was the maiden name of Norma Jean's mother. The blonde bombshell starred in a string of popular movies during her relatively brief career, including *Gentlemen Prefer Blondes* (1953), *The Seven Year Itch* (1955), and *Some Like It Hot* (1959), for which she won a Golden Globe award.

Esther Williams: Glamorous When Wet

Esther Williams was one of the biggest female box-office draws of the 1950s, enchanting America with her big-budget aquatic musicals and her daring on-screen stunts. Despite a wholesome, athletic image, the oft-married actress had a passionate and tempestuous personal life involving a string of Hollywood heartthrobs. Let's set the record straight and revisit her fascinating life.

✳ ✳ ✳ ✳

ESTHER WILLIAMS WAS an accomplished swimmer who earned a spot on the 1940 Olympic team; unfortunately, the games were canceled due to the outbreak of World War II. But it didn't take long for movie producers to notice the striking, athletic beauty. Williams made her film debut in 1942 alongside Mickey Rooney in *Andy Hardy's Double Life*. She wowed audiences with her grace and natural beauty, much to the delight of executives at MGM, who had been courting the statuesque young woman for some time in hopes of featuring her in a series of aquatic films to counter the success that rival 20th Century Fox had enjoyed with ice-skating star Sonja Henie. Within two years, Williams was starring in her first musical—the hugely successful *Bathing Beauty* (1944)—and America had a new darling of the silver screen.

Box-Office Bombshell

Knowing they had a hot property on their hands, MGM spent six figures converting a soundstage into an elaborate aquatic set rigged with fountains, fireworks, and other special effects. For the next 15 years, Williams made use of the set to headline two dozen films—mostly aquatic musicals—and bring in more revenue than any other female film star of the era. She was paired with some of Hollywood's hunkiest leading men, including Peter Lawford, Van Johnson, Jeff Chandler, Fernando Lamas, and Victor Mature, but in every film, Williams remained the main attraction.

In addition to her comely features and strong-willed all-American image, Williams consistently thrilled audiences with her graceful and daring maneuvers in the water. But those thrilling moments did not come without cost. She nearly drowned while filming *Texas Carnival* (1951) and once ended up in a body cast with three broken vertebrae thanks to a heavy tiara that her director insisted she wear while performing a high dive in *Million Dollar Mermaid* (1952). While doing a water-skiing routine for *Easy to Love* (1953), she was almost maimed by a boat propeller, but she did successfully pull off a dangerous jump over a full orchestra on a floating platform. That same film also called for a spectacular 80-foot dive out of a helicopter, but Williams drew the line and insisted on a stunt double—because she was three months pregnant!

By the late 1950s, Williams was reaching the end of her athletic prime, and she attempted to broaden her range in dramas such as *The Unguarded Moment* (1956) and *Raw Wind in Eden* (1958). Though a capable actress, she was not able to pull off the transition. Her film career petered out by the early 1960s, so she retired.

Rocky Romances

Williams was breathtakingly beautiful, and she found herself courted by men of all stripes from the earliest days of her career. Sadly, most of these relationships took a considerable toll on her. Johnny Weissmuller, who was known almost as well for his lascivious behavior as for his world-famous performances as Tarzan, pursued the unwilling starlet relentlessly when they worked together in the Billy Rose Aquacade, a swimming and diving show, in San Francisco. Her first marriage ended badly when her husband objected to her entering the film industry, and her second husband squandered much of the fortune she had earned with MGM. In the 1950s, she indulged in passionate affairs with costars Jeff Chandler and Victor Mature before taking Fernando Lamas as her third husband. Though dedicated and often tender, Lamas was fiercely jealous and vain, which made life difficult for Williams. After his death, she married a French literature professor who supported her post-Hollywood career in swimsuit design. A true show business trouper, Williams never let physical challenges or her rocky personal life interfere with her climb to the top of the Hollywood high dive.

Hey, I Never Said That!

"Judy, Judy, Judy"

Hollywood icon Cary Grant appeared in more than 70 movies, and the utterance most frequently attributed to him is "Judy, Judy, Judy." The problem is that he didn't say it.

✳ ✳ ✳ ✳

BORN ARCHIBALD ALEXANDER Leach in Bristol, England, in 1904, Cary Grant would grow up to become one of Hollywood's most popular leading men. His early career included a stint as a stilt walker in a traveling sideshow that toured the United States, where he eventually decided to live and work. While performing in a series of roles in light comedies on Broadway, he signed with Paramount Pictures and took his stage name.

By 1932, Grant was starring with screen sirens Marlene Dietrich and Mae West, and he soon became one of Alfred Hitchcock's favorite leads. His films with costars like Katherine Hepburn, Rosalind Russell, Ingrid Bergman, Grace Kelly, and Audrey Hepburn are considered some of Hollywood's all-time classics.

Along with film icons such as Jimmy Stewart and Humphrey Bogart, Grant became a favorite subject of impersonators. But the scripted line he is most often tagged with was never heard by a movie audience. The closest Grant ever came to uttering the line was in the 1939 film *Only Angels Have Wings*, with Rita Hayworth as his ex-girlfriend, Judith. Grant says, "Hello, Judy," "Come on, Judy," "Now, Judy," but never "Judy, Judy, Judy."

Intriguing Individuals

Joan Crawford

Movie megastar or box-office poison? Loving mother or wire hanger-hating madwoman? During the course of her long career in Hollywood, Joan Crawford amazed and confused millions of people as they sought to understand her.

✳ ✳ ✳ ✳

Reaching for Stardom

ON MARCH 23, 1905, Lucille Fay LeSueur was born in San Antonio, Texas. In her late teens, she joined a traveling theatrical company, and by age 20, she was performing in a chorus line on Broadway.

In 1925, Lucille was contracted by MGM to appear as an extra in six films, receiving her first credit on *Pretty Ladies* (1925). MGM then picked up her option, though studio execs, including Louis B. Mayer, insisted on a name change. In one of the most famous publicity stunts in Hollywood history, MGM held a contest for fans to select a suitable name for her. The starlet made her debut as Joan Crawford in *Old Clothes* (1925). Crawford did everything the studio asked of her, and more— from appearing in unworthy films to making herself available for all photo opportunities. All of this led MGM screenwriter Frederica Sagor Maas to utter the now-famous words: "No one decided to make Joan Crawford a star. Joan Crawford became a star because Joan Crawford decided to become a star."

Douglas Fairbanks Jr. and the Clark Gable Affair

After a short courtship, Crawford married Douglas Fairbanks Jr. on June 3, 1929. Trouble started brewing when Crawford began filming *Laughing Sinners* (1931), and then *Possessed* (1931), with Clark Gable. Rumors quickly began to circulate that Crawford and Gable were having an affair, and the couple was anything but discreet with their behavior. Studio execs demanded that the pair curtail the affair, which they did, more or less. But the chemistry between the two was palpable, so the studio cast them in eight films together.

In May 1933, Crawford filed for divorce from Fairbanks. Less than two years later, she married actor Franchot Tone, with whom she appeared in seven films. But the studio made much of Crawford's level of stardom compared to Tone's, which created a lot of tension in the marriage, and the couple filed for divorce in 1939. That same year, Crawford appeared as the villainess in the film *The Women*. She campaigned for the role, and studio execs finally gave it to her, though they disliked the fact that she played a hard-edged, unrepentant homewrecker.

Box-Office Poison

In 1932, when the *Motion Picture Herald* released its poll of the top ten moneymaking movie stars, Joan Crawford topped the list. In fact, she held down the top slot in the poll for the next four years. But by 1937, Crawford had not only fallen from the top spot, she didn't even make the top ten. Perhaps that's why the following year, the *Independent Film Journal* referred to her as "box-office poison," though she was in good company because Katharine Hepburn, Greta Garbo, and Marlene Dietrich were also labeled as such by trade magazines in the late 1930s.

Adopting Children

In 1940, although unmarried at the time, Crawford adopted a daughter, Christina. Then, after Crawford married her third husband, Phillip Terry, in July 1942, they adopted another child, Christopher. But when Christopher's birth mother found out who had adopted her child, she petitioned the court and was awarded custody. Crawford was outraged and immediately took steps to adopt another boy, whom she named Phillip Terry Jr. When Terry and Crawford divorced in 1946, the eccentric actress received full custody of the two children and legally changed Phillip Jr.'s name to Christopher Crawford. The following year, Crawford adopted two more girls whom she named Cindy and Cathy.

Crawford continued to accept whatever movie roles were offered to her, but they were coming less frequently. In 1943, when her contract with MGM was terminated by mutual consent, Crawford moved to Warner Bros., who gave her more control over her material and directors.

Despite the fact that she won a Best Actress Oscar for her role in *Mildred Pierce* (1945) and appeared in a handful of solid dramas, Crawford left Warner Bros. in 1952.

Al Steele and the Pepsi-Cola Company

In May 1955, Crawford married her fourth and final husband, Alfred Steele, the president of Pepsi-Cola. Soon after, Crawford made herself an unofficial spokesperson for Pepsi and began traveling extensively to promote the beverage. When Steele died unexpectedly of a heart attack in 1959, Crawford took his spot on the Board of Directors, even though she had no background in running a business.

In 1961, Crawford was offered a starring role in *What Ever Happened to Baby Jane?* (1962). She played Blanche Hudson, a former A-list actress who had become confined to a wheelchair; Bette Davis portrayed Blanche's sadistic sister. The two actresses were reputedly engaged in a bizarre feud that may have stemmed from the 1930s, when both were interested in Franchot Tone. Legend has it that Crawford complained that Davis intentionally kicked her during a scene. Seeking revenge,

Crawford allegedly strapped weights to her body for the scene in which Davis was required to lift her.

Feigning Illness?

When director Robert Aldrich cast Crawford and Davis in *Hush...Hush, Sweet Charlotte* (1964), everyone warned him that he was asking for trouble—and he got it. According to some reports, the two stars were constantly bickering and would often go out of their way to anger each other. Davis seemed to take great pride in trying to get Crawford to snap and appeared to have succeeded when Joan claimed to have fallen ill and left the set.

Aldrich begged Crawford to come back, and she did, but when she again claimed she was ill, Aldrich demanded that she be examined by a company physician. Crawford refused and several days later checked into a hospital with an "undisclosed illness." Believing Crawford was faking, Aldrich promptly fired her, scrapped all of the existing footage she appeared in, and replaced her with Olivia de Havilland. Crawford reportedly cried for 39 hours straight after hearing of her replacement.

Turning to Television

With movie scripts no longer coming her way, Crawford turned to the world of television. In 1968, Crawford's daughter Christina, who was also an actress, took medical leave from *The Secret Storm*, the soap opera on which she was a regular. Somehow, Joan convinced producers that she should fill in until Christina returned, despite their 30-year age difference. But during taping, Crawford repeatedly muffed her lines, which caused her to get so angry that she lost it altogether and was reportedly sent home and told not to return.

Joan had several other appearances on TV shows and starred in one final movie, *Trog* (1970), but she was never able to recapture the level of stardom that she once had. Still, by 1972, with her final acting appearance on the TV series *The Sixth Sense*, Crawford's career had spanned an amazing 45 years.

Seclusion and Death

In 1973, when Crawford was told that her services were no longer needed at Pepsi-Cola, she began to withdraw from society. When she saw some unflattering photos of herself at her last known public appearance on September 23, 1974, she is said to have remarked, "If that's how I look, then they won't see me anymore." With that, Joan Crawford was rarely seen again until her death on May 10, 1977.

When Crawford's will was read, her two youngest children, Cathy and Cindy, each received roughly $78,000. As for Christina and Christopher, Crawford's will simply stated that "for reasons which are well known to them," they were to receive nothing.

Mommie Dearest

Roughly 18 months after Crawford's death, Christina published *Mommie Dearest,* a book that candidly discussed Joan's (alleged) erratic behavior. (The book was later made into a movie of the same name, starring Faye Dunaway as Crawford. Dunaway described feeling typecast or shunned after playing this divisive role.)

Christina described how her mother choked her, drank excessively, obsessed over her appearance, and had a revolving door of lovers. But far and away, the most infamous scene in the book—and movie—was the one in which Joan found wire hangers in Christina's closet, which sent Joan into a rage, and she screamed, "No wire hangers! No more wire hangers ever!"

Christina maintains that everything was described in the book exactly as it happened. Crawford's other children and her friends claim that they never saw any of the strange behavior related in the book. True or not, the book has overshadowed Crawford's decades-long career and her glamorous image.

16 Unexpectedly Influential Film Directors of the 20th Century

Many celebrated film directors have influenced their peers and artistic descendants, and even casual film fans know their names: Alfred Hitchcock, George Lucas, Orson Welles, Steven Spielberg, and D. W. Griffith, just to name a few. The following is a list of some noteworthy directors who are considerably less well known, yet played a significant role in inspiring future directors. Let's look closer at these influences on our favorites.

✳   ✳   ✳   ✳

1. **Oscar Micheaux:** Before Oscar Micheaux, African-Americans had only a marginal presence in American movies, and only then as figures of menace or derision. In 1919, Micheaux made a film of his book *The Homesteader*, and followed it with *Within Our Gates* in 1920, a tough-minded drama designed to expose the ugliness of racism. For the next 30 years, Micheaux wrote, produced, and directed nearly 40 films that portrayed the difficulties of black Americans.

   Hollywood regarded his productions as unimportant "race films" that were played only in segregated theaters. But to African-American audiences and the black actors he employed, Micheaux was a trailblazer who addressed contemporary concerns. Today's black cinema—and the mainstream stardom of Denzel Washington, Forest Whitaker, and others—has roots in the work of Oscar Micheaux.

2. **David Hand:** For years, Walt Disney allowed the general public to believe that he alone was the creator of his cartoons and live-action movies, and even the originator of such stories as *Robin Hood, Cinderella,* and *Alice's Adventures in Wonderland*. But Disney's landmark 1937 release, *Snow White and the Seven Dwarfs,* was

directed by a longtime animator and animation supervisor named David Hand.

Snow White was the first feature-length cartoon, and its visual beauty and mammoth commercial success inspired generations of future animators, including those who work today with computer-generated images instead of pen and ink. Hand also directed *Bambi* (1942) and remained active until 1980's *Mickey Mouse Disco*.

3. **Anthony Mann:** Anthony Mann was a highly skilled Hollywood studio director who pushed the limits of film noir in the late 1940s with *T-Men* (1947) and *Raw Deal* (1948) and later reinvigorated the Western via driven, neurotically vengeful antiheroes. Many of these Mann productions star James Stewart, including *Winchester '73* (1950), *Bend of the River* (1952), and *The Naked Spur* (1953). From this new approach came the concept of the "adult Western," which carried through Clint Eastwood's *Unforgiven* (1992) and beyond.

4. **Robert Aldrich:** Though highly influential in the development of the contemporary Gothic thriller (*What Ever Happened to Baby Jane?*, 1962) and the war film (*The Dirty Dozen*, 1967), Aldrich's most penetrating influence comes from his 1955 adaptation of Mickey Spillane's crime novel *Kiss Me Deadly*. With disorienting camera angles, grotesque violence, and a bleak portrayal of a world out of control, it knocked audiences back in their seats and made a tremendous impression on Jean-Luc Godard, François Truffaut, and other important young directors of the French "New Wave" of the late 1950s.

5. **Roger Corman:** Roger Corman, the legendary "King of the Bs," directed scores of films in just over 15 years (sometimes six or seven a year), and became not just a busy director, but Hollywood's most successful and prolific independent

producer. From Westerns to Gothic horror, science fiction, crime, juvenile delinquent, and hot rod flicks—Corman made them all with a sense of fun, and continues to sponsor and inspire low- and no-budget filmmakers today.

6. **Russ Meyer:** When he was unable to crack the Hollywood unions, this robust, perpetually grinning cameraman and glamour photographer became an independent filmmaker. Meyer's first feature, *The Immoral Mr. Teas* (1959) brought humor, color film stock, and even a shred of plot to the "peekaboo" genre. Teas was a boisterous financial success and led to other Meyer films including *Lorna* (1964), *Mudhoney* (1965), *Vixen!* (1968), and the highly regarded *Faster, Pussycat! Kill! Kill!* (1965).

In 1970, 20th Century Fox financed and released Meyer's most elaborate production, *Beyond the Valley of the Dolls* (with a script by film critic Roger Ebert). Adult movies became drearily explicit in the late 1970s, and Meyer lost interest in pursuing his career, but before that happened, he inspired hundreds of films by other, lesser directors.

7. **Herschell Gordon Lewis:** This Chicago ad exec and junk-mail marketer partnered with financier Dave Friedman to invent the "gore" genre in 1963 with the ineptly made *Blood Feast.* Lewis elaborated on his no-holds-barred approach to violence with *Two Thousand Maniacs!* (1964), *Color Me Blood Red* (1965), and many others. He earned the dubious title "Godfather of Gore" and helped create the climate that made possible latter-day gore fests such as *Saw* (2004).

8. **Richard Lester:** British director Richard Lester's free-wheeling approach to The Beatles' first two films, *A Hard Day's Night* (1964) and *Help!* (1965), gave swingin' London a visual style marked by handheld cameras, flip humor, and breakneck pacing. Every other director who worked with a Brit pop group followed Lester's lead, including

the talented John Boorman, who guided the Dave Clark 5 through *Having a Wild Weekend* in 1965. On a broader level, Lester's influence was felt in a variety of British films that were made in the mid-to late 1960s, such as John Schlesinger's *Darling* (1965).

9. **Mike Nichols:** An iconoclastic American director, Mike Nichols came to movies after a successful live comedy career with partner Elaine May. Nichols's first splash was *Who's Afraid of Virginia Woolf?* (1966), which came along at a time when America was on the verge of a great liberalization of thought and cultural mores. With *The Graduate* in 1967, Nichols wittily examined youthful angst with the story of a freshly minted college grad who desires the daughter but beds the mother. Hollywood grew up in the mid-1960s, and Nichols was at the forefront.

10. **Frederick Wiseman:** Documentary filmmaker Frederick Wiseman made a controversial splash with his first picture, 1967's *Titicut Follies*, a harrowing look at a Massachusetts institution for the mentally ill. The movie became the template for Wiseman's subsequent work—a keen interest in the everyday but frequently hidden aspects of American life. *Titicut Follies* was followed by a score of poignant documentaries, and Wiseman's work is a direct link to latter-day socially conscious documentaries, such as *Hoop Dreams* (1994), *Stevie* (2002), *The Thin Blue Line* (1988), and even *Fahrenheit ⁹/₁₁* (2004).

11. **Gordon Parks:** Brilliantly talented African-American photographer and filmmaker Gordon Parks revolutionized black cinema with *Shaft* in 1971. For the first time, audiences saw a black man—here, a private detective named John Shaft—pursue his own agenda in the white world and control his own life, establishment be damned. The movie launched the so-called "blaxploitation" genre that brought stardom to Jim Brown, Fred Williamson, Pam Grier, Ron

O'Neal, and Shaft's Richard Roundtree.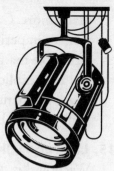
Blaxploitation flourished throughout the
1970s and has lately been honored—and
gently parodied—by nonconformist
directors Quentin Tarantino and Larry
Cohen.

12. **Tobe Hooper:** In 1974, Tobe Hooper
    was a young indie filmmaker in Texas.
    Hooper and his partner, writer Kim
    Henkel, wanted to do something more commercial, so they
    decided to make a horror thriller, which they called *The
    Texas Chainsaw Massacre*. This tale of college kids victim-
    ized by a family of demented cannibals shocked audiences
    who thought they saw gore where there was none (blood
    appears only once, when a man purposely cuts his thumb).

    Texas Chainsaw Massacre exploited extreme psychological
    unease as audiences witnessed the helplessness of innocent
    victims. Other filmmakers followed with similar films that
    were heavy with gore but lacking Hooper's flair for bilious
    suspense and sick humor.

13. **Robert Altman:** With his peerless skill at guiding ensem-
    ble casts through a rich tapestry of interwoven stories
    (*Nashville*, 1975), Robert Altman made films that were
    short on explosions and shootouts, and long on thought-
    ful characterization, rueful wit, and the complexities of
    emotion and desire that nudge (or sometimes propel) us
    through life. Altman inspired some equally intelligent later
    filmmakers, including Paul Thomas Anderson (*Magnolia*,
    1999).

14. **John Carpenter:** A lifelong fan of horror movies, John
    Carpenter reinvented the genre in 1978 with *Halloween*,
    and unwittingly inspired a flood of "holiday" horror films:
    Mother's Day, *My Bloody Valentine*, *Friday the 13th*, and

many more. Carpenter laid the ground rules with a young woman in peril inside a weirdly shadowed house, an indestructible maniac on the loose, dark rooms that the heroine has an inexplicable urge to enter, and fiendishly effective shock moments. *Halloween* is a perennial favorite, and still a high point of blunt, low-budget moviemaking.

15. **Lana and Lilly Wachowski:** Usually credited as The Wachowskis, American writers and directors Lana and Lilly Wachowski brought a fresh spin to blackmail and murder with *Bound* (1996), and became highly influential with *The Matrix* (1999) and its sequels. These science-fiction thrillers brought a fresh approach to special effects, notions of space and time, and virtual reality. Widely imitated and frequently parodied, The Matrix films may have outstayed their welcome, but their reverberations will be felt for many years.

16. **Steven Soderbergh:** Steven Soderbergh is a versatile American director who moves easily between smart action films (*Ocean's Eleven*, 2001), social commentary (*Erin Brockovich*, 2000), and crime epics (*Traffic*, 2000). Soderbergh's eclectic career is noteworthy, but his greatest influence may come from *Bubble* (2005), a low-budget drama about three underachieving employees at a doll factory and the circumstances that lead to jealousy and murder. Unassuming but extraordinarily powerful, *Bubble* shook up the film industry because Soderbergh elected to release it in theaters, on DVD, and to pay-per-view TV all on the same day. Since *Bubble*'s release, this model has become more and more common.

Have I Seen that Scene Before?

If you've ever watched a movie and thought a particular scene looked familiar, you might be correct. Many movies "borrow" scenes and elements from earlier films as a sort of homage or visual inspiration. While there are parodies and spoofs—what is Austin Powers but a take on James Bond—other films are more sly. Think of it as a way for the writers and directors to acknowledge their influences through allusion.

✳   ✳   ✳   ✳

Stairways Not to Heaven

IN BRIAN DE Palma's gangster saga *The Untouchables* (1987), the train station shootout takes place on a stairway. This scene was inspired by the Odessa steps sequence in *Battleship Potemkin* (1925), which was directed by Sergei Eisenstein. Ironically, De Palma wanted the shootout to be on a period train, but cost concerns made this impossible. Instead, it was decided that the scene would pay homage to the earlier film through the use of the baby carriage falling precariously down the stairs. And, if you have a keen eye, you'll notice several sailors caught in the crossfire—also a nod to the Russian film.

Gold and Oil

James Bond seems to face many villains with unique plans for world domination, but these foes often employ strangely similar methods. One of the most memorable images of the 007 classic *Goldfinger* (1964) was actress Shirley Eaton covered in gold paint from head to toe. *Quantum of Solace* (2008) features a scene with Gemma Arterton as Strawberry Fields, who meets a similarly gruesome end, though this time the erstwhile Bond girl was covered in thick black oil. Bond may always get the girls, but the girls seem to get it in the end.

Bridges Too Far

Picture this: A hero in an exotic land is chased across a long rope bridge, only to find himself trapped. Sounds like the climax of *Indiana Jones and the Temple of Doom* (1984), but actually, Tommy Lee Jones found himself in a similar predicament a year earlier in *Nate and Hayes*. In fairness, *The Man Who Would Be King* (1975) offered up a scene with Sean Connery trying to get out while the getting's good. Of course, all these may have been inspired by *Perils of Nyoka* (1942), a Republic serial that also featured a hero in trouble on a bridge.

City Shootout

Quentin Tarantino's *Reservoir Dogs* (1992) paved the way for the writer/director to make *Pulp Fiction* (1994). However, *Reservoir Dogs*, a story about jewel thieves, is itself guilty of a heist. Tarantino made no secret of the fact that he was inspired by Hong Kong action cinema, but *Reservoir Dogs* features a remarkable number of moments lifted from the Ringo Lam-directed *City on Fire* (1987), starring  Chow Yun-Fat. Not only do both stories feature an undercover cop in a gang in which the criminals don't know each other, but there is also a similar "Mexican standoff" climax just before the credits roll.

When Is a Western a Western?

A Fistful of Dollars (1964), starring Clint Eastwood, put a new spin on the traditional Western. Shot in Spain—yet considered a "Spaghetti Western" because it was directed by Sergio Leone and produced by an Italian film studio—this movie was actually a remake of Akira Kurosawa's 1961 film *Yojimbo* (*The Bodyguard*), which itself was a samurai flick influenced by Hollywood films, including Westerns. *Yojimbo* was remade again by Walter Hill as the gangster film *Last Man Standing* (1996), which starred Bruce Willis.

The Hidden Inspiration

Ever wonder why George Lucas included R2-D2 and C-3PO as comic relief in the original *Star Wars* (1977)? Well, take a gander at Akira Kurosawa's 1958 epic *The Hidden Fortress*. It features a very similar duo of secondary characters arguing as they attempt to escape the main enemy's army. Throw in a princess-saving plot, and you get the idea that heroic stories don't only happen in a galaxy far, far away.

Name-dropping

In *Batman Returns* (1992), Christopher Walken plays corrupt business mogul Max Shreck. This is director Tim Burton's homage to German Expressionist actor Max Schreck, who portrayed the vampire in F. W. Murnau's original *Nosferatu* (1922).

Monster Mash

The sight of pitchfork-wielding townspeople bent on burning the monster and putting an end to Dr. Frankenstein's experiments is a cinematic device that has been parodied and spoofed many times. But the original sequence from *Frankenstein* (1931) was re-created almost shot for shot—and in black and white—for the beginning of *Van Helsing* (2004).

It Came from the 1950s!

The sci-fi genre blossomed in Hollywood in the 1950s, with all the major studios offering films with alien invaders, mutation, and end-of-the-world scenarios. Film scholars suggest that these tales reflected popular fears of technology stemming from the remarkable scientific advances of the era such as nuclear power and space flight. Whatever the underlying themes, the result was a spate of imaginative and innovative sci-fi flicks.

✳   ✳   ✳   ✳

The Day the Earth Stood Still (1951)

GENERALLY CONSIDERED ONE of the best sci-fi offerings of the era, this thoughtful morality tale sees a powerful alien named Klaatu come to Earth to warn humanity that it must reject war and aggression or face annihilation from alien civilizations. The film was remade in 2008 as a vehicle for Keanu Reeves, but it bombed and was widely panned by critics.

The Thing from Another World (1951)

A group of scientists at the North Pole battle a savage alien in this sci-fi classic produced by the great Howard Hawks. The film offers an interesting take on the theme of technology, as the humans find their modern weapons and scientific devices ineffective against the creature and must resort to natural forces such as fire and electricity to defeat it. Director John Carpenter helmed *The Thing,* a successful remake of the film in 1982.

When Worlds Collide (1951)

When scientists discover that a planet is on a collision course with Earth, a privately funded group builds a rocket ship to send a few dozen men and women into space to ensure that humanity carries on. A predecessor to the second wave of sci-fi disaster films, including *Independence Day* (1996), *Deep Impact* (1998), and *Armageddon* (1998), this early entry from sci-fi producer George Pal offered state-of-the-art special effects and a thrilling storyline.

The War of the Worlds (1953)

This rousing action tale, based on a story by H. G. Wells that Orson Welles famously narrated on the radio in 1938, has ruthless Martian invaders laying Earth to waste. Filmed in Technicolor and lauded for the creepy, sterile design of the Martians and their powerful war machines, it set a new standard for visual effects. Tom Cruise and Dakota Fanning starred in Steven Spielberg's 2005 remake of this sci-fi classic. Their efforts fared far better at the box office than Keanu Reeves's take on *The Day the Earth Stood Still*.

The Creature from the Black Lagoon (1954)

A small group of scientists deep in the Amazon jungle mix it up with a prehistoric man-fish. In this tightly crafted allegory of passion gone awry, the creature's interest in the sole female member of the expedition mirrors the unwanted romantic advances of the expedition's leader.

Them (1954)

Giant ants run amok in the American Southwest in one of the first films to caution against the potentially dire consequences of tampering with nuclear radiation. This memorable movie offers plenty of mystery, thrills, drama, and even a touch of humor along with its terrifying mutant insects.

Forbidden Planet (1956)

Best remembered for its amazing special effects, including Robbie the Robot, this was one of the first films with high production values and an A-level cast to be set on another planet. A retelling of Shakespeare's *The Tempest*, *Forbidden Planet* suggests that even the most futuristic technology is no match for the destructive power of the human mind.

Invasion of the Body Snatchers (1956)

This classic story, cleverly directed by Don Siegel, has emotionless aliens taking over the identities of the residents of a small town, while the one man who knows the truth desperately tries to warn authorities. Remarkably, it has been interpreted as a commentary on both the threat of Communist infiltration and on the misguided conformity demanded by the infamous Senator Joe McCarthy in response to that threat.

The Incredible Shrinking Man (1957)

After being exposed to a mysterious radioactive cloud, a man finds himself growing smaller and smaller in size, and he must learn to adjust to a world in which mousetraps and household spiders have become potentially deadly. While its subtext clearly alludes to fears about technology, the film's conclusion also offers an inspiring bit of pulp philosophy about humankind's place in the universe.

The Blob (1958)

Though shot in just a few weeks on a shoestring budget, this alien-attacks-small-town story wowed audiences and remains a much-loved sci-fi staple. The villain, a gelatinous mass that feeds on everything in its path and grows larger with every meal, is eventually stopped by the teenage hero, played by Steve McQueen in his first starring role.

Switcheroo!

It's hard to imagine different actors playing the characters in your favorite movies. Could anyone but Jon Heder have been the goofy title character in Napoleon Dynamite *(2004)? Who but Julia Roberts could have played opposite Richard Gere in* Pretty Woman *(1990)? Surprisingly, roles can change hands many times before a movie starts shooting—sometimes actors get switched around even after the cameras roll. Read on for a few actor "switcheroos."*

✳   ✳   ✳   ✳

✳ Michael J. Fox was the original choice for Marty McFly in *Back to the Future* (1985), but his work on *Family Ties* caused scheduling conflicts, so producers went with Eric Stoltz instead. When they decided Stoltz was "miscast" as McFly, they were already six weeks into filming and had to reshoot several scenes when Fox finally came onboard.

✳ Director Francis Ford Coppola fired Harvey Keitel two weeks into filming *Apocalypse Now* (1979). Martin Sheen replaced Keitel as Capt. Benjamin L. Willard in the famously troubled production of this war flick.

✳ The villain played by Colin Farrell in Steven Spielberg's *Minority Report* (2002) was originally a character meant for Matt Damon. But Damon was busy filming *The Bourne Identity* (2002) and couldn't take the part.

✳ *The Godfather: Part III* (1990) presents Sofia Coppola as the daughter of mobster Michael Corleone. Sofia (the real-life daughter of *Godfather* director Francis Ford Coppola, and a successful director in her own right) was a replacement for Winona Ryder, who gave up the part due to exhaustion. Her performance has entered the public imagination as a place-holder for bad and debatably nepotistic casting.

* Will Smith turned down the role of Neo in *The Matrix* (1999) in order to star in the flop *Wild Wild West* (1999). Although Smith admits the decision was a mistake, he feels Keanu Reeves played the role better than he would have himself. In ten years, there may be a remake of *The Matrix* starring one of Smith and wife Jada Pinkett's talented kids.

* The Oscar-winning script for *Forrest Gump* (1994) was originally offered to directors Terry Gilliam and Barry Sonnenfeld, but Robert Zemeckis ended up taking the helm. Bill Murray was considered for the role of Forrest, as was Chevy Chase, but both turned down the role that eventually went to Tom Hanks. (It's difficult to picture Clark Griswold disappearing into the role.) The role of Bubba was passed up by David Alan Grier, Dave Chappelle, and Ice Cube before Mykelti Williamson took it on.

* Sandra Bullock replaced Lori Petty as Lt. Lenina Huxley in *Demolition Man* (1993). The temperamental Petty—known for her roles in *A League of Their Own* (1992), *Tank Girl* (1995), and Netflix's *Orange is the New Black*—had been on set for several days before being let go. All of her footage had to be reshot.

* Vivien Leigh made history as Scarlett O'Hara in *Gone with the Wind* (1939), but many of Hollywood's top female stars tested for the part, including Bette Davis and Paulette Goddard. Both were considered front-runners until Leigh was signed.

* Marilyn Monroe wanted to have *Breakfast at Tiffany's* (1961), but the equally iconic Audrey Hepburn was the actress who brought the beloved character of Holly Golightly to life. Monroe campaigned for the role, partly because she was encouraged by Truman Capote, who wrote the novella and felt she was a good fit.

Monroe even worked on scenes for her audition in Lee Strasberg's acting class. But Paramount had no intention of hiring Monroe after her behavior on their production of *Some Like It Hot* (1959), during which she was late to the set, emotionally distraught, and unable to act some days.

✳ In the psychological thriller *Panic Room* (2002), Jodie Foster plays an appropriately freaked-out mom facing intruders. The role was first offered to Nicole Kidman, but an injured knee kept her from accepting it.

✳ The 1964 big-budget comedy *What a Way to Go!* featured the legendary Robert Mitchum in one of the film's five male roles, but the part changed hands several times before he got it. The studio wouldn't pay Frank Sinatra's asking price; they wanted Gregory Peck, but he was unavailable; and finally, a recommendation from costar Shirley MacLaine got Mitchum the role.

✳ Fred Astaire and Judy Garland sing and dance their way through *Easter Parade* (1948), but it would've been a different duo if fate hadn't intervened. Gene Kelly was supposed to be Garland's dancing partner, but a broken ankle put him out of commission and out of the running.

✳ Can you imagine Sylvester Stallone—Rocky himself—as Axel Foley in *Beverly Hills Cop* (1984)? Stallone was replaced by comic Eddie Murphy because Sly demanded that the writers add more action to their comedic script. Murphy made the cut and then made history as everyone's favorite 1980s funny cop.

Sci-Fi Flicks that Leaped from the Printed Page

Most movie fans may not know it, but quite a few classic science-fiction flicks have deep literary roots. In some cases, the source material is well known: The Time Machine, The War of the Worlds, *and* The Invisible Man *by H. G. Wells, for instance, or Jules Verne's* Twenty Thousand Leagues Under the Sea. *But many other movies are based on books or short stories so obscure that only the geekiest sci-fi fans are aware of them.*

✳ ✳ ✳ ✳

Farewell to the Master by Harry Bates

CONSIDERED BY MANY critics to be one of the best science-fiction stories ever written, this tale of a visit from a technologically advanced alien being and his robot guardian hit the big screen in 1951 under the title *The Day the Earth Stood Still*, starring Michael Rennie as the extraterrestrial Klaatu. Keanu Reeves starred in a 2008 remake of the film.

Flowers for Algernon by Daniel Keyes

This poignant story of a developmentally challenged young man whose intelligence is temporarily boosted through a scientific breakthrough made a star out of Cliff Robertson, who played the lead character in the 1968 screen adaptation, *Charly*.

Who Goes There? by John W. Campbell

This chilling short story about a shape-shifting alien who terrorizes the crew of a remote Arctic outpost has been adapted twice for the big screen—once in 1951 as *The Thing from Another World* and again in 1982 as simply *The Thing*. The 1982 version, which starred Kurt Russell and was directed by John Carpenter, adheres more closely to the original text.

The Sentinel by Arthur C. Clarke

Film fans know this short story better by the title *2001: A Space Odyssey* (1968), which was directed by Stanley Kubrick.

However, *The Sentinel* provides only a basic framework for the movie; don't expect a lot of mind-blowing psychedelic space travel in the book.

Do Androids Dream of Electric Sheep? by Philip K. Dick

This compelling story of humanlike "replicants" and the cop who hunts them down when they go bad was made into the much-heralded Ridley Scott flick *Blade Runner* (1982), which starred Harrison Ford.

We Can Remember It for You Wholesale by Philip K. Dick

If you're an Arnold Schwarzenegger fan, you probably know this story better as *Total Recall* (1990). In this film, Schwarzenegger plays a man who doesn't know whether his memories of a trip to Mars are real or not. Author Philip K. Dick has become well known among screenwriters in recent years, and many of his stories have received the Hollywood treatment.

The Racer by Ib Melchior

Before Sylvester Stallone hit it big as underdog pugilist Rocky Balboa, he costarred with David Carradine in the film version of this futuristic thriller retitled for the big screen as *Death Race 2000* (1975). A 2008 remake of the movie, simply titled *Death Race*, starred Jason Statham.

Eight O'Clock in the Morning by Ray Faraday Nelson

This sly story of alien infiltration and subliminal manipulation became a showcase for wrestler "Rowdy" Roddy Piper when director John Carpenter brought it to the silver screen in 1988 under the title *They Live*.

The Cosmic Frame by Paul W. Fairman

This short story, first published in 1955, follows a young couple after they accidentally run over an alien. It was adapted—rather loosely—as the low-budget 1957 Edward Cahn flick *Invasion of the Saucer Men.*

The Fly by George Langelaan

Two movie adaptations have been made of this short story, which was originally published in the June 1957 issue of *Playboy* magazine. The first film, which was released in 1958, starred Vincent Price, but the remake, directed by David Cronenberg and released in 1986, was a much more graphic version that starred Jeff Goldblum in the title role.

The Many Deaths of Wile E. Coyote

Come on, admit it: After all these years, wouldn't it be nice to see Wile E. Coyote succeed in his futile quest to capture the Road Runner—even just one time?

✳ ✳ ✳ ✳

CREATED BY WARNER Bros. animation director Chuck Jones, cartoon character Wile E. Coyote is renowned for the outlandish inventions—all of them purchased from the shady Acme company—he uses in his vain attempts at capturing the Road Runner. These contraptions, which run the gamut from dehydrated boulders to jet-propelled skis, inevitably cause nothing but insult and injury to Wile E., yet he refuses to give up, turning to Acme again and again.

Wile E. Coyote made his debut in the 1949 cartoon "Fast and Furry-ous" (written by Michael Maltese, who would go on to script another 15 stories depicting the creative coyote). Although Wile E. tried desperately to catch the Road Runner with an electric motor and a super outfit, such tools were no match against his fleet-footed nemesis. The coyote had tasted defeat—and not for the last time.

Over the years, Wile E. Coyote has appeared in a total of 45 shorts, a short film, and—more recently—in three brief shorts that aired only on the Internet. He has also appeared in a handful of television shows—primarily compilations of earlier cartoons—and in the motion pictures *Space Jam* (1996) and *Looney Tunes: Back in Action* (2003).

Wile E. Coyote has assumed a variety of personas and has encountered many different foes over the course of his career. In a separate set of cartoons, he is known as Ralph Wolf and spends his time trying to steal sheep from a laconic but very effective sheep dog. And in a few cartoons, his foil is Bugs Bunny instead of the Road Runner. At the end of the day, however, the results of his actions are the same: abject failure and an empty stomach.

Creator Chuck Jones and the cartoons' animators conceived a series of strict rules governing Wile E. Coyote's behavior and his relationship with the Road Runner. Among them: The Road Runner cannot harm the coyote except by saying "beep beep." Also, no outside force can harm the coyote—only his own ineptitude or the failure of the various Acme products can derail the animal. In several cartoons, Wile E. is also thwarted by the unexpected arrival of various trucks and trains.

There's no doubt that Wile E. Coyote has suffered tremendous harm at the hands of the Acme devices he places his trust in time and again. He should really have shopped for villain gear somewhere else. Following are some of the outlandish ways that the long-suffering desert dog has dispatched himself, along with the cartoons in which they were featured:

* Anvil, "Gee Whiz-z-z," 1956

* Axle grease (guaranteed slippery), "Zip N Snort," 1961

* Bumble bees (one-fifth), "Zoom and Bored," 1957

* Do-It-Yourself Tornado Kit, "Whoa Be Gone," 1958

* Earthquake pills, "Hopalong Casualty," 1960

* Explosive tennis balls, "Soup or Sonic," 1980

* Giant mousetrap, "Chariots of Fur," 1994

* Giant rubber band, "Gee Whiz-z-z," 1956

* High-speed tonic, "Hip Hip Hurry," 1958

* Instant icicle maker, "Zoom at the Top," 1962

* Jet-propelled pogo stick, "Hot Rod & Reel," 1959

* Lightning bolts (rubber gloves included), "Chariots of Fur," 1994

* Little Giant Do-It-Yourself Rocket-Sled Kit, "Beep Prepared," 1961

* Mouse snare, "Hip Hip Hurry," 1958

* Nitroglycerin, "Beep Beep," 1952

* Road Runner lasso, "Freeze Frame," 1979

* Rocket-powered roller skates, "Beep Beep," 1952

* Triple-strength battleship steel armor plate, "Gee Whiz-z-z," 1956

* Triple-strength fortified leg muscle vitamins, "Stop! Look! and Hasten!," 1954

* Water pistol, "Whoa Be Gone," 1958

Five Obvious TV Cast Changes Maybe No One Will Notice

Ill health, educational pursuits, and a dislike for the job are just some of the reasons an actor may choose to depart a series. But do TV execs really think viewers don't notice the difference?

✳ ✳ ✳ ✳

Batman Holy cast changes! Let's see . . . two Riddlers (John Astin and Frank Gorshin), three Mr. Freezes (Otto Preminger, Eli Wallach, and George Sanders), and two Catwomen (Julie Newmar and Eartha Kitt—three if you count Lee Meriwether in the *Batman* movie). The man behind the cowl, however, was always Adam West.

Bewitched The "original" Darrin—Dick York—left the comedy in 1969 due to back problems. He was replaced by the "new" Darrin— Dick Sargent. And no one ever said a word. (The series actually had multiple actor/character changes, though none as notable as the two Darrins.)

Cagney & Lacey Chris Cagney's badge was passed around a lot before landing in the hands of Sharon Gless. It started with Loretta Swit (of M*A*S*H fame) in the made-for-TV movie, then was passed to Meg Foster, who was dismissed for being too "aggressive," before being turned over to Gless.

Roseanne Oldest daughter Becky (Alicia Gorenson, who left to attend college) became oldest daughter Becky (Sarah Chalke) who became oldest daughter Becky (again, Gorenson). A few passing references to the switch were made, most notably in the series' final episode. The series also poked fun at the switch in one version of the opening credits.

The Munsters Beverley Owen never liked the role of "Marilyn Munster" on *The Munsters*, so few people (including the actress herself) were upset when the character was replaced after 15 episodes by Pat Priest. They made 55 more episodes. Priest became a part of TV history; Owen . . . did not.

Offscreen Accomplishments

Most actors are famous for the movies in which they appear. Typically less well known are their non-Hollywood accomplishments, some of which are quite impressive. Who were the real people behind the screen?

Lionel Barrymore

ACADEMY AWARD WINNER Lionel Barrymore, the star of *Grand Hotel* (1932) and *Dinner at Eight* (1933) as well as the *Dr. Kildare* film series and others, composed a symphony titled *Tableau Russe*, part of which was featured in the 1941 film *Dr. Kildare's Wedding Day*.

Wallace Beery

Wallace Beery, who won a Best Actor Oscar for *The Champ* (1931), once held the world record for the largest black sea bass ever caught. He hooked the 515-pound behemoth off Catalina Island in 1916. Beery's record stood for 35 years.

Chief John Big Tree

Chief John Big Tree, who costarred with John Wayne in *Stagecoach* (1939) and *She Wore a Yellow Ribbon* (1949), was also the model for the 1912 Indian head nickel.

Rossano Brazzi

Rossano Brazzi, who costarred in *Three Coins in the Fountain* (1954), *The Barefoot Contessa* (1954), and *South Pacific* (1958), among many other films, was at one time the featherweight boxing champion of Italy.

Lon Chaney

Lon Chaney startled the world with his portrayals in the silent-screen versions of *The Hunchback of Notre Dame* (1923) and *The Phantom of the Opera* (1925), for which he designed his own makeup. Chaney also wrote the entry on theatrical makeup for the *Encyclopedia Britannica*. The article has been reworked through various editions.

Bebe Daniels

Bebe Daniels, whose acting career began with the 1910 version of *The Wonderful World of Oz* (in which she played Dorothy Gale), was a reporter for the BBC during World War II. She was the first female civilian to land in Normandy after D-Day.

Irene Dunne

Irene Dunne, who received five Academy Award nominations for Best Actress (but never won), was an alternate delegate at the 12th session of the U.N. General Assembly in 1957.

Clint Eastwood

Clint Eastwood, one of Hollywood's most stalwart leading men and most respected directors, was elected mayor of Carmel, California, in 1986. His first act as mayor was the legalization of ice cream parlors. The Carmel City Council wanted to ban ice cream sales within the city limits because they felt ice cream was making the sidewalks sticky. This is the kind of silly bureaucracy that made Eastwood decide to run for mayor in the first place. He accomplished much during his two-year tenure but decided not to run for a second term.

Ethan Hawke

As a child actor and teen heartthrob, Ethan Hawke worked hard to be taken seriously as an actor. He also worked hard as an author of fiction, penning two books, *Ash Wednesday* and *The Hottest State*. Many actors write or cowrite their biographies, but Hawke's modest success in the fiction world suggests that he's the real deal.

Hedy Lamarr

Exotic Austrian beauty Hedy Lamarr played sultry women of mystery and was once billed as "the most beautiful woman in the world." And like her name implies, Hedy had a good head on her shoulders: Together with composer George Antheil, she developed the idea of switching frequencies in order to create torpedo radio signals that could not be jammed by the Nazis. The idea was not practical until transistors made the switching of frequencies easy, and now the concept has applications in cell phone technology and satellite communications. In 1997, she was acknowledged at the Computers, Freedom, and Privacy Conference for "blazing new trails on the electronic frontier."

Steve Martin

"Wild and crazy guy" Steve Martin is also a knowledgeable art connoisseur. Martin has been collecting 20th-century American art since he was 21 years old and has amassed an important albeit eclectic collection that he lends to museums for exhibitions. Tops in his collection are two major works by Edward Hopper—*Hotel Window* and *Captain Upton's House*—which toured the country in a Hopper retrospective in 2008–2009. Martin has also released bluegrass albums and novels, making him quite the Renaissance *Jerk*.

Talk to the Expert

Best Boy

This job has nothing to do with gender or favoritism despite its name. Here's the scoop on that strange-sounding job we've seen in film credits.

Q: What does a best boy do?

A: That depends whether she's the best boy electric or the best boy grip. I'm a best boy electric, making me chief assistant to the gaffer, who's in charge of lights. A best boy grip is chief assistant to the key grip, who's in charge of camera dollies and cranes, mechanical stuff.

Q: So you rig up the lights?

A: Not usually, because my job is supervisory. I hire, fire, and oversee the people who rig up the lights. If someone has a union complaint, they bring it to me. I buy new equipment and supplies, make sure people work safely, and establish procedures. If the director or cinematographer wants something done with lighting, he might go to the gaffer or to me, but normally I'm the go-to gal. We produce the right lighting conditions for the time of day.

Q: How did you learn to be a best boy?

A: In high school, I discovered school plays and cinema and knew that's what I wanted to do. We shot our own movies on the side. I loved being up there manipulating the lights, making things work in the background. I started as a trade electrician in construction. Meanwhile, I kept putting in for film work and finally got my chance. I can tell the electricians what to do, because they know I've done it myself—and sometimes still do.

Q: It must be hard to break into your business.

A: It takes a good deal of skill and a lot of luck. When your moment comes in Hollywood, you have to perform really well. I carry spares of everything, especially fuses, because something can always go wrong.

They Also Served: Hollywood's Real Heroes

On the silver screen, they often seem invincible—able to leap tall buildings in a single bound, fearlessly enter a burning building to save the damsel in distress, or calmly capture the bad guy. But for the actors who served in the armed forces and defended their country against all odds, the bullets were real, the action unscripted, and the danger unimaginable. For these classic Hollywood heroes, art really did imitate life. Audie Murphy is the most well known war hero turned movie star, but let's shed some light on a few others.

✳ ✳ ✳ ✳

Eddie Albert

EDDIE ALBERT, THE star of the sitcom *Green Acres*, had a successful Hollywood career that lasted six decades. But few know that he was also a bona fide World War II hero. On November 21, 1943, while serving in the Marines in the South Pacific, Albert took command of several landing craft and raced to the rescue of 13 wounded marines trapped on an exposed reef at Betio Island. With the tide coming in and under enemy fire, Albert successfully retrieved them all.

Humphrey Bogart

Humphrey Bogart enlisted in the navy in 1918, but the war ended before he saw any combat. He completed his training at the Naval Reserve Station in Pelham Park, New York, and was assigned to the USS *Leviathan*, the navy's largest American troopship, and then the USS *Santa Olivia*. Bogart made several transatlantic trips, helping ferry American troops back home. During World War II, he joined the Coast Guard Auxiliary and regularly reported for duty when he was in California.

Michael Caine

Michael Caine was drafted into the British Army in May 1951 and was initially stationed in Germany as a member of the peacekeeper forces in the occupation army. He later became a rifleman in the Royal Fusiliers and was sent to Korea during the height of the Korean War, seeing extensive battle action at the Sami Chon River. Shortly after arriving in Korea, he contracted malaria, a disease that continued to affect him long after his release from the army in 1953.

R. Lee Ermey

Best remembered for his roles in *Full Metal Jacket* (1987) and *Mississippi Burning* (1988), R. Lee Ermey served in the Marine Corps for 11 years, rising to the rank of staff sergeant. He served 14 months in Vietnam and did two tours in Okinawa.

Dennis Franz

Born, raised, and educated in and around Chicago, Dennis Franz (*Die Hard 2*, 1990; *American Buffalo*, 1996; *NYPD Blue*) was drafted into the U.S. Army after graduating from Southern Illinois University and spent 11 months in an airborne division reconnaissance unit during the Vietnam War. During his tour of duty, Franz was awarded 17 accommodations, including the National Defense Medal, the Vietnam Cross of Gallantry–Individual Medal, the Vietnam Service Medal, and the Parachute Badge.

James Garner

In 1944, at age 16, James Garner left home, lied about his age, and joined the Merchant Marines. Later, he enlisted in the army and served in the Korean War. During his 14 months of service overseas, Garner was wounded twice. He earned his first Purple Heart after sustaining face and hand wounds from shrapnel from a mortar fired by North Korean troops. He was later wounded by his own troops during an exchange of gunfire with the enemy, but it wasn't until 1983—32 years later—that he finally received a second Purple Heart.

Tim McCoy

The film industry was still in its early days when World War I erupted, so very few Hollywood heroes served in the conflict. Tim McCoy was one of those few. He was also a real cowboy and a noted expert on the history of the Old West, particularly Native Americans. During the 1920s, he made more than two dozen movies, including *War Paint* (1926) and *Frontiersman* (1927). He also served in World War II, winning a bevy of medals including a Bronze Star.

Audie Murphy

The most notable performance in the line of duty goes to Audie Murphy, World War II's most decorated soldier with more than 30 medals on his chest, including the Medal of Honor and French Croix de Guerre with Silver Star. Murphy returned to America a national hero and went on to star in more than 40 major motion pictures, including *The Red Badge of Courage* (1951) and *To Hell and Back* (1955), which was based on his autobiography of the same name.

Lee Powell

The first actor to portray The Lone Ranger on the silver screen, Powell was the only "name" actor who died overseas during World War II. Powell enlisted in the Marines in 1942 and was assigned to the 2nd Battalion at Camp Elliott, California. After shipping overseas, he saw sustained action at Tarawa and Saipan and was promoted to sergeant. After fighting in a battle on Tinian in the Marianas Islands, he became ill after drinking home-brewed methyl alcohol—methanol, which is poisonous in even tiny amounts—and died after a brief hospital stay.

Harold Russell

As a sergeant in a demolition squad at Camp Mackall, North Carolina, Harold Russell was handling a half-pound chunk of TNT when a defective fuse detonated the explosive. He lost both hands in the accident, becoming one of approximately 1,200 double amputee victims of World War II. He later starred as a disabled veteran in the 1946 film *The Best Years of Our Lives*, a performance which earned him an Oscar for Best Supporting Actor and an Honorary Oscar for his courage and dedication. He is the only person to receive two Academy Awards for the same performance.

Jimmy Stewart

Jimmy Stewart joined the Army Air Corps as a private in 1941, studied painstakingly to become a military pilot, and served stateside for two years as a training instructor until his request for active duty was granted in 1943. Stewart flew a B-24, an aircraft known as The Liberator, for the remainder of the war, partaking in 20 dangerous combat missions as a command pilot, wing commander, or squadron commander. He was awarded the Distinguished Flying Cross with two Oak Leaf Clusters, the Air Medal with three Oak Leaf Clusters, and the French Croix de Guerre with Palm. By the end of the war, Stewart had risen to the rank of colonel. Throughout his film career, he continued to be a member of the U.S. Air Force Reserves and was promoted to brigadier general in 1959.

Lewis Stone

Lewis Stone, who first served in combat during the Spanish-American War, appeared in only a handful of movies before he rejoined the U.S. Army in 1916. He returned from the first World War and appeared in more than 140 more films, including *The Prisoner of Zenda* (1922) and *Grand Hotel* (1932).

What's in a Name?

A good movie title should compel moviegoers to line up for tickets on opening weekend. So it's surprising to find out that some of Hollywood's biggest hit movies started out with very different names. Let's find out what might have been.

Blade Runner (1982)

RIDLEY SCOTT'S FUTURISTIC sci-fi classic starring Harrison Ford as a policeman tracking down human-looking cyborgs was based on the Philip K. Dick novel *Do Androids Dream of Electric Sheep?* The movie adaptation initially kept the same title, but the studio considered it too long and "uncommercial," so it pushed for a change. Before settling on *Blade Runner*, however, the movie was known by a variety of other titles including *Android*, *Mechanismo*, and *Dangerous Days*.

Field of Dreams (1989)

W. P. Kinsella's book *Shoeless Joe* was the source material for this poignant story of redemption about an Iowa farmer (Kevin Costner) who builds a baseball diamond in his cornfield because he heard a voice. He is surprised and pleased to learn that the spirit of disgraced ballplayer Shoeless Joe Jackson inhabits the field.

The film's producers were content to use the novel's title for their film adaptation, but according to their marketing departments, the title confused test audiences. The "shoeless" part of the title suggested the story of a homeless person, while those who were familiar with the real Shoeless Joe

thought Costner would be playing him. This is one case where Hollywood actually improved on a book's title, because the film proved so inspirational that the real Iowa cornfield used for location shooting has attracted movie tourists who were touched by the story.

Pretty Woman (1990)

In 1990, this hugely popular romantic comedy made a star out of Julia Roberts and resurrected the career of Richard Gere. But it was nearly a very different movie with a very different title. Originally called *3,000*—in reference to the amount of money Gere's character pays Roberts's character (a prostitute) to spend the weekend with him—the script was first written as a dark drama about prostitution.

Even after it was reworked to be a romantic fairytale, the title *3,000* remained until test audiences complained that it sounded like a story about hookers in outer space. While considering songs for the film, director Garry Marshall came across Roy Orbison's 1964 hit "Oh, Pretty Woman." The rest is history.

Unforgiven (1992)

Clint Eastwood directed, produced, and starred in this one, which won four Oscars and is considered one of the best Westerns ever made. The script, however, had been bouncing around Hollywood for nearly 20 years before Eastwood picked it up, during which time it carried the less-than-snappy title *The Cut Whore Killings*. During production, the movie's working title was changed to *The William Munny Killings* before Eastwood finally settled on the more succinct *Unforgiven*.

While You Were Sleeping (1995)

In this romantic comedy, Sandra Bullock plays a Chicago public transit employee who has a serious crush on a man who loses consciousness for several days after a fall, thus the original title of the film—*Coma Guy*. Disney wisely decided to change the somber-sounding title when they realized that, in 1991, *Dying*

Young had proved a box-office disappointment, despite the fact that star Julia Roberts was at the top of her game. Studio execs figured that couples looking for a romantic escape would probably avoid a movie with words like *dying* or *coma* in the title, so they went with *While You Were Sleeping* instead, and it grossed $81 million—more than twice as much as *Dying Young*.

G.I. Jane (1997)

This Disney flick starring a very buff Demi Moore as a female Navy SEAL recruit carried several different titles before its release in 1997. The film would have been titled *In Pursuit of Honor* or *Navy Cross* had Disney not eventually paid several hundred thousand dollars to purchase the rights to license the name G.I. Jane from toy company Hasbro.

American Pie (1999)

The title *American Pie* probably doesn't immediately make you think "teenage sex comedy," but the title proved hugely successful for the movie. The original script carried the more apt, but far too lengthy postmodern title *Teenage Sex Comedy that Can Be Made for Under $10 Million that Your Reader Will Love, But the Executive Will Hate.*

When Universal purchased the project, the title was changed to *East Great Falls High*, but the final decision came down to a choice between *American Pie* or *Comfort Food*. Perhaps it was shrewd executives time traveling to the possibility of having sequels called *Comfort Food 2* and *Comfort Wedding* that helped cement their decision.

Hollywood Heroes

Hollywood celebrities tend to make the tabloid pages for all the wrong reasons. Every now and then, though, they find themselves in the headlines for heroic deeds rather than scandals.

✳ ✳ ✳ ✳

Mark Harmon

THE ACTOR, BEST known for his roles on *St. Elsewhere*, *The West Wing*, and *NCIS*, became a real-life hero in 1996 when two teenage boys crashed their Jeep near his Brentwood home. Harmon's wife, actress Pam Dawber, was the first on the scene, so when she saw the car in flames, she yelled for her husband to bring a sledgehammer. Harmon smashed a window, wrestled one of the boys from his seatbelt, and then pulled him to safety. The boy was on fire so the actor rolled him on the ground to extinguish the flames. A fire department spokesman praised Harmon for his heroics, stating, "These boys certainly owe their lives to the quick and selfless action of Mr. Harmon." No wonder he was so believable as C.J. Cregg's protective personal Secret Service detail.

Harrison Ford

This movie star doesn't confine his heroics to the big screen when he's playing Han Solo or Indiana Jones. Ford has twice turned real-life hero to rescue stranded hikers by flying his Bell 407 helicopter. In July 2000, the accomplished pilot picked up a distress call from two female hikers on Table Mountain in Idaho. One was overcome with altitude sickness after a five-hour climb, so Ford flew in to airlift her to the hospital. The woman didn't recognize her famous rescuer until after she'd vomited in his hat.

A year later, Ford's flying skills were called upon again in the rescue of a 13-year-old Boy Scout who went missing in Yellowstone National Park. After scouring the area for two hours, Ford spotted the boy and swooped down to rescue him.

He even shared a joke with the boy, who had managed to survive overnight wearing only a T-shirt and shorts. "Boy, you sure must have earned a merit badge for this one," said the actor.

Cuba Gooding Jr.

On the night of Memorial Day 2007, Cuba Gooding Jr. picked up dinner for his family from Roscoe's House of Chicken 'n' Waffles in Hollywood. When the Oscar-winning actor saw a young man collapse, bleeding from a gunshot wound, he ran to help. He called into the restaurant for towels and managed to stem the bleeding. The *Jerry Maguire* (1996) star hailed a passing police car and cradled the injured man until an ambulance arrived at the scene.

Gerard Butler

Before he became famous in the U.S. as the heroic lead in *300*, the 2007 movie adaptation of Frank Miller's graphic novel, Gerard Butler was honored for real-life heroism. The Scottish actor received a Certificate of Bravery from the Royal Humane Society of Scotland in 1997 after he risked his life to pull a drowning boy from the River Tay, the longest river in Scotland. Butler was enjoying a picnic nearby when he saw the child drowning and immediately dived in to rescue him.

Tom Cruise

Tom Cruise has a history of coming to the aid of folks in trouble, though the tabloid press seems to focus more on his couch-jumping and religious beliefs than his good deeds. In 2006, he and then-wife Katie Holmes assisted a young couple who had been in a car accident. Ten years earlier, Cruise rescued a young woman who had been hit by a car. He called an ambulance for her, then paid her emergency room bill. However charitable these acts were, they pale in comparison to an incident in London in 1998. While out walking, Cruise came across a woman being mugged. The woman was sitting in her Porsche when a man opened the car door and began grabbing the jewelry from her hands and arms. The woman screamed, and Cruise ran to her aid, chasing off the mugger in mid-theft. Reportedly, he prevented the loss of at least some of the jewelry the woman was wearing—worth between $120,000 and $150,000, so about ten minutes of the actor's time on set.

Todd Bridges

After his role as Willis Jackson on the popular sitcom *Diff'rent Strokes* came to an end in 1986, actor Todd Bridges tended to make headlines for all the wrong reasons. He endured a much-publicized battle with cocaine addiction and, in 1990, even stood trial for the attempted murder of a drug dealer. In 2001, however, Bridges made headlines for rescuing a paraplegic woman from drowning in Lake Balboa in Los Angeles. The 50-year-old woman was fishing while buckled into her motorized wheelchair. When the chair accidentally rolled into the lake and fell on its side, her head was trapped underwater. Bridges and his brother James ran to the woman's aid and managed to pull her to safety.

What Really Killed John Wayne?

The Conqueror (1956) wasn't exactly John Wayne's masterpiece. According to "The Duke" himself, the film was written with Marlon Brando in mind for the lead role, and this historical drama has been criticized for miscasting Wayne in the part. However, The Conqueror *has been connected to far worse things than box-office failure: Some say the movie is to blame for Wayne's death from stomach cancer two decades after its debut. What's more, Wayne isn't the only person believed to have died as a result of the project. Was the nearby nuclear testing site to blame?*

✳   ✳   ✳   ✳

Radiation Exposure

THE QUESTIONS SURROUNDING *The Conqueror* come as a result of its filming location: The movie was shot near St. George and Snow Canyon, Utah, an area in the vicinity of a nuclear testing site. In the early 1950s, the U.S. military set off nearly a dozen atomic bombs just miles away from the location, sending clouds of radioactive dust into St. George and Snow Canyon. Work on *The Conqueror* began just two years later, even though the film company and cast knew about the radiation.

To make matters worse, after the location work had wrapped, the film's crew transported dirt from the area back to soundstages in Hollywood to help re-create the setting for in-studio shooting. (At the time, the effects of radiation exposure were not as well documented as they are today.)

In the years following the filming of *The Conqueror*, numerous members of the cast and crew developed cancer. Aside from Wayne, at least 45 people from the group died from causes related to the disease, including actress Agnes Moorehead, who died in 1974 from uterine cancer; actress Susan Hayward, who died from brain and skin cancer at age 57 in 1975; and director Dick Powell, who, in 1963, passed away at age 58 from lymphatic cancer. Actors Pedro Armendariz and John Hoyt and both took their own lives after learning of their diagnoses.

An article published in *People* magazine in 1980 stated that 41 percent of those who worked on the movie—91 out of 220 people—later developed cancer. That figure reportedly didn't include the hundreds of Utah-based actors who worked as extras. Still, the numbers far exceeded any statistical normality for a given group of individuals. A scientist with the Pentagon's Defense Nuclear Agency was quoted in the article as saying: "Please, God, don't let us have killed John Wayne."

Broader Findings

While many of the actors were heavy smokers—Wayne included—the strange circumstances surrounding the filming of *The Conqueror* have turned into an underground scandal of sorts. And the general findings from the city of St. George certainly don't help quell the concerns.

In 1997, a study by the National Cancer Institute found that children who lived in the St. George area during the 1950s were exposed to as much as 70 times the amount of radiation than was originally reported because of contaminated milk taken from exposed animals. Consequently, the study reported that the children had elevated risks for cancer development. The report further stated that the government "knew from the beginning that a Western test site would spread contamination across most of the country" and that the exposure could have easily been avoided.

The government eventually passed an act called the Radiation Exposure Compensation Act, which provided $50,000 to people who lived downwind of the nuclear testing site near St. George and had been exposed to radiation. At least 40,000 people are thought to have been exposed in Utah alone. While John Wayne is the most famous of them, the true cause of his cancer may never be definitively known.

* The actor known as John Wayne was born Marion Morrison. The name John Wayne came about in 1930 in the months before filming began on *The Big Trail*. Twentieth Century Fox wanted a catchier moniker, and the name Anthony Wayne—from the Army general known as "Mad" Anthony—caught their attention. They substituted "John" for "Anthony," and Marion Morrison became John Wayne.

All that Glitters

When the producers of the James Bond film franchise heard the rumor that Shirley Eaton, who portrayed the gold-plated woman in Goldfinger, *had died from skin suffocation, they were shaken—and stirred. Let's find out what really happened.*

❋ ❋ ❋ ❋

SHORTLY AFTER THE release of *Goldfinger*, the third spool in the James Bond library, rumors spread that the actor who portrayed the damsel Jill Masterson—who dies in the film's opening sequence after being painted from head to toe in gold varnish—had passed away from paint poisoning. The actor whose body was used as a human canvas by the sinister smuggler Auric Goldfinger and his parasitic sidekick Oddjob was Shirley Eaton, who was alive then and is still among us today.

In fact, the brass behind Bond were so cognizant of the dangers inherent in dabbing a person from head to toe in gold paint that they instructed Eaton to wear a strategically placed undergarment and left an area of her stomach unpainted to allow her body to "breathe." Although she was exposed in the movie only for a matter of moments, her alleged celluloid demise became legendary, even warranting her placement on the cover of *Life* magazine. Eaton went on to appear in dozens of other movies and played the title character in the notorious (and notoriously awful) *The Million Eyes of Su-Muru* with beach-boy Frankie Avalon before retiring in the late 1960s to raise her family.

In fact, the glistening glamour girl that most people associate with the movie isn't Eaton at all. Margaret Nolan, who is best known as one of the bodacious babes in the *Carry On* gang films, played the gold-fleshed filly in the movie's title sequence, and she was the model prominently featured on the subsequent movie-poster advertising blitz.

Celebrities Who've Encountered Ghosts

Who says that ghosts only show themselves to everyday people in out-of-the way locations? The following list just might convince you that when it comes to ghosts, not even the Hollywood elite is safe from a supernatural scare!

❋　❋　❋　❋

Vincent Price

WHILE HE WAS alive, the great, spooky Vincent Price frightened the heck out of millions of moviegoers, but Price himself experienced a ghostly shock while he was on an L.A.-to-New York flight on November 15, 1958. Most of the trip was uneventful, but at one point, Price glanced out the window and was shocked to see giant letters that were "lit up with blinding light from within the clouds" spelling out "Tyrone Power is dead."

Price, who was a close friend of Power, was shocked by what he saw, but he was even more perplexed by the fact that no one else on the plane seemed to notice the words, even though some were looking out the windows. Before Price could speak, the words vanished as quickly as they had appeared.

Upon reaching New York, Price dashed to a phone and tried to call Power. That's when he learned that Power had just died of a heart attack in Madrid, Spain. Price originally thought that he'd had a psychic premonition, but as the years passed, he did not experience any similar events, which ultimately led him to believe that he'd been given a single otherworldly message.

Paul McCartney

In 1995, Paul McCartney, George Harrison, and Ringo Starr entered a studio to record as The Beatles for the first time in decades. They had chosen to record the song "Free as a Bird," which was written by their dearly departed bandmate John

Lennon, gunned down in 1980. While recording the song, McCartney had the distinct feeling that Lennon's ghost was present for the session. McCartney said that they kept hearing strange noises coming from inside the studio and that the equipment malfunctioned from time to time. "There was just an overall feeling that John was around," McCartney said later.

Sugar Ray Leonard

In 1982, after ruling the boxing world for several years, Olympic Gold Medalist and World Champion Sugar Ray Leonard found himself in a bad place. At age 25, he had been forced into an early retirement due to a detached retina. He wasn't happy with himself or with life. But all that changed when he and his wife were awakened one night by what sounded like children running in the attic above them. Leonard went to investigate, but his search came up empty. The next day, an exterminator was summoned, but he too found nothing.

The following night, Leonard woke up feeling as though he was being watched. Looking across the darkened bedroom, he saw the silhouette of a child, which he initially thought was one of his sons. But as the shape approached the bed, Leonard realized that it was a young girl. He was transfixed for several moments before he decided to reach out to touch the figure. When he did, the girl's image began to distort, taking on the look of someone who had been horribly burned. It was then that Leonard smelled gas.

Forgetting all about the ghost, Leonard woke his wife. She too smelled the gas, so the couple immediately grabbed their two sleeping children and fled to a relative's house. The following morning, Leonard called a repairman and asked him to check for a gas leak. Several hours later, the repairman called to tell Leonard that not only was there no leak, there weren't even any gas lines in or near the Leonard residence.

Leonard interpreted seeing the ghostly young girl as a sign that he needed to recognize the importance of family. And although

Leonard never saw the apparition again, he later discovered that a young girl had burned to death inside the home.

Anson Williams

Years before he would work his way into America's heart as the lovable Potsie Weber on *Happy Days*, Anson Williams had his own guardian angel. Both of Williams's parents told him that on many occasions, they would walk by his room at night and see the ghost of his grandmother standing watch over him as he slept. As he grew older, Williams would take comfort in that, especially since his grandmother had died before he was born and he never had the chance to meet her.

One night in 1971, Williams drove his car into an intersection and was broadsided by a car that had run a red light. Williams states that just as the cars collided, time suddenly began to move in slow motion, and as his head moved toward the windshield, he saw the face of his grandmother in the glass; he also heard her voice telling him, "Everything's fine." And although both cars were smashed beyond recognition, Williams walked away from the accident with only a scratch.

Marilyn Manson

You'd expect shock-rocker Marilyn Manson to have at least one creepy ghost story to tell, but you'd probably never guess that it happened to him at, of all places, a farm in Ohio.

As a teenager in 1986, Manson (then known simply as Brian Warner) befriended a classmate in rural Canton, Ohio. In an attempt to scare Manson, the boy took him to his family's barn, where the boy's older brother had created a sort of makeshift satanic altar, complete with strange symbols and rotting animal carcasses. The boy then picked up a book that was alleged to contain incantations intended to summon evil spirits and ordered Manson to read aloud from it. Before Manson could get very far, the older brother showed up, causing Manson and the other boy to flee into the woods with the book in tow.

After running for a while, the boys came to an old, abandoned house. They made their way to the building's basement, where Manson was once again ordered to read aloud from the book. As he did, Manson became aware of strange symbols written on the cellar walls, along with what looked like handprints. As he continued to read, the boys began to hear people walking just outside the cellar door, followed by voices. Some of the voices were whispering, while others were clearly saying phrases such as, "Do you believe in Satan?" In a panic, Manson dropped the book and the two boys ran home.

The following day, Manson and his friend returned to the abandoned house to retrieve the book only to find no sign that a house was ever there. Manson called it "the most supernatural strange thing" that he ever experienced, which says a lot coming from him, right?

Michael Imperioli

Actor Michael Imperioli, who gained fame on *The Sopranos*, counts himself among those who have seen the mournful spirit of Mary, which haunts New York's Chelsea Hotel. Mary wasn't a poet or an artist like many of the Chelsea's guests; she was just a woman from Buffalo, New York, who was waiting for her husband's boat to arrive in New York City. Unfortunately, her husband was on the RMS *Titanic*, and when Mary received news of his fate that cold April night in 1912, she hanged herself in her room.

Typically, guests spot Mary on the eighth floor of the Chelsea; she is seen crying or staring longingly into the mirrors. While living on the eighth floor in 1996, Imperioli saw a woman weeping at the end of the hall. He approached her and noticed that she was wearing clothes from the early 1900s. When he asked if she needed help, he heard a lightbulb pop behind him and instinctively turned toward it. A second later, when he turned back around, the woman had vanished. Imperioli moved out of the hotel shortly after discovering that the woman he had encountered was Mary... and that she was a ghost.

The Amityville Horror: Haunted House or Horrible Hoax?

It seems that nearly every town has a haunted house—the one home that animals and locals avoid like the plague. But when it comes to haunted houses that can chill your bones with just one glance and give you nightmares for weeks, nothing can hold a ghostly candle to the foreboding Dutch Colonial in Amityville, New York, which once glared down at passersby with windows that seemed to resemble demonic eyes. The house and its years of misadventures have spawned almost countless movies.

✳ ✳ ✳ ✳

Brutal Beginnings

MOST HAUNTINGS BEGIN with tragic circumstances, and the house at 112 Ocean Avenue is no exception. In the early morning hours of November 13, 1974, someone fatally shot six of the seven members of the DeFeo family—parents Ronald Sr. and Louise and four of their children: Mark, John, Allison, and Dawn. The only family member to escape the massacre was 23-year-old Ronnie "Butch" DeFeo, who was arrested and charged with all six murders. He eventually confessed and was sentenced to 25 years to life in prison. During the trial, rumors suggested that demonic voices had directed DeFeo to commit the murders, although prosecutors claimed that he was merely trying to collect the family's $200,000 insurance policy.

The DeFeo house stood unoccupied until December 1975, when new owners came calling.

The Horror Begins

George and Kathy Lutz knew that they had found a bargain when their realtor showed them the house at 112 Ocean Avenue. It had six bedrooms, a pool, and even a boathouse, all for the unbelievable price of $80,000. Of course, an entire family had been murdered in the house, and some of their belongings were still inside, but the Lutzes decided that it was too good a deal to pass up. So George and Kathy moved in with their three young children: Daniel, Christopher, and Missy. Shortly thereafter, the Lutzes' nightmare began. It quickly became obvious to them that demonic forces were at work inside the house. Here is some of the paranormal activity that allegedly took place there:

* George had trouble sleeping and continually woke up at exactly 3:15 A.M., which was believed to be the time that the DeFeo murders took place.

* Daughter Missy began talking to an imaginary friend—a girl named Jodie, who sometimes appeared as a pig. Standing outside the house one night, George looked up and saw a giant pig with glowing red eyes staring back at him from Missy's room. Later, cloven hoofprints were found in the snow outside the house.

* Even though the family moved in during the middle of winter, certain rooms in the house—especially the sewing room—were constantly infested with flies.

* A small room painted blood-red—which was dubbed "the Red Room"—was found hidden behind shelving in the basement. The Lutzes felt that an evil force inhabited the room; even the family dog refused to go near it.

* During an attempt to bless the house, a priest suddenly became violently ill and heard an inhuman voice tell him to "Get out!" When George and Kathy attempted to bless the house themselves, they heard voices screaming, "Will you stop?"

* Green slime oozed from the toilets and dripped down walls.

* George unintentionally began to take on the mannerisms of Butch DeFeo; he even grew a beard, which caused him to resemble the murderer. Apparently the likeness was so

uncanny that when Lutz walked into a bar that DeFeo used to frequent, patrons thought he *was* DeFeo.

On January 14, 1976, unable to cope with the unseen forces at work in the home, George and Kathy Lutz gathered up their children and their dog and fled the house in the middle of the night. The following day, George sent movers to collect their belongings. The Lutzes never again set foot inside the house at 112 Ocean Avenue.

Searching for Evil

In an attempt to understand exactly what had happened to his family inside the house, George hired paranormal experts Ed and Lorraine Warren, who arrived at the house with a local news crew on March 6, 1976. Lorraine said that she sensed a very strong evil presence in the house. Several years later, the Warrens released time-lapse infrared photographs from the investigation; they seem to show a ghostly boy with glowing eyes standing near one of the staircases.

Jay Anson's book *The Amityville Horror: A True Story* was released in September 1977. The book, which chronicles the Lutz family's harrowing ordeal, was compiled from more than 40 hours of tape-recorded interviews with George and Kathy Lutz and became a best-seller almost immediately. After the book became a cultural phenomenon, however, people started taking a closer look into what had really happened at 112 Ocean Avenue.

Controversy Begins

When people started to scrutinize the specifics in Anson's book, the story began to fall apart. For example, a check of weather conditions showed that no snow was on the ground when George claimed to have found the strange cloven footprints in the snow. Likewise, windows and doors that ghostly forces had supposedly broken were found to be intact. Reporters who interviewed neighbors along Ocean Avenue found that not a single person could remember seeing or hearing anything strange going on at the house. And despite the book mentioning numerous visits by the local police to investigate strange noises at the Lutz house, the Amityville Police Department publicly stated that during the time that the Lutzes lived at 112 Ocean Avenue, they never once visited the home or received a single phone call from the family.

The Lawsuits

In May 1977, George and Kathy Lutz filed a series of lawsuits against numerous publications and individuals who had either investigated 112 Ocean Avenue or had written about the reported hauntings there. They alleged that the accused had invaded their privacy and caused their family mental distress. There was one other name in the lawsuits that raised a few eyebrows: William Weber, Butch DeFeo's defense attorney. Even more surprising was that Weber filed a countersuit for $2 million for breach of contract.

Weber contended that he had met with the Lutzes, and "over many bottles of wine," the three made up the story of the house being haunted. When Weber found out that the Lutzes had taken their story to Jay Anson and essentially cut him out of the book deal, he sued. In September 1979, U.S. District Court Judge Jack B. Weinstein dismissed all of the Lutzes' claims and made some telling remarks in his ruling, including his belief that the book was basically a work of fiction that relied heavily upon Weber's suggestions. Weber's countersuit was later settled out of court for an undisclosed amount.

What Really Happened?

Even though it's been decades since the Lutzes occupied the house at 112 Ocean Avenue, many questions still remain unanswered. A series of books and films bearing the name *The Amityville Horror* continued to blur the lines between what really happened in the home and what was fabricated. In 2005, a remake of the original *Amityville Horror* movie added many new elements to the story that are unsubstantiated, including a link between the house in Amityville and a man named John Ketcham, who was reportedly involved in witchcraft in Salem, Massachusetts.

Kathy Lutz died of emphysema in August 2004, and George passed away of complications from heart disease in May 2006. Both went to their graves claiming that what they said happened to them at 112 Ocean Avenue was not a hoax.

The house itself still stands. One would think that a building as infamous as the "Amityville Horror" house would be easy to find; not so. In order to stop the onslaught of trespassing curiosity seekers, its address has been changed, so 112 Ocean Avenue technically no longer exists. Also, the distinctive quarter-moon windows have been removed and replaced with ordinary square ones.

Since the Lutz family moved out, the property has changed hands several times, but none of the subsequent owners have reported anything paranormal taking place there. Some have acknowledged being frightened from time to time, but these scares are usually caused by trespassers peering into the windows, trying to get glimpses of the inside of this allegedly haunted house.

Spirited Celebrities

By their very nature, celebrities seem larger than life—but some seem to be larger than death, too. Were the egos within this group so immense that even death couldn't contain them? Might they have something important to tell us? Or are these notables simply performing an afterlife version of a curtain call? For whatever reason, something seems to be keeping these celebrity spirits earthbound.

✳   ✳   ✳   ✳

Marilyn Monroe

AS FAMOUS IN death as she was in life, screen legend Marilyn Monroe (1926–1962) continues to captivate. Plagued with insecurities from the start, the blonde bombshell's three marriages ended in divorce, and she eventually developed a dependency on substances to counter the overwhelming weight of her celebrity. Nevertheless, when Monroe exited the mortal world at age 36, the coroner's pronouncement of "probable suicide" didn't ring true for many. Since then, countless conspiracy theories concerning Monroe's death have taken root.

In life, a favorite haunt of the sexy siren was the Hollywood Roosevelt Hotel. It was at this retreat for Tinseltown's elite that Monroe found peace and could rest, safe in the knowledge that her private moments would remain private. Perhaps she is still searching for such moments in death: That might explain the sightings of her sashaying across the hotel's ballroom and lingering near the room that she often occupied. It might also explain why her haunting image can sometimes be seen in a mirror that hangs in the hotel's lobby.

In recent years, guests at the Hotel del Coronado in Coronado, California, have also reported seeing Marilyn Monroe's ghost.

She loved "the Del" when she stayed there while filming *Some Like It Hot* (1959). She is supposedly seen as a fleeting, translucent apparition near the door to the hotel or on the beach nearby. Those who have seen her specter comment on its windswept blonde hair and its fringed shawl that flutters in the breeze. Others claim to have heard Monroe giggling.

Carole Lombard

Another spirit that is said to haunt the Hollywood Roosevelt Hotel is that of actress Carole Lombard (1908–1942). The golden-haired beauty made her mark in notable films such as *My Man Godfrey* (1936) and *Mr. & Mrs. Smith* (1941). Despite her talent, Lombard is perhaps best remembered as the wife of screen legend Clark Gable. The couple married in 1939, but only three years later, on January 16, 1942, fate played its cruel hand when the actress was killed in a plane crash.

Lombard's death had a profound effect on Gable: The word *devastated* only begins to describe the depth of the actor's grief. Despite two subsequent marriages, Gable said that with Lombard's passing, he had lost the greatest love of his life. When he died in 1960, he was buried beside his beloved Lombard. But death may not have signaled the end of their romance: Sightings at the Hollywood Roosevelt suggest that this great love carries on. Lombard's apparition has been spotted moving about the hotel's 12th floor. It was there that the famous couple's love first blossomed, and it is there that it apparently continues . . . for eternity.

Lon Chaney Sr.

Known for playing such frightening characters as Quasimodo in *The Hunchback of Notre Dame* (1923) and the title character in *The Phantom of the Opera* (1925), Lon Chaney Sr. (1883–1930), the "Man of a Thousand Faces," scared viewers silly during the silent-film era. With his haunting legacy, it's not surprising that Chaney can still be found wandering the catwalks above Soundstage 28 at Universal Studios. Horror-film buffs know that this is the stage where *Phantom* was shot. Chaney's ghost reportedly moves about in full Phantom garb, flipping lights on and off and opening and closing doors.

Rudolph Valentino

Before "talkies" (movies with sound) came along, silent films ruled the silver screen. In those early days of filmmaking, the strikingly handsome Rudolph Valentino (1895–1926) made women swoon. Moviegoers happily plunked down a quarter to see the "Latin Lover" in films such as *The Sheik* (1921). His immense popularity made Hollywood moguls rich, but the actor's earthly days were sadly limited. Due to complications from a ruptured appendix and gastric ulcers, Valentino left the human realm at age 31. Nevertheless, there are some who say that he never left at all.

Before his former mansion—Falcon Lair—was demolished in the 2000s, Valentino was spotted standing in his bedroom and peering from a second-floor window. He was also seen inside the estate's barn: It was there that a stable worker saw Valentino's ghost petting his favorite horse.

Valentino sightings at Paramount Studios may be even more dramatic. There, the ghost of the eternal ladies' man has been seen wandering around the costume department wearing his costume from *The Sheik*. The handsome apparition has also been spotted looking down from a catwalk high above Soundstage 5. For a brief time, this was his world.

George Reeves

If a post-death appearance suggests unfinished business in the mortal world, the spirit of George Reeves (1914–1959) may be trying to tell us something. Reeves acquired his acting chops long before the popular *Adventures of Superman* TV series (1952–1958) turned him into a household name: Before he was "The Man of Steel," Reeves appeared in several TV shows and movies, including the classic *Gone with the Wind* (1939).

On June 16, 1959, Reeves held a party at his Benedict Canyon home. The get-together suddenly turned tragic when a loud bang was heard in the actor's upstairs bedroom. Upon investigation, Reeves was found dead of an apparently self-inflicted gunshot wound to the head. His death was ruled a suicide, but not everyone was convinced that he killed himself. After all, Reeves had recently launched a career as a TV director and seemed to be riding a happy wave in life. Some began to wonder if the actor's death was, in fact, a *murder* that was made to look like a suicide. Reeves certainly had his enemies—most notably an insanely jealous ex-lover who resented being jilted for another woman.

Perhaps we'll never know just what occurred in Reeves's bedroom on that sad day, but some believe that his spirit is trying to tell us. Numerous people have claimed that Reeves's ghost inhabits his former residence. Strange noises, moving beds, tossed linens, and a variety of other surreal incidents have kept subsequent owners on their toes. Once, Reeves's ghost was spotted—dressed in Superman garb—lingering in the living room where the ill-fated party had taken place. The apparition hung around until the residents fled in panic. Was the "Man of Steel" trying to relay a message about his stolen life?

Lucille Ball

After a long and successful career as Hollywood's most beloved comedienne, Lucille Ball died in 1989 at age 77. Although she died during surgery, her spirit apparently returned to her beloved home on Roxbury Drive in Beverly Hills. After Lucy died, her husband Gary Morton sold the home, and the new owners subsequently demolished it. When a friend of Lucy's stopped by the home to assess the destruction, he saw her ghost lingering at the construction site, looking bewildered.

Elvis Presley

Graceland will never be the same without Elvis Presley. But according to some, Elvis hasn't left the building. Visitors have caught glimpses of his apparition walking through the gates of his beloved estate. One tourist claims to have seen "The King's" face reflected back at her from a glass jewelry case, and it's rumored that his ghost still resides in his old private quarters—an area that is closed to the public.

Since his death in 1977, Elvis's spirit has also been spotted near Music Row in Nashville. Workers at a studio there say that whenever Presley's name is brought up, lights flicker, ladders fall down, and unusual noises are heard over the sound system.

Elvis appears as the resident ghost in Dean Koontz's mystery series about an eccentric, spirit-seeing young man named Odd Thomas.

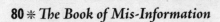

Chapter 2

Cooking

Talking Turkey

Did the Pilgrims start a tradition by eating turkey at the first Thanksgiving—or was that Tiny Tim's doing?

✳   ✳   ✳   ✳

Which came first, the turkey or Thanksgiving?

GOVERNOR WILLIAM BRADLEY's journal from around that time indicates that "besides waterfowl there was great store of wild turkeys, of which they took many." Another record notes that "our governor sent four men on fowling . . . they four in one day killed as much fowl, as with a little help beside, served the company almost a week."

Of course, "fowl" doesn't necessarily mean turkey, so the best we can say is that the Pilgrims may have eaten it. The only food we know for certain they ate was venison, and that was provided by their guests, the Native Americans (who may have been a little surprised by the meager spread their hosts had laid out). They probably also ate codfish, goose, and lobster, but not a lot of vegetables—you can catch fish and fowl, but it takes time to grow crops. And mashed potatoes? Nope—potatoes hadn't yet been introduced to New England.

So how did the gobbler become the centerpiece?

It may have had something to do with the prevalent diet at the time the national holiday was founded in 1863. Beef and chicken were too expensive to serve to a crowd. Even if you had your own farm, you needed the animals' continuous supply of milk and eggs. Venison was an option, but you couldn't always count on bagging a deer in time for the holiday.

Turkey was readily available, not too expensive—and very popular, perhaps in part due to the scene at the end of Charles Dickens's *A Christmas Carol* in which Scrooge buys "the prize turkey" for Bob Cratchit's family. The novel, published in 1843, was immensely popular in America and may have secured the humble fowl's center-stage spot on the Thanksgiving, and oftentimes Christmas, table.

Turkey Tracking

Exactly how this Thanksgiving favorite got its name is frequently debated, but one thing is certain: Turkeys are not so called because they originated in Turkey.

✳   ✳   ✳   ✳

TURKEYS ARE NATIVE to North America. Spanish settlers originally brought the bird back from Mexico in the early 16th century. English merchants picked up the birds in Eastern Mediterranean trading ports, which were then part of the Ottoman Empire, an area that included modern-day Turkey. Believing that the bird originated in this part of the world, the English dubbed it a "turkey bird" or "turkey cock."

The turkey was domesticated and bred specifically for its meat and plumage and was then taken by the British to its colonies in America. Of course, the bird was already living there and had been hunted for centuries by Native Americans. The name stuck nonetheless, and eventually "turkey bird" was shortened to plain old "turkey."

Strangely, it was only the English who believed the bird originated in Turkey. Most other Europeans, including the Turks, believed the bird came from India and so dubbed it some variation of "bird of India." This confusion is most likely due to the fact that the Spanish referred to the newly discovered territories of the New World as the Spanish Indies or the New Indies, believing that Mexico was part of Asia.

Overkill: A Matter of Degrees

Boiling water kills bacteria, but it also wastes energy. Here's how you can have your clean water and save the environment, too.

✳ ✳ ✳ ✳

WHEN IN DOUBT about the potability of your water supply, you can ensure its cleanliness (well, at least its "antimicrobialness") by boiling it. But if you don't have an updated wilderness manual, you may not know that boiling water for extended period of time doesn't make it any cleaner, and in fact, boiling isn't even necessary.

It's a misconception that water must reach the boiling point—212 degrees Fahrenheit—to kill pathogens. The temperature needed to knock off most critters (excluding extreme varieties such as bacteria living in volcanoes) is just 185 degrees Fahrenheit. Bacteria, microbes, viruses, and parasites are killed off after just a few minutes at that temperature. Disease-causing pathogens, then, are already dead by the time the water begins to boil. (That's good news, but also, *gross*.)

In developing countries where firewood is scarce and water is filled with bacteria, it is imperative to adhere to recommended boiling times. Since you're unlikely to have a cooking thermometer handy, the prudent route is simply to wait for the water to boil so you know for sure it's over 185 degrees.

Yet various safety guides recommend boiling water for 5, 10, even 20 minutes. At this point much of the water will evaporate, and fuel will have been wasted. In light of criticism about wasting energy to boil water, the Centers for Disease Control and the Environmental Protection Agency recently lowered their suggested boiling times. Both now recommend heating water to a rolling boil for only one minute.

Cholesterol Confusion!

You know the old saying, "You can't judge a book by its cover"?
Well, you can't judge your cholesterol level by your cover, either.

✳   ✳   ✳   ✳

YOU'VE PROBABLY HEARD about someone who runs daily and eats a lean, healthful diet but is suddenly struck by a heart attack. The culprit: undiagnosed clogged arteries because of high blood cholesterol. But it's a common misconception that high cholesterol is always the result of poor diet. Although diet can play a significant role in boosting (and lowering) cholesterol levels, other factors may also be involved.

Our genes partly determine how much cholesterol our bodies make, so high blood cholesterol often runs in families. Dietary cholesterol found in eggs and other foods seems to make very little difference, despite the infamous "Is Your Breakfast Killing You?" rash of headlines in the mid 20th century. Other potential causes include:

✳ **Excess weight.** Being overweight boosts cholesterol levels; losing weight can bring down bad LDL cholesterol and increase good HDL cholesterol.

✳ **A sedentary lifestyle.** Being inactive is a major risk factor for high cholesterol. Increasing physical activity will help lower LDL cholesterol and raise HDL levels.

✳ **Age and gender.** Cholesterol levels tend to rise naturally as we get older. Before menopause, most women have lower total cholesterol levels than men of the same age. But after menopause, women's LDL levels frequently rise.

Putting the "C" in "Panacea"

Vitamin C is an essential vitamin. It plays a critical role in the formation and repair of collagen, the connective tissue that holds the body's cells and tissues together. It promotes the normal development of bones and teeth, and it is a potent antioxidant. But it is not a cure-all.

✳   ✳   ✳   ✳

Vitamin c was catapulted into the limelight in the 1960s when Nobel Prize–winning scientist Linus Pauling began touting vitamin C megatherapy, claiming high doses could reduce the frequency and severity of colds. Sales of vitamin C exploded after Pauling's book *Vitamin C and the Common Cold* was published in 1970. Pauling went on to claim that megadoses of vitamin C could also prevent or slow the growth of cancer, among other diseases. Even though Pauling's methods (and findings) have been soundly debunked, the myth that vitamin C is a cure-all persists.

Found especially in uncooked fruits and vegetables, vitamin C is a water-soluble substance that humans don't produce naturally. The body's tissues can't absorb more than 100 milligrams a day, so it's a waste of money to take megadoses. High doses are not known to be toxic, but too much vitamin C (more than 2,000 mg/day) can cause gas, diarrhea, and kidney stones, as well as impede the absorption of other vitamins.

However, there is still debate over vitamin C's role in disease prevention and treatment. Some studies show a positive impact on heart disease, cancer, and other illnesses, while others do not—a few even indicate that it can be harmful. More medical research is needed for definitive answers.

Don't Hold the Pepperoni

For years, spicy foods and stress took the rap for causing ulcers.
The real culprit, however, has a Latin name.

✳   ✳   ✳   ✳

YOU CAN HAVE an ulcer and eat your pepperoni pizza, too.
Research has proved that certain foods—including hot
chilies, coffee, and curry—do not cause ulcers. Nor does stress,
no matter how much you have to endure on the job or on the
home front.

Your lifestyle is not to blame for the gnawing pain in your gut,
though it can exacerbate your symptoms. Ulcers are most frequently caused by a bacterial infection. The little bug is called
Helicobacter pylori, a corkscrew-shape (helico-, like "helix," a
root shared by helicopters) bacterium that commonly lives in
the mucous membranes that line the stomach and small intestine. Antibiotics are usually successful in eliminating H. pylori.

Ulcers can also be caused by excessive use of nonsteroidal anti-
inflammatory drugs (NSAIDs) such as ibuprofen or aspirin.
That's because these medications inhibit the production of an
enzyme that plays an important role in protecting your sensitive stomach lining. And it's why they're best taken with food or
a nice tall glass of insulating milk.

Drinking alcohol and smoking, once also indicated as ulcer-
causing habits, don't have primary responsibility for the development of ulcers, but they can be contributing factors. And
they can definitely make an existing ulcer worse. Alcohol is an
irritant that increases the amount of stomach acid you produce.
The nicotine in cigarettes increases stomach acid, too, and pre-
vents healing of ulcerated tissue.

Don't confuse heartburn symptoms—burning, pressure, belch-
ing, and a bitter taste after eating—with those of an ulcer.
Spicy foods *can* aggravate heartburn and gastroesophageal

reflux disease (GERD), which are much more common than ulcers. If you have ulcers, you don't have to worry about spicy foods. But if you have frequent heartburn, stay away from the chicken curry.

How Sweet It Is

High fructose corn syrup is worse for us than sugar, right? Well, it's complicated.

✳ ✳ ✳ ✳

MYTHS AROUND SUGAR and other sweeteners are invasive and insidious because of the complicated politics involved. The United States grows more corn than any other country—more than the next three top producers combined, in fact. When given the choice between tariffs on imported sugar or subsidies on domestic corn syrup, American food manufacturers made the financially logical decision to turn to corn, and their powerful lobbyists followed with the charm offensive.

Birth of an Industry

The same qualities that bakers value in traditional corn syrup—ease of use, soft-baked texture, and moisture—made it ideal for processed and packaged foods as well. But the problems began when manufacturers realized they could make the same quantity of corn syrup taste sweeter by using natural chemistry to convert some of the existing glucose to fructose. This added to the existing market incentive to use corn sweeteners, and high fructose corn syrup is nutritionally almost identical to much more expensive refined white sugar. So what's the problem?

High Fructose, Low Veracity

There is a huge amount of misinformation about high fructose corn syrup swirling around. Isn't fructose naturally found in fruit and therefore not unhealthy? Yes and no. Fresh fruits have varying amounts of fructose but little overall. Dried fruits have higher concentrations of fructose and are very calorie dense—you could easily eat a harmful amount of sugar if you're indiscriminately eating dried fruit or drinking fruit juice. But the amount of sugar in whole fresh fruit is not impactful for the average person. Fruit is high in water and fiber, both of which help to slow down how quickly sugar is absorbed by the body. There's a world of difference between a juicy summer peach and the added sugar in a cherry yogurt or a granola bar. Even the starchy, dense banana is nearly $3/4$ water.

Case Study: Weight Watchers

The false equivalence of calories in fresh fruit versus calories in processed foods led the Weight Watchers corporation to make a landmark change to its plan in 2010. Local and regional leadership noticed that members were choosing so-called "healthy" packaged snacks over fruit because these foods had the same value in proprietary "points," but food science was demonstrating that fruit calories are digested differently. Weight Watchers wanted to incentivize choosing whole foods like fruit, and they changed their points system in order to make this change worthwhile for members, who were encouraged to fill up on fruit with no impact on their daily counting.

Drawing Conclusions

What's the bottom line with high fructose corn syrup? Nutritionally, it isn't any different from white sugar. But its cheapness has made it ubiquitous in even savory packaged foods, and studies show that a diet with too much added sugar (where "too much" is a quantity *far below* what the average American eats daily now) increases risk for obesity and life-shortening diseases. Choosing a convenient whipping boy has allowed the packaged food industry to rally around "pure cane sugar" as its savior, when really, all added sugars are created pretty equal. Handle with care.

MSG: The Powdered Stuff of Legends

Is MSG bad? There's no sound evidence that it is.

✳ ✳ ✳ ✳

REPORTS OF HEALTH effects of MSG (monosodium glutamate)—such as causing headaches, flushing, or mental cloudiness—have not been proven, let alone specifically linked with Chinese food. People experiencing a reaction of this kind would also react to tomato paste, Parmesan and blue cheese, and many other common foods with high levels of naturally occurring MSG and MSG-like compounds.

Bins of MSG powder can be found alongside other condiments at food stalls and eateries in parts of China and probably elsewhere. Most major world cuisines have an ancient "umami bomb" condiment, too: not only soy sauce and other fermented soy foods but also varieties of yeast, fish, tomato, and mushroom sauces from around the world. Half the world's population does not have a chemical headache after each meal.

Modern recipes that seek to boost flavor and "meatiness" still use anchovies, tomato paste, yeast, browned mushrooms, and other glutamate-heavy foods to add umami. This is especially effective in soups, where layering flavors historically required hours of work and careful simmering.

In packaged, instant, and frozen foods, MSG fills the gap left by short preparation time and shelf stabilizing recipes, and in flavor-boosting it can make up for costlier spices or flavors. MSG is also used in foods that are made mostly of flavor-neutral foundations like soy and grains, especially vegetarian or vegan meat analogs. Some unwarranted ballyhooing surrounds MSG, so eat what you like and choose for yourself.

The Texas Pig Stand Introduces Front-Seat Dining

The drive-in restaurant wasn't born in California, nor did the McDonald brothers invent the fast food genre. Carhops, curb service, and the Pig Sandwich are what started it all.

✳   ✳   ✳   ✳

IN 1921, TEXAS mercantile wholesaler Jesse Granville Kirby made the proclamation, "People in their cars are so lazy that they don't want to get out of them to eat!" At the time, he was trying to hook Reuben Jackson, a Dallas physician, to invest $10,000 in a new idea for a roadside stand, one that paired the Lone Star State's love for the automobile with another beloved pastime: eating barbecue.

For the era, Kirby's idea was revolutionary: Texans were to drive up to the food stand and make their requests for food directly from behind the wheel of their cars (or trucks, of course, this being Texas). A young lad would take the customers' orders directly through the window of the car and then deliver the food and beverages right back out to the curb. The novelty of this new format was that hurried diners could consume their meals while they were sitting in the front seat.

Convenience Over All

When Kirby and Jackson's Texas Pig Stand opened along the busy Dallas–Fort Worth Highway in the fall of 1921, legions of Texas motorists tipped their ten-gallon hats to what was advertised as "America's Motor Lunch." Prepared with tender slices of roast pork loin, pickle relish, and barbecue sauce, Kirby and Jackson's Pig Sandwich quickly gained a loyal following among cabbies, truckers, limousine drivers, police officers, and other mobile workers.

But curbside cuisine wasn't the only attraction at America's first drive-in restaurant. The daredevil car servers who worked the curb—or carhops, as someone coined the phrase—were a sight. "Carhops were very competitive," recalled Richard Hailey, successor to the Pig Stand throne and former president of Pig Stands, Inc. "As soon as they saw a Model T start to slow down, they'd race out to see who could jump up on the running board first, while the car was still moving."

An Explosion of Pork Barbecue

With its good food and derring-do curb service, the legend of the Texas carhop grew as the reputation of the Pig Stands and its signature sandwich spread. Propelled beyond the borders of Texas by franchising, the number of pork stands multiplied. Between 1921 and 1934, more than 100 Pig Stands were serving up "A Good Meal at Any Time" across America. Drive-in curb service had gone nationwide, and scores of operators duplicated the successful format.

In 1930, Royce Hailey, future patriarch of the Pig Stands clan and father to Richard, started as a Dallas carhop at age 13. Moving up through the ranks to take the president's job, he became sole owner in 1975. A self-made Texan with a knack for food, he's credited with inventing the chicken-fried steak sandwich and the super-sized slice of grilled bread called "Texas Toast." Food historians also cite onion rings as one of his more famous works of culinary art.

Modern Hard Times

Unfortunately, the novelty of the drive-in restaurant and the nostalgic comfort food it served wasn't enough to carry the operation into the new millennium. In recent years, all of the Texas locations have ceased car and dining room service for one financial reason or another. A single exception exists in San Antonio. Although it was closed with the others, what is now known as Mary Ann's Pig Stand was saved from the scrap heap of history when longtime employee Mary Ann Hill came up with the money to reopen it. Starting as a carhop at age 18 in 1967, Hill had never worked anywhere else. With its original

Georges Claude neon pig-shaped sign, vintage Coke machine, shelves of pig memorabilia, and canopied lot, the restaurant operates under trustee status.

Fortunately, then, longtime fans and curious newcomers can still get a milkshake, a Pig Sandwich, and many of the classic fast food entrees that Hailey pioneered—including his signature Texas Toast and giant onion rings. For fans of "The World's First Drive-In Restaurant," there's still nothing that compares with chowing down in America's favorite dining room: the front seat of the car.

All Choked Up

Recollections of Mama Cass Elliot should include a powerhouse singing voice, multimillion-selling singles, garish garments, and a flamboyant stage presence. Instead, she is often remembered for dying with a hoagie gorged in her gob. Let's satisfy the public's hunger and set her record straight.

✳   ✳   ✳   ✳

A S RENOWNED FOR her prodigious girth as she was for the rich timbre of her singing voice, Ellen Naomi (Mama Cass) Cohen knew no half measures—she lived life to the fullest. Although the musical Mama had an appetite for substances of all quantities and assortments, the details surrounding her untimely demise have been distorted and exaggerated to the point of inaccuracy.

Shortly after news of her death in a London apartment was announced to the public, rumors abounded that the corpulent chanteuse had punched her ticket to the great beyond by choking on a ham sandwich. The genesis for the gossip was a notation on the official police report, which stated that a half-eaten sandwich had been found near her expired form. However, the autopsy report, a far more reliable document, revealed that there was no evidence of food particles in her trachea.

The simple truth is that Mama Cass died a rather pedestrian death. The vocalist perished from heart failure, most likely because of her unhealthy habit of alternating periods of food and substance abuse with intervals of crash dieting.

Junk Food Verdict: Not Guilty

Your complexion may be bumpy, but if you eat a lot of junk food, you can at least have a clear conscience.

✻ ✻ ✻ ✻

PIMPLE-PRONE ADOLESCENTS ARE often told to skip the pizza, fries, and potato chips to keep their faces acne-free. But greasy foods only affect your appearance if you're a messy eater. Research shows that breakouts are caused by a surge in hormones, which stimulates the body's secretion of oils.

When the oil glands in the skin are overactive, pores get clogged from the secretions and become perfect hosts for a bacterium called *Propionibacterium acnes* that thrives without oxygen. It's the bacteria's activity that produces pimples.

Chocolate has also been blamed for causing acne, but it's not at fault either. A University of Pennsylvania study compared people who ate a bar of chocolate with those who ate a bar with similar amounts of fat and sugar. The study found no evidence that chocolate had an effect on producing acne. (Besides, chocolate has an abundance of antioxidants, which may help prevent wrinkles.)

You might want to think twice about eating dairy, though. A recent Harvard study found that women who drank two or more glasses of skim milk a day were 44 percent more likely to report severe acne as teenagers. Researchers believe that hormones or whey proteins found in dairy products might be the cause. With more and more hormones fed to cows, who knows?

Does Searing Lock In Moisture?

Many recipes for cooking meat or poultry start with a sear. But searing does not "seal in moisture"—it only adds tasty browning.

✳ ✳ ✳ ✳

I N FACT, SEARING can dry out your food if done for too long. There are different kinds of reactions and processes that cause what we think of as browning. Fruits and vegetables turn brown due to oxidation, and we won't get into that because it is an accidental and gross kind of browning. (Scientists have patented some genetically modified varieties of apple that purportedly don't brown after cutting! Packaged sliced apples use safe, natural preservatives like lemon juice or citric acid to stanch the browning effect. Also, mild browning can't hurt you.)

The Maillard Reaction

Searing meat triggers the Maillard reaction, where simple sugars and amino acids react and rearrange each other's molecular structures to create new brown compounds on the surface of the meat. Avid omnivore cooks know that meat has to be dry in order to sear in hot fat—water disrupts the Maillard reaction—and dredging meat in flour helps to create an even drier surface that quickly breaks down into helpful simple sugars. This is one reason why simply dredging meat once in flour yields such different results than dredging followed by an egg wash and a second dredge. And a fun fact: dulce de leche is made not by caramelization but by the Maillard reaction!

Golden Brown

Fast-food French fries use Maillard-friendly additives to get predictable, fast browning. Some franchises add a tiny amount of starch, whether by itself or in the form of some kind of flour. Some use sugar or dairy instead. Foodie culture places a high premium on whole and simple foods with fewer additives, but major fast-food chains don't have the option to get a bad batch of potatoes when trying to deliver thousands of consistent meals each day. Certainly their harried employees can't look into the deep fryer to check for doneness on a variable French fry. But ""fast casual"" chains like Five Guys offer a simpler potato product if that's what you're looking for, or you can make your own at home.

Layers of Flavor

What about caramelization? Are caramelized onions different from the browning on seared meat or French fries? The results of all three are delicious, but yes, onions undergo a completely different chemical process. Remember that the Maillard reaction involves protein—caramelization is instead the controlled chemical change of just sugar. If you heat granulated white sugar in a pan, it will eventually go through all the stages of caramelization used in candymaking. Compare this with melting white sugar into water to make simple syrup, where there is no color change. Where do onions fit in? Most onions don't taste sweet, but they contain enough sugar, trapped inside of caramelization-friendly insulated layers, to brown over time and create the delicious base for French onion soup. But when you caramelize onions, you must add liquid very slowly to avoid interrupting the caramelization process. This is also why recipes call for browning onions before you add any liquid, because that's the only window for browning.

Are French Fries Really French?

No one is certain that French fries are French at all.

⁑　⁑　⁑　⁑

CERTAINLY "FRENCH FRIES" had their moment of ill repute when they were briefly renamed "freedom fries," after the U.S. invaded Iraq and was not supported by the French. But there is a century-old dispute over where French fries came from. The Belgians, who are rightfully proud of creating the perfect food in pommes frites, claim they invented all French fries and are only over-looked because of confusion over the shared French language. Did Americans cause this mild rift by attaching a demonym in the first place? No one but us seems to call pommes frites, chips, or anything else "French fries." Whatever the case, these fried potato wands are a delicious cornerstone of American fast food. Just don't ask for ketchup in a Belgian bar.

The Base of the Neo Food Pyramid

Hostess Twinkies will not survive the apocalypse—they'll barely make it through next month.

⁑　⁑　⁑　⁑

THE ORIGINAL TWINKIE, manufactured through 2012, had a shelf life just under 4 weeks. Hostess then reformulated the Twinkie to glean a shelf life of over 6 weeks. There are many processed foods that last a lot longer than Twinkies, so the snack cakes aren't an obvious choice as the whipping boy of processed-food alarmists, at least not based on the single data point of shelf life. Both the sponge cake and the hydrogenated-oil-based filling have a very uniform texture that holds up at room temperature.

Slowing Rapid Turnover

Much of modern processed-food science revolves around making stable, shippable products that don't separate or otherwise deteriorate before they can be sold and consumed. American consumers are used to constant availability of any food they want, and the idea of discarded unsold food also makes us queasy—at least those of us who aren't dumpster divers. Grocery stores operate on razor-thin profit margins as is, let alone if the short shelf life and urgent turnover of the meat and dairy sections applied to the entire store. Independent restaurants and bakeries must wrestle with this issue every day, planning for future demand and deciding how to mitigate money lost to wasted inventory.

Some Baking Science

Cake as we know it today is usually a sponge cake, made not from a yeasted dough but from a batter that does not need to rise, rest, or be kneaded. The oldest cakes we would recognize as such were seriously labor intensive, requiring cooks to whip eggs by hand in order to manually add air to the batter. Modern baking soda and baking powder gave cooks a much-needed time saver by using chemistry to add air. One much-loved Depression-era cake recipe uses the reaction of applesauce with baking soda to replace the eggs in a traditional cake. This cake may last longer than its egged counterpart, especially if it's made with oil rather than butter.

Adapting to Modern Tastes

Baking is unique even among food sectors. Customers will wait for food to be cooked and brought to them at a restaurant, but they will not wait the several hours it takes to prepare, chill, bake, cool, and frost their favorite desserts. In Great Britain, they already favored relatively dry digestive biscuits (crispy cookies) or shortbread that lasted longer from the getgo. Americans prefer their cookies soft and very sweet—even Oreos, whose cookie halves are the closest major American consumer cookie to a British biscuit, have a layer of hydrogenated filling to sweeten the deal. So it did not take long for the creators of the Twinkie to realize they needed a product that stayed fresh and saleable for more than a couple of days, and they didn't face this dilemma alone. Mass-market bakeries used burgeoning food science to replace the vulnerable ingredients in their recipes, like eggs, milk, and butter, with stable imitators.

A Note About Hydrogenated Oil

The single most robust engineered ingredient is hydrogenated oil, whether fully or partially hydrogenated. Animal fats like butter and lard are solid at room temperature because of their chemical makeup. Most vegetable fats are liquids at room temperature, and the few that are more solid have saturated fat content on par with animal fats. Scientists developed hydrogenated fats like Crisco by adding hydrogen to liquid vegetable fats in order to change how the fat molecules bond together. Since there's no added moisture, these fats are solid and shelf stable at room temperature. The downside is that partially hydrogenated fats contain trans fats, which the FDA has ordered food manufacturers to eliminate from their products within the next few years.

The Tall and Short on Kids and Coffee

A cup of java may keep kids up at night, but it won't affect their height.

✳ ✳ ✳ ✳

I N PAST GENERATIONS, parents didn't allow their children to drink coffee, believing that it would stunt their growth. But today, kids are consuming coffee in record numbers and at younger ages. In fact, young people are now the fastest-growing coffee-drinking group in the United States.

Does this trend indicate a corresponding shrinkage in the younger generation's adult height? No, say researchers. There is no evidence that drinking coffee affects growth or a person's eventual height.

At one time there seemed to be a link between caffeine consumption and the development of osteoporosis, and that may be how coffee originally got blamed for inhibiting growth. Early studies suggested that drinking lots of caffeinated beverages contributed to reduced bone mass.

More recent studies have debunked that idea. Dr. Robert Heaney of Creighton University found that much of the preliminary research on caffeine and bone loss was done on elderly people whose diets were low in calcium. Other researchers have noted that even if caffeine does affect bone mass, its influence is minimal and can easily be counteracted with a sufficient amount of calcium-rich foods.

The myth that coffee stunts growth was laid to rest by a study that followed 81 adolescents for six years. At the end of the study, there was no difference in bone gain or bone density between those who drank the most coffee and those who drank the least.

In other words, don't worry about letting your kids have an occasional cup of joe, but unless you want to be up all night while they bounce off the walls, make sure they drink it in the morning.

The Alcohol All Cooks Off?

Alcohol does not "cook off" completely when used in recipes like risotto or bombe Alaska.

❋ ❋ ❋ ❋

OVER A COOK time of several hours, such as a very long braise of a huge cut of meat, virtually all the alcohol you use in a recipe does cook off. But for bombe Alaska, bananas foster, and other flambéed recipes, the very brief cook time leaves most of the alcohol in. Osso buco and risotto retain about a quarter to a third of the alcohol. Most cooks prefer to add wine to risotto very early in the cooking anyway in order to let the flavor steep and mellow as they continue to add broth for the rest of the cook time.

In a single serving of any of these dishes, there shouldn't be enough alcohol to impair anyone—but some people may want to avoid alcohol altogether for health or other personal reasons. The safest bet (in many senses!) is to ask before you light everyone's desserts on fire.

Espresso Has More Caffeine Than Coffee?

Espresso does not always or even usually have more caffeine than a cup of brewed coffee, let alone the behemoth coffees from Starbucks.

❋ ❋ ❋ ❋

THERE'S THREE TIMES more caffeine per ounce in espresso versus Starbucks brewed coffee, but an espresso is about two ounces compared with a "tall" 12 ounces. For those who still drink a standard heavy diner mug of coffee, which is 6–8 ounces, that cup of coffee usually has less caffeine than an espresso shot. Haute coffee, so to speak, has moved the goalposts on how much caffeine we can expect.

What about energy drinks? Four-ounce energy shots like 5 Hour Energy and its imitators have a relatively small amount of caffeine compared to coffee. Larger energy drinks like Red Bull and Monster have gotten into trouble over the years for their high levels of caffeine, so these recipes are constantly being tinkered with and complained about. Red Bull and vodka became the go-to drink for a certain demographic at the turn of the millennium, but physicians caution strongly against mixing uppers and downers like caffeine and alcohol.

Monster, now the main sponsor of NASCAR's keystone racing series, has been the defendant in many individual and class action lawsuits for its high levels of caffeine. Plaintiffs in these cases claim that they or their loved ones suffered catastrophic health effects linked to overconsumption of caffeine. The court of public opinion is a different matter altogether, and energy drinks are an enormous and growing industry. Monster and its competition have all reduced the amount of caffeine in their products in response to lawsuits and FDA concerns.

Why Does My Microwave Heat Food Inside-Out?

Food does not heat "from the inside out" in a microwave—at least, not usually.

✳　✳　✳　✳

MICROWAVES WORK BY making the water molecules inside of any food move rapidly and therefore generate heat.

(Yes, your food, like anything else in this world, is just vibrating nanothingies all the way down.) Most foods have the highest water concentration and most freedom of movement in their centers: imagine spending a dance party standing next to the wall versus in the very middle of the room. This is how the infamously nuclear-hot center of a fast-food fruit pie gets that way. Watch your mouth!

Accidental Melting

Microwave ovens were invented after the discovery that microwaves, the bandwidth one step up the spectrum from radio waves, generated noticeable heat. The legend goes that a scientist walked past a microwave experiment with a chocolate bar in his pocket and noticed that the chocolate had melted. Radio waves are able to travel through walls—that makes them sound a bit like superheroes!—but microwaves are confined to so-called "line of sight," meaning they can be harnessed and safely contained within a microwave oven. Microwaves are also used to cauterize surgical cuts.

Laser-Sharp Heat Science

Infrared light is the next step up the spectrum from microwaves, and it, too, was discovered by serendipity when a scientist wanted to measure the temperature of different colors of light. Astronomer William Herschel placed thermometers in each color of light projected by a prism (as seen on the cover of *Dark Side of the Moon*) and included one final thermometer outside the visible spectrum as his control. His due diligence in the scientific method paid off when this control thermometer registered a very high temperature, indicating to Herschel that some unseen phenomenon was at play. The heat of infrared radiation is used in consumer laser cutters!

Will My Fork Explode in the Microwave?

Leaving a fork in your microwave dinner will not necessarily destroy your microwave.

❋ ❋ ❋ ❋

METAL ACTS LIKE a sort of lightning rod that draws electricity, which can create super high temperatures that damage the inside of the microwave and can burn your food as well as your skin when you touch it. A version of the same phenomenon can happen inside your oven if a misplaced bit of metal or a cookie sheet touching the oven wall creates a path for far increased heat to travel—leaving cookies burned on just the bottom, for example.

Some tiny bits of metal, like the staples used on tea bags or folded Chinese-food containers, are fine to microwave in most cases. Chef and television personality Alton Brown includes a single staple in many of his recipes for microwave cooking.

But what about our microwave favorites that come in metallic packaging? The metal-ish sleeves used for Hot Pockets and other microwaveable foods use specially made materials called susceptors. These can be made from metal or even ceramic. They gather up microwave-generated heat and use that heat to create low-level browning.

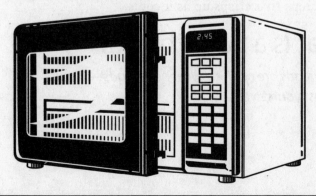

"Chinese" Fortune Cookies

Fortune cookies are synonymous with American Chinese food, but they don't originate in China.

✻ ✻ ✻ ✻

A SIMILAR COOKIE EXISTS in Japan and may have inspired American fortune cookies. Several people and groups claim to have invented the crimped cookie with a fateful surprise inside, but there's no real demonstrable chain of custody. As with cookie urban legends like the Neiman Marcus chocolate-chip cookie recipe, it's all improbable speculation. That's apt for a cookie whose goal is to cold read our futures.

How does the fortune get inside the cookie? This we can answer for sure. Fortune cookies are baked in circular discs that are picked up and folded while they're still warm and pliable. Home cooks often bake fortune cookies on a silicone baking mat or parchment paper to facilitate this step. Many recipes for fortune cookies use corn flour to help create a super fine and uniform texture, and the cookie dough is more like a pancake batter. It's not all that incorrect to think of a fortune cookie as a baked crepe that crisps up as it cools.

What Is a Sweetbread?

Sweetbreads are neither sweet nor breads—discuss amongst yourselves.

✻ ✻ ✻ ✻

NY VERBAL RESEMBLANCE to shortbread is strictly a coincidence when it comes to these...organ-ic flavors. Sweetbreads aren't very common anymore outside of fine dining, an absence that lays the groundwork for a memorable *Gilmore Girls* bit. Rory and Lorelei joke to each other that the foods they like best at rich matriarch Emily's house always turn out to be something gross—in this case, sweetbreads, an umbrella term that refers to glands and other miscellaneous animal innards.

Like brain, sweetbreads are carefully prepared to neutralize their, uh, insides-y flavor. But since that *Gilmore Girls* gag in 2002, a trend for nose-to-tail dining and a revitalized interest in offal have brought this delicacy way back into vogue: look for sweetbreads in a gastropub near you.

Point Me to the Welsh Rabbits

It's not rabbit, and it's likely not Welsh.

✳ ✳ ✳ ✳

CHEESE ON TOAST (an open-faced grilled cheese sandwich, to translate it into American) is a mainstay of British comfort food, and Welsh rabbit is a variation where a cheese sauce is poured over toast. Think of it as an extremely British version of nachos. The dish dates back hundreds of years and even has its own later adulterated name: Welsh rarebit.

The American term "grilled cheese" is probably British in origin as well, involving a musical chairs of cooking implements. What we call the broiler, Britons call the grill. What we call the grill, Britons call the barbecue. So our grilled cheese originates under a British oven grill rather than in the frying pan we use today. But if we called our sandwich a "fried cheese," we'd step on the toes of many other international delights, like queso frito or fried halloumi.

Waiter, There's Meat in My Mincemeat

Is mincemeat made of meat? Not anymore—at least not usually.

✱ ✱ ✱ ✱

MINCEMEAT PIE, AMERICAN style, is a common wintertime and Christmas treat alongside pumpkin pie and fruitcake. Recipes combine what we think of as "pumpkin pie spice," dried fruits soaked in alcohol, and vegetable or animal fat to make a rich, hearty pie filling. The original mincemeat often included minced meat, hence the name, and was made using animal fat called suet in both the pastry crust and the filling.

Both spices and sugar were cherished luxuries for most of human history, which led to their addition to savory dishes that sound a bit unsettling to us today. But in today's era of added sugar, even ketchup is very sweet. Maybe our ancestors' cooking wouldn't seem strange after all. Mincemeat's carnivore-friendly reputation endures: in 2015's season of *The Great Australian Bake Off*, the hosts referred to a modern fruit mincemeat as "vegetarian mincemeat."

Ich Bin Ein Myth

Did JFK call himself a German donut?

✱ ✱ ✱ ✱

PRESIDENT JOHN F. Kennedy's "Ich bin ein Berliner" comment, made in 1963 during a landmark speech to the stressed-out citizens of free West Berlin, is a matter of fact in the public record. But all discussion of any mispronunciation or incorrect word choice is based on a myth. The German capital city of Berlin was divided into multiple parts following Germany's surrender at the end of World War II, and in 1961, the Soviet Union built a fortress-like wall patrolled by guards in order to stanch the flow of East (Soviet) Berliners through West Berlin and into the free world.

President Kennedy immediately added this issue to his portfolio of speeches and mentioned the isolated American and other western citizens of West Berlin as a population in dire need. In 1963, he prepared for a state visit to West Berlin by studying the German translations of some of his key political leitmotifs and writing these phrases down phonetically for use in his public remarks. When he said "Ich bin ein Berliner," the crowd cheered and applauded. The President poked fun at his own Boston-inflected German pronunciation and the crowd laughed with him.

A Berliner is a donut in the same way a Cuban is a sandwich: Context is king. In fact, most Germans use a different term for the Berliner pastry. The myth that sprang up in response to President Kennedy's famous comment developed in the years and decades afterward, when it was easy to create a legend that was humanizing or humiliating, depending on one's political party affiliation.

Certainly the German language is complex enough that we find it plausible to make an obscure grammatical error that completely changes the meaning. But it's even more plausible in tonal languages like Mandarin Chinese, where a rising or dipping pronunciation of the same syllable may mean, for example, your mother or a cow.

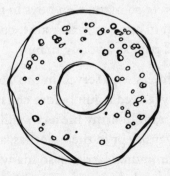

Chapter 3

The Civil War

Belles in Battle

In the American Civil War, which raged from 1861 to 1865, Union and Confederate armies forbade the enlistment of women. But it is a mistake to think that there were no female soldiers in action.

✳   ✳   ✳   ✳

FOR MANY YEARS after the Civil War, the U.S. Army flatly denied that women had played any part in the conflict, making it difficult to know for certain just how many women had served on each side. The best estimates indicate that the number was at least 750.

It's hard for people today to imagine that women could have passed themselves off as men and served undetected, but life in the military was very different back then. Army recruiters for both the North and South never asked for proof of identity, and they conducted only farcical physical examinations.

Doctors at the time hardly knew enough to conduct what today's school-age children need in order to enroll each fall. And because there were so many teen boys in the ranks, it was possible for a woman to adopt a male name, cut her hair short, bind her breasts, and pass as a young man.

Most of the male soldiers who served in the war were former civilians who had never fired a gun before enlisting and were therefore just as ignorant of army life as a similarly oriented woman. Soldiers always slept in their clothes, and many refused to use the massive communal latrines, so many of the women soldiers were detected only by accident.

Spotlight on: Loreta Velazquez

Loreta Velazquez joined the Confederate army in order to be close to her fiancé.

✳ ✳ ✳ ✳

Loreta Velazquez served under the name Harry T. Buford, wore a false mustache, smoked cigars, and padded her uniform to make herself look more masculine. It wasn't until she was wounded at the Battle of Shiloh and an army doctor examined her that her gender was finally revealed. She was discharged from the military and then wrote a book about her experiences titled *The Woman in Battle*. In it, Velazquez also claims to have worked as a double agent for the Confederacy, usually dressed as a woman.

Spotlight on: Albert Cashier

A mysterious past led this Irish immigrant to join the Union army.

✳ ✳ ✳ ✳

Not much is known about Union soldier Albert Cashier, born Jennie Irene Hodgers in Ireland in the 1840s. It seems that a hardscrabble family life led Hodgers to begin dressing as a boy in order to find work and contribute to the family income even as a child. Hodgers responded to President Lincoln's call for enlistment in 1862 and signed up as "Albert Cashier." Cashier served and was honorably discharged in 1865, and living as a man meant that Cashier could also vote after returning to Illinois after the war. A handful of nurses and physicians discovered Cashier's "secret" biological identity over the years but did not disclose it.

Spotlight on: Frank Thompson

She escaped an arranged marriage to be a wartime nurse—as both a man and a woman.

* * * *

CANADIAN IMMIGRANT SARAH EDMONDS was motivated to disguise herself as a man when she needed to escape in order to avoid becoming a young teen bride. She adopted various male names during her life and seemed to view her disguises as means to an end rather than an identity—as a man she could travel without notice, come and go as she pleased, and largely be overlooked rather than chaperoned and coddled. She signed up for the Union army as Frank Thompson and worked as a male nurse on the battlefield. Later, an illness forced her to desert rather than be discovered at a military hospital. She served as a female nurse after that.

Behind Southern Lines

Some Southerners were antislavery, while others just wanted to be left alone—although there's no doubt that slavery was the major issue in the Civil War. There were many reasons for Southerners to support the Union, and many people went to great lengths to follow their beliefs.

* * * *

WHEN THE SOUTHERN states seceded from the Union in 1860 and 1861, it wasn't exactly a unanimous decision. Plenty of citizens throughout the South opposed secession and weren't particularly inclined to don the grey fatigues of a Confederate soldier. Large groups of nonslaveholding citizens felt that they and their homelands had been hijacked for the benefit of wealthy plantation owners looking to secure their own right to keep slaves—and to keep making money.

Nickajack

Upon Abraham Lincoln's election, Alabama's governor gathered a convention of elected delegates in an attempt to protest by leaving the Union. It quickly became apparent to the representatives of northern Alabama that the state's slaveholding southern half was trying to dominate the vote.

The northern delegates wanted the decision to be made by popular vote, while the southern delegates, whose number was increased by the slaves they "represented," wanted the issue kept within the convention. Secessionists couldn't muster a two-thirds majority, but its simple majority of 61–39 was enough to pull out of the Union. Disgruntled northern Alabamans discussed seceding from Alabama itself. Along with parts of Tennessee, they intended to form an independent state called Nickajack that would exist as a neutral entity within the South.

Events soon caught up with the state, however, and after Fort Sumter was attacked and Lincoln began mustering troops to respond to the Southern provocation with force, the people of Alabama clung together, and the idea of forming Nickajack all but disappeared. Though there was no formal separation, the people of northern Alabama still refused to embrace the Confederacy, and many fled north to join the Union army.

Republic of Winston

For Christopher Sheats and his neighbors in Winston County, Alabama, however, the story did not end when the shooting started. Sheats had been the Winston County representative to the secession convention, and his stubborn refusal to go along with the state's plan to leave the Union got him thrown in jail in 1861. The people of Winston County were enraged, and more than 3,000 of them gathered at a local tavern to officially wash their hands of the whole thing. Their demand was simple: that both the Union and Confederacy leave them alone. It was there in Looney's Tavern that the idea of an independent, neutral Republic of Winston was born.

The county never did actually secede, but when the population of the "Republic of Winston" tried to maintain its sovereignty, the withering Confederate army exploited them through violence and coercion. Food, supplies, and even men were hauled away to support the Southern cause against their will. These incidents, while difficult for the people of Winston, never completely broke them, and their remote location deep in the hills of rural Alabama made it impossible for the Confederacy to exert complete control over the area.

Today, this tumultuous time in the history of Winston County is memorialized with a statue of a solider, like any other you'd see all over the United States, except one half is dressed in Union blues, and the other in Confederate grey. The plaque reads, in part, "Johnny Reb and Billy Yank, disillusioned by the realities of war, shared dual destinies as pragmatic Americans in a reunited nation."

Red Strings

Other Southerners took a more subtle approach to subverting Confederate interests in their areas. Small bands of Union supporters and pacifist Quakers in the slavery-free foothills of Virginia and North Carolina developed a covert organization to undermine the Confederacy from within. Their secrecy was so total that most members did not know who their compatriots were—they could only identify each other by a display of red strings on their clothing.

Their cautious and meticulous attention to covering their tracks made the Red Strings nearly invisible in the South. Confederate officials, attempting to disrupt these rebels' efforts to harbor deserters and aid escaping slaves, were flummoxed and unable to root out the subversives. The Red Strings are said to have numbered 10,000 strong.

One Red String, Byron Scott of Kentucky, was swept up into Southern State's Guard and used his proximity to vital military information to become a spy. He would gather intelligence on

Confederate plans and strategies and pass it on to the Union. Within the Confederate army, Scott personally obstructed the pursuit of several Southern draft dodgers, directing the posse that had been formed to capture them away from their actual location, allowing the resisters to escape.

Much of the anti-Confederate sentiment in the South drew from a vast reservoir of poor and disaffected citizens who saw the war as a rich man's folly. The popularity of organizations such as the Red Strings proves that the lines of battle were not always clearly drawn.

Wave the Flag

It took the Confederacy the entire war before it settled on a flag everyone could agree on, which means the colors never officially flew, although it has certainly flown since.

✳ ✳ ✳ ✳

RECEIVE, THEN, FROM your mothers and sisters, from those whose affections greet you, these colors woven by our feeble but reliant hands; and when this bright flag shall float before you on the battlefield, let it not only inspire you with brave and patriotic ambition of a soldier aspiring to his own and his country's honor and glory, but also may it be a sign that cherished ones appeal to you to save them from a fanatical and heartless foe."

These were the words Idelea Collens proclaimed as she presented a flag to a Louisiana regiment. As Collens stated, flags typically served two purposes in battle: to display pride in state and country for those in battle and to act as a beacon around which the members of a regiment would form and fight. Therefore, it was important to both Union and Confederate soldiers that much care was taken in the design of their flags.

Throughout the Civil War, Union regiments carried at least two flags: a national flag, or colors, and regimental colors. Many Confederate regiments also carried the national colors and a battle flag, although no single battle flag design was adopted by the Confederacy during the war.

First Flags

Soon after the Confederacy was born, a congressional committee was formed to choose a design for a national flag. The first design proposed was what they called "The Stars and Stripes," so named because it was very similar to the U.S. flag, with 13 red and white horizontal stripes and a blue field in the upper left corner with 13 stars. It was quickly rejected by Confederate Congress delegates as being too similar to the Yankees' flag.

Their second choice was called the "Stars and Bars" and featured two thick red horizontal stripes separated by a thick white horizontal stripe, with seven stars on a blue background in the upper left corner. This design was a compromise between those delegates who wanted a unique design and those who wanted to keep the Union's national colors.

The Stars and Bars, however, created confusion at the First Battle of Bull Run—without any wind to waft the flag, its colors made it look too similar to the Union flag. Along with the fact that the colors of the Union and Confederate uniforms were also so similar, the Stars and Bars made it difficult for soldiers to tell if other troops were friend or foe. As a result, some rebels fired on friendly troops. Following the battle, the Southern commanders began designing a new flag.

A Battle Flag Is Born

The Beauregard battle flag was adopted on October 1, 1861,

by the Confederate Army of the Potomac (which later changed its name to the Army of Northern Virginia). This design is familiar to people today—a St. Andrew's Cross on a field of red, with 13 stars aligned across the blue cross. Instead of a rectangle, however, the Beauregard battle flag was a square. The Stars and Bars remained the national colors, yet many Confederate citizens and politicians identified with the battle flag and demanded that it replace the unpopular Stars and Bars as the national flag.

Not every Confederate regiment adopted the Beauregard battle flag, especially in the western theater. Many flags had a similar design, but others were unique to a particular regiment. The Confederate Navy adopted a rectangular form of the Beauregard battle flag in 1863, called the "Confederate Navy Jack," and this is the flag that today is often mistakenly believed to have been the national flag of the Confederate States of America.

I Surrender?

Throughout all of this, many continued to seek a flag that could take the place of the Stars and Bars. A third national flag, the "Stainless Banner," was adopted on May 1, 1863. Its design featured a rectangular white background—intended to signify the purity of the Confederate cause—with the Beauregard battle flag in the upper left corner. One of its initial displays was over the coffin of General Stonewall Jackson. Criticism of the new design poured into Richmond soon after it was adopted. Some said its dimensions created the impression of a long tablecloth; others thought it looked like a flag of surrender. The flag was also too long to float properly in the wind.

Too Little, Too Late

In response to these criticisms, yet another new flag design was sought. Major Arthur Rogers, gravely wounded during the Battle of Chancellorsville in May 1863, proposed that a shorter version of the Stainless Banner be adopted with a thick vertical red stripe running along the right side. As the fortunes of the Confederacy slipped away, its Congress took time to debate the design until finally adopting it on March 4, 1865. Ironically, it took the Confederacy its entire lifetime before it finally adopted a flag that met the approval of the nation. General Lee surrendered his Army of Northern Virginia a little more than a month after the new flag was adopted. As a result, it never flew over the Confederate capitol or any of its armies.

After the War

Until 1890, Confederate flags were closely held either by the War Department in Washington, D.C. or by organizations like the Daughters of the Confederacy for use at funerals and other solemn, official ceremonies. But that year, a statue of Robert E. Lee was dedicated as part of a weeklong celebration that was decked out with Confederate battle flags in a showing that journalists from the north found shocking. Why was the "flag of treason" on full and proud display? Black journalists were especially distressed.

As the idea of Confederate heritage gained popularity, so did the Confederate flag. It was adopted by so-called heritage fraternities at southern universities, and over generations of college students who were further and further from the time when their ancestors had served, it was easy to disconnect the "flag of treason" from its origins as the battle flag of the seceding Confederate States of America. These young men brought the flag with them when they were drafted into their generations' wars and were surprised when it spread beyond their reach—as it had spread beyond the reach of the Daughters of the Confederacy in the first place.

Mixed Messages

At some point, white southerners decided that enough time had passed for them to reclaim the Confederate flag and insist that it no longer had its original meaning as the battle flag of the failed state that declared war on the United States over slavery. But the thin veil of "states's rights" reemerged when civil rights and desegregation were adopted by the Democratic Party. The Dixiecrat Party, built on a platform of continuing segregation, used the Confederate flag pointedly as a reminder of their heritage as whites who wished to remain very separate. Southerners who opposed civil rights waved this flag to make a statement. It was no longer confined to college football games or ostensibly solemn occasions, and this wide usage continues today through the United States.

Life in the Camps

Army life during the Civil War was not all it was cracked up to be. Soldiers certainly experienced their share of adventure and drama, but daily life was often quite the opposite.

✳ ✳ ✳ ✳

WHAT WAS THE difference between Confederate and Union soldiers? When it came to daily life, not much. Although their viewpoints and goals may have been wildly different, they were, in essence, mostly cut from the same cloth. With 38 percent of Union generals and 35 percent of Confederate generals having graduated from West Point, it stands to reason that many of these officers had been classmates and close friends. Since they had trained together, it's no surprise that many of them ran their armies in similar ways. Whether Northern or Southern, most participants agreed on a single sentiment: The majority of a Civil War soldier's life was very tedious. "Soldiering is 99 percent boredom and 1 percent sheer terror," wrote one soldier to his wife.

Daily Doldrums

When not campaigning, soldiers settled into camps that were temporary in warm weather and long-term in winter. For North and South both, an average day in camp began when reveille was blown at 5:00 A.M. in the summer and 6:00 A.M. in the winter. There was little difference in the condition of the troops who answered the call on one side of the fight or the other. "Some wore one shoe," observed Union correspondent George Townsend, "and others appeared shivering in their linen. They stood ludicrously in rank, and a succession of short, dry coughs ran up and down the line."

Following roll call, soldiers ate breakfast, which was usually followed by the first of several one- to two-hour drill sessions. "The first thing in the morn-ing is drill," said one soldier. "Then drill, then drill again. Then drill, drill, a little more drill. Then drill, and lastly drill." The type of drills depended on the type of soldier. A squad of infantry would drill with each other, practicing marching, parad-ing, and moving together.  Cavalry would perform sword drills, either on horseback or on foot. Anything a soldier needed to do was subject to a drill.

Everybody practiced loading and readying their firearms. One activity that didn't get a lot of drill time, surprisingly, was actu-ally firing the weapons. There wasn't a lot of extra ammunition, and the military brass wanted to use it on targets that mattered.

Between drills, a soldier would perform necessary chores around the camp, such as picking up waste, digging latrines, or standing on guard duty. When on his own, a soldier engaged in a variety of activities to keep busy, including playing games such as chess and baseball, reading, and writing letters to loved ones who were, hopefully, safe at home.

Much less wholesome (and far more popular) was the trio of gambling, whiskey, and women. "If there is any place on God's fair earth where wickedness 'stalketh abroad in daylight,'" one

Confederate wrote to his family, "it is in the army." A new recruit also wrote about the activity of camp: "There is some of the onerest [sic] men here that I ever saw, and the most swearing and card playing and fitin [fighting] and drunkenness that I ever saw at any place."

Eat Up

As addictive as such self-indulgences were to a soldier, nothing was more important than food, which was plentiful for both sides in the opening months of the war. "We have better meat hear [sic] than you have in St. James," one Confederate soldier wrote to his sister. "We have Ice Water & Coffee three times a day." If the army didn't serve what the soldier liked, he either asked his family to send it or, when he had money, bought it from one of the sutlers who followed the armies and set up businesses near the camps.

Troops were formed into four to eight messes, and the men were expected to share in the food preparation. Some soldiers cooked while others cleaned up or went foraging for any foodstuffs available within the camp or from neighboring civilians. They cleared out nearby areas, so the longer the troops were in camp, the further they had to travel for firewood and other necessities.

While on the march, however, food was not as plentiful because of the logistical difficulty of carrying all the supplies an army would need. While camping, food supplies were far more abundant, though as the war progressed, the Confederates weren't able to find the amount and quality of food necessary to sustain the energies of an army.

In Sickness and in Snow

Due to a lack of sanitary conditions, the longer the armies camped, the more susceptible soldiers were to disease, which could bring down even the heartiest of them. "Camp streets and spaces between tents [were] littered with refuse, food and other rubbish," one Union soldier noted, "sometimes in an offensive state of decomposition; slops deposited in pits within the camp limits or thrown out broadcast; heaps of manure and offal close to the camp."

Such filthy living bred disease, which in turn resulted in many deaths. More soldiers died of disease during the Civil War than died in battle. Armies sometimes remained camped for six months or more, and the problems of boredom and disease were particularly intense during the winter. Ingenuity was necessary at this time to make both work and play bearable.

To get out of their tents, soldiers built cabins with chimneys when wood was available. If there was little or no building material during the winter, they still needed fires to keep themselves warm, so they built chimneys in the openings of their tents.

Both Union and Confederate soldiers found ways to entertain and amuse themselves and each other throughout the winter. Music played an important part in camp life, whether it was singing songs around the campfire or even formal orchestral concerts. To break up the boredom, snow fights between regiments or even brigades would break out at a moment's notice. And for those less inclined to participate in the usual debauchery of gambling, whiskey, and women, religious tent revivals could also be found.

Life in camp was a trial for all soldiers no matter their rank, but those battle-free days or months were far preferable to time spent marching or fighting.

A Union Leader By Marriage

As the wife of one of America's greatest leaders, Mary Todd Lincoln had to fight rumors—and reality.

❋ ❋ ❋ ❋

MARY TODD LINCOLN was a Southerner born into a slave-holding family, and she had very little interest in being a role model for keeping the Union together. But that was the position she held due to the man she married.

By all appearances, the marriage of Abraham and Mary Todd Lincoln was an unlikely one. By the time he met Mary Todd, the future president made little secret of his frontier upbringing and his lack of any significant formal education. Throughout his life, Lincoln carried himself with the bearing and demeanor of the quintessential common man.

By contrast, the early life of Mrs. Lincoln, née Mary Todd, was one of refinement and culture. Raised by a large and wealthy family in a genteel Kentucky home, Mary Todd was as well educated as it was possible for a young woman at that time in America to be. She moved to Springfield, Illinois, at age 20 and was a society belle when she met the older Lincoln in 1841.

The Heat Is On

Mrs. Lincoln's Kentucky roots and her closeness to her family members—some of whom owned slaves—stirred the Washington gossip mill as Lincoln ascended to the presidency in 1860. As fear of an imminent war over slavery became more pronounced in the capital, Mrs. Lincoln's loyalties were repeatedly questioned by various elements of Washington society. She particularly felt heat from those who opposed her husband's efforts to find some sort of agreement on states' rights issues and questions concerning slavery.

Although Mrs. Lincoln several times pledged her support for the Union cause both publicly and privately, rumors continued that she was a Southern spy. The rumors were outlandish, but there's no denying that Mrs. Lincoln had a strong connection to the Confederacy. She kept excellent relations with her brother-in-law, Confederate General Benjamin Helm. Her father had married again after her mother's death and had fathered several more children.

By 1861, Mary Lincoln's extended family included several brothers and half brothers who'd enlisted in the Confederate army. In 1861 and early 1862, the Union military was bogged down, and a Confederate attack on Washington was a constant concern to the populace. Union forces seemed unable to deal decisively with the enemy, and the gossip about Mrs. Lincoln's true loyalties and her influence over the conduct of the war never lessened.

As the war effort deepened in Washington, Mrs. Lincoln's detractors turned their attention from her suspected Union disloyalty to her spending habits in the White House. From 1862 to 1864, she exceeded her permitted White House domestic budget, often going so far as to hide the true cost of purchases from her husband. She told a confidante about her utter relief at Lincoln's reelection victory in 1864—not from any sense of sharing a political triumph with her husband, but because her personal debts far exceeded his annual presidential salary of $25,000. Her husband's victory would give her a longer grace period with her many creditors. The accumulation of such debts by the President's wife—especially during wartime—was ripe for scandal.

After the Fall

Few women in American public life have sustained the personal tragedies that Mrs. Lincoln did. She and her husband had four children, but only one survived to adulthood and outlived both his parents. The death of their 11-year-old son Willie in 1862 caused great depression for Mrs. Lincoln—in many ways, she never fully recovered.

She had a reputation for being tempestuous, a trait that led Lincoln's private secretary John Hay to call her a "hell-cat" in his published private diaries. Her emotional troubles became worse after President Lincoln's assassination in April 1865.

Mrs. Lincoln left Washington with very little fanfare after her husband's murder. It's inconceivable to us in our media-drenched age that a former first lady could exit public life so quietly. The combined effect of her Confederate connections and her reckless spending, however, proved extremely difficult for her in the summer of 1865. She lived in Europe for a time, dreading the possibility of a life of poverty.

Her fears were not rational, however, as she often kept more than $50,000 in securities and cash in her skirt pocket. Despite her pleas to the federal government for financial support befitting a presidential widow, Mrs. Lincoln got nothing from the government until 1870, when she received a $3,000-a-year pension. The amount was increased in 1882, and she received a one-time gift from the Senate of $15,000.

In 1867, Mrs. Lincoln tried to sell her entire White House wardrobe and most of her jewelry through a New York estate agent. Although she intended to make the sale anonymously, her identity became known, and she was the subject of both ridicule and disgust.

One of the dresses she tried to sell was the dress she'd worn the night of Lincoln's assassination, still stained with her husband's blood. The entire transaction took on a distasteful, macabre tone—imagine if Jackie Kennedy had auctioned her outfit from the day JFK was assassinated—and the sale of these possessions was never completed.

Mrs. Lincoln's mental health continued to deteriorate, and in 1875, a court committed her to an asylum in Batavia, Illinois. Her son, Robert Todd Lincoln, had arranged this against her will, and Mrs. Lincoln fought to be released. She remained in the asylum for only a short time and was helped in her efforts to be released by attorney Myra Bradwell, one of the first women licensed to practice law in the United States.

In part to escape her son's efforts to have her recommitted, Mrs. Lincoln lived for a few years in France. She returned to Springfield, Illinois, in 1880 and lived with her sister Elizabeth Edwards and her family until her death two years later. And until the time of her death, she signed every letter she wrote as "Mrs. A. Lincoln."

The 1863 "Draft Riots": African American Pogrom

New York City played a heralded role in the Union's Civil War victory. How then did the city explode into riot over conscription in July 1863?

❋　❋　❋　❋

WHEN WAR BROKE out between United and Confederate states in spring 1861, New Yorkers rushed to the colors. Dozens of New York volunteer infantry and cavalry regiments formed in the city. Like their Southern counterparts who donned gray, dashing young New Yorkers put on blue in high spirits, sure of victory.

Such a grand adventure it seemed, with ladies moved to tears by the gallant, manly sight of the Army of the Republic marching to war!

Reality soon set in. War wasn't a gallant spectacle, nor was victory sure. War meant inept, politically appointed generals ordering inexperienced, politically connected colonels to send their men forth to die. Many would perish moaning for water, and for mothers they would never see again. For most of the first two years of war in the East, Union forces got spanked. "Johnny Reb" had proved himself a tough, obstinate foe.

Manpower Crisis

By 1862, Union staff officers ran short of volunteers to replace the dead and the AWOL, the amputated and the captured. Late that year, New York elected as governor Democrat Horatio Seymour, a staunch Lincoln opponent. Seymour's election warned of growing discontent with the "rich man's war, poor man's fight."

While the Union's manpower dilemma was tame compared to the Confederacy's, in March 1863 Congress enacted the long-discussed conscription solution. Able-bodied males from ages 20 to 45 became liable for three years' involuntary military service. The most divisive proviso in Congress's legislation was the means to *avoid* service. A conscript who could scrape up $300 (about $5,300 in 21st-century purchasing power) could buy his way out. Failing that, he could hire a substitute. New York City was full of destitute immigrants, mostly Irish and German, ready to risk their lives for a stake that could elevate them from dire poverty.

Racial Overtones

The issue, though, wasn't simply about money. On New Year's Day 1863, President Lincoln signed the Emancipation Proclamation, freeing slaves in the core Confederate states. This raised a question in the mind of the average soldier: *What am I fighting for?* To risk his life for his country was one thing. Risking it for African Americans (for whom the typical Union soldier would use a racial slur) was quite another.

The fact that the Union did not have slavery does not mean white northerners were immune to racism and xenophobia—remember that even different white European immigrant populations were thought of as different races during this time, let alone free or liberated African Americans.

If the Union won, slavery would almost surely end nationwide. Our typical white soldier envisioned himself returning home only to find that he had helped liberate a whole lot of new competition for employment, a concern that echoes in modern anti-immigration politics. Some regiments became mutinous. The racial factor, then, would play a very sordid part in the city's antidraft explosion.

On July 11, 1863, the NYC provost marshal held the first draft lottery. African Americans were not included in the draft—not that they needed to be; free and freedman alike, they would soon volunteer in great numbers. Recent war news may have contributed to draftee dissent, namely the pivotal Union victories at Gettysburg and Vicksburg. *If we've turned the tide, why do we need a draft?* At the time, of course, no one knew exactly how long the Confederacy might fight on.

July 13, 1863

A sultry day began with a protest in Manhattan. Germans, Irish, men, women, workers, and firefighters gathered numbers as they marched toward the offices of the provost marshal at 47th Street and Third Avenue. Hopes of a peaceful protest ended when the mob torched the marshal's building. The arson had a professional touch: A rioting fire engine company took the lead in torching the place.

Monday dissolved into pandemonium as rioting and arson spread throughout lower Manhattan. Many firefighters were unavailable for service, having joined the rioting. The state militia was away in Pennsylvania, leaving the NYPD ill-equipped to contend with angry mobs. Overwhelmed police resorted to nightsticks and pistols. Undeterred, a gang beat and slashed NYPD Superintendent John Kennedy.

The violence fell most heavily upon African Americans. Many were beaten, sometimes to death. Residents of homes that sheltered African Americans received similar treatment. Rioters even burned an African American orphanage. Other primary targets were homes and businesses of major Republican supporters, such as Horace Greeley's *New York Daily Tribune.*

July 14

A night of rain didn't quench the desire to riot. Mobs barricaded the streets of lower Manhattan. What began as a draft protest had become open warfare on vocal Republicans, African Americans of any station, and war-profiting businesses.

The only Federal troops close enough to play a part on Tuesday were fortress garrison troops from the harbor and West Point. As always, Federal troops played rougher, but the rioters matched them. The 11th New York Volunteers opened fire on rioters at 34th Street and Second Avenue with a six-pounder howitzer. Noting the identity of the colonel in command, a mob hunted him down and beat him to death near his home. The state militia and other nearby regiments hurried to the city.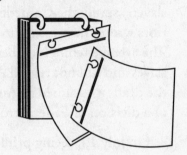

July 15

The violence focused still more intensely on African Americans, who were now unsafe in any part of lower Manhattan. By Wednesday, authorities had identified all areas under mob control. Calling them "infected areas," military and police units moved to contain the rioters inside them. The strategy wasn't entirely successful, however, as the rioting spread to Staten Island and Brooklyn—never mind newspaper reports that the draft had been suspended.

July 16

The arrival of more Federal troops quashed the remaining rioters, with the final fight taking place on 22nd Street between Second and Third avenues.

Cleaning Up and Taking Stock

The official death toll was 119; the true toll may have been higher. Thousands were injured, and thousands of African Americans chose not to stay in Manhattan. Estimates of property damage ranged as high as $5 million (today, that would be about $88.5 million).

The lasting damage was to the city's diversity and the justice of the Union cause. While the Union did not go to war to end slavery, surely the Confederacy went to war to preserve it. The riots wrote the message in letters of blood underlined in fire: The average white Northerner was uninterested in a war to free slaves and did not regard African Americans as equals. As for the draft, it resumed in August—this time with the equivalent of a division of Federal troops in town.

❋ On July 14, seeing prime political opportunity, Tammany Hall's infamous Democratic machine started drafting a bond issue to cover the $300 fee for any New Yorker drafted.

❋ By 1863, the Five Points area had become an important center of African American social life in Manhattan. The area experienced little violence, with white and black New Yorkers joining forces to drive mobs away.

❋ One of the burnt businesses was Brooks Brothers, which made uniforms for the military then (and now).

❋ The real winners in the riots were Tammany politicos, whose power increased when antidraft immigrants saw in the Tammany machine a way to assert their position in the city's political life.

General Sherman Marched Straight into History

William Tecumseh Sherman seemed to come alive on the battlefield. Before the war and at its beginning, he was viewed as a man unsure of himself. By the time the war was over, he had evolved into a general full of bravado, one of the most fearsome warriors the United States has ever seen. What is the truth behind the legend?

✳ ✳ ✳ ✳

WILLIAM TECUMSEH SHERMAN was born in 1820 in the Ohio town of Lancaster. When he was only nine years old, his father died, and his mother, overwhelmed, put him in the care of Thomas Ewing. Ewing later became a U.S. senator and secretary of the interior and used his influence to get Sherman into West Point at age 16, where Sherman graduated sixth in his class in 1840.

His military career thereafter was lackluster, however. He served mostly in Southern states, and he regretted missing the action of the Mexican War. He wrote to his future wife, "I feel ashamed having passed through a war without smelling gunpowder." Seeing little future in an army career, Sherman quit and became a banker in 1853, running the San Francisco branch office of Lucas, Turner and Company of St. Louis. Accounts differ concerning his success; some historians say he was cautious and prudent in the role, while others call him a failure. In any case, he soon left banking to become a lawyer, a field in which he didn't gain much more success: He lost his only case and quickly moved on.

Tired of moving from one place to another and being too often separated from his wife and children, Sherman once wrote, "I am doomed to be a vagabond, and shall no longer struggle against my fate." In 1859, he finally settled for a short time into the job of superintendent of Louisiana State Seminary of Learning & Military Academy (which later changed its name to Louisiana State University). He proved himself an efficient administrator there, and he became a popular storyteller among young professors and students.

Taking a Stand with the Union

Though Sherman enjoyed his job and loved the South, he knew that he could not follow Louisiana out of the Union if it came to that. When Louisiana seceded in 1861, he went north and took a position with a street railway company in St. Louis. Two months later, when he realized war was inevitable, he volunteered to return to his Army uniform.

Sherman continued his mediocre career performance through the first half of the Civil War. He was made a colonel and saw his brigade routed along with everyone else in the Union defeat at Bull Run, although he himself was said to have performed well. Transferred to Kentucky, he blundered politically by stating that it would take a force of 60,000 to hold that state and another of 200,000 to open the Mississippi Valley. Newspapers and Northern politicians called him insane for these estimates. By the end of the war, however, his estimates were proven right.

Sherman had backed himself into a corner and was relieved of his Kentucky post, but he'd made an important friend while in the West: General Ulysses S. Grant. In Sherman's next few battles—Vicksburg, Jackson, and Chattanooga—he had minor success but was highly praised by Grant. His career was on the upswing and he had high hopes.

Sherman Comes into His Own

When Grant was called to take command of all military operations for the war in March 1864, Sherman took over command of the West. As was the case for many Union generals, his early, less successful battles had served as a training ground. In his new position, Sherman understood that his objective went beyond the military force opposing his vast army. "War is cruelty and you cannot refine it," he wrote, "and those who brought war into our country deserve all the curses and maledictions a people can pour out."

Militarily, Sherman led his army against that of Confederate General Joseph E. Johnston. He pushed Johnston all the way to Atlanta and crushed Johnston's successor, John Bell Hood, in three battles outside that pivotal city. Then began his famous March to the Sea, which cemented his reputation and his place in American history. Sherman finished the war marching north through the Carolinas up until the hostilities ended. He accepted the surrender of Johnston's army a little more than two weeks after Lee surrendered to Grant.

After the War

Sherman remained in the Army after the fighting was finished, but his performance in the last year of the war had made him a high-profile political figure. Because he had spent so much of his time in the South before the war, he had a lot of friends in the areas undergoing Reconstruction. He always advocated a light Reconstruction policy, falling on the side of those who preferred to "welcome back" the seceding states.

When Ulysses Grant was elected to the office of president, Sherman took his place as general of the Army, the top military officer of the day. He continued to hold that position until his retirement in 1883.

Sherman remained popular after the war, even—surprising as it may sound today—in the South. In 1879, he toured the sites of many of his Southern victories, such as Atlanta and Savannah, and received a friendly reception.

Many expected that he would follow in Grant's footsteps and run for president, but Sherman never had any interest in the office.

When supporters threatened to draft him as a Republican candidate in 1884, he wired back a famous response: "I will not accept if nominated and will not serve if elected." The nomination that year went instead to James G. Blaine, who lost to Grover Cleveland. Sherman died in 1891. Joseph E. Johnston, the Confederate general who surrendered to him in North Carolina, served as a pallbearer at his funeral.

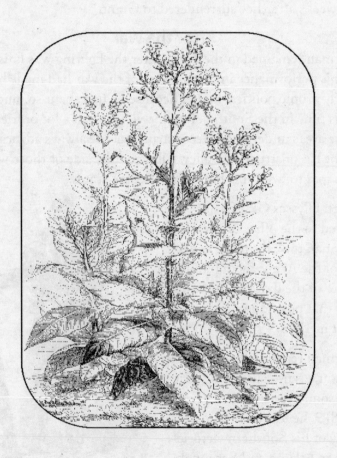

Unlikely Ends

A few Union and Confederate military leaders had less-than-heroic ends—to their careers and even sometimes their lives.

❋ ❋ ❋ ❋

Earl Van Dorn

CONFEDERATE GENERAL EARL Van Dorn's notoriety wasn't due to success on the battlefield—his efforts to defend Missouri from Union forces had gone about as well as can be expected from a man at the bottom of his West Point class. His incompetence was on display at Pea Ridge, Arkansas, in March 1862—Van Dorn lost 4,600 troops, and Arkansas and Missouri were left defenseless against Union forces.

Van Dorn was known as an unrepentant womanizer, wrecking homes not with cannonballs but with his charming demeanor. He also had a reputation for being hot-blooded and impulsive. After an argument over supplies for troops in 1863, Van Dorn pulled a pistol on his superior, General Nathan Bedford Forrest, to challenge him to a duel. Forrest—older, wiser, and more experienced—turned up his nose and told Van Dorn that he had enough Union soldiers to fight without worrying about his own troops, too.

Ultimately, Van Dorn proved affairs of the heart could be just as dangerous as matters of war. In 1863, he and Forrest had routed a Union force into surrender, and Van Dorn made his headquarters in Spring Hill, Tennessee, where he could settle in with his soldiers and reconstitute his forces while awaiting further orders.

During this time of rest, his wandering eye caught sight of Mrs. Jesse Peters, the wife of a local doctor. Van Dorn wooed the woman, taking her on romantic rides in his carriage and even visiting her in her home, barely concealing his improper intent. So self-assured and without fear of discovery was Van Dorn that he barely batted an eye when Mr. George Peters, her husband, appeared at his headquarters on May 7, 1863, requesting a pass to travel to the front lines. Perhaps figuring it might be a good way to get the man killed, Van Dorn happily bent over his desk to scrawl out the permission slip.

Mr. Peters calmly walked up behind the lascivious general and put a bullet in his head. Peters argued in court that he acted in defense of the sanctity of his home, and the court agreed, giving him no punishment. He even reconciled with his wife.

William "Bull" Nelson

When Van Dorn threatened to shoot Forrest, cooler heads prevailed and both men emerged unscathed. But when Union General William "Bull" Nelson had a run-in with one of his peers, General Jefferson C. Davis, no such luck was with them.

Nelson had ordered Davis to organize a militia of citizens to help defend Kentucky from the Confederates. Davis's work was apparently unsatisfactory and took too much time, so Nelson angrily dismissed him and ordered him shipped off to Ohio, effectively cutting Davis out of the thick of the war. Davis took this as an insult and was determined to take revenge on Nelson. On September 29, 1862, he strolled down Main Street in Louisville and entered the Galt House, a hotel where Union officers had been meeting. Davis confronted Nelson, angrily asking why he had been treated so shabbily. Nelson slapped Davis in the face, and before anyone could step in to diffuse the situation, Davis's pistol flew up and a single round was fired, killing Nelson.

Killing a superior officer is generally not acceptable in the military, and this should have been a career-ending decision for Davis. But with the Confederates bearing down on Kentucky and a significant lack of experienced generals, no one pressed charges against him. He returned to combat, and though he never was punished, he was never afforded any promotions or honors, either.

John Reynolds

While Van Dorn got into trouble by sleeping around, Union General John Reynolds got into trouble by just sleeping. A well-respected commander, Reynolds fought bravely until his death by a stray bullet at Gettysburg. His troops saw him as a competent and exceptional leader who rode hard with them and had a consummate knowledge of military strategy. His first few months on the job, however, were not quite as impressive.

Reynolds had been separated from his troops after intense fighting at Gaines' Mill, Virginia, in 1862. Taking refuge in a nearby community named Boatswain's Swamp, he intended to rest and rally with his unit later. Unfortunately for Reynolds, a crew of Confederates snuck into town while he slept and captured him with ease. His embarrassment was only compounded by the fact that the Confederate general to whom he was presented was an old friend from before the war, General D. H. Hill.

After a few weeks in awkward captivity, Reynolds was traded for Confederate prisoners of war and returned to duty.

Edwin Stoughton

Union General Edwin Stoughton was also enjoying a pleasant night's sleep when he was abruptly roused with a slap to his backside. He was furious, kicking away the sheets and confronting his assailant with a bellow, asking, "Do you know who I am?" The unfamiliar voice replied that yes, he did know the general and then asked Stoughton whether he was familiar with a reviled Confederate raider named John Mosby.

Suddenly, Stoughton's anger turned to optimism. "Have you got the rascal?" he asked, excitedly.

"No," replied the voice, "but he has got you." Mosby had made a daring raid deep into Union-controlled territory, picking up Stoughton in Fairfax County, Virginia. Stoughton became a prisoner of war.

While his victory was a great morale boost for the Confederacy, Mosby had not captured a very popular general. Stoughton was the youngest general in the army at only 24 years old. His inexperience, coupled with a preoccupation with his appearance and a finicky personality, made his troops wary of him. Even Abraham Lincoln hardly cared when he was captured, expressing more concern over the loss of 60 horses.

When Stoughton was released to the North, he was immediately discharged to civilian life.

Going Down to Mexico

Defeated and unwilling to face their shattered lives in the South, a number of Confederates crossed the border to create a new life in Mexico… at least for a moment.

* * * *

AFTER THE CONFEDERACY collapsed in the spring of 1865, some of its leaders, refusing to admit surrender to the United States or return to their now-ruined plantations, fled the country to begin new lives in Mexico. Their attempt to recreate the Confederate lifestyle south of the Rio Grande began with Confederate diplomat Matthew Fontaine Maury. He was a man of many talents, also having a background as an ocean explorer and the inventor of an early torpedo. Maury sought help from a close friend of his: Emperor Maximilian I.

The Situation in Mexico
Maximilian, an Austrian archduke, was struggling to hold on to his position in Mexico after France's Emperor Napoleon III placed him in power as part of a short-lived stab at expand-

ing French ambitions into North America. Poorly informed about the actual political situation in Mexico, Maximilian had accepted the crown in 1864 under the mistaken belief that the Mexican people had chosen him to be their emperor. In fact, only a conservative faction of Mexicans supported Maximilian and his French benefactors, while the liberal armies of the ousted Zapotec president Benito Juarez were actively fighting back to topple the new monarchy.

Into this situation came Maury, who had been overseas when peace between the United States and the Confederacy had been declared and the Confederacy dissolved. Instead of returning to his defeated homeland, he went to Maximilian with an idea that the emperor quite liked. Together, they could build support for Maximilian's government by inviting Confederate settlers to come and settle plots of land. The widely admired Southerner spread word among defeated Confederates that 500,000 acres were available for the taking at bargain rates in the Mexican kingdom—and tax-free the first year.

Agrarian Heaven

Among the Confederate exiles who answered the call was General Sterling "Old Pap" Price, who at the end of the war found himself in Texas at the head of a beaten army, having failed to take Missouri for the Confederacy. He and General Joseph Shelby led their troops and their families across the border to the new colony. Protected by Maximilian's French army, the former Confederates started new lives and farms. In the colony of Carlotta, named for the emperor's wife, Price set himself up in a bamboo house. The combination of sun, cheap labor, and fertile soil seemed to promise agrarian heaven.

But it couldn't last. Now that the American Civil War was over, the United States was able to pay more attention to the activity across its border. The federal government turned up the heat on the French presence in North America, which it viewed as an intrusion under the Monroe Doctrine. With 80,000 American troops, General Phil Sheridan rushed to the border to rattle his saber and run guns to Juarez's rebel army. The French decided a Mexican colony wasn't worth all the trouble or the resources, so they withdrew, leaving Maximilian to face whatever fate the Mexicans had for him.

Back to Reality

When, in 1867, a Mexican firing squad put Maximilian against a wall, the exiled Confederates again found themselves without a country, or, in this case, a benefactor. The reinstalled government of President Juarez lowered the boom on their land rights, and the new colony was gone. Confederate colonists, including Price and his followers, fled back to the United States to face Reconstruction.

"Old Pap" died later that year under U.S. rule in Missouri. Maury held out a bit longer, returning to Virginia the following year. He stepped back into American public life with a professorship at the Virginia Military Institute.

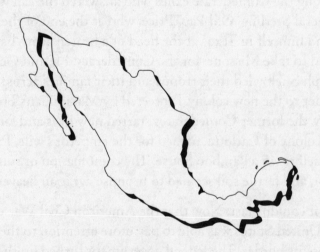

Chapter 4

Science

Monkey See, Monkey Be?

Everyone knows what a monkey is…or maybe they just think they do. Is a chimpanzee a monkey? How about an orangutan or an ape?

※ ※ ※ ※

To ANSWER THESE questions, one must wander into the confusing world of animal taxonomy, where scientists attempt to lump species together, figuring out which ones are closely related and which just look similar. Monkeys, prosimians, tarsiers, chimpanzees, and humans are all examples of the order known as primates, a relatively inclusive taxonomic category. Monkeys represent a suborder of primate that is more closely related to humans, genetically speaking, than to primates such as tarsiers.

All in the Family

After the primate category comes a less inclusive grouping known as a family. This is where apes come in. All apes belong to a family called Hominidae, which includes gibbons, gorillas, chimpanzees, orangutans, and humans. This family is subdivided into the "lesser apes" and the "great apes," and the latter category is reserved for chimpanzees, gorillas, humans, and orangutans (gibbons get chucked). Great apes are unique in that they have no tail, are larger than other primates, have unusually long gestation periods (eight to nine months), and have an extended adolescence.

Of the great apes, humans are most closely related to chimpanzees. To further complicate things, there are actually two main types of chimpanzees: common chimpanzees and bonobos, also known as pygmy chimpanzees. It seems that humans are equally related to both common chimpanzees  and bonobos. Chimpanzees are known for their aggressive social relations, while bonobos prefer to make love instead of war. Many have wondered about the fact that humans seem to represent a fusion of the social behaviors of our two closest biological relatives, who most definitely are not monkeys.

Snakes Alive!

If you're bitten by a poisonous snake, leave your pocketknife alone and use your mouth to call for help.

✳   ✳   ✳   ✳

IT'S A DRAMATIC scene in many old Westerns: After a cowboy is bitten by a rattlesnake, he bravely carves an "X" into the wound and sucks out the venom. This first-aid approach has become so common in popular culture that most people assume it's the right thing to do. But here's why it doesn't work:

Cutting into the site of a snakebite can damage underlying tissue and increase the possibility of infection. Sucking the wound is unlikely to remove any venom—and it puts the person at risk of absorbing the poison through mucous membranes. Instead, the bite should be washed thoroughly with soap and water, if it's available. Otherwise, your best snakebit kit is the car that takes you to the hospital.

Milk for Cats

It's an image straight out of a Norman Rockwell painting: a kitty lapping up a saucer of milk as happy children look on. But now we know better—cats and milk don't mix.

* * * *

* Cats may like milk—chances are they even crave it. But just as people should avoid certain things that we enjoy, cats are better off without milk (especially cow's milk).

* The notion that Fluffy favors dairy products could have originated on farms, where cats roam freely and help themselves to a quick lap out of the pails when cows are being milked. The question is, are the cats coveting a special source of milk or just quenching their thirst when water isn't readily available? Hard to say. But because it's a common behavior, people assume that cats prefer, and perhaps even need, milk.

* Once kittens are weaned, they no longer need milk in their diets. What's more, most grown cats are lactose intolerant. In the same way humans do, cats can experience stomach pain and diarrhea when they drink milk. Because cats don't know to stop drinking something that actually tastes good, they can have continuous diarrhea, which leads to a loss of fluids and nutrients and can endanger their health.

* Can you ever give your cat milk? As always, your veterinarian can tell you what's best for your particular pet. To be on the safe side, consider one of the latest products at pet-supply stores: milk-free milk—for cats! At the same time, though, remember that milk and milk substitutes are really a form of food rather than a beverage. The best way to quench your cat's thirst is with a handy source of fresh, cool water. Your cat may prefer several different water bowls, and they should all be placed in spots that aren't right next to the food.

Canines Are Anti-Perspirant

Do dogs "sweat" through their mouths by panting?

✳ ✳ ✳ ✳

No, THEY DON'T. This myth just fundamentally misunderstands the way sweating works. Humans, who are relatively hairless, have a large and smooth surface area from which moisture can evaporate. The evaporation itself is the cooling mechanism, and this action doesn't translate to the small, wet surface area inside your mouth. Try it: open your mouth and imitate a panting dog. Odds are good that the only change you feel is that your mouth is more dry, and the air being exhaled from your lungs is warm, not cool. Then run water over your forearm and blow gently to evaporate the water. You'll feel cooler or even cold almost right away. When dogs pant, the goal is to bring fresh air into their lungs and cool their bodies from the inside out, not to cool the actual surface area inside of their mouths. It's apples and oranges—both refrigerated, of course.

Lest We Forget

"Have we met before? Sorry, I have the memory of a goldfish."

✳ ✳ ✳ ✳

THE ALLEGED SHORT memory of goldfish is embedded enough in our shared psyche to be the subject of common jokes ("Look, a castle!...Look, a castle!"). But researchers find that goldfish remember months worth of stimuli and act accordingly. Those with goldfish or koi ponds (both kinds of fish are in the carp family) can attest that the fish can gather and hang around during regular feeding times, demonstrating an ability to remember and therefore predict. A viral YouTube video even shows a group of goldfish waiting for a bird that drops seeds into one corner of their pond on a daily basis. Studies of fish memory date back more than 100 years, and it isn't clear where the goldfish myth began.

We're Gonna Need a Bigger Myth

Sharks are bloodthirsty and easily mistake human swimmers for dolphins. It's an easy myth to believe.

✳ ✳ ✳ ✳

Do SHARKS SEE human swimmers and believe them to be dolphins or other marine mammals? The short answer is no, and the important part is "see." This myth hinges on the incorrect idea that sharks have poor vision—easy to believe when you see their black, almost opaque eyes. But sharks' eyes have complexity equal to or greater than that of the human eye, which makes sense for the apex predator of the ocean. In fact, eyes evolved beginning over 500 million years ago, and fossils found in the world-famous Burgess Shale show a veritable kaleidoscope of eyeball setups during this time, including one creature with five eyes on individual stems. These eyeballs already existed before any living thing tiptoed onto dry land and survived.

Sharks can see the lights, darks, and colors that humans see, so their rare choice to bite down on a human swimmer is likely out of curiosity and exploration instead of predation. Since they don't have hands or other ways to use sensory touch, they use their teeth. Think of how human babies put things in their mouths before they grow strong enough to be confident in their hands and fingers. Sharks may not mean to hurt us at all. But as we all learned from *Of Mice and Men*, innocent intentions are not enough. Sorry sharks, you'll need a better PR rep.

Here's a fun fact: Life began in the ocean and crawled out, but at some point, newly evolved mammals decided to crawl back in and become marine mammals. Scientists still don't know why. Maybe the ancestors of dolphins and whales knew that humans were arriving at some point to wiggle their toes and draw all the sharks back to the beach.

Cape Fear?

A bullfighter may be the only one in the ring seeing red.

✳   ✳   ✳   ✳

Red Receipt

MATADORS—THE WORD ITSELF means roughly "killers" in Spanish—wave a classic red cape in the bullfighting ring, and we're told that the red cape enrages the bull. But does it really? Scientists can't seem to agree about the eyesight displayed by bulls, and it's hard to imagine getting a duplicable result in experiments with angry cattle anyway. Some claim that bulls are colorblind. Whether or not bulls can see red,

the cape probably agitates them because it's being waved in their face, not because it's a particular color. This myth is easily perpetuated in light of humans' perception of red as a fast, sexy, exciting color. Straight men find women more desirable when they wear red. Perhaps they've projected some of their own color psychologies into the bullfighting ring.

Widely Red

The idiom "seeing red" is usually traced back to bullfighting, so it's unlikely that this busted myth will ever change. And the phenomenon isn't limited to English, with phrases like *rojo con rabia* ("red with rage") included in many other world languages. But the red cape contrasts with most current uses of red flags, like the caution in an automobile race. A so-called red flag on a first date means you're unlikely to accept the invitation for a second date. In sports, a red card usually means you're ejected from the game for bad behaviors. Historically, red flags were also used by ships in battle and military groups conducting exercises with live ammunition.

Let's Take This Outside

If you don't want to retire your red cape, consider staging a fight with an animal that can indeed see red. Birds, squirrels, and most other animals that are likely to eat brightly colored fruits and berries can see more of a human-like spectrum of colors. Even many insects see a full visible light spectrum—why would the beautiful coloring of a butterfly or beetle matter otherwise? For a next-level challenge, consider an ultraviolet cape that will draw honeybees and other pollen-seeking creatures that have evolved to see special flower markings that are hidden to the naked human eye.

After You; No, After You

Do lemmings mindlessly follow each other to their dooms? They don't.

✳ ✳ ✳ ✳

Dilemma-ing

THE DISNEY CORPORATION has always been known for its sanitized, family-friendly versions of classic fairytales, stories, and world mythology. But during its golden age of live-action narrative and documentary films in the 1950s and 1960s, Disney singlehandedly created the urban legend— natural legend?—of mindlessly suicidal lemmings jumping to their watery deaths. During filming of their Academy Award-winning theatrical documentary *White Wilderness*, filmmakers used an unseen merry-go-round (the playground kind) to launch the lemmings, and they used other camera tricks to create the rest of the narrative leading up to the dramatic waterfront scene. In fact, all the lemmings were brought in for the shoot, and the location and its geographical features were also misrepresented in the final film. *White Wilderness* was about as authentic as the tearful confessional scenes in reality shows.

Long-Tailed Tall Tale

Much like the "frog in boiling water" myth, this animal tall tale has legs because of its easy use as an analogy. A popular early video game franchise called Lemmings used the mechanic of a neverending stream of mindless walkers to prompt players to create safe, contiguous paths. This idea is mimicked in later games like the Pikmin franchise, where herds are led and used to trigger events. As an invective, "lemming" is hurled at almost anyone who believes in almost anything at some point. And last but not least, we spoke with your mom, and she wanted us to remind you that if everyone else were jumping off a bridge, would you do it too? It turns out, neither would lemmings.

The True Story

In reality, lemmings are Arctic rodents with well developed survival instincts. The rodent family was one of the groups that flourished in the aftermath of the mass-extinction event that killed off almost all dinosaurs, and these small, scrappy mammals will live and thrive in almost any conditions on the surface of the earth.

Lemmings live beneath the snow and, like many Arctic and other extreme-climate animals, are not well understood. Many math students study the example of animal population booms to help illustrate equilibrium—most animals stop breeding at a certain point because they instinctively know to avoid overpopulation, or the natural predators and other factors in the area cull the population back to equilibrium anyway. Lemmings seem to breed rapidly without any usual sense of reaching the saturation point in their local habitats. This overbreeding leads to a large, omnidirectional exodus that may have inspired the myth of the suicidal lemming. Scientists don't understand why lemmings breed so rapidly.

Nine Feet Tall and Bulletproof

The tallest, heaviest, and most powerful bird on Earth doesn't need to hide.

❊ ❊ ❊ ❊

Unjust Deserts

OSTRICHES DON'T BURY their heads in the sand. Why would they ever need to? These nine-foot-tall, 300-pound flightless birds can kill almost anything by kicking or pecking, and they can run up to 40 miles an hour to get away from anything else. Plus, any air-breathing animal would suffocate under the sand, so an ostrich hiding this way would literally be scared to death. The whole myth is pretty mysterious and hard to explain. *National Geographic Kids* guesses that someone looking from far away might mistake an ostrich picking at the ground for burying its head in the sand. Ostriches are born from eggs that are kept in burrows in the sand (like sea turtles), so technically all ostriches have their heads in the sand during their baby lives, along with the rest of their bodies. Zing! An observer may have seen an ostrich caring for her eggs and wondered if ostriches bury their heads in the sand for protection.

Bird-Brained Ideas

Perhaps that anecdote misled Pliny the Elder, whom many credit as the progenitor of this myth based on a passage from his most famous work:

"[Ostriches] have the marvellous property of being able to digest every substance without distinction, but their stupidity is no less remarkable; for although the rest of their body is so large, they imagine, when they have thrust their head and neck into a bush, that the whole of the body is concealed."

Pliny isn't wrong about the diet of the ostrich, which is as "flexitarian" as that of a barnyard chicken. His information is likely from Aristotle rather than any firsthand knowledge or observation, but he also projected psychological motives onto an animal behavior, which even today's scientists hesitate to do. But no one was trying to libel the ostrich; Pliny was simply mistaken. At other points in his book, he recommended hundreds of superstitious folk remedies, like eating mice to prevent toothache or wearing animal body parts as amulets to ward off disease. Pliny was very influential, smart, and thorough in his research of what was available to him. He was also wrong about almost everything.

The Moral of the Story

Pliny took a spiritual approach to his study of nature, and it's interesting to wonder if he valued his observations of animals in the same way we rely on proverbs and other folk wisdom today: as advice that reflects on human nature by proxy.

As in Aesop's fables, animals appear in Pliny's work in order to teach some lesson to his readers. The ostrich is "stupid" because it hides in the sand, but the act is also cowardly and shows a distateful denial of reality. And the contrast between its large size and this cowardice is funny. If Pliny knew the truth, perhaps the ostrich wouldn't have made it into his book at all.

Foley Me Once, Shame On You

Dramatic animal documentaries capture our imaginations in unique ways, but most viewers don't realize how much of this footage is doctored, staged, or otherwise "performance enhanced."

✳   ✳   ✳   ✳

IN THE AGE of high-definition television, big-budget draws like *Planet Earth* use the latest, greatest technology to zoom in on rare animals and habitats. In these shots, the sounds are added by the same kind of foley work that accompanies our mental image of old-timey radio dramas—humans with headphones on, crinkling cellophane or playing back recorded zoo animals in time with the footage. If not, the crew would need to get much, much closer to record audio than they do to record video because of the difference in the two technologies.

Long-Distance Video

Think about tabloid stories where celebrities are photographed on secluded beaches in their skimpy swimsuits. Photographers use huge, expensive telephoto lenses to take these photos from very far away, claiming, if asked, that they were on public lands when they took the photos. The same technology enables the astonishing shots of wild animals that we've grown used to seeing in every nature documentary.

Audio Stopgaps

Physicists and other scientists have had more success with long-distance photography than with audio recording, so there is simply not a similar audio technology to match telephoto lenses for faraway footage. Why is this? An armchair scientist might speculate that sounds travel out in all different directions at once, meaning the sound waves are hard to capture. Many noises animals and people make have to reverberate inside our throats, mouths, or noses in order to be heard, and this is hard to capture as well. Imagine using a spray bottle with an adjustable nozzle set to shoot one stream versus a wide spray. Could you aim well or at all with the wide spray?

Going Deeper

Sound isn't the only way these documentaries are doctored. Close-up scenes of animal families and dens or nests are often recreated using domesticated animals on constructed sets, like the soundstages used for movies and television. And hyper-realistic computer-generated imagery (CGI) can bring animals to life almost seamlessly. All these techniques sound familiar to even a casual consumer of Hollywood movies, but no one is calling *Jurassic Park* a documentary by any definition. Concerned filmmakers have cited short time frames and budget crunches as reasons they've made ethically gray choices, and most point out that these documentaries have disclaimers in their credits, so perhaps no ethical line has been crossed. But the public seems to revere nature documentaries as insight into the unvarnished world of animal behavior.

Drawing the Line

Sometimes these choices seem arbitrary. Why do filmmakers insist on following journalistic conventions of standing by while animals are killed or eaten but then doctor the sound effects and cut to a captive animal filmed on a soundstage? It's all a slippery slope. Some animal rights activists encourage the use of humanely kept captive animals in these documentaries in order to avoid distressing or harming wild animals in their natural habitats.

One major accomplishment in recent years is the use of battery-powered, motion-activated cameras to film the most elusive animals on earth without installing a filmmaker for months at a time—or introducing the observer effect, where the act of watching itself affects the outcome. We can see beautiful snow leopards in their natural habitats, and the cameras are close enough to record sound, in theory. And without a filmmaker in the mix, there's no temptation to interfere in the animals' lives.

No Cats Were Harmed

What's the story with so-called "catgut," the material used in tennis and musical-instrument strings? It is really made of guts, but the guts don't come from cats.

* * * *

Intestinal Fortitude

THE INTESTINES OF cattle and other livestock are cleaned, stripped of fat, and prepared with chemicals before they can be made into catgut string. Preparation of string from animal tissue dates back thousands of years in recorded history and likely much longer ago in reality. Intestines are uniquely

suited because of
their combination of
strength and elastic-
ity, even in compari-
son to other pretty
robust naturally
occurring strings like
horsehair or silk.

This makes sense intuitively because of the role our intestines
play in our bodies, but let's not think too hard about that. One
downside is that the prepared gut fibers are still very absorbent—enough so that even atmospheric humidity can warp
them out of shape.

In Stitches

Historical humans realized surprisingly early that gut string
was a good way to sew up wounds, and in this case the absorbency is a bonus. These humans weren't aware of issues like
infection, so their ingenuity with gut string was a matter of
simple craftsmanship: you should sew with the strongest
material you can find, whether for clothing or shelter or for a
wound. Thousands of years later, scientists experimented and
realized that gut string could dissolve in the human body. With
the eventual rise of germ theory, doctors were able to create and
use sterilized dissolving sutures that would be recognizable to
the ancient Egyptians who first documented their sewing of
wounds. In fact, most dissolvable stitches are still made with
prepared animal fibers or with synthetics that were designed to
mimic animal fibers in the body.

High Strung

For musical instruments, gut strings also date back thousands
of years. In both Latin and Greek, the terms for strings and
bowstrings (and our modern words chord and cord) were from
the original Greek term meaning guts. Musicians found that
gut strings made the best sound, but the strings warped, frayed,
and broke quite quickly because of the effects of moisture in

the air and from musicians' touch. Modern musicians can use strings with a core of gut that's surrounded by a snug winding of very fine metal. In a fine example of art imitating nature, this structure mimics the way our flexible gut fibers are arranged in our intestines, with both lengthwise fibers and circular bands.

The Gut Racket

Gut strings are still considered the gold standard by many high-level tennis players and manufacturers. In tennis, the absorbency of gut strings is counteracted with topical wax that seals the strings. Choosing and making gut strings for tennis rackets is still an artisan craft, and some cattle—most if not all tennis gut strings come from cattle—apparently produce finer quality gut strings than others, creating a Wagyu-beef-like hierarchy among cattle ranchers.

Digesting the Information

Humans have shown remarkable ingenuity since we first diverged from our most recent ancestor, but even by human standards, it's unusual to have a found material that works as both a durable tool and a nourishing food—depending on how you prepare it. Whether you're preparing for your Wimbledon debut or a period-correct Baroque chamber orchestra, consider the millennia-old tradition of the gut string.

Brain Power

Mental gymnastics are not the only way to keep your brain sharp. Physical gymnastics—or any form of exercise—are just as important.

✳ ✳ ✳ ✳

Looking to roll back the cognitive clock? Or maybe just remember where you put your car keys? Cognitive "training"—that is, doing mentally challenging activities such as crossword puzzles and sudoku—has been all the rage lately because it's been shown to help preserve brain function. But there's another kind of workout that could be the real ticket to keeping your brain young.

Stay Sharp and in Shape

Studies show that regular, moderate exercise helps our brains stay sharp. Researchers have found that one hour of aerobic exercise three times a week can increase brain volume, which in turn may delay some age-related changes. It takes only a few months to start seeing results, suggesting that it's never too late to start exercising. Other studies done on animals concur that more exercise equals better brain function. Even the dormant neural stem cells in elderly mice "wake up" once the critters hit the running wheel.

In one study that examined older men and women with memory problems, mental workouts (in the form of brain teasers and puzzles) produced encouraging results when combined with physical exercise and a heart-healthy diet. What's good for the cardiovascular system appears to also be good for our gray matter, giving us another reason to lower our blood pressure, weight, and cholesterol levels.

Experts caution not to waste money on dietary supplements and vitamins that claim to have "anti-aging" benefits, and we don't need to buy special "brain fitness" computer programs. Engaging in a pleasurable activity, such as studying a foreign language, reading, or playing a musical instrument, is a great way to keep us thinking and learning.

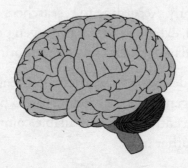

Wound Care Catastrophe!

Hydrogen peroxide isn't the miracle cure it's cracked up to be.

✳ ✳ ✳ ✳

YOU'LL FIND A brown plastic bottle of hydrogen peroxide in most medicine chests, right next to the iodine and calamine lotion. It's been touted for decades as the ideal treatment for cuts, scrapes, and other minor wounds.

There's just one problem, medical experts say: Applying hydrogen peroxide to open wounds may actually do more harm than good.

Hydrogen peroxide became an integral part of most home first-aid kits because people had the mistaken belief that it killed germs and helped wounds heal faster. However, recent studies have found that hydrogen peroxide can actually damage the healthy tissue around a wound, which slows the healing process. Worse, it's a lousy germ fighter. Many other compounds, such as over-the-counter antibacterial salves, work much better.

In recent years, hydrogen peroxide has been touted as a cure for everything from cold sores to foot fungus to arthritis. Few of these claims have been confirmed by the Food and Drug Administration (FDA), which warns that hydrogen peroxide in high concentrations can be dangerous and even deadly if swallowed. The FDA has approved just one home use for hydrogen peroxide—as a mouthwash. But even then it should be used infrequently. According to researchers at Massachusetts General Hospital, extended use of hydrogen peroxide as a mouth rinse can damage cells and soften tooth enamel.

Hydrogen peroxide comes in a variety of strengths. Most household hydrogen peroxide products are 3 percent solutions. Much higher concentrations are available commercially for disinfectant and other uses.

So when you scrape your skin, don't reach for the hydrogen peroxide. There are better products to use on your wound.

A Tired Misconception

Most people associate yawning with sleepiness, but the cause of the open-mouthed reflex remains a mystery. According to researchers, humans (and many other animals) yawn for a variety of reasons—fatigue is just one of them.

❋ ❋ ❋ ❋

SCIENTISTS HAVE TRIED for decades to figure out the physical mechanism behind yawning, and they still don't have a definitive answer. A popular older theory held that yawning was a way to bring more oxygen into the bloodstream and move carbon dioxide out. That theory was shot down, however, after experiments showed that increased oxygen intake didn't decrease the rate of yawning.

Another theory suggests that yawning is the body's way of boosting heart rate and blood pressure in anticipation of an energetic or strenuous activity. There may be something to this concept, because it's well documented that Olympic athletes often yawn before a competition and paratroopers yawn before a jump. But that doesn't explain the millions of other times we yawn.

We may not yet know why we yawn, but we do know when. Yes, we yawn when we're tired. We also yawn when we're bored or nervous, and sometimes we yawn for no reason at all. In fact, just thinking about yawning can bring one on.

So the next time someone yawns in your presence, make no assumptions about his or her state of mind or degree of fatigue. Go ahead and yawn right back—yawning, after all, is contagious.

Or is it?

✳ Yawning is also common in the animal world. Dogs, for example, yawn when tired, just like their owners. But they also yawn when excited or tense, and they do it as a way to tell other dogs that they're stressed and need to take a break.

Seeing Double

Can't tell which identical twin is which? Check their fingerprints. Identical twins may look like carbon copies, but research shows they are not exact duplicates of each other. Indistinguishable to the naked eye, some differences are skin deep—but most run much deeper.

✳ ✳ ✳ ✳

IDENTICAL TWINS RESULT when a zygote (a fertilized egg) divides in half, forming two embryos. The embryos develop in tandem and, at birth, are identical twin siblings. In the past it was largely assumed that identical twins were exact replicas of each other. After all, they formed from the exact same genetic material. But scientists have found that there are variations in identical twins' individual gene segments. Researchers believe these disparities occur in the womb, when dividing cells cause small genetic differences in each twin. This explains why one identical twin can develop a genetic disorder while the other twin remains healthy. It also is the reason one twin may be right-handed and the other left-handed.

In addition to subtle differences in their genetic blueprints, there is another difference in identical twins—their fingerprints. Fingerprints are formed while a fetus is growing and are the result of DNA and environmental influences in the womb. By the second trimester of pregnancy, the ridges and loops in our digits are permanently etched into our skin. Factors such as contact with amniotic fluid and the pressure of bone growth affect the unique patterns. Although no two fingerprints are alike, identical twins often have similar patterns.

The unique fingerprints can also assist confused parents who return home from the hospital with their newborn identical twins, remove the ID bracelets, and then can't figure out who is who. The babies can be identified by refingerprinting them and matching the prints with the originals on file at the hospital.

Out of Body, Out of Mind?

Does having an out-of-body experience (OBE) mean that you're out of your mind? Absolutely not. In fact, statistics show that between 5 and 35 percent of the population has had at least one OBE. And many of the people who have had them don't even know it.

✳ ✳ ✳ ✳

So What the Heck Is an OBE Anyway?

DEFINITIONS IN SCIENTIFIC journals can get pretty technical, but the simple explanation of an out-of-body experience is that it's the feeling that you've left your physical body and can see yourself and the world from outside of your earthly vessel. Some people describe the OBE as a state in which a person's consciousness separates from his or her body, usually for a very short period of time. Sometimes those who experience an OBE report hearing or seeing something that they couldn't have seen or heard from within their own body.

People seem to find out-of-body experiences fascinating, but we don't really know much about what causes them at this point. What *is* clear is that an OBE can happen to anyone at any time. It can happen just as easily to a paranormal skeptic as it can to a believer. And although an OBE can occur during a near-death experience (NDE), the two are not one and the same. An OBE occurs when the mind separates from the physical body, but the spirit remains in the physical world. During a near-death experience, the person may or may not experience an OBE. The person may look down at her body lying on a hospital bed or see herself in a wrecked car, which would be considered an OBE, but the rest of the NDE involves *leaving* the physical world and traveling to "the Other Side." Most people who experience an NDE report seeing a bright light, traveling through a tunnel, and seeing deceased relatives; those components are not part of the simple OBE, during which the person remains in this realm.

One survey asked people who'd had an OBE to describe the circumstances surrounding it. More than 85 percent of respondents said that they'd had their OBEs while they were resting, sleeping, or dreaming. Others reported being sick in bed or even medicated. But still other people—especially those moving at fast speeds like in an airplane or on a motorcycle—have reported feeling as if they were floating above themselves.

Do It Yourself...or Not

While many OBEs simply occur, researchers have confirmed that some people are able to create their own out-of-body experiences. Using relaxation techniques and isolating sensory input, subjects have succeeded in making OBEs happen. Those who can do this at will report a greater feeling of control, as if they are out of their regular body but remain empowered in the situation; many even describe a "silver cord" that attaches their corporeal body to their ethereal form. The silver cord and the feeling of empowerment are much less pronounced among those whose OBEs are spontaneous. Many subjects reported a sense of great energy. They saw bright colors and heard loud noises. Everything was vivid and vibrant, yet more like being awake (except that the person observed it from above) than like the hallucinatory quality of a dream. OBEs seem to be more grounded and feel more "real" than dreams.

Tell Me More

We could analyze OBEs and NDEs all day, but it's more fun to read about actual experiences rather than the science behind them. Here are some reports from people who have actually experienced them.

No Fear of Flying

Eileen T. said that she had an out-of-body experience when she was nine, so she wasn't afraid when she had another one more recently. When it happened to her as a child, she simply rose to the ceiling and hovered above her body; during her adult experience, Eileen was lying near her grandson, who was very ill. Suddenly, she felt herself leave her body through the bottoms of her feet. She reported feeling as though she was flying feet-first for a hundred miles. After a short time, her ethereal form—which seemed as though it was still attached—reentered her physical body. Initially, reconnecting was uncomfortable, but she eventually settled back in. When she awoke, her body was lying calmly with its feet crossed, as though she hadn't a care in the world.

Scared Back to Reality

Although it happened in 1980, Paul R. said that he remembers his OBE like it occurred yesterday. He had gone to bed with his wife and was drifting off to sleep when, suddenly, he awoke to hear a loud humming noise and felt his entire body vibrating. The next thing he knew, he was looking down at himself and his wife in the bed. He decided to visit an aunt who lived nearby, but as he left the apartment, he encountered a strange man who tried to hand him a small scroll. Something about the man or the paper must have frightened Paul because he swiftly returned to the bedroom, where he "slammed" back into his body. He said that it was like nothing he had ever experienced before, but he's certain that he wasn't dreaming, and he hadn't been under the influence of any mind-altering substances.

A Campfire Story

A nine-year-old boy had an out-of-body experience while camping and told his mother about it when he returned home. His parents were divorced, and the boy was vacationing with his father and his father's girlfriend in early 2004. While the youngster was drifting off to sleep, he felt a huge burst of energy. Suddenly, he found himself back at the campfire, where he could see and hear the adults quite clearly. However, glancing back at the tent, he was surprised to see that his body was still inside—fast asleep.

A Spiritual OBE . . .

Kevin G. of Toronto described his out-of-body experience as being something of a religious experience. It occurred one night in 1990, when he was feeling especially tired and went to bed a bit earlier than he normally would. He thought that he fell asleep right away, but the sensation that he experienced was not at all like a dream: He "woke up" and realized that he was about six feet above the bed, where his body was still lying. Kevin said that he felt an incredible peace and happiness. He was raised in a religious home and has always been interested in spiritual matters. He felt his personal OBE was a message to him that each person's spiritual journey is just a part of life; he remembers that message each and every day.

. . . And a Spiritual NDE

When Baptist minister Don Piper was on his way home from an out-of-town conference in the early 2000s, his vehicle was hit head-on by an 18-wheeler. Pronounced dead at the scene, his spirit was immediately transported to the Great Beyond. According to his book *90 Minutes in Heaven*, Piper experienced an out-of-body experience like nothing he had ever imagined. He had no memory of the crash or of hovering above his body; instead, he went directly to heaven and was reunited with deceased friends and relatives. He knew that he was no longer on earth because he was in a place that was more beautiful than anything he had ever seen. All of his senses were heightened, and he recognized people who were no longer living. After

90 minutes, he was sent back to earth, where he found himself awake and in pain, with heaven nothing more than a memory.

Escaping Earthly Illness for a While

Linda S. had been ill for some time when she made the decision not to fight her disease anymore. No more doctors, no more medication; she was going to be free. And free she was. Shortly thereafter, Linda had a near-death experience during which she felt supreme quiet followed by a detachment from her body. In fact, she watched her spirit leave her physical body: She could see her diseased body lying there, but she no longer had a connection to it. Suddenly, she felt no pain. Gone was her struggle to breathe. As her weightless spirit lifted, so did her depression. Linda felt a profound sense of calm. When she made a conscious decision to let go of her lifeless body, she felt a powerful force lift her upward. Linda described the rest of her experience as a peaceful and loving journey to heaven, which ended when God told her that she must return to earth. She could not recall her trip back to this world, but she has since recovered from her illness.

25 Steps to a Healthier You

In the late 20th century, along came aerobics, isometrics, Richard Simmons, Dr. Atkins, and a nonstop barrage of exercise gadgets, all of which have left the average person dazed, confused, and in worse shape then ever! So what really works? Here are some helpful tips for getting in shape.

✳ ✳ ✳ ✳

1. **Follow a balanced exercise program:** A brisk 30-minute walk while enjoying the sunset will burn 1,500 calories per week—that's 78,000 calories a year! Cardio is great for your heart and lungs, but add a couple sessions of weight training to tone or build muscle.

2. **Schedule family fitness time:** Play basketball, chase a Frisbee, or hike the hills together. You'll be getting closer to each other as you shape up.

3. **Invest in a jump rope:** It's a great workout anytime. Set a goal of skipping rope for ten minutes per day and watch those love handles melt away.

4. **Get a training partner:** Knowing that someone is waiting is great motivation to get on with it. You'll also have a ready-made spotter.

5. **Exercise in water to relieve stress on the joints and back:** Check out the aerobics programs at your local pool and go aqua—the wave of the future.

6. **Get active at work:** Walk around outside on your breaks. When in front of a computer, sit up and pull in your abs.

7. **Eat more frequent, smaller meals:** It is better to eat six small meals a day than three large meals. The smaller the meal, the less your stomach will stretch.

8. **Hydrate with water:** Drink at least eight glasses of water every day. This does not include coffee, soda, or fruit-flavored drinks, which have extra calories.

9. **Don't pollute your body:** Avoid tobacco, excess alcohol, and illegal drugs. These are bad for health and can also inhibit weight loss.

10. **Always eat a good breakfast:** Skipping breakfast is a method of dieting for many people. But studies have found that people who eat breakfast are actually less likely to be obese.

11. **Start cooking healthy:** Stop frying your food and opt for roasting or grilling instead. Frying only adds unnecessary calories to food.

12. **Enjoy every morsel of food:** When eating, chew food

slowly. Relish it and pay attention to flavors and taste. The longer you chew, the fuller you'll feel!

13. **Be an early riser:** Start your day early. Rising with the sun helps reset your body's clock. This builds better sleep patterns so you're energized througout the day.

14. **Be sun smart:** Skin cancer is the most common type of cancer. Sun exposure increases your risk, so when you're in the heat of it, either cover up or slip, slap, slop on a high SPF sunscreen!

15. **Stay emotionally in shape:** Poor emotional health can weaken your body's immune system. Don't ignore what's going on in your heart and mind. It is healthy to acknowledge your emotions.

16. **Keep your teeth healthy:** A common cause of tooth loss after age 35 is gum disease. Keep your teeth and gums healthy and free of plaque by brushing and flossing every day.

17. **Eat five or more servings of fruits and veggies per day:** Keep fruits and vegetables on the front shelves of your refrigerator so they are easy to get to when you reach for a snack!

18. **De-stress your life:** Stress can cause or aggravate many health conditions. So, don't sweat the small stuff!

19. **Know thyself:** Knowing your family's health history can help you stay healthy. Many diseases are hereditary and preventable with early screening.

20. Look after your mental health: Depression is a serious illness that needs to be treated. It's not your fault, so you shouldn't be afraid to talk to a doctor for help.

21. Get a good night's sleep: Lack of sleep causes stress on the body: It increases cortisol and insulin, promoting fat storage and making weight loss difficult.

22. Ladies, perform regular breast examinations: The best time to perform a breast self-examination is the week after your menstrual period, when breast tissue is less tender and swollen.

23. Take a nap: Many have commended the benefits of a good 30- to 45-minute nap a day to keep refreshed and lower stress. Try it—it doesn't mean you've passed your use-by date!

24. Open your lungs: Sing your heart out! It doesn't matter what you sound like! In the shower, in the car, or wherever you are, sing out loud. It's a great stress reliever.

25. Take time to enjoy your life: While it's important to do a good job and take care of responsibilities, life is also meant to be enjoyed. Loosen up! Laugh at yourself, and play as hard as you work!

Hard As Nails

You may be soft at heart, but you want your nails to be as hard as … well, nails. Can gelatin help?

✳   ✳   ✳   ✳

GELATIN CAN TURN a liquid into a solid—think Jell-O after it sets. So perhaps it makes sense to think that ingesting it or soaking your fingertips in it would strengthen your nails and make them more resistant to chipping and cracking.

The logic may be flawed, but millions of people fell for a marketing scheme that connected gelatin with strong nails. And it's a tribute to that wildly successful advertising campaign that millions of people still believe it today.

In 1890, Charles Knox developed gelatin, a product made from slaughterhouse waste. He sold the public on it by touting its nail-enhancing benefits. The animals (cows and pigs) used to produce gelatin had strong hooves, Knox reasoned, so eating their by-products would give people nails just as strong. Consumers fell for it, lock, livestock, and barrel.

The Truth of the Matter

But no matter how many people swear by it, there is no scientific proof that gelatin hardens nails. Gelatin is made from the skin, connective tissue, and bones of cattle and pigs, and so it is full of protein and collagen. The protein is not, however, in a form that's usable by humans. And unless your diet is deficient in protein, which is unlikely, eating more protein is not going to solve your nail problems. The best thing you can do for your nails is to pick up some petroleum jelly and use it to moisturize them.

Color Me Toxic

Mares eat oats, and does eat oats, and little kids eat crayons. But should Junior wear a HAZMAT suit as he munches on Burnt Sienna or Cadet Blue?

✳   ✳   ✳   ✳

O N MAY 23, 2003, the *Seattle Post-Intelligencer* fired a shot heard by parents around the world. In independent tests of eight brands of coloring crayons, three brands (Crayola, Prang, and Rose Art) had colors that contained more than trace levels of asbestos.

The three manufacturers immediately dismissed the findings as wrong, citing their own industry tests. Despite the denials, this report set off a firestorm of fear, criticism, and consumer panic.

"Asbestos" is a general term for several minerals that break easily into fibrous threads, and that have been linked to various forms of cancer, especially when inhaled. In these cases, asbestos is likely mixed with the mineral talc, which was used as a binding agent in crayons. Talc and asbestos are found together in rock formations and frequently are combined in the mining process.

In follow-up tests, the Consumer Product Safety Commission (CPSC) found traces of asbestos in Crayola and Prang crayons, but it assured the public that the amount was insignificant. Similar but non-hazardous "transitional fibers" also appeared in the tests. Although the CPSC wasn't concerned about children ingesting any of these materials and found no airborne fibers even after 30 minutes of simulated scribbling, it requested that the manufacturers reformulate their products. All three companies agreed, and later tests showed all of the crayons to be asbestos-free.

When Cold Burns

Frostbitten skin may feel like it's burning, but that doesn't mean you should try to cool it down.

✳ ✳ ✳ ✳

IF YOUR MOTHER told you to rub snow on frost-nipped digits or append-ages, chances are she was born before the 1950s—or else she was getting her treatment advice from a very old first-aid manual. Rubbing snow on frostbit-ten skin had been standard treatment since Napoleon's army surgeon, Baron Larrey, proposed it in the frigid winter of 1812–13, during the retreat from Moscow. Larrey saw the disastrous results when soldiers defrosted their hands and feet by holding them over fires, and he decided that using snow was a better way to minimize infection.

The good doctor had it wrong, however. Physicians' discoveries during another military endeavor, the Korean War, followed by a landmark study a few years later, debunked the popular snow-on-frostbite treatment theory. Frostbitten skin should not be thawed unless it won't be refrozen. Refreezing warmed frostbitten tissue is more harmful than leaving it alone. Of course, the soldiers did not have an option. They were stuck outdoors on the battlefield, and a great number of them ended up amputees afterward.

Lock-Picking Know-How

Regardless of what is portrayed in cops-and-robbers flicks, you need at least two tools to pick a lock.

✳   ✳   ✳   ✳

WHETHER YOU'RE A wannabe ruffian or a forgetful home-owner, you should know that it is nearly impossible to pick a lock with only one paper clip, one bobby pin, or one of anything else. Although you can certainly accomplish the task with simple tools, you will need two of them—one to act as a pick and a second one to serve as a tension wrench.

The simple pin-and-tumbler locks on most doors contain a cylinder and several small pins attached to springs. When the door is locked, the cylinder is kept in place by the pins, which protrude into the cylinder. When a matching key is inserted into the lock, the pins are pushed back and the cylinder turns. The key to lock-picking, then, is to push the pins back while simultaneously turning the cylinder. This is why two items are required—a pick to push the pins and a tension wrench to turn the cylinder. Professional locksmiths often use simple lock-picking techniques to avoid damaging the offending lock.

Common household items that can serve as tension wrenches include small screwdrivers and bent paper clips. Items you can use as picks include safety pins, hair fasteners, and paper clips. The determined apprentice may be happy to learn that there is a situation in which one paper clip may suffice in picking a lock: Small, inexpensive padlocks sometimes succumb to large paper clips that are bent in such a way that one end is the pick and the other end is the tension wrench. Even so, the process involves more than just jamming something into the lock and turning the doorknob. Seasoned lock-pickers rely on their senses of hearing and touch to finish the job success-fully. They're anticipating a vibration accompanied by a distinct "click" that means each pin is in alignment.

The Memory Fallacy

"I have a photographic memory," a television or movie character conveniently says; then she recites specific details from a crime scene or piece of evidence and solves the Big Case.

✳ ✳ ✳ ✳

The Super Good Guys

AMERICAN TV AND movie viewers may have superhero fatigue, but our procedural dramas are also stuffed with superhuman abilities of the mind. Characters have savant or genius intellects for everything from diagnostics and mathematics to forensics and legal history. They turn probabilities into hard facts and catch the bad guy every time. What a magical world!

Memory in particular is a well worn plot device. On one end of the spectrum is convenient amnesia, brought on by an otherwise benign bump on the head and often cured the same way. (If only because of the tragically affected NFL players, we know repeated head traumas don't cancel out like double negatives.) On the other end is the so-called photographic memory, illustrated with spliced footage where an investigator mentally examines a crime scene and zooms in on the relevant details.

Un-Total Recall

Does this phenomenon exist? No one has ever observed a case that passed regular scientific muster. Photographic memory like the kind seen in TV savants has probably never existed, but eidetic memory, a slightly different real-life condition, may exist in a limited form.

The subject of exceptional memories continues to be studied and debated because of the difficulty of standardizing those studies. If there were a uniform test for memory, someone would leak its contents, and potential takers could memorize the answers. If a test taker got the right root word of an answer but confused "walked" with "walking," does that count? There's simply too much room for human error and gray areas in testing memory. Scientists also don't yet understand how memories are formed and stored.

Case Study: Marilu Henner

Actress Marilu Henner is the most famous face of exceptional memory, with a self-help book on the subject and many appearances on TV talk shows to discuss and promote it. But her memory is of the type known as hyperthymesia, where people recall their own lives in extraordinary detail.

This is fundamentally different from the visual nature of the so-called photographic memory. Scientists theorize that people with hyperthymesia use very strong cues, maybe even unconsciously, to remember specific details that come in patterns most people simply don't grasp. It may be a form of mnemonic device that its users don't always know they're using because it comes more easily to them than to others.

Facts Versus Fiction

The closest real-life analog to photographic memory is eidetic memory, a term coined in 1924 to describe people who are able to visualize whole scenes and images in much more detail than nearly everyone else. There are virtually no adults known to have had true eidetic memory, where they don't rely on mnemonic devices of any kind and can recall a lot of visual detail. What's interesting is that those with eidetic memory can still add, subtract, and distort the details, as the rest of us do in our average memories.

Psychology and criminology instructors who teach the limitations of eyewitness testimony often use a fun real-life exercise that you can do with any group. Have a friend or other passerby put on specific clothes and accessories, enter the room in a specific way, say a specific phrase, wave a specific object like a book or keychain, and make a specific exit. Afterward, ask everyone who witnessed the event to write down what happened. Participants will swear they saw something that didn't exist, just moments after it took place in front of their very eyes.

Wasted On the Young

Children have much more plastic and reliable memories for details than adults, and rates of eidetic memory in children are quite high—as many as 1 in 10 may have eidetic memory for a time. But as with other side effects of growing up, this special memory fades as children get older. It may be that turning our perceptions into better and better language skills makes this level of memory feel unnecessary to our brains, causing it to dissipate as we reach adolescence or adulthood.

There's also evidence that babies and toddlers have a totally different intuitive way to think about numbers than what most children are taught in school. The preverbal brain is an enigma!

Improving Your Memory

Photographic memory may not be real, but there are many ways to improve your memory, especially for things like daily tasks and people's names. Marilu Henner's book offers techniques based on her own experiences. Journalist Joshua Foer, brother of novelist Jonathan Safran Foer, studied under a "master of memory" and became the American memory champion in 2006, which he documented in a 2011 book. The idea of the memory palace, a mnemonic where you associate facts and other desired memories with physical locations inside a house that you visualize, plays a prominent role in the British detective-savant TV series *Sherlock*.

Exaggerating memory and other abilities is fine for fictional TV, where producers must make an entertaining and viewable version of what their characters are thinking. But photographic memory of this kind just doesn't seem to exist. Certainly if anyone in your life shows evidence of one, you should talk to your friendly local cognitive scientist! Until then, we'll have to stick to fictional examples.

Amongst the Very Old at Heart

Was the average life expectancy in ancient times short, with basically everyone dead by 30? Think again.

❋ ❋ ❋ ❋

IN THE 21ST century, there's no health headline scarier than declining life expectancy. What could more pointedly indict our culture as backsliding toward primitivity? After all, medical science has brought the average life expectancy in the U.S. from under 40 in 1850 to the mid 70s in 2000. Well, yes and no—it depends on how you measure.

Infant and Child Survival Rates

The greatest factor in overall life expectancy has always been infant and child mortality, and these numbers are powerfully affected by dozens of different factors in everyday life, not to mention the specific practices around childbirth and childrearing. In fact, this one statistic is so far-reaching that it can pretty accurately predict whether a national government will fail.

The U.N. reports that world infant mortality, defined as a baby who dies during or after birth, dropped from nearly 16% in 1950 to about 7% in 1980 and about 5% by 2000.

Adult Life Expectancy

There have always been adults who lived a relatively long time by modern standards. Historians divide life expectancy for prehistoric people, ancient Egypt or Rome, and so forth into categories that try to account for child mortality. As a template, if an ancient child lived to age 10, 15, or adulthood, she could expect to live an additional 20, 30, 40 years, depending on the documents historians are able to read and parse.

Different ancient groups had varying life expectancies that map to differences in lifestyle and location. The same is true today, when pockets of people who share unusual longevity factors— cleaner air, lower stress, healthier staple foods—are anomalies.

It's fun to consider the globetrotting explorers of the 1500s embarking on *Gulliver's Travels*-like adventures among groups and cultures with noteworthy numbers of healthy older people. More importantly, these anecdotes illustrate how important environmental and lifestyle factors could be even centuries before modern medical science emerged.

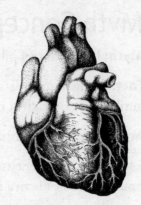

Old News

Today, reports of declining life expectancy cite the specific health dangers that plague our era, like coronary artery disease, HIV and AIDS in the developing world, and opioid overdose in the United States.

Life expectancy has fallen sharply in specific nations like North Korea, where the stifling autocracy has created food shortages and medical crises along with the general risk factors like low general education or access to information. But any declines in the 21st-century developed world are small, especially compared to the almost history-ending severity of the waves of Black Plague that ravaged Europe in the late middle ages.

As the U.S. government takes action to curb opioid addiction, for example, the lives saved will help to buoy the life expectancy overall. But public health researchers are rightfully concerned that the same socioeconomic factors that can lead to opioid addiction may also lead to a rise in infant mortality, and the U.S. already has one of the highest rates of infant mortality in the developed world—even as its single richest nation. This is a much more worrisome statistic in terms of life expectancy in the broad historical sense.

Myth Conceptions

Myth: Birth control pills don't work as well with antibiotics.

Fact: Medical scientists have officially concluded that common antibiotics don't affect the efficacy of birth control pills.

Myth: Humans use only about 10 percent of their brains.

Fact: Actually, scientists have proven that there is no part of the brain that is not active in some way.

Myth: Most of your body heat is lost through your head.

Fact: Sorry, there's nothing special about your noggin—at least when it comes to heat loss. You'll lose heat through any uncovered body part.

Myth: Marijuana use causes brain damage.

Fact: Modern brain-imaging techniques have found no signs of brain damage or killed brain cells in marijuana users, even in those who smoke multiple times per day. No widely accepted scientific studies have proven long-term damage resulting from marijuana use, either.

Myth: Crashing is the worst thing that can happen on a plane.

Fact: Not to be a downer here, but actually, in most airplane accidents, there's an on-board fire. And when there's a fire, the biggest threat is actually the toxic smoke, which can spread fast in a closed cabin, obstructing everyone's view of the emergency exits and making it difficult to breathe or speak.

Myth: It never snows in the desert.

Fact: Believe it or not, the largest desert in the world is Antarctica, where it snows a lot—the mean annual precipitation ranges from 5.9 to 10.2 inches. So why is Antarctica considered a desert? The definition of a desert is a region that receives very little rain. To be precise, a desert landscape exists where rainfall is less than 10 inches per year. Rain, of course, is needed to sustain certain types of plants and animals, but snow doesn't count as rain. So Antarctica is dry enough to be considered a desert and too dry for a person to survive without water.

Bringing the Plagues of Exodus to Life

Do we need to explain the plagues of Egypt in terms of modern science? No, but for the most part, we can, if you take each description with a grain of salt.

✳   ✳   ✳   ✳

Do It or Else!

GOD TOLD AARON and Moses to give pharaoh one more chance, in the name of the Lord, to release the Israelites from forced labor. Pharaoh had a bad attitude about this, saying (yes, we're paraphrasing): "Not familiar with this Lord of yours. This is Egypt, and you may have noticed that *I'm* its lord. Now run along, and make your bricks like good forced laborers. In fact, no straw for you, but your brick-making quota remains the same. That'll teach you." God more or less told his people's leaders: "Okay, I'll fix this. Time to bring the pain."

The Bloody Nile

The first lesson involved God turning all the water in Egypt—whether in someone's glass or flowing down the Nile—into blood. Yuck. This killed all the fish (try to imagine the smell of fermenting dead fish in a sunny climate) and made the water undrinkable. While the modern Nile has never turned to actual blood, a couple of known conditions could create this effect. We now know that algae can create red tides in fresh water as well as seawater, causing massive fish kills and reddening the water. Another fair explanation could involve volcanoes in Ethiopia, far up near the headwaters of the Blue Nile, which can fill the river with nasty reddish silt that could kill fish.

Frogs

A week passed, and pharaoh didn't yield. "Tell him I will swamp Egypt with frogs," said God. Pharaoh wouldn't budge, and soon Egypt looked like an Alfred Hitchcock version of *The Muppet Show*. This time pharaoh showed signs of getting with the program, but after God killed all the frogs—leaving Egypt buried in dead frogs—pharaoh went back on his word. Well, the Old Testament Hebrew word for "frogs" also includes toads; both are common enough in Egypt. It's possible that the mess in the Nile caused the frogs and toads to jump out on land en masse.

Gnats and Flies

After pharaoh reneged on his commitment, God said: "Okay, have some gnats." The little insects drove everyone crazy. The Exodus account may be describing the dog fly, a very nasty biting insect native to the Nile Delta, or it could simply describe plain old gnats in great clouds; some accounts interpret the word as "lice" (pretty common in the ancient world to begin with). God sent flies, which concentrated especially on pharaoh's house and those of his officials. Now pharaoh began to waver, but when God called off the flies, pharaoh flip-flopped again. These flies could also be dog flies—it's hard to specify exactly based upon scripture's rather general description.

Dying Livestock

"Pharaoh doesn't learn, does he?" mused God. "Okay, time for the heavy stuff." Moses warned pharaoh again and got rejected again. Suddenly most camels, horses, cattle, and other livestock in Egypt got sick and died, while the Israelites' livestock kept happily munching grass. The ancient Egyptians knew any number of livestock diseases, including African horse sickness, bluetongue, rinderpest, foot-and-mouth, and anthrax (in descending order of likeliness based on scripture). A combination of outbreaks is quite plausible.

Boils

Pharaoh didn't give in, so God played a little rougher: He sent a plague of boils. This one affected both animals and humans, causing huge disgusting sores that broke and festered. What could this have been? One strong possibility is *glanders*, a disease people can catch from animals. It causes the lymph nodes to swell up and can be fatal even with early modern medical detection; imagine how hard it might have hit the Egyptians.

Thunder and Hail

God next had Moses warn pharaoh to get his people and livestock into shelter, for he was about to send a monster hailstorm. Some did. Those who ignored the warning (plus all the flax and barley crops) perished. Pharaoh again seemed ready to give in, then he reneged again. (By any measure, the guy was a slow learner.) Hail is simple to explain: While rare on the Nile, it isn't unknown there today.

Locusts

God's next plague, the grasshopper (called a locust in its swarming phase), simply ate Egypt alive: crops, trees, anything with leaves. While pharaoh didn't give way yet, this plague is known to anyone who lived through the Dust Bowl days in the American Midwest. When the locusts got thick enough, they could and did eat even the clothes off clotheslines, so no wonder they scoured Egypt, as scripture says.

Darkness

God then socked Egypt with three solid days of darkness. While it didn't bend pharaoh, this also has a very plausible explanation. Egypt is in North Africa, where the *khamsin* (Sahara sandstorm) can last up to three days, burying everything in sand and blotting out the sun. In fact, the *khamsin* has preserved numerous archaeological wonders simply by burying them over the years.

Death of the Firstborn

By now God was absolutely fed up with pharaoh, so he made it personal: He struck down the firstborn of every Egyptian family, from pharaoh's to prisoners' to livestock. The Israelites were untouched. "Okay, enough, get out!" said pharaoh.

While there are numerous candidate toxins and diseases that could have caused this, it may not have a corresponding modern explanation.

Whatever the plagues actually were (and giving a scientific explanation doesn't lessen God's power), the Israelites were now free to find a new land where they could worship and live in accordance with the Lord's commands.

Diamonds Are Forever

While there's little doubt that the billion-dollar diamond industry has captured the romantic machinations of modern couples, some are beginning to challenge the notion.

✳   ✳   ✳   ✳

THE BIRTH OF a diamond is not as exciting as you might think. Diamonds are made of carbon, one of the most commonly occurring substances on the planet. Carbon is found in unimpressive forms, such as graphite (also known as pencil lead). But, when crystallized and pressed for millennia, something rather interesting happens. Eventually, all this pressure and a good dose of heat work to create diamonds—the hardest naturally occurring substance in the world. When harvested, cut, and polished, a diamond becomes the kind of shiny object that's desired the world over.

What's Behind the Demand?

Committed couples have been wearing simple metal bands since ancient Rome, and by the 13th century, betrothal rings *sans* diamond were a mainstay of Christian tradition. In 1477, the first recorded instance of a diamond engagement ring appeared: The Archduke Maximilian of Austria commissioned a diamond ring (modest by today's standards) for Mary of Burgundy. By the 1800s, Americans were offering diamond rings to their betrothed as a matter of course.

The 1930s, however, changed everything. Smartly mastered diamond advertising campaigns upped the ante. These advertisements played on emotion and captured the attention of an entire nation. Behind it all: De Beers diamond company, who lobbied fashion designers to put the weight of their favorable opinions behind diamonds; talked Hollywood celebrities into flaunting large diamond rings during public outings; and convinced men everywhere that they should spend three months' salary on an engagement ring. And the campaigns worked. By 1941, diamond sales were up more than 50 percent in the United States.

To prompt continued sales, jewelers marketed diamonds as a rarity and as a symbol of eternal devotion. Indeed, what is arguably the most successful marketing campaign slogan of the 20th century still rests on the lips of many: "A diamond is forever." Frances Gerety, an on-deadline copywriter at Philadelphia-based advertising agency N. W. Ayer & Sons, authored the phrase for De Beers in 1947.

The diamond's popularity became a constant humming after 1953, when Marilyn Monroe sang the now famous line "Diamonds are a girl's best friend" in the movie *Gentlemen Prefer Blondes*. Anita Loos's 1925 book of the same name seemed to capture Americans' future love affair with this sparkly gem: "So I really think that American gentlemen are the best after all, because kissing your hand may make you feel very, very good, but a diamond and sapphire bracelet lasts forever."

Still the world's largest diamond mining company, De Beers continues to fund advertising campaigns that marry myth with emotion, and today, although times are changing, almost all engaged women wear a ring—with at least one diamond.

Why All the Fighting?

For many betrothed couples, knowing that some diamonds cost not only money, but also human lives, is troubling. Dubbed "blood diamonds" or "conflict diamonds," these stones are used to fund wars, particularly in central and western Africa, before they ever become part of a romantic setting in the West.

The problem became so widespread within the diamond industry that, in 2003, the United Nations adopted a system to track the origins of all rough diamonds. The idea was to stem the flow of conflict diamonds by ending sales of diamonds from areas that were hot spots for conflict. The process was also meant to encourage the humane treatment of those who mined the diamonds.

Today, the Kimberley Process Certification Scheme (KPCS) is an international effort that's had debatable success. And while the average American may not follow the inner workings of the United Nations, some of the controversy surrounding diamonds became a part of the cultural landscape in 2006 with the movie *Blood Diamond*, which was set against a backdrop of enslaved diamond miners and fueled a growing debate.

Despite the intentions of many brides and grooms to buy "conflict-free" diamonds, it's still difficult to determine if this is the case. The jewelry store where a diamond engagement ring is purchased isn't likely to guarantee the stone has conflict-free origins. Fortunately, there are other options.

Some companies, like Brilliant Earth, offer buyers a certification of diamond origin that tracks each diamond back to its conflict-free source. The iconic Tiffany & Co. reportedly deals only with suppliers using conflict-free, environmentally conscious mining. Some jewelers provide a KPCS or System of Warranties statement that illustrates the diamond's journey from mine to store. Some work with vintage diamonds, because no new diamonds need to be mined with potentially unethical ramifications. Others used lab diamonds.

What if You Just Want a Shiny Ring?

Enter the cultured diamond. A far cry from the cubic zirconia monstrosities of decades past, the modern version of a faux diamond is a brilliant imposter. Cultured diamonds, also known as synthetic diamonds, are gemstones created in laboratories. These gems are large and pure enough to mimic the real diamonds typically atop engagement bands—without the hefty price tag. Plus, the process doesn't create toxic byproducts or pollutants, according to Diamond Nexus Labs, one of the largest players in the cultured diamond manufacturing market.

Diamonds were even usurped during the 2009 Miss USA pageant, when Miss Venezuela, Stefania Fernandez, received a crown comprised entirely of cultured diamonds. Later that year, the Miss Universe and Miss Teen USA pageants followed suit by switching to cultured diamonds.

Before long, it may be impossible to tell whether a "diamond" engagement ring is sporting the real deal—unless you're the one who paid for it, of course. And so-called synthetic diamonds may eventually surpass their mined counterparts.

What Causes the Wind to Blow?

Judging by the graphics your local TV weather person uses during the nightly forecast, you'd think that wind is caused by cartoon clouds that expand their billowy cheeks and blow. But don't believe it.

✳ ✳ ✳ ✳

WIND IS THE result of Earth's atmosphere constantly trying (and failing) to maintain equilibrium. The sun warms the atmosphere and Earth's surface, but that warmth is spread unevenly. This inconsistent heating creates global patterns of high and low air pressure. Wherever there are differences in atmospheric pressure, air rushes from the high-pressure areas to the low-pressure regions to try to make up the difference.

This mass movement of air creates wind. The patterns of this air movement vary based on a number of factors. Close to the planet's surface, winds rotate around low-pressure areas (called cyclones) and high-pressure areas (anticyclones). Meanwhile, up in the atmosphere, ridges of high pressure and troughs of low pressure create waves that push air around and often dictate the travel of the cyclones that are close to the ground. In addition, certain geographic features like mountains or bodies of water create local wind systems. Even the rotation of the planet affects the way that air flows.

It all makes weather prediction kind of a crapshoot—especially for people who make drawings of wind-blowing clouds for a living. And don't even get us started on the ludicrous notion that the sun would ever actually need to wear sunglasses.

Can Tornadoes Cross Rivers?

Yes, they can.

❋ ❋ ❋ ❋

A SPECIFIC TYPE OF tornado known as a waterspout forms on water and is typically less powerful than a land-based tornado. Waterspouts occasionally move from water to land, but they are usually fairly weak when they make this transition. There is also evidence that thunderstorms, which can spawn tornadoes, weaken as they cross larger bodies of water, such as lakes. Yet even in this case, a tornado can form once the storm reaches shore. Rivers appear to have no effect on the strength of tornadoes that form on land. Weather records reveal that tornadoes have crossed every

major river east of the Rockies. When it comes to surviving a tornado, the safety of a basement beats the false security of a nearby river.

The Real Millennials

Turning back the clock with young-earth creationists.

❋ ❋ ❋ ❋

CHARLES DARWIN AND his 19th-century contemporaries, all scientists and anthropologists who were hot on the trail of the theory of evolution, would be shocked to know how many so-called "young earth creationists" there are in the 21st century—people who believe the entire universe is just 10,000 years old, based on close literal reading of the Bible. Maybe this is why dinosaurs, people, and prehistoric mammals like woolly mammoths or sabertooth tigers are often shown hanging out together, despite the fact that dinosaurs died off more than 60 million years before humans evolved. But it's fun to imagine these uber-ancient times with our human selves included, even if only for scale. The majority of religious believers of all faiths treat science with due respect, and the creation story in particular is often placed in context as an allegorical version of the real role a given deity played in the creation of the universe.

Lightning Strikes Once, Fire Strikes a Match

Is it true that the cigarette lighter predates the match? This myth is no "match" for the truth.

❋ ❋ ❋ ❋

THE CENTERS FOR Disease Control and Prevention reports that rates of cigarette smoking among both adults and high-school students continue to decline over time, and about

1 in 7 American adults is a smoker. Some have probably heard the myth that the lighter was invented before the match, a snazzy-sounding "gotcha!" that is misleading at best. Humans have used anything they had at hand to start fires for as long as there have been fires, so it can be challenging to draw bold lines in the sand in any case. But some history is clear.

The lighter usually cited as predating modern matches is more like a lantern than a Zippo, so it doesn't really count. Matches—also known as friction matches, because their heat is created by the friction of the striking action—have existed in clumsier but recognizable forms for almost 200 years. Before that, scientists and other curious pipe-smoking intellectuals experimented with matches that were like bingo cards worth of potential dangers, and thankfully those ideas never took off. The invention of ferrocerium, an inexpensive manmade alloy of iron and the element cerium, led to handheld fuel lighters and spark fire starters. But none of that happened until the 20th century, leaving matches the clear winner.

A Refined Industry

Plastics are ballyhooed as one of the great bogeymen of modern life, but use of plasticky materials dates back thousands of years, and continues to evolve.

✳ ✳ ✳ ✳

Roots in the Ancient World

ANCIENT HUMANS USED natural rubber, wool, and animal horns in ways we recognize in modern life. These materials are strong and elastic because of cellulose, a naturally occurring, strong, fibrous compound that gives wood (and subsequently paper) its utility and durability as well.

The Modern Age

The age of plastics we live in now was enabled by scientists who found ways to turn natural plastic-like materials into distilled, uniform versions that could be mass produced, usually relying on fossil fuels. Climate change and the impending "peak oil" have pushed some scientists to explore a return to the natural roots of plastics, whether for sustainability, recyclability, or simply our inevitable future with less petroleum.

Casein Point

One early modern plastic was made with milk, and school-children still often make a version of this for science fairs and other experimental fun. Milk has a strong, consistent structure called a colloid, which means a drop of milk is always the same as any other drop of milk—nothing settles at the bottom and there are no "particles" moving around. Melty cheese is not just stretchy but elastic, meaning it bounces back into shape at least a little. This is because of a protein called casein, which does for dairy products what gluten does for wheat: adds strength, stretch, and elasticity. Casein is the reason milk can be turned into a usable plastic.

Making plastic from milk is simple, and in fact it's the same way many world cultures make fresh cheeses like ricotta, quark, paneer, mascarpone, cottage cheese, and queso blanco. Vinegar or lemon juice is added to milk, which is usually heated before or after the acid is added to speed up the curdling. This process creates curds and whey. (Sorry, Miss Muffet, you'll need to bring your own tuffet.)

If you want to eat the fresh cheese, this is the time. But to make it into plastic, you should drain the whey and press the curds dry in a clean dishtowel or other absorbent material, then knead it until it forms a dough that you can mold like modeling clay. Google it and double check the details before you dive into this experiment—only you can prevent dairy wastage.

Glutenous Maximus

Twenty-first-century supervillain gluten, enemy number one in trendy restaurants and yuppie homes, plays the same role for wheat that casein plays for dairy. Bread bakers mix ingredients and let the dough rest and rise, which both activates the yeast that will leaven the bread and lets gluten begin to form the long structural chains that make bread strong and elastic.

Making gluten-free bread is a challenging task for a lot of reasons, but the main one is that gluten is simply impossible to mimic. Really talented bakers have found great substitutes that often mean adding different starches, like that from potatoes, corn, or tapioca, and sometimes more scientific ingredients like xanthan gum. (Despite its sinister name, xanthan gum is a harmless food additive made by fermenting sugars with bacteria. But it does have a laxative effect, so be careful.)

The upshot to all this gluten talk is that scientists are exploring ways to use gluten as the foundation for more sustainable plastics. Especially as more and more people seek to avoid gluten, which has historically been added to other processed foods as a stabilizer, there's a real *glut* of gluten on the commodities market. Plastics made with gluten may be more biodegradable or recyclable than the plastics made with petroleum.

The Future of Plastics

Plastics have symbolized the world's future, first as an optimistic and cutting-edge convenience and later as the primary culprit bulking up our landfills. But a changing relationship to plastic could be emblematic of the next step in our future, especially if scientists can make biodegradable natural plastics that are easy to manufacture.

Eco-friendly restaurant and grocery chains may already use biodegradeable flatware made from corn or other strong starches, so there's an existing market for this category of product. Plastics may be our future one way or the other, but science lets us see a less polluted vision.

The Myth of the Dumb Dinosaur

Are language, arts, and mathematics the real culmination of a successful dominant species? Or did the dinosaurs have something right?

✳ ✳ ✳ ✳

DINOSAURS CAN SEEM a bit clumsy to us because of their size and, perhaps, because of how different they are from humans. We see our human selves as the dynamic apex predators that we are today, and due to casting in movies and TV shows, we even imagine alien species that are basically humanoid in shape and behavior. How could dinosaurs, so strong in resemblance to geckos or Gila monsters or barnyard chickens, be the most capable and adapted group on Earth at any point? But dinosaurs dominated the planet for well over 100 million years, and they were killed off by an extraordinary mass-extinction event that affected three-fourths of the planet's species. They did not go blindly into that good night—instead they were wiped off the planet in a single stroke. If Earth's history were compressed to a span of one year, dinosaurs roamed for a couple of weeks of December, but humans evolved just 25 minutes before the New Year. Perhaps in 150 million more years we can cast a judgmental eye on the dinosaurs.

The Meek Shall, Motionlessly, Inherit the Earth

Hold still and the T. rex won't see you—if you're a movie character.

✳ ✳ ✳ ✳

Visual Aid

DID TYRANNOSAURUS REX really only see moving objects? The makers of the *Jurassic Park* franchise drew fire during production of *Jurassic World* because they chose not to update their dinosaurs with the feathers scientists now believe dinosaurs had. But in 1993, the original movie was not controversial in its depiction of *T. rex*. Paleontologists and other scientists were actually inspired by the movie to do research of their own in order to explore the issue. They now believe *T. rex* had vision close to what many birds have today, if not better.

Based on the shape of its eye socket and the vision of its closest extant relatives, *T. rex* likely had vision far better than ours and even better than its modern descendents. It may all be a moot point, though—does anything in nature ever really stand still, making it invisible to this fictitious *T. rex*? An animal that only saw objects in motion would see exactly what everything else sees, because everything is always in motion. Humans have stereo vision because of our two front-facing eyes positioned close together, so motion and dimension are what give meaning and weight to objects within our field of vision.

Moving On

Our intuition may be to blame for the *T. rex* myth, because it seems like anything as large, heavy, and prehistoric as a long-extinct dinosaur couldn't be as evolutionarily advantaged as we are. And certainly it was convenient for Michael Crichton's massively bestselling novel and the film franchise it inspired. But dinosaurs were massively diverse and well suited to the earth, with a larger range of sizes, shapes, diets, and so forth than almost any other family of organisms in billions of years of history. What might the earth look like if dinosaurs hadn't been killed off by a gigantic mass-extinction event? They might be cloning us in *their* fictional laboratories.

Myth Conceptions

Myth: The "10 second rule" applies.

Fact: Many people believe that if food drops on the ground and is picked up quickly, it's perfectly fine to eat. Not so fast. Scientists discovered food that has touched the ground does pick up large amounts of bacteria. So just get a new potato chip, okay?

Myth: Single people have more active sex lives than marrieds.

Fact: Actually, in one recent survey, 43 percent of married men reported having sex two to three times per week, compared to only 26 percent of single men.

Myth: If you swim on a full stomach, you'll get a cramp and drown.

Fact: Nah. It's true that when you eat a big meal, your body has to work harder to digest it. You might be uncomfortable if you swim with a belly full of food, but you'll probably not get a cramp and drown at your cousin's barbeque this summer—even if you ate six bratwursts.

Myth: My dog humps my leg. It's a sex thing.

Fact: Actually, it's a domination thing. Both male and female dogs do it, and it's much more of an act of aggression or dominance than it is a sexual behavior.

Myth: Your hair and nails keep growing after you die.

Fact: What actually happens is the retraction of skin as it dehydrates during the breakdown of the body. The shrinking skin on a cadaver makes it appear as though hair and nails are still growing, but they're not.

Chapter 5

Technology

On the Autobahn

Owners of high-performance cars dream of pushing their vehicles to maximum speeds, and the road of their dreams is the German autobahn. But this expressway isn't entirely a pedal-pusher's playground.

✳ ✳ ✳ ✳

Go, Speed Racer!

MOST PEOPLE AGREE that if you like to speed, Germany is the place to be. The autobahn has long stretches where you can legally drive as fast as you want, and it is not uncommon for cars to top 150 miles per hour. But driver, beware: The autobahn does have speed limits. In fact, almost half of the system is under some sort of speed control. As you approach major interchanges, cities, or difficult terrain, you'll start to see speed-limit signs. And even though you will rarely encounter any *autobahnpolizei* (highway patrols), if you speed and get caught, it will be expensive. Radar-linked cameras positioned over interchanges photograph the license plates of all speeders, who then receive considerable traffic fines in the mail.

Green Concerns

The era of high-speed driving in Germany may actually be coming to an end. Concerns about fuel consumption and global warming have increased pressure from environmental groups to bring Germany's traffic laws in line with the rest of Europe— that is to say, a maximum speed limit of 130 kilometers

(81 miles) per hour. Studies have shown that CO2 emissions would be cut by 15 percent in the long term once more fuel-efficient cars are on the roads. But German car companies are working to keep this from happening, arguing that high-speed driving is an integral part of the "German brand." The Germans themselves are passionate about driving—and driving fast—and it is doubtful they will give up their speedy ways without a fight. In the meantime, if you have the opportunity to drive through Germany on its famous freeway, do so with a lightened foot and a cautious eye.

The Long Extension Cord of History

Hybrid and electric cars are so twenty-first century…if they hadn't been invented in the 1800s.

❋ ❋ ❋ ❋

EVERYONE UNDERSTANDS THAT VHS tapes surpassed Betamax, but similar older rivalries are a bit more obscure. Automotive history buffs know that early cars were electric, and they were beaten out by the internal combustion engine because of logistical issues that still exist today.

A Current Affair

Electric cars are the environmentally friendly alternative to fossil-fuel vehicles, at least by most measures. For consumers with an international frame of mind, electrics also represent a way to work toward energy independence from the chaotic Middle East. They're quiet—electric luxury cars sometimes have engine sounds piped back in—and often they don't need traditional transmissions or many of the other trappings of fossil-fuel vehicles. But these pros and cons are cutting edge compared to the factors affecting consumers in the late 1800s.

Plugged In to Safety

Electric cars—still often called "horseless carriages" at the time—outsold fossil-fuel cars by a factor of 10 to 1 in 1890. Internal combustion engines were still frightening to many people, so choosing electric was a matter of safety and comfort. Today, refueling at a gas station is very structured and sterile, but carrying gasoline around in the 1800s probably didn't give anyone confidence. At the time, new car garages were built far from their corresponding houses in case of explosions or fires.

And gas cars needed to be hand-cranked to start their engines, which required physical strength and then catlike reflexes to get out of the way of the spinning crank starter. In 2007, *Top Gear* hosts James May and Jeremy Clarkson visited England's National Car Museum and drove what many consider to be the first modern-layout car, the 1916 Cadillac Type 53. But in the same visit, they drove an antique car with a crank starter, which Britons call the starter handle. May joked, with sincerity, that the crank starter nearly broke his arm.

The Feminine Mystique?

So there were great reasons to choose electric in the early automobile age, despite the fact that electrics cost more at the time and were less practical—does that sound familiar? The crank starter issue alone meant that many who drove electric cars were women, and the cars developed a reputation as something of a "woman's car." Automotive journalist Gary Witzenburg wrote in 2013 about the way some manufacturers "bolted dummy radiator grilles on the fronts" to help stanch this stigma. Presumably this didn't fool anyone.

Ford Every Revenue Stream

Henry Ford worked closely with Thomas Edison to introduce an electric car for consumers. He felt strongly about electric motors and believed this to be the way forward for city travel and trucking. But their deal fell through in a similarly modern way, as the media were given different excuses and postponed release dates with little concrete information. Henry Ford told the *New York Times* in 1914, "The problem so far has been to build a storage battery of light weight which would operate for long distances without recharging."

Edison was no stranger to generating, so to speak, his own buzz. He crusaded against alternating current technology, insisting that his own direct current was safer and better. In the course of this public relations war, Edison electrocuted more than a dozen animals in public demonstrations. His intentions were good, but this barbaric campaign just didn't work. Alternating current (AC) worked at higher voltages than direct current, but the relative danger of AC was mitigated after electrical engineers in Hungary invented the electrical transformer. Edison is largely looked back on as a sore loser as well as an inventive genius.

So electric-car skeptics doubted that Edison could help to make the affordable electric car he was shilling—he and Ford claimed that multiple prototypes existed, but just a couple were ever seen. The project dragged on for years and overstayed the public's attention span. Eventually, after an estimated investment of $1.5 of Ford's money, his electric car dreams went up in environmentally friendly smoke: Edison didn't have a battery suitable for the car, and he covertly swapped a much heavier battery in its place. The bromance ended on this sour note.

The Decline of Production Electrics

Costly consumer electric cars were made for decades beginning in the 1880s, and the only revolutionary thing about Edison and Ford's plans, decades later, was that their electric car would

hypothetically be more affordable. In the meantime, high-end customers continued to buy and drive electric cars in small but steady numbers.

What led to the near disappearance of electric car technology was partly Ford's own doing: His assembly-line Model T brought the price of a gasoline car down to a level a more average American could afford. A few years after the introduction of the Model T, prolific inventor Charles Kettering developed the electric starter motor. Production cars no longer needed to be cranked by hand, opening the market to anyone previously discouraged by the hand crank.

But the electric car wasn't simply bested by the gas car. As technology continued to improve, the electric car stood still while progress marched on. Even today, affordable, durable, practical batteries are an obstacle to many electric-car development programs—imagine the issues faced 100 years ago before many Americans even had electricity in their homes. In 1925, half of American homes had electricity, which probably trickled out the way internet service did in the 1990s and 2000s: cities first, everyone else much later. And these folks lived further apart than their city counterparts, meaning they needed vehicles that could carry them more miles than an electric car could manage. Filling up a gas tank takes a matter of minutes; charging an electric car took hours, even back then. Electric cars were slower, too.

In the Interim

Electric concept cars were made on and off throughout the decades between the decline of early electrics and the revival with cars like the Toyota Prius in the 1990s. A modified Chevrolet Corvair known as the Electrovair was shown in 1964, with the Electrovair II in 1966. The Electrovair II was packed with over $150,000 in batteries that still amounted to a range of 80 miles at most—you'd be better off wearing the Heart of the Ocean while you tooled around on an electric scooter.

It was inventor Charles Kettering who inadvertently led Americans back to environmentally friendly electric vehicles. Along with the electric starter motor, he invented both leaded gasoline and freon coolant. These two inventions meant that Kettering almost singlehandedly punched a hole in the ozone layer, and it was the discovery of this hole by scientists that really kickstarted modern environmentalism.

The Rest Is Modern History

Toyota introduced the Prius in Japan in 1997 and began introducing it to the rest of the world in 2000. The idea of a hybrid vehicle combines the safe modern use of internal combustion with the environmental savings of a rechargeable battery, and the women driving electric cars in the 1890s would probably love to know the part they played in this very long story. One notable early adopter was fictional Rory Gilmore, whose very ugly early Prius was a graduation gift from her grandparents. You can still see these first-generation Priuses—rarely—on highways today. And they are where America's love affair with alternative fuel sources began all over again in the 21st century.

Red Whine

Are red cars pulled over more often than their neutral neighbors?
There's no evidence that they are, and there are plenty of biasing
factors at play in this belief.

✳ ✳ ✳ ✳

ARED SPORTS CAR may be noticed more than a classic family car, but a red Honda Civic isn't much more eyecatching
than a blue one. Sporty cars are more likely to be offered in red,
often as one of only a couple of non-neutral available colors.
Think about it: Do you remember the last red car you saw? On
the other hand, do you remember the last exotic car you saw,
whatever the color? The theory of increased tickets and thefts
for red cars remains firmly planted in the area of anecdata. Of
course, a myth this prevalent may reinforce itself over time—
making an interesting topic for some future Ph.D. student's
research.

What's in a Name? It's Complicated

Rube Goldberg was not an inventor. The reason we call Rube
Goldberg machines Rube Goldberg machines is quite a Rube
Goldberg machine in itself.

✳ ✳ ✳ ✳

AMERICAN CARTOONIST RUBE Goldberg tapped into a
goldmine of popularity when he began drawing overcom-
plicated situations. You can easily build one in your imagination: a hamster in a ball runs toward a treat, pushing over a
book, which falls onto a seesaw, tipping a toy car onto a track.
The possibilities are infinite and we've loved to consider them
for over 100 years—"Rube Goldberg machine" makes its first
known dictionary appearance in 1915.

Around the world, cultures have their own versions of Rube
Goldberg in the likes of Sukumar Ray, Robert Storm Petersen,

Zihni Sinir, and countless others. The German term for a Rube Goldberg machine is the best, though: *Was-passiert-dann-Maschine*, meaning "what-happens-next machine."

Monckying Around with the Truth

Is the monkey wrench named for Charles Moncky? Was it invented by boxer Jack Johnson?

✳ ✳ ✳ ✳

NOTHING GETS HISTORIANS in a lather faster than an unfounded claim, in this case the origin story of the monkey wrench. One story is that an inventor named Charles Monk, Moncke, or Moncky made the wrench and named it for himself. In another version, others name it "monkey wrench" after his invention. Another story altogether claims that boxer Jack Johnson, the first black world heavyweight boxing champion, invented the wrench in the 1920s and found it was nicknamed "monkey wrench" as a racial epithet.

None of these stories is 100% true, but don't they all sound plausible? The most damning evidence against them is that the term monkey wrench exists in print long before these explanations popped up. Jack Johnson did invent a wrench that he patented in 1922, but his patent was for an improvement to a wrench that already existed, and not a monkey wrench. Charles Moncky is usually credited as the inventor of the monkey wrench, but historians disagree about its name, which could also be because its operation can resemble twisting a monkey's tail.

Babysittin' Joe

Did Joe DiMaggio really play a part in the discovery of the breast cancer gene? This delightfully strange but true fact is one of the most satisfying morsels in the public imagination.

✳ ✳ ✳ ✳

CELEBRITIES DABBLE IN science and invention, like Abraham Lincoln's boat-safety patent or Danica McKellar's math books and activism. But Joltin' Joe happened to be in the right place at the right time to help someone out, and that someone made a world-changing discovery.

Genetic scientist Dr. Mary-Claire King told her story to *The Moth*: She had plans to meet with the National Institutes of Health about a careermaking grant when a series of obstacles nearly derailed her. Her husband left her, causing her aggrieved mother to refuse to babysit Dr. King's daughter. While trying to accommodate her mother's wishes to return home, Dr. King had to choose between making her own flight and helping her mother.

It was then, in line, that Joe DiMaggio appeared—retired for 30 years at that point but still just 67 years old. He offered to watch Dr. King's daughter and they became fast friends. Dr. King traveled with her daughter and secured the grant that began her brilliant march toward the eventual discovery of BRCA1, the breast cancer gene.

Floating a Presidential Idea

Abraham Lincoln's background as a flatboat crewman led to the lightbulb moment that helped him become the only U.S. president with a patented invention.

✳ ✳ ✳ ✳

I N 1843, FUTURE greatest president Abraham Lincoln wrote to a friend and joked that he was "a stranger, friendless, uneducated, penniless boy, working on a flatboat at ten dollars per month"—the implication being that he was an incongruous Whig, the more upscale political party at the time. Lincoln lost the 1843 election for a House seat, but his roots as a crewman instead of a yachtie soon helped him to massive populist success that endures today. And they're the reason he's the only U.S. president to ever hold a patent.

The Mother of Invention

Lincoln was finally elected to Congress in 1847, and he traveled home between House sessions in 1848. On the way there, his boat was stranded on a sandbar—all too common when taking a flat-bottomed passenger boat on rivers that constantly changed because of currents and rainfall. Waterways with heavy freight traffic are dredged, meaning deepened by regularly raking out the sediment. But to dredge entire rivers is not possible for many reasons.

According to the story, Representative Lincoln didn't jump in to help dislodge the boat, but he must have had flashbacks to his own career as a flatboat navigator. The usual way to shift a boat off of a sandbar was to basically wedge buoyant things, meaning all the loose wood on the boat, underneath the boat until it was able to move more freely over the sandbar. These pieces of wood would just be left behind.

Floating an Idea

His boat soon moved on, but the seeds of invention were planted in Lincoln's mind. He had also witnessed a grounded boat being lifted out of its quagmire near Niagara Falls. He asked a mechanic friend for help and built a model of a new piece of equipment that could deploy to dislodge a boat from a sandbar. When this was finished, he applied for a patent—Lincoln admired patent law and felt that it encouraged ingenuity and constant improvement.

Lincoln's invention was, as far as we know, never built for use on a real boat. His political career probably precluded any interest he had in really pushing the design. But the model survives in the Smithsonian Institute's National Museum of American History collection. Lincoln was a curious, brilliant thinker who constantly wondered how he could improve the world—a high tide may raise all boats, but Lincoln sought to lift one at a time until then.

Topsy Turvy

Did Thomas Edison famously electrocute an elephant? This myth quickly turns into a metamyth, because people love to debunk it with a similarly misguided take on the truth. Let's get to the bottom of it.

✳ ✳ ✳ ✳

I N A VERY brief motion picture released in 1903, a disgraced circus elephant named Topsy is electrocuted by alternating-current lines hooked to two of her feet. The details are upsetting and so is the footage.

The Life and Times of Topsy

Topsy was captured in Asia and smuggled into the United States for a contemporary competitor of Barnum & Bailey Circus. She was about 27 years old when she was sold from the circus to an amusement park in Coney Island. She already had a few alleged deaths on her record. Just several months after they bought Topsy, the amusement park owners decided she was not worth keeping, and after trying to give her away, they claimed the only remaining option was to euthanize Topsy.

At first, the owners planned to hang the elephant and charge admission to the execution. The ASPCA stepped in only to ensure that there was no spectacle and that the execution was humane—a far cry from today's ASPCA, who vocally object to any exotic or wild animals in shows like circuses. In fact, Ringling Bros. and Barnum & Bailey Circus phased out its elephant act in 2016 in response to changing public attitudes toward performing animals, and the circus shut down completely in 2017. The elephants were sent to "retire" at a wildlife conservation facility.

Topsy was not as lucky as the retired Ringling elephants. There were simply not any good options for the circus owners once they decided Topsy was a nuisance and a danger. Her handler was a heavy drinker and they felt he couldn't be trusted either. But the owners' desire to cash in on the spectacle, or even their "compromise" that the event was closed but could be filmed instead, is inexcusably crass.

Topsy was hooked up to copper wires and electrodes that were fashioned into sandals for her feet. She was fed poison, electrocuted for ten seconds, and hung, all at the same time. The ASPCA believed the redundant methods would help make the experience as quick and humane as possible for Topsy.

But how does any of this involve Thomas Edison? For that, we need a bit of background.

Long Tail of the Current Wars

In the late 1800s, Edison started his own electric utility company to bring direct current (DC) into homes. His rival, a company called Westinghouse, wanted to bring *alternating* current (AC) into homes instead. Edison felt, somewhat correctly, that AC was dangerous compared to DC. So during the "Current Wars," Edison traveled and made demonstrations where he used AC to electrocute animals in front of crowds. He did this more than a dozen times.

By 1902, this time in Edison's life was long, long over. But he had a burgeoning film production company and a proprietary technology called the Kinetoscope to show his motion pictures. Viewers stepped up and looked into a peephole, one at a time, to view a precursor of modern movie film. At the turn of the century, Edison sought to film very short documentaries to offer in his Kinetoscopes. An Edison film crew was on hand at Topsy's execution.

The resulting film wasn't very successful, and it's not clear why anyone thought it would be. But the public imagination is malleable, and Edison's history of executing animals as part of the Current Wars became linked with the footage of Topsy's execution, perhaps because there's no surviving film of Edison's own animal executions. In this case, the myth may be misguided, but the truth is actually more sinister.

Edison's Kinetoscope lost out to the modern movie theater format we recognize today.

An Open Secret

Was Amelia Earhart the victim of some kind of conspiracy? Her choice not to keep up with technological knowhow is more likely to blame for her disappearance.

✳ ✳ ✳ ✳

PIONEERING AVIATOR AMELIA Earhart set records and made headlines because of her talent, courage, tireless work ethic, and willingness to craft her own image. But no one is perfect, of course. Earhart failed to keep up with the technologies that helped other pilots to call for help and made flying a much less dangerous job.

Opening the Books

After Orville and Wilbur Wright made the first powered airplane flight in 1903, an ugly patent war began among inventors in the U.S. A huge number of researchers from all kinds of backgrounds—the Wrights themselves were bicycle mechanics, publishers, and journalists—had made incremental improvements on one another's work, brainstormed similar ideas, and generally squabbled over who was making the best progress. Think of it as a grade-school classroom where all the students are grown men, and they've propped up folders and textbooks to hide their tests from their classmates.

These aviation pioneers were out-pettying today's worst startup companies in Silicon Valley. They went to court over fine details of one aircraft versus another, citing their own notes and evidence that had largely been kept secret. But after a decade of brutal lawsuits and public fighting over who was first, who invented what, and where the credit was due, the United States entered World War I. Aviation companies were de facto forced to pour their proprietary research and patents into a large pool shared by all of America's aircraft industry.

Making their technology "open source" was part of the war effort, but as with software and other inventions today, the open industry led to better and more rapid developments. After World War I ended, pilots began to set records left and right using ingenious inventions like the artificial horizon—something pilots still use in cockpits today, in a modernized form, of course. And some pilots made their livings in traveling airshows as airplanes became more and more familiar, but no less mesmerizing, to the American people. Amelia Earhart was one of these pilots, traveling to build buzz for her own career.

The Morse the Merrier

Earhart was a gifted and remarkable pilot, the first woman to *ride* in a plane (as a passenger) across the Atlantic and then to fly across it as the pilot. She started a professional organization for women pilots and took a faculty position at Purdue University. She and fellow groundbreaking pilot Charles Lindbergh were like movie stars by the 1930s, and Earhart was witty and engaging when she spoke with the press or members of the public. Her career was at a perfect point for her to make an outsize gesture in the form of a trip around the world. She wasn't the first, but she was definitely the most famous.

Technology leapt ahead during her career, and Morse

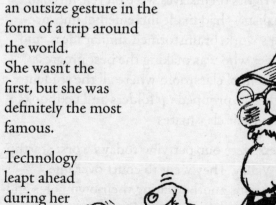

code was in wide use by the time Earhart began her trip around the world. The world's leading navigation instructor offered to teach Earhart radio operation, Morse code, and cutting-edge navigation, but she didn't have time before her trip, which had already been delayed by a failed first attempt. The navigator she chose also didn't know Morse code. When they grew disoriented in poor weather over the Pacific Ocean, they could not call for help in Morse code, and their radio reception was too poor to send or receive verbal messages from the Navy ships assigned to support the open water sections of their flight.

The "what ifs" of Earhart's failed final journey stoke pop culture across the decades, and who can say what could have happened if she and her navigator were able to get help? Without specific coordinates or landmarks, which Earhart likely could have relayed to her support team, even modern rescuers can't cover large swaths of open ocean with success. Morse code might have made the critical difference.

The Mystery Control

Surfing the Air Waves

The Lazy Bones remote control, invented by Zenith in 1950, was not the first device used in the home to control an entertainment system. Some radio and phonograph manufacturers also offered remotes for their products as early as the 1930s. Philco, for example, sold one whose name speaks to the novelty of the technology at that time—the Mystery Control. This bulky contraption had a rotary dial much like a telephone. Each "number" on the dial controlled a different function by emitting radio waves that were recognized by the radio or phonograph. Remarkably, the very first remote control devices of any sort appeared at the end of the 19th century; one of the earliest patents was awarded to famous inventor Nikola Tesla. These remotes were intended to operate machinery or even vehicles, but the applications never proved practical.

If the Shoe Fits...

Contrary to what manufacturers claim, costly sneakers aren't always your best bet.

* * * *

IN THE UNITED States alone, people buy some 400 million athletic shoes every year, and their price creeps ever higher. Although manufacturers attribute the rising costs to advanced technological features, they also reflect the price of celebrity endorsements and advertising.

Save Your Money

Despite conventional wisdom and manufacturers' claims, a higher number on the price tag does not guarantee a better athletic shoe. In fact, more expensive shoes could be a waste of money. A study in the *British Journal of Sports Medicine* concluded that low- and medium-price shoes provided the same—if not better—shock absorption and cushioning as the more expensive ones. Study participants who tested the shoes by walking or running on treadmills did not find the pricier models to be more comfortable, either.

Shoe Shopping

Finding the right workout shoe is important. The wrong footwear can cause discomfort and even injury. You should shop in a store with knowledgeable employees who are trained to properly evaluate your gait. And buying a shoe designed for your specific sport makes sense, since those designed for, say, basketball, have different features than those for aerobics or running.

The best time to try on shoes is within an hour of exercising, when your feet are still expanded. Even if you know your size, get measured, because feet change over time.

Be sure to retire your favorite sneakers when they wear out. Experts advise replacing exercise shoes after 300 to 500 miles of use. For most people, this means getting a new pair at least every six months—another reason to check out lower-price sneakers, or sniff out your local factory outlet.

Orange You Glad You Didn't Say Black?

An aircraft's black box isn't legally allowed to be black.

* * * *

THINK BACK, WAY back, to math class. At some point, your teacher may have used a common technique to teach the class about functions: a large square with a chute going in and a chute leading out. You put a number into the mystery machine and something happens to it inside. A number, usually a different number, comes out the other side. This is a basic form of the idea of the black box—it's not black in color but rather shrouded in mystery. Our figurative name for an airplane's flight recorder comes from this idea.

In reality, flight recorders are bright orange, in order to be as visible as possible in an emergency or wreckage situation. Imagine if we called orange traffic cones "black cones," and you can begin to understand why the aeronautics industry chafes at the misnomer.

The flight recorder notes so many different parameters and details that a human pilot in realtime could never absorb them all, and the pilot really doesn't need to. The information is only called on in the case of a mishap or foul play. Think of it as a much more solemn version of the instant replay camera used in professional sports, or a closed-circuit video taken inside a convenience store. In a perfect world, no one would ever need to view the footage.

Leave No Trace?

Movie bad guys are always trying to sand or burn off their fingerprints, but can it really be done?

✳ ✳ ✳ ✳

An Ancient Art

THE USE OF fingerprints as identifiers or signatures dates back thousands of years, when different ancient civilizations used fingerprints on official documents. By the 1300s, someone had already noted, in surviving documents, that all the fingerprints he had seen in his life were unique. Scientists now know that fingerprints emerge during the first trimester of human embryo development and last in the same form for the entire human lifetime. Older people can naturally have very shallow fingerprints that are hard to read, but the shapes of these fingerprints are still the same.

People who work in certain fields are more likely to sand their fingerprints off during their regular daily routines. Construction workers who build with brick, stone, concrete, and other abrasive materials can end up losing their fingerprints. So can people who handle a lot of paper or cardboard. These changes are temporary: since only the topmost layer of skin is abraded, it will come back with the same pattern.

A Modern Problem

In the 21st century, people noticed a new form of fingerprint annihilation. A small number of cancer patients being treated with a chemotherapy drug called capecitabine found that they no longer had fingerprints. In the past, people easily went entire lifetimes without ever noticing their fingerprints, but modern banking and security often require them, and fingerprints are the next big thing in protection of personal devices like smartphones and laptops. Patients have been questioned in banks, locked out of their own computers, and stopped in security lines—as if being treated for cancer wasn't hard enough.

Researchers aren't sure whether or not these cancer patients' damaged or obliterated fingerprints will eventually grow back. But how could it be ambiguous like this? The answer is in the makeup of our fingerprints, which grow up into the topmost layer of skin *from* the layer beneath. If you trimmed down your rose bushes for the winter, would you expect tulips the next spring? Without doing major damage to your fingertips, you simply can't get rid of your fingerprints.

The Imperfect Solution

Villains of the past have tried a lot of superficial ways to scrub off their identities. The first known and famous case was a gangster in the 1930s named Handsome Jack, who made cuts to disrupt his fingerprints. His case made a huge splash in the press, but his mutilated prints were even easier to spot than they had been. Most documented attempts to change fingerprints fall into this category, where the actions taken to obscure the fingerprints create a new, even more identifiable, scarred fingerprint.

To truly distort and alter your fingerprints, you would need to disrupt the connection between the two layers of skin where fingerprints root and grow. As of yet, there's no reasonable way to do this. Criminals and other wannabe disappearers may have more luck in the future.

Three Sheets to the Wind of History

Vellum, papyrus, parchment, parchment paper, oh my! How do we crack the code…or codex?

✳ ✳ ✳ ✳

PAPYRUS PREDATES PAPER by thousands of years. By the 3000s BC, Egyptian citizens were gathering papyrus plants, reedy sedges that were plentiful in Egypt's harsh climate shot through with wetlands. People were probably using papyrus as a foundational crop for building boats, housing, and more long before they began processing it into a writing material.

In the Beginning

Ancient writing materials that seem alike still differ in the ways they were made. Papyrus sheets were made by peeling papyrus plants to reveal the more tender pith inside the stems—imagine an artichoke heart or heart of romaine compared with the outsides of these vegetables. The pith was thinly sliced into ribbons that were lined up to create a wide sheet. A second layer of slices was arranged perpendicular to the first, and the two layers were hammered or pressed until they bonded. No one is sure if the papyrus was treated with a chemical to make it bond together, if the Egyptians used some kind of glue, or if they did something altogether different that we can't guess.

The Boiling Point

In the Americas, indigenous people made their own paper out of a local tree's bark, but their process was more of a halfway point between papyrus and modern paper. The tree bark was prepared and soaked or boiled, then it was laid out on a marked surface that helped the artisan know where to spread and press the fibers. If papyrus is like the woven pastry top on a pie, this American protopaper, *amate*, is more like a crumble topping.

Cai Lun's Invention

The first ancestor of modern paper was made in China, using strong fibers from local plants mixed with discarded and recycled pieces of hemp rope and other materials. A celebrated court eunuch, Cai Lun, is credited with developing paper, but many theories compete to explain how he came up with the idea. Did he see a paper wasp building its nest from recycled fibers? Did he notice a fibrous layer of textile lint left to dry at the bottom of a laundry pot? Whatever the case, he helped to find the best way to mix new fibers with discarded rags or nets to produce the wet pulp that is pressed and dried into paper.

Developing Better Materials

Ancient people had no vocabulary to explain why certain parts of certain plants made better, stronger papyrus or amate or paper. Now, we know that plant cellulose is what gives stems, bark, and other plant fibers their strength and flexibility. People in ancient times used their common sense to do a version of the scientific method, where they experimented with the materials they had on hand. Will the amate be stronger if we soak the fibers for a longer time? Could we speed up the process if we added salt or other chemicals to the water? Any writing material that was too labor intensive to make was not practical, by the principle of diminishing returns.

The Need for Parchment

Market forces of supply and demand led to the invention of parchment. People throughout the ancient Mediterranean region loved papyrus and exported it from Egypt to as far as they could travel at the time. The papyrus plant was harvested nearly to extinction because of high demand, and scribes—often religious figures who viewed their written products as sacred—needed a reliable substitute in order to continue their important work.

Parchment was made from animal skins which were treated with chemicals in a process similar to tanning leather. Thicker skins were divided into layers, a process which continues today in order to produce cheaper leather goods. Vellum, a term from the same root word as veal, refers to the finest parchment usually made of calfskin. But parchment makers were flexible and adaptable and they used all manner and sizes of animal skins in their work. As with the recycling of rags and pieces of net to make paper, parchment was a way to use leftover animal skins that were less desirable for clothing or other uses.

What Is Parchment Paper?

Modern parchment paper used by cooks and bakers is a "regular" pulp paper treated with silicone or another nonstick coating. There's also a modernized parchment made by treating pulp paper with a chemical bath that creates an authentic-looking parchment for use in ceremonies and events where tradition is valued.

So-called paper vellum, familiar to architects and crafters, is made either from treated cotton rag paper or from an industrial polyester called Mylar—the same material used to make metallic birthday balloons. This paper is tough and transparent, making it ideal for tracing and copying blueprints, schematics, or anything else that needs to be reused and archived.

Tugging on a Loose Thread

Spider silk is not stronger than steel. But it has plenty of interesting potential uses.

✳ ✳ ✳ ✳

Spinning Yarns

THIS MYTH REALLY has legs—eight legs, in fact. (Sorry to all the arachnophobes who've just closed this book and thrown it across the room in disgust.) Why is that? Well, there are many possible factors. Something appeals to us on a basic level in the idea that a totally natural product like spider silk could be stronger than steel. It feels like a David and Goliath story, although not a David and Goliath birdeater spider (*Theraphosa blondi*) story.

Spiders are also one of the creatures that seems most alien to humans, from their strange-seeming number of legs to their array of differently sized, opaque, black eyeballs. Severe fears that qualify as clinical phobias are more studied, but researchers find that up to 75% of people are casually afraid of spiders, with an emphasis on women over men. There are compet-

ing explanations for the gender gap, but the overall fear of spiders comes from their unpredictability and seeming strangeness. Very few people are harmed by spiders, and most spider bites are hardly worse than a mosquito bite.

Think of the related myth that an average person "eats" eight spiders per year while sleeping. There's no rational reason to believe it! Why would a spider want to crawl into the moist, windy cave of your snoring open mouth? There isn't even anything for a spider to eat in there, hopefully. But our shared pessimistic imagination around spiders seems to have no limits.

Many Threads of Study

Spider silk is definitely strong, and scientists do study its strength. But other qualities about spider silk are more interesting from a scientific and technical standpoint. Manmade strong and light materials like Kevlar are made with chemicals that can be very costly, and these processes may create caustic or otherwise dangerous waste products. Spider silk is made by the same general family of body processes that make human hair or nails, and we don't generate caustic byproducts. Proteins like spider silk are generated in living cells and have no byproducts other than water.

Steel and other strong alloys need to be superheated in almost sterile settings in order to perform their best as manufactured products. This requires a great deal of energy, both to generate the heat in the first place and to absorb and neutralize the heat after it's used. Alloys require mined raw materials in addition to simple, abundant elements like carbon, but spider silk uses only the abundant elements to make remarkable results at room temperature.

These factors give scientists different ways to approach and play with spider silk. They can study the chemical makeup of the strands and mimic this using synthetic fibers. They can try to create biological factories to string out their own strong natural proteins. They can even experiment with combinations of abundant elements to make new kinds of strands altogether.

A Tale of Two Armors

Spider silk may not be as strong as steel, but it weighs a small fraction as much and works in much different applications. Could spider silk be used to make body armor? Unbelievably, could corn starch?!

✳ ✳ ✳ ✳

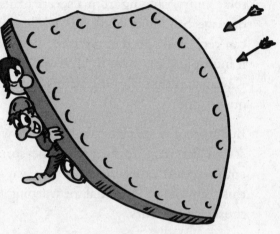

IT'S HARD TO browse the cable guide or Netflix homepage without seeing a handful of crime shows, if not more. Americans can't get enough of watching actors pretend to be law-enforcement agents, detectives, prosecutors, or military versions of any of those jobs. Terms like "armor-piercing round" are floating around in the vernacular now, but what does it really take to pierce the armor worn by law enforcement or private security?

Arming and Armoring

Sorting out the language of the ballistic or "bulletproof" industry and its armor-piercing counterparts is a slippery task. The language isn't standardized, and marketing has affected how makers describe their products. Traditional armor-piercing rounds are meant for use against armored vehicles or ships. Bullets designed for use in rifles, and therefore to shoot individuals, must be manufactured with super rigid materials like tungsten carbide in order to be able to penetrate body armor.

The goal with armor on a ship or person is to slow down a projectile enough to drastically reduce how much harm it does. We might picture bullets bouncing off of armor, but the truth is that plated armor seeks to smash the front of a bullet into a flat "mushroom" shape that won't get any further. Kevlar slows the bullet with layers of densely woven, incredibly tough man-made fibers. The person wearing the armor feels the full force of the bullet's mass and speed but the force is distributed over and absorbed by a larger area.

Sounds great, right? And it is . . . but the wearer can also expect *some* injury, ranging from a severe bruise to internal organ damage. Someone who's shot while wearing a "bulletproof" vest can very easily need to go to the hospital afterward, especially if multiple shots were fired. Armor can warp after impact, even Kevlar, and that warping affects how the armor absorbs subsequent shots.

Bulletproof vests save countless lives with technology that seems like magic to the average person, and scientists spend entire careers experimenting with ways to improve and update this technology. Potential for warping is a great place to begin those experiments.

Mysteries of Oobleck

If you have, know, teach, or exist near one or more children, you almost definitely know what oobleck is, if not by name alone. Oobleck is the term for a mixture of corn starch and water that reacts as a solid sometimes and a liquid sometimes. You can "walk on water" across a kiddie pool of oobleck if you move quickly. It's more like a run on water—check it out on YouTube. But if you stand on the oobleck, you'll sink in, and the oobleck will try to hold you down.

These special qualities make oobleck one of very few known "non-Newtonian fluids," meaning it literally defies the classic laws of physics as touched off by the lifetime's work of Sir Isaac Newton. And in 2014, an Air Force Academy cadet (meaning student) made the connection between oobleck and the liquid binders or epoxies used in body armor. She wanted to replace traditional gluey fillers that dried into a solid with a fluid that stayed flexible and loose.

The cadet and her advisors worked together to make layers of oobleck sandwiched between layers of Kevlar. They tried different setups and numbers of layers until they found an arrangement that can, in fact, stop bullets. Kevlar is a trademarked product, but oobleck is as close by as an 80 cent box of cornstarch. It's flexible until an impact and then again immediately afterward. It could be lighter than traditional armor and cost a lot less. The possibilities are endless.

Arach-ing Our Brains

Spiders produce strong natural proteins in the form of silk strands. Maybe a scientist started to wonder about the tensile strength of spider silk after walking through a web and trying to remove all traces of it for the rest of an entire day. This strong, durable, biological product requires no unusual ingredients or energy sources. In strength, flexibility, and other attributes, it could rival Kevlar, without the hangups of patent law or petrochemicals.

The U.S. military loves the idea of spider silk as a part of the armor kit soldiers wear. Its flexibility compared to Kevlar means it could be used to build comfortable underlayers that still offer protection, the same way consumer "worm silk" makes superlative long underwear. Scientists are working with the military to genetically engineer stronger, more versatile, or simply more abundant spider silk. They've bred silkworms that can make spider silk, because worms are much faster at silk production than spiders are.

Scaling to a military application is still a huge problem, literally. The U.S. Department of Defense employs over 2 million active duty or reserve military personnel. Can there ever be enough spider silk to supply these soldiers with even their smallest piece of armor? Will spider silk be used as one component in a much larger application?

So far, the investment in spider silk research is tiny compared to almost any other Department of Defense project. And the military has a terrific track record with technologies that trickle down to the civilian level: GPS navigation, the jet engine, walkie talkies, duct tape, and the Internet were all originally invented for military use.

Carrying the Weight of the Medieval World

Full suits of metal armor must have weighed a ton, right? This popular misconception has seeped into almost every depiction of medieval combat, tournament, and ceremony.

✳   ✳   ✳   ✳

"Well, a man that is packed away like that [in armor] is a nut that isn't worth the cracking, there is so little of the meat, when you get down to it, by comparison with the shell. The boys helped me, or I never could have got in."

MARK TWAIN, *A CONNECTICUT YANKEE IN KING ARTHUR'S COURT*

Thinking Logistically

Knights, samurai, Viking raiders, and other medieval warriors were the soldiers of their times. They were swift, agile fighters who aimed to kill, and they needed to move as freely as possible in order to use all the skills at their disposal. A cumbersome suit of armor could make the difference between winning or losing, not because of its defensive qualities, but because a fighter in lighter-weight armor could move faster and with more agility.

Chain of Fools

Could these knights have favored chainmail instead of solid metal? Chainmail seems lighter to the modern observer, perhaps because we're used to fabric mesh, metal window screens, and other lightweight modern materials. In reality, chainmail was super costly and less protective than plate armor. A blacksmith had to spend massive manhours extruding iron into thin rods, bending into rings in the right formation, and welding the rings closed. There might be solid circles of iron to punch and attach using rings.

The resulting chainmail felt comparably heavy while offering less protection. A sharp sword or spear tip could either penetrate the rings of the mail or simply drive them into the body. Ouch! Mail was simply not a plausible alternative after the invention and perfection of plate armor. For the record, a modern combat soldier's complement of armor and equipment weighs far more than a suit of plate armor from medieval times. Protecting against firearms and explosions is an inconceivably huge task compared to hand-to-hand or sword combat. And this armor actually can be prohibitively heavy—the soldiers who wear it are *tough*.

Why the Myth?

Human empathy may play a part in the myth of heavy plate armor. A full suit of metal sounds heavy, and it looks cumbersome! People who've worn welding gear, ski boots, lead aprons, or any other protective-but-prohibitive equipment know that it feels heavy and uncomfortable. And it also feels right that the metal gear that protects you in a swordfight needs to be heavy—after all, swords are razor sharp and made of heavy metal themselves.

But were swords heavy, either? Yes and no. At around three pounds, a medieval sword was not as easy to swing as an aluminum baseball bat. But a swordsman trained from a young age to carry a sword quickly grew used to the weight. Shelvers at grocery stores lift bags of flour or cat food countless times without an issue. Cooks wield cast-iron pans as their weapons of choice in the kitchen. The tiniest dumbbell you can picture is probably 3 pounds.

There were exceptionally heavy swords, especially *zweihänders* ("two handers"), which could weigh up to or over 10 pounds.

These were often a hybrid of a traditional sword and the longer polearm. They weren't more capable of piercing armor than a similar smaller sword.

Jousters mounted on horseback for tournaments wore heavier armor than fighters going into combat. They didn't need flexibility of movement, and their horses could still easily support their weight. Mark Twain may have had this heavy armor in mind when he wrote *A Connecticut Yankee in King Arthur's Court*, but this impression spread and endures today. So lighten up!

Grilljóns and Grilljóns Served

A "bajillion" isn't a real number. A "jillion" isn't a real number. So why does a bajillion sound bigger than a jillion? And why do we love these pretend numbers?

✳　✳　✳　✳

TO BE FRANK, no one is sure. Lexicographers—people who study word usage over time—have found usage of pretend numbers like jillion and zillion from nearly 100 years ago. Zillion likely began in African-American communities during the literary heydays of the 1920s before seeping into white usage in a pattern that has repeated throughout U.S. history with all manner of language, arts, and culture.

Mega-Mellifluous

It's probably impossible to separate how we "hear" these words from the shared mindset that led us to hear them that way. American children grow up learning about metric prefixes, ranging from nano to tera and far beyond with nearly infinite waypoints. Even infinity becomes "infinity plus one" in playground insults long before a burgeoning math student learns that there's some meaningful difference between infinity and *more* infinity.

How Do Numbers Feel?

Named large numbers like googol and googolplex sound a bit silly and are unfathomably large. These huge numbers may blend together into one big ball of hyperbole that lends itself to zillions and bazillions based on how far from reality they seem to us. After all, the average person's ability with language is far more developed than their ability with numbers. We intuit meaning, tone, and context from language that is leagues outside our comfort zones with mathematics. What is a jillion or zillion but a different way to say "infinity plus one"? Exaggeration in language carries specific meanings that we share with others to help them understand our feelings. Waiting in line *feels like* it takes *literally forever*.

A Zillion Kinds of Fun

It's interesting to wonder why people don't exaggerate using real named numbers. But the clinical names for these—quadrillion, septillion—aren't satisfying to say in the way zillion or bajillion are. A googol is the same as 10 duotrigintillion, but Earth's favorite search engine isn't named after a duotrigintillion. Those who speak other languages probably know different fictional number words that sound pleasing to the ear trained in those languages. Icelandic linguist Andri Erlingsson says that Icelanders use "grilljón," a mix of the words for grilled and billion. Sounds delicious!

Mis-Nomed

How did Nome, Alaska get its name? No one is really sure, but adventurous cartographers with sloppy penmanship may be to blame.

✳   ✳   ✳   ✳

NOME IS A city of just under 4,000 people in the only state where 4,000 people is comfortably termed a city. The area was populated by Alaska's native peoples since prehistory, but white explorers surveyed and named it in the 1850s. Nome boomed during the 1890s after gold was discovered, and Nome still has a great deal more amenities and local services than you'd guess for such a small town.

The legend goes that explorers marked the location on a hand-drawn map with a notation that said "? Name" and a reader misread this as Nome. The misnomer (zing!) cascaded to the nearby Nome River and Port Nome.

But did the *misnamer* really exist? Unless the person reading the map was literally born yesterday, it's hard to imagine him misreading the zillionth time he saw that someone had written a question mark on a freshly drawn map. Then again, a piece of paper hand-lettered in ink had a lot of opportunities to smudge, tear, or otherwise be corrupted.

There are other theories but none so charming. "Misnomer" jokes aside, Nome is close to the Latin root *nomen* meaning name—a root shared by *nomenclature*, literally to call by name. Unfortunately, Nome nomenclature is none closer to closure.

Pressing Ye Issue

Ye Olde Pretend Old English has planted "ye" in the public imagination, but this was never meant to be pronounced "yee"— it's "the." Blame the confusion on the printing press.

✳ ✳ ✳ ✳

A Curious Inventor

ASPECIAL SET OF circumstances helped Johannes Gutenberg to invent the movable type printing press in 1440. He was a metalworker with a curious, entrepreneurial spirit that led him to experiment and learn at least a little bit about many different fields. He adapted the tech-

nology used in the wine press, which had evolved over thousands of years, to build his printing press. For the type itself, he made individual letter stamps from a strong, durable alloy of his own devising. As a goldsmith, he had learned firsthand how soft metals like gold could warp and distort with wear.

Character vs. Character

Movable type was originally developed in China, with its own set of fortunate circumstances. Mandarin and other dialects of Chinese use characters arranged in columns, reading top to bottom, and the characters are designed to be the same width. Artisans could make consistent square "blanks" with characters on them and slide them into fixed columns that were the same from job to job. The cost of labor was high but different artisans could work in parallel to the same specs.

English used an alphabet of letter characters with different widths, mostly from the Latin alphabet but with a handful from the Norse runic alphabet. Crafting letter stamps that were all the same width would make awkward type and be an inefficient use of space on costly paper or parchment pages, especially compared with the fine, thoughtful work done by hand in monasteries or by scribes.

Ye Olde Printing Mix-Up

Space-saving Middle English signpainters and calligraphers shortened the word "the" using the runic letter thorn (þ), but typesetters didn't have access to thorns and used "y" instead—it looked very similar in the typeface styles of the time. So all those Ye Olde Pubberies are just the old pubs after all. The pronoun ye, as in "We hardly knew ye," is separate and pronounced phonetically.

The letter switch may seem foreign to us, but modern life is filled with the same misapprehensions. Surely you or someone you know writes "would of" instead of "would have," or "all intensive purposes"? Let they who are without syntax cast the first stone.

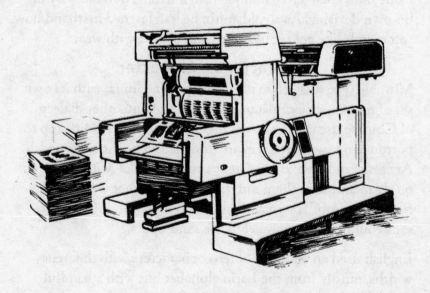

Dodging a Different Kind of Draft

Around the world, a huge variety of cultures have a handed-down fear of drafts, air conditioning, or room fans. But why?

✳ ✳ ✳ ✳

I F YOU'RE A longtime American resident, chances are good that you have air conditioning in your home or know of the best coffee shops, public libraries, and other places near you that have air conditioning. Your workplace may be downright frigid during the summer, a hot topic (so to speak) that comes up in annual think-pieces. But in other countries, you might find summer news stories about alleged "fan death" or the illnesses caused by drafts.

Draft Fear

Former *Daily Show* correspondent John Hodgman acts as a kind of *People's Court* for petty squabbles on his podcast *Judge John Hodgman*. In 2014, a couple that had just moved in together in Berlin asked for help deciding whether or not to get an air conditioner or even a box fan. The American in the relationship said that almost no one had air conditioning in Berlin, and ceiling fans were unusual because of a cultural fear of drafts. "Germans dislike rushing air," she said. The German in the relationship said he thought it was only Germans like him who believed this, and the fear is based on the old wives' tale that moving air causes colds and other diseases.

Prevalence in the World

The phenomenon of draft fear is widespread. English-speaking transplants abroad have blanketed the internet with accounts of their confusion about not just the lack of air conditioning but a refusal to open the windows. German, French, Portuguese, Italian, and Serbian—and likely other languages!—have specific terms for their feared or loathed drafts. Many other European nations have related wives' tales. Believers cite pseudoscience and repeat the wisdom of the ages to back up their traditional opinion.

The Airing of Grievances

Certainly an abrupt change from hot, humid air to cold, dry air can induce a mild headache at times or trigger a migraine in an affected person. But the alternative pushed by Germans in particular is to air your home for a few minutes in the morning or during home cleaning and then close up the "fresh air" for the rest of the day. That sounds just as unpleasant in a different way. What about people who live on the top floor of a building and absorb all the heat of the sun? No one needs to live in a greenhouse.

Europeans also seem to dislike ice cubes and cold beverages. Americans were inundated with commercials for a Coors can that turns a different color when it's "super cold" at the same time Germans were using branded beer warmers to bring beers back to room temperature. Certainly there are no Big Gulps filled to the top with crushed ice.

Fans of Fan Death

Korea has an even more extreme take on moving air. The old wives' tale there is that running a fan in a closed room can literally kill you, based on a variety of handwavey theories, the least absurd of which is that circulating air can cause hypothermia. The belief is mainstream enough to regularly appear in newspapers and other media. It's shared by some other parts of East Asia as well. There is confirmation bias when a sudden death from cardiac arrest or another cause can instead be linked with fan death.

Any suggested explanation for fan death rings false to those of us not raised with this belief, but every culture has its own reality-denying legends and sayings. Believers insist that a fan can lower your body temperature—this is only true when your body is warm enough to sweat, triggering evaporation that cools the body. Otherwise, anyone who's spent a long night in a sweltering room with only a fan can confirm that the room doesn't get any cooler because of the fan, despite their fervent wishes. Some claim that an electric fan churns carbon dioxide in a way that suffocates its victims—but it makes no sense to blame this on the fan, and anyone in a room small enough to suffocate them in the course of a night's sleep, less than 5 feet on a side, has bigger problems with their living situation.

Blown Away by Evidence

Ultimately, people around the world choose stories and myths that confirm their views. If you're comfortable in a hot room and others want to change your behaviors, you fall back onto explanations that reinforce your comfort zone. But these regional fears and beliefs are not grounded in science and can't stand up to scrutiny. The only real danger lies in the pseudo-scientific ways people seek to justify their favorite old wives' tales. Americans have a growing fear of gluten despite thousands of years of thriving human life fed on gluten-riddled bread products. No one is immune, so to speak, from regionally biased health quackery.

Dammed by the Truth

How many workers fell to their deaths in the freshly poured concrete of Hoover Dam? There were around 100 deaths during construction, but none died in this horrific way.

✳ ✳ ✳ ✳

THE MASSIVE HOOVER Dam, completed in 1936, joins its contemporary Golden Gate Bridge in the category of things we almost can't believe were built so long ago. The dam soars over 700 feet high and holds back the largest reservoir in the United States. It is shaped so that water pressure helps to press strength into the dam, like the keystone of an architectural arch is pressed into the rest of the arch.

Estimates of worker deaths vary between high 90s and somewhere in the 100s. There were terrible falling deaths, equipment malfunction, and even a purported conspiracy to cover up illnesses caused by work hazards as pneumonia. It was dangerous work, and six different construction companies had to combine resources to raise a workforce of more than 20,000 men by the time the dam was finished.

There's a related myth that the Great Wall of China is filled with the remains of dead workers. Because parts of the wall were build in ancient times and no longer exist, historians will likely neither prove nor disprove the myth at any point. Archaeologists may unearth some new site in the future, of course. But in extant portions of the wall that were built later, they haven't yet found any human remains.

The Great Wall had a mortality rate closer to that at other major ancient builds like the Great Pyramid at Giza. Ancient technology, no safety, poor nutrition, and a host of other factors meant workers were taking their lives into their hands.

Chapter 6

Life of the Law

Dude, What Time Is It?

The stoner term 420, celebrated both daily and once a year on April 20, is rumored to come from the California legal code number for a marijuana-related crime. But 420 doesn't match any state's listings, including California's.

✳　✳　✳　✳

THE TERM HAS always referred to the time of day, and it began with a group of teens who were loosely socially linked with the Grateful Dead. The term went viral. No one in the 1970s could have predicted the long tail of this niche counterculture term, including California's 2004 medical marijuana initiative named Senate Bill 420. The state of Colorado went so far as to replace its "mile 420" marker signs with ones reading "mile 419.99" to deter theft.

Vi Coactus

Can you sign a contract in such a way that a judge knows you signed under duress?

✳   ✳   ✳   ✳

THIS QUESTION IS a sticky wicket with a variety of potential answers. The myth at play is that you can add "VC" to your initials, meaning *vi coactus*, Latin for "by coercion," in order to show that your signature shouldn't be valid. (Coactus looks at a glance like it might be related to coach, but coach evolved from Romance words like *coche*.)

Everyone seems to agree that adding VC, UD ("under duress"), or even full words like "signing under protest" show that the signatory felt their signature was not binding. But that intention doesn't translate to legality. Think about it: Cases of true coercion and duress involve other crimes or egregious ethical violations, like threatening an employee's future, holding someone against their will, or saying or suggesting that they will be harmed.

But in a contract negotiation or other straightforward business transactions, which is when VC signatures come up the most, experts seem to agree that the best way to "protest" is simply not to sign. The party applying pressure may renegotiate the contract, or you may simply walk away from the deal.

Rest Uninsured

If you're an uninsured driver and someone hits your car, are you excluded from benefits?

✳ ✳ ✳ ✳

DRIVERS WITHOUT AUTO insurance make up about 1 in 8 nationwide, with individual state rates ranging from 1 in 25 to 1 in 4. Every driver is legally obligated to have valid auto insurance, and you can be ticketed and charged with driving without insurance. But there's an insidious myth that an uninsured driver is on their own if they're struck by another car and the other driver is at fault.

The truth is, unless the at-fault driver is also uninsured or underinsured, their insurance will pay (in accordance with their policy) the costs and bills of the victim. The victim may still have their license suspended for driving without insurance or whatever the local policy is.

And if you continue to drive on a suspended license, you join the most dangerous group of U.S. drivers. The American Automobile Association (AAA) estimates that nearly 1 in 5 fatal car accidents in the time period 2007–2009 involves an unlicensed or invalidly licensed driver. For the age group 21–34, the number was almost *half*.

As it is almost impossible to get car insurance without a license, these dangerous unlicensed drivers are almost always uninsured as well. If you have valid insurance but a suspended license, your insurance may not cover any claims.

Uncommon Law

What is a so-called common law marriage?

✳ ✳ ✳ ✳

ABOUT ONE THIRD of U.S. states have laws that define or recognize common law marriage, meaning unmarried partners who live together as spouses and have evidence of a combined, permanent lifestyle. A handful of these states have grandfathered common law marriage, so new relationships can't be recognized, but existing ones are still considered valid for legal purposes.

Those states that recognize new common law marriage relationships have codified it enough to protect these de facto spouses the same way they protect legally married spouses, including that they require separating common law spouses to legally divorce. In fact, some experts recommend that cohabitating partners in common law marriage states think about protecting themselves in writing *from* common law marriage if they don't wish to be considered married at any point.

But as with an LLC, the major obstacle to a common law marriage is lack of thoughtful supporting actions. Common law spouses must be able to show that their lives are meaningfully combined in the same way legally married spouses share major purchases and ownership, banking, and other financial and logistical decisions. They must present as spouses in their own communities.

In the other two thirds of U.S. states, cohabitating couples can never be considered married unless they legally marry. These partners may still choose to protect themselves legally by completing paperwork for issues like power of attorney, inheritance, and shared ownership of assets. At the end of the day, legal marriage is a contract, and many elements of it can be recreated by other legal paperwork.

A Card of Many Colors

What color is my so-called green card?

✳ ✳ ✳ ✳

IMMIGRATION TO THE United States forms a huge part of the U.S. economy, both by boosting tax bases for foreign-born workers and through secondary effects to productivity, innovation, and other factors. And the general "streets of gold" image of the U.S. means that almost nothing in the world is so coveted as a green card, the documentation of a person's status as a lawful permanent resident. People can remain lawful permanent residents for decades without needing or necessarily wanting to become citizens of the U.S., although there are downsides to that choice as well.

Some stable countries with low immigration to the U.S., like Morocco, have an available number of spots each year for green card lotteries. These people don't have to go through the harrowing journey to squeeze into a tiny number of available places in the U.S.

But What Color Is the Card?

The green card *was* green in its first iteration from 1946 to 1964. It was also actually paper cardstock, like many Social Security cards still are. As these cards grew more and more precious during the Cold War, the government began changing the design in an attempt to thwart counterfeiters. The cards were also made of the same tough plastic as driver's licenses. (Imagine if the document you legally had to have on your person at *all times* could be destroyed in the washing machine.)

In 2010, they released a new design that capitalizes on the fraud protection technologies used in paper currency or drivers licenses: holograms, shadow images, complex chemical printing. The designs look like items from Tom Cruise's wall display in 2002's *Minority Report*. And through the decades, the cards have been almost every color there is: green, yellow, purple, peach, blue, and multi.

Desperate Times

Movie hitmen are almost superheroes, but the reality is much more boring—and sad.

✳   ✳   ✳   ✳

Fantasy Roles

JASON BOURNE IS pulled from the dark and stormy ocean after a failed mission, and he finds his identity stored in some kind of laser pointer bullet sewn into his skin. Leon (The Professional) commits coldblooded crimes before a tragic and redemptive final story arc. Jack Reacher's foes are often part of far-reaching criminal conspiracies and they plow through civilians and other victims without breaking a sweat.

Why do we love assassins? This even translates to our fixation on conspiracy theories around the assassinations of Presidents John F. Kennedy and Abraham Lincoln—movies and books about them marvel at links between the two men's lives, keeping the stories as fresh in our minds as if they happened last year. The shadowy CIA, and hypothetical super secret uber-CIAs, is an elephant in the TV room.

Antiheroes are the new heroes, beginning in the dark resurgence of good bad guys in HBO's *Oz* and *The Sopranos*. But in the Bourne franchise and the reborn (and re-Bourne) Bond movies of the oughts, the relatable but murderous main character really hit his stride. By the time *Breaking Bad*, *Boardwalk Empire*, *Daredevil*, and other ambiguously evil and righteous ensemble casts took over in the 2010s, viewers were definitely mixed up about assassins.

Deflating the Killer Image

Our cultural love for sociopaths is a far cry from the reality of hitmen. Most people who end up taking on these jobs are desperately broke. They're first-timers, not suave careerists. Their work is not subtle. Matt Damon isn't going to meet them in hand-to-hand combat using a ballpoint pen as a miniature polearm. No one is following them to cover up the act or ensure that they aren't arrested—and they usually *are* arrested, as can be the person who hired them. They also aren't generally very well paid considering the scale and moral toll of the crime.

As far as the skilled, easy-lying sociopaths in real life, these people usually end up having normal-appearing family lives and careers. Don't think about that part for too long.

New York City?!

Legendary western outlaw Billy the Kid was born in New York City! His family followed a common path out west during the twilight of the Manifest Destiny era.

✳   ✳   ✳   ✳

Lonely Boy

HENRY MCCARTY WAS born and baptized in Manhattan before moving with his family first to Indianapolis and then to New Mexico. After his mother died, he took a job working in exchange for room and board at a boardinghouse in town. But before long, he had begun committing petty thefts and crimes in town and was unceremoniously escorted out and unwelcome to return. Billy stayed briefly with his stepfather, from whom he also stole before absconding. He continued to alternate working, losing money, fighting, and stealing, until he eventually shot and killed a fellow bar patron and had to flee to Arizona. This was all by age 18.

A Worsening Spree

Billy's crimes—now we understand why he changed his name around this time!—escalated to the point that Arizona's governor got involved in the bounty on Billy's head. Billy was arrested but shot and killed his way out of custody, which only increased the resources poured into the manhunt. Eventually, a sheriff named Pat Barrett, who'd sought Billy for months or even years, found Billy and shot him to death. Billy was 21.

The Legend Begins

A conspiracy theory sprang up almost immediately that Sheriff Barrett had been in the wrong to kill Billy or that the killing had been dishonorable, which seems ludicrous given Billy's crimes. As with Bonnie and Clyde and other true-crime legends, Billy's actions were more egregious and capricious than they're painted in hindsight. He was a scared teen with no family who refused to stay put and work for a living. Certainly today there are orphaned teens, many in frightening group homes, who would love the opportunity for room, board, and independence in exchange for their work.

Fame and Legacy

Billy appears in a cameo role in the 2014 video game *80 Days*, in which an adapted Phileas Fogg and Passepartout make their way around the world from an array of transit options between major cities. He boards their train in the American west, more like a Doolin-Dalton outlaw gang member than his own biography. But no other outlaw has the level of recognition that Billy has. If Bill Doolin boarded the train, no one would bat an eye.

The contrast between New York and the Old West was less pronounced in Billy's lifetime than it is today—think of the clashing gang culture immortalized in *Gangs of New York* or the relative anarchy in Mark Helprin's novel *Winter's Tale*. But today, when this biographical tidbit makes many of us think of the "New York City?!" commercial for Pace picante sauce, Billy's birthplace and life's work seem at odds.

You Need a Lawyer

If I'm not guilty, I don't need a lawyer, and I won't be convicted.

✳ ✳ ✳ ✳

Fair Play

HUMANS HAVE A strong sense of fair play. We don't like to
see a badly lopsided sporting event, and we invented the
so-called "slaughter rule" to end these games early. If guilty people are arrested for crimes, we think they should be punished.
How could the same system find us guilty if we aren't? But this
belief becomes dangerous when the accused person translates it
to not needing a lawyer.

Preventive Care

If someone says you look unwell, but you feel okay, you might
go to the doctor anyway. We consider that a reasonable precaution to take, especially if we have young kids or others around
us who might get sick too. The same idea applies to legal
defense. If you aren't sure, take it anyway. Your loved ones and
others will appreciate and benefit from your precaution, and
you'll benefit directly from the support of an attorney.

Vulnerable Groups

There is an unsavory truth in America that people in some
racial or ethnic groups are far more likely to be arrested than
others, and far more likely to be convicted than others under
similar circumstances. For these vulnerable people, taking
advantage of the right to an attorney is even more important.
Studies estimate that about one in 25 inmates on Death
Row is innocent of the crimes for which they're serving death-
penalty sentences.

Staggering Numbers

Other crimes are less studied than death-penalty cases. But as
law professor Samuel Morse puts it, in a nation with two million prison inmates at any given time, if even one percent are

innocent, that amounts to 200,000 people. The odds of becoming part of that percentage of innocent prisoners may be very long, but someone still becomes part of that figure. That alone is a reason to defend yourself to the best of your ability.

Separation of Church and State From the Truth

The first amendment includes separation of church and state.

✳ ✳ ✳ ✳

WHAT THE FIRST amendment explicitly says is, "Congress shall make no law respecting an establishment of religion, or prohibiting the free exercise thereof." In the time since, the Supreme Court and Congress have expanded on this single sentence to apply it to funding for religious charities, worker rights on religious holidays, and all manner of other issues.

But the fine-toothed comb of policy doesn't apply to the single biggest message: Congress, and therefore the lawmaking arm of the United States, can never make any religion or establish an official U.S. religion. Supreme Court cases virtually always deal with the "prohibiting the free exercise thereof" part, because working on the Sabbath could be impeding the free exercise.

Oral Tort-y

There are many gotcha moments on TV, including when—it turns out!—an oral agreement counts as a legally binding contract. Does this happen?

✳ ✳ ✳ ✳

ORAL AGREEMENTS, LIKE those made over solemn hand-shakes, can be legally binding. Trying to prove these agreements exist can be a far messier process, so it's common for a he-said-she-said legal quarrel to end in an unsatisfying decision. But if both parties admit there was an agreement, it's basically smooth sailing. Complications arise if the verbal contract turns out to be too big, too long a time, or certain other qualifications that can all trigger something called the statute of frauds.

Each state has standards at which an agreement must be written and signed in order to be valid. These standards protect people from scams or exploitation by others who know the loopholes of oral agreement rules. Think of it as a form of insurance that applies without us even realizing it. You can't verbally agree to sell your multimillion dollar corporation to hoodwink someone. Also, there's a reason that Nigerian prince always gets it in writing.

One-Way Ticket

If the police officer makes an error on my ticket, it can be voided.

✳ ✳ ✳ ✳

ONE OF THE worst scourges of life in the internet age is the drive-by pedant—no moving-violation pun intended. This person wants to correct your grammar and remind you that it's "you're," not "your." They share Facebook memes about commonly confused words. They're upset about this use of the singular they, which dates back to at least the 1800s so is actually not a sign of the apocalypse. The myth of the error-riddled ticket appeals to these sticklers. Aha, a typo!

But the truth is more generous. Police officers are not just human; they're stressed and busy, with huge responsibilities on their shoulders. Your boss probably wouldn't void your day's work because of a typo, and neither will a judge void a ticket because of an error made in simple good faith. Your rights include just two things: notification that you have been charged with something, and notification of how and when you may dispute that charge.

Certainly if the mistake on your ticket is that your Uncle Billy was driving instead of you, and the cop mixed up your licenses, that mistake needs to be corrected—but you still have to do that, and it won't simply resolve on its own.

Gone in 60 Seconds

Our heroes finally reach the kidnapper by phone. One sweaty detective stammers into the phone while another, sitting in front of a computer, makes the universal hand gesture for "keep talking."

✳ ✳ ✳ ✳

THE RULE THAT it takes 60 seconds to trace a call has been out of date literally since the end of manually routed calls—40 or more years. This fact makes intuitive sense and is not shocking in itself, but why is it perhaps *the* most used crime show cliché decades after it went out of practical use?

The answer is probably as simple as that the time delay builds suspense. After all, landlines and cell phones are all traceable virtually instantaneously, landlines since the end of manual operator connection and cell phones since the placement of GPS chips inside them. There's no mystery left anymore, except to wonder why television criminals don't use burner phones like all the real criminals in the world do.

We as the viewing audience may also have a few different ideas mixed up, only one of which is how long it takes to trace a call. Sometimes, it seems like officials want to keep a suspect on the phone in order to make a connection with the suspect, prevent further harm to hostages, or keep the suspect's actual human body in the same place long enough for police to arrive on the scene.

How to Break a Contract

Once I sign a contract, it's impregnable.

✳ ✳ ✳ ✳

MANY PEOPLE IN the workforce sign employment contracts and even non-disclosure agreements, but the most common way Americans encounter contracts is in finance: car loans, mortgages, apartment leases, buying a home. These are huge commitments that can feel very intimidating. Most of the time, the best idea is to have a lawyer review whatever you're signing before you sign it.

But if you've already signed, there's almost always some way out. It may be very costly, professionally damaging, or otherwise inconvenient. But it may not be! The best way to find out is to ask an attorney.

Try Another Way

It can be difficult to get out of a contract completely, but many people don't know how easily a contract can be modified, amended, or otherwise updated to suit a new agreement both parties agree on. Nothing is set in stone, and a broken contract is a pain for both sides. Rewriting or modifying could be the difference between breaking a contract and moving forward together—it's usually worth a shot.

One way to build a contract that you may feel better about signing is to write in "landmarks" that your project needs to reach, so that either party can exit the contract if those landmarks are not reached in the terms you've chosen. You may also want to include a "kill switch" that lets either party exit with fair notice, if that's appropriate for your project or business.

Ask for Help

The bottom line is, of course, to ask your attorney and work together to understand any contract you're ever asked to sign. Nothing is forever, and nothing is set in stone.

This Land Is My Ground, This Land Is Your Ground

Trayvon Martin's killer George Zimmerman used Florida's stand-your-ground law in his defense, right? No, not explicitly.

✳   ✳   ✳   ✳

MEDIA COVERAGE OF the George Zimmerman case mentioned "stand your ground" a million times a minute. Florida's law is fairly open-ended about the idea of deadly force as applied when someone feels threatened or in imminent danger, and it explicitly says the threatened person has no duty to retreat. But the jury in Zimmerman's case acquitted him even without this legal concept being mentioned outright in court. Proponents and critics alike say that the idea of choosing deadly force over retreat is a cultural way of life in states that have enacted and cherish their stand-your-ground laws.

Everywhere Is "Your Ground"

What makes stand-your-ground laws so distasteful to those that oppose them? First, these laws go a step beyond the preexisting castle laws—nicknamed by the saying "A man's home is his castle"—where a home's occupants can defend their home by meeting force with force, so to speak. In a stand-your-ground law, the name is literal. The ground where you're standing belongs to you enough for you to meet force with force, rather than retreating to different ground that's out of harm's way.

Safe Retreat

The idea of retreat is part of another major criticism of stand-your-ground laws. American self-defense laws have encouraged or even required retreat when the threatened or fearing party had a safe way to do so. Stand-your-ground laws explicitly say that state residents have no duty to retreat, effectively rewriting our shared culture around self defense. Critics argue that an aggressive enough "self defense" policy eventually becomes an offense policy.

Florida's stand-your-ground law has gone through multiple iterations since its introduction in 2005. Debate rages on over the constitutionality of aspects of the law, although it may represent the shifting culture around guns and deadly force in the states where these laws have been enacted.

Too Hot to Touch

That old lady sued McDonald's because she spilled hot coffee on herself. It sounds ridiculous. But the real story, and thinking about your own grandmother, may change your mind.

✳   ✳   ✳   ✳

AMERICA IS THE land of the ambivalent loyalties. We dislike "huge corporations" and their products, unless their products are cheap. We like the right to sue, unless it seems like someone else is suing for the wrong thing. The McDonald's coffee case is one such lawsuit, or, at least, it's purported to be. The truth is much more complicated.

The Story

Elderly Stella Liebeck was riding with her grandson when they stopped at McDonald's, and she waited until the car was parked to open her coffee in order to add cream and sugar. Nowadays, it's standard practice for McDonald's, Dunkin' Donuts, and other fast-food coffee joints to ask how many cream and sugar you want and put them in. At Starbucks, you're already inside the store so it's easy and safe to open your cup to add sugar and cream; even so, they'll put it in for you if you ask them to. But imagine a handful of loose packets handed through your car window. Liebeck made the prudent choice to wait until the car was stopped, and she rested her cup between her knees. It's what anyone would do.

The Third Degree

Here's where the important overlooked piece of information comes into the story. The coffee served at McDonald's at the time was between 180° and 190° Fahrenheit. This is far hotter than is the general practice—an "extra hot" drink from Starbucks is around 180°. Scalding hot liquids can cause third-degree burns in a matter of seconds, and although "scalding hot" is a figurative usage, scalded milk is heated to 180°.

The McDonald's range began at what was already an unsafely hot temperature compared to the average person's usual cup of coffee. It's hot enough to kill germs, as we learned earlier in this book: 185° Fahrenheit, which people intentionally overshoot because boiling is easier to observe. Even scalded milk has a slightly different chemical makeup than from before it was scalded, because the heat breaks down some elements.

The Burning Truth

Anyone who's cooked regularly for any period of time has probably burned themselves at some point, and when that burn occurs, we're likely to drop what we're doing. Steam can scald our skin and catch us off guard. Liebeck had third-degree burns, which must be treated immediately by a medical professional, and that usually means an emergency room. She asked for just $20,000, which McDonald's refused to settle for. You may still think the lawsuit was frivolous, but now you at least have more of the facts.

Riding While Intoxicated

Cycling is growing in popularity for people who live in bike-friendly places, but bicycles have always offered a fallback plan for those without licenses or whose licenses were revoked for traffic offenses or DUI. But can you get a DUI when you're "driving" a bike?

✳ ✳ ✳ ✳

Changing Times

OVER TIME, THE number of Americans using bicycles for daily travel needs continues to go up. Rather than fitting their mountain bikes into bike racks for weekend trips, these commuters are suiting up on narrow-wheeled city bikes and riding on major thoroughfares. Many U.S. cities are building bike lanes on these major roads, both to encourage cycling as an alternative to cars and to try to better protect cyclists from harm at the hands of motorists.

And Consequences

Laws regarding bicycles don't seem to be written with this level of traffic mingling in mind. Most states have clear laws about the cycling "rules of the road," like how bikes must follow right-of-way in the same order as cars and obey traffic signals. Cycling activists argue that bikes should have more leeway because it's so much more difficult to stop and then restart a bike's forward motion than to simply press the gas pedal.

The major problem with this idea is that cars have outsize power over cyclists in almost any collision. A person on a bike is basically a pedestrian in terms of safety, and cars already struggle to obey pedestrian crosswalks. If cyclists were given legal right of way over cars, they would be trusting drivers in a way that is simply not supported by car crash statistics. It's a difficult situation without an easy answer.

Mutual Misunderstanding

In the meantime, every driver has stories about a bicyclist scofflaw who blows through a red light during their commute. In a climate where there are relatively few cyclists along the major commuting roads, cyclists feel they can use their own discretion rather than adhere to the law as it is. But if the number of cyclists multiplies in the future and all make their own individual judgment calls, the need for standardized and enforced bicycle *plus* automobile traffic laws will become clear.

The Gray Status Quo

Right now, there are almost no laws about riding a bike while under the influence. The same gray area that muddles bike traffic behaviors means that bikes aren't considered "vehicles" for legal purposes in most states, so operating one while drunk is not illegal. As more and more cyclists use their bikes for daily travel, these rules will likely also need to change.

For now, choosing to ride while intoxicated is another apparent individual judgment call for cyclists. They may be stopped and cited for more pedestrian intoxication crimes like drunk and disorderly, but these citations have far fewer consequences than DUI.

Taking Video of Police

More and more police wear bodycams or have dashcams in their cars, but bystanders or people who've been pulled over are sometimes harassed for taking video. What's okay to do or not?

✳   ✳   ✳   ✳

THESE SITUATIONS ARE complicated and the best way to know for sure is to do your research or consult a lawyer. But here are some general guidelines on what's okay and what's not okay in terms of what courts will likely determine. In the heat of the moment, it's always better to be safe and take care when you're making assertive choices. Cloud storage has made it easier for street photographers to instantly upload their work to a secure third party location where it can't be deleted by others.

Helpful Hints

Photos and video are not only protected as free speech—they're a cornerstone of the government transparency that contributes to the freedom of American citizens.

✳ You can't break a law in order to lawfully film someone else you suspect of breaking the law.

✳ Spaces considered public, like streets, transit, and government buildings like police and fire stations, are all fair game to photograph. Anything you can see from a public street is considered fair game as well, which is the defense invoked by papparazzi who use telephoto lenses to zoom in on actors on family vacations.

✳ If you are filming a law enforcement encounter and the way or place in which you're filming is interfering with the officers' work, they can order you to move, leave, or stop filming.

✳ Private property owners can order you to leave their property at any time.

✳ Law enforcement can't legally delete your photographs or video. They can only ask to look at your equipment or look at your work if they have a warrant, and it is still illegal to delete anything.

Poor Man's Patent

My awesome new idea is protected, because I mailed it to myself and kept the sealed envelope.

✳ ✳ ✳ ✳

THIS URBAN LEGEND may have been more factual at some point in history, because the postmark on a sealed, mailed envelope counts as an official timestamp, comparable to a notary public. Postmarks are often still used as the determining timestamp for filing tax returns or applying to college.

But the so-called "poor man's patent" is no longer valid. The patent office now has a mechanism in place where you can file a kind of placeholder saying that you have an idea and are preparing a patent. This eliminates the need for a stopgap, because the placeholder itself shows when you first conceived of the idea in its developed form.

Limits of Limited Liability

Forming a limited liability corporation (LLC) means my stuff is safe if my business fails.

✳ ✳ ✳ ✳

STUDIES FIND THAT, usually, a majority of Americans wish they could or plan to start their own businesses. And about 1 in 8 working Americans is a business owner—the number varies by the level of inclusiveness of the term "working Americans," but the variance isn't very big. Many of these entrepreneurs rely on LLCs to protect their assets in case of business failure, and this is especially important in industries like sit-down dining that have astronomical failure rates.

Yes, an LLC draws a legal circle around business assets, but it's only as good as the work and due diligence the entrepreneur continues to put into it. Letting LLC documentation get badly out of date, failing to keep the right records, and other simple mistakes can really hurt a business owner. The stress and daily chaos of starting a business can leave owners feeling as though they must do the most critical tasks first, and clerical tasks can be left behind. It's understandable but still risky.

Silence Is Golden

Americans have the right to remain silent, in many contexts.

✳   ✳   ✳   ✳

OUR MIRANDA RIGHTS, which apply to interrogations, include the explicit right to remain silent. But many people don't realize you can and should stay silent when possible in almost *every* context with legal officials. After an incident like a car crash, what you say—exactly as it says in the Miranda warning—can be used against you. That line is not a harmless disclaimer or cover-your-seat statement.

Taking responsibility, even indirectly, can reverberate through the rest of your legal dealings. If you're not comfortable saying nothing, you can answer questions directly and simply without adding extra information. In stressful times that involve police, it's hard to stay cool, but if you can, it is a great benefit.

The same is true in courtroom settings. If you're serving jury duty, acting as a witness, or even just sitting in court, it behooves you to sit quietly, stick with the simplest form of the truth, and let the professionals draw you out further if necessary. And if any of this, or issues like whether or not you can refuse a sobriety test or vehicle search, is a concern for you, ask an attorney and do your research. The best defense is a thoughtful and prepared offense.

Serial Killers Aren't That Smart

Fictional serial killers are smart, resourceful, and ruthless. With rare exceptions, real-life serial killers are just ruthless.

✳ ✳ ✳ ✳

D<small>R. MIKE AAMODT</small> of Virginia's Radford University maintains a database of serial killers, which he defines as someone who commits two or more murders with a "cooling off period" between. This parameter excludes spree killers or mass murderers, who have a different psychological profile and are studied separately.

Dr. Aamodt has compiled the findings from trials of the serial killers who have been caught and tried in the U.S. and his statistics show that the average serial killer IQ is below the general population's average IQ, with a median much further below that. The IQs range between 54 and 186 overall, and the average and median show that this range is much more heavily weighted toward the lower end, with a handful of very high IQs distorting the range.

One specific highlight of interest is the breakdown of method of killing compared with the IQs of those that chose it. Bomb users had the highest IQs, nearly double that of the group that bludgeoned victims to death. The numbers in these groups are too small to be statistically significant but they're interesting to think about.

Dr. Aamodt points out in his own report that recent numbers are also distorted by the "lag" between a murder and the identification and arrest of the killer. With serial murders, this lag can be years or even decades. So the statistics are a dynamic set that adapts to new information over time.

Attorney-Client Privilege

Like doctor-patient confidentiality, attorney-client privilege helps form the backbone of the strong relationship of trust between the provider and recipient of a complex and vulnerable service. But where doctors are mandatory reporters, meaning they must report suspected child abuse and a litany of other legal or ethical issues related to injuries, attorney-client privilege is almost inviolable.

✳ ✳ ✳ ✳

Violating Privilege

THERE ARE EXCEPTIONS, although almost all are related to actions the client takes on their own, not anything the attorney decides to disclose. The exception to this is if a client tells an attorney that they plan to imminently harm someone, which attorneys are usually allowed to reveal. Here are some other common exceptions.

✳ In some examples, clients tell information to an attorney that they previously shared with another non-attorney person, making the "confidential" communication less exclusive.

✳ When a will is challenged, attorneys may be asked to share pieces of confidential communication that shed light on the deceased client's wishes.

✳ Attorneys can use certain details in public proceedings when their clients refuse to pay them, because otherwise they would all need to be paid up front—a financial hardship for many and an actual impossibility in some cases.

✳ *There are other examples, like when attorneys are in their "off time" in roles that may have legal aspects they are not involved in. An attorney in the world isn't a client to everyone they meet.

No one knows better than attorneys themselves what they need to keep confidential. Violating attorney-client privilege without adequate cause almost always means suspension or disbarment and is a gravely serious offense. Any evidence obtained from an attorney who broke privilege is probably not admissible in court. There's a reason attorneys are also called "counselors"—their services are private and insightful and require a trust relationship.

Limits of Blood Alcohol

In the 1990s, states began lowering the blood alcohol content (BAC) that constituted a DUI or DWI charge in that state. All 50 states now have a .08 BAC standard, but you don't have to reach .08 in order to be arrested and charged with DUI.

✳ ✳ ✳ ✳

Rapidly Shifting Opinions

DRUNK DRIVING HAS experienced one of the biggest pivots in public opinion in U.S. history in just a few decades. As our shared national culture has realized the error of its drunk-driving ways, laws about drunk driving have sprung up and been fine tuned and expanded. These laws help police arrest those who choose to drive under the influence, yes, but our attitude toward drunk driving as a criminal act helps to prevent others from making the choice. Ultimately, lives are saved.

Adding Complexity

Some U.S. states have codified their lower limits for different categories of drivers, like those who drive trucks or city buses. Some states have lower-tier drunk driving laws for those above .05, like the tiered categories of speeding tickets. More and more, the legalization of marijuana for recreational or medical use has put states in a whole new world of lawmaking, because this kind of "influence" needs to be quantified too, especially when combined with alcohol. How should we combine BAC and marijuana intoxication levels to form one aggregate blood intoxication scale? These questions are being asked and debated now.

Officer Discretion

The baseline drunk driving laws in most states mean that officers have no compunction in arresting someone above .08, but officer discretion can easily turn a lower breathalyzer into a DUI charge. How a suspect acts, responds to questions, and performs in any field sobriety tests all factor into this decision. If a suspect takes medication that interacts with alcohol or uses other drugs in addition, they're likely more impaired at the same BAC as another person who doesn't take those same drugs or medications. You can also be charged with impaired driving or other crimes if you've taken *only* non-alcohol drugs like opioids or sedatives.

Prozac Nation

Anyone who believes "pleading insanity" is a way out of criminal punishment has too much faith in the underfunded American mental health system ... and prosecutors.

✳   ✳   ✳   ✳

Background and Stigma

THE INFAMOUS "TWINKIE defense" was more of an insanity defense—an unusual craving for Twinkies and other abrupt changes in diet, energy level, and mood indicated the suspect's severe depression, his defense team claimed. Bystanders want to believe people pleading not guilty by reason of insanity are faking it, but it's not clear *why* people want them to be faking it. Is our attachment to the idea of swift, severe justice so firm that even debilitating mental illness can't shake it?

Our understanding of this complex issue is made even cloudier by the fact that different states use different standards for what qualifies as "insanity" in the legal sense. (No doctor, clinician, or other medical professional uses "insane" anymore, in any other context than the rest of us should too: as an adjective to describe the insanely good Buffalo wings we had last night, for example.)

Varying Standards

Policies change, but as of 2017, there is just one U.S. state without any form of insanity defense: Kansas. Three more states, Idaho, Montana, and Utah, have the option of a "guilty but mentally ill" verdict, but this subtle distinction usually doesn't translate to a different sentence, including that these convicted "mentally ill" people can still be sentenced to death. New Hampshire uses the strictest standard of any state with an insanity plea: the defendant must prove that the crime was a direct result of their mental illness and wouldn't have happened if they didn't have that mental illness. (New Hampshire also still has the death penalty. "Live Free or Die," indeed.)

The rest of the states use one of two protocols to define their standards that must be met for a valid insanity plea. Details vary, of course. In some states, the defendant must assert their own legal insanity and satisfaction of the standard using medical records, expert witnesses, and more. In other states, the prosecution must assert the "sanity" of the defendant by highlighting expert findings, lucid interviews, or anything else they feel is relevant.

Reality Check

The insanity plea is overrepresented in fiction but makes up less than 1% of criminal cases in reality. And, of course, the overwhelming majority of mentally ill people are not violent or criminal.

What about so-called "temporary insanity"? This is a true novelty, with limited applications in the last two centuries. There isn't protocol or a standard to define it. Examples in pop culture are most likely an exaggeration for drama's sake.

Lawyers Are Bad

Lawyers are evil bottomfeeders, and anyone who hires one is trying to play hardball.

✳   ✳   ✳   ✳

THE JUSTICE SYSTEM of the United States, and much of our Bill of Rights, is built on the idea of fair due process for all Americans. These rights are one of the cornerstones of a free and functional democracy, because citizens must be heard in order for a society to be held accountable. Qualified representation by an expert is one of these rights too.

Like Almost Any Other Job

Lawyers are convenient whipping boys when we feel unsatisfied with how our justice system is working, but their performance is no better or worse than that of any other professional. No one likes every doctor they ever go to. People hate and fear their dentists in statistically notable numbers. But our dislike doesn't mean that we don't *need* these professionals.

Times when people need lawyers are often among the most stressful, draining, and confusing in their lives. They or someone they love have been accused of something, sued, wronged in some way, or harmed. There is a power dynamic between the average person and the maze of courts that make up the U.S. justice system, and people grasp for meaning wherever they can when they feel frustrated and powerless. An advocate helps to bridge the gap between those average people and the system that is scrutinizing them or their loved one.

The Dark Side

Certainly there *are* evil attorneys, the same way there are evil bus drivers, CEOs, or bank tellers. But even the idea of the ambulance-chasing attorney is confusing. People who have been injured have the right to sue to recoup their medical expenses. There may be a factor to blame that someone in a place of business should have noticed and fixed. No one is a villain for simply asking these questions—if the answers are no, then everyone can find closure and move on.

Criminal law seems to speak directly to our hearts, and the idea of someone spending their career helping to "get guilty people out of jail" certainly sounds bad. But every American to ever be arrested for anything has the right to consult a lawyer, and there are countless reasons that accused people owe it to themselves and their families to do exactly that. A fair day in court is built into the bedrock of this nation.

Port in a Storm

A legal expert is there to proverbially hold the accused's hand. To simply railroad everyone we suspect is a criminal is what authoritarian governments do—not the beacon of democracy for the world. If an accusation and the evidence supporting it were not gathered legally or are otherwise vulnerable to attack by a defense attorney, that's a sign that the justice system is functioning as it was intended to.

We live in the "plea bargain" era of American jurisprudence, an issue that's hotly debated by legal scholars and civil rights activists because of the misleading and unethical ways prosecutors present plea bargains much of the time. Average people are not experts and they have no reasonable way to know the whole story of what's being offered to them. A competent lawyer can be the difference between the plea that inconveniences you but adequately addresses your crime, and the plea that puts a black mark on your criminal record and ruins your career.

On the Bright Side

These are complicated questions that demand nuanced attention. Most attorneys offer consultations for exactly these reasons, because counseling people on the best course of action—not just in court after they're hired, but at every step, beginning with the first phone call—is their legally defined and regulated job. Corporate attorneys may still seem like "sellouts" or whatever the relevant term may be, but the same could be said of any highly paid corporate worker, and none of it is unique to lawyers.

If you're ever in a position when you or someone you know needs a criminal attorney, keep this in mind: State's attorneys who manage staffs of prosecutors have to run for reelection and campaign on numbers of convictions and other statistics. Private attorneys and public defenders are hired with no elections to answer to. They work for you. Public defenders may be overworked or relatively new attorneys, but they hold your interest at the core of their work, not their political careers.

Show Me the Money

If a police officer can't prove I was speeding, I can't get a ticket.

✳   ✳   ✳   ✳

THIS MYTH IS redolent of wishful thinking, right? We can smell the hopeless cause. Police officers use radar guns to clock the speed of passing cars, but there are many other ways in which they can ticket you for speeding.

If you're a driver, consider a time you were on the interstate going at or near the speed limit when a reckless vehicle blew past you. You likely thought or even said aloud, "They must be going a hundred miles an hour." Cops are no less aggrieved by this kind of driving, and at high speeds they can simply ticket for reckless driving. Cars that are climbing rapidly in speed may not give a clear radar gun reading, and it's nonsensical to believe that exempts them from speeding tickets—"80 miles per hour and climbing" is the accepted parlance for someone with a lead foot in progress.

Obstructing traffic by driving too slowly or disrupting it by driving too fast are both easily spottable by police, as is going at or above the speed limit during inclement weather that should cause you to slow down. Some states even allow a regular old speeding ticket for a cop's impression of your speed. And the radar gun works better than you think, so the times at which you can in fact be clocked at speed are more often than you'd guess.

Independence Days

The U.S. Declaration of Independence was not signed on July 4.

✳   ✳   ✳   ✳

MOST PEOPLE KNOW that Christmas is a somewhat arbitrarily chosen date to celebrate a specific event, but few know that the U.S. Declaration of Independence was signed on August 2. Independence Day is celebrated on the day that the final text was approved, which is quite a publishy choice for the national holiday, especially when independence was *declared* on July 2. Future president Thomas Jefferson wrote the first draft, which was returned by the Continental Congress reduced in volume by about 25%. Who did Jefferson think he was— Charles Dickens? Perhaps this is why they picked the day of final edits to become the nation's official day of independence.

If July 2 were celebrated as the date instead, that would perhaps rule out one of the nation's favorite pieces of founding-father trivia: President John Adams and President Thomas Jefferson died on the same day, July 4, 1826, exactly 50 years after approving the final Declaration. The story would be less pithy if it were 50 years . . . and two days.

The Right to Trans Fat

Since the beginning of the 1980s, the so-called "Twinkie defense" is mentioned as shorthand for an outlandish defense plan in a criminal case—the same way the hot McDonald's coffee suit came to embody nanny-state frivolous lawsuits. But the truth is that Twinkies were invoked as the evidence of defendant Dan White's clinical depression.

✳ ✳ ✳ ✳

CHANGES IN WEIGHT and appetite are still listed among the symptoms of major depressive disorder in the Diagnostic and Statistical Manual of Mental Disorders. You could argue that the Twinkie defense was ahead of its time in that way. White was accused of murdering gay rights pioneer Harvey Milk and the mayor of San Francisco, so to use an unconventional defense drew even more attention to a high-profile injustice.

During his brief political career as a social conservative, White had strong support from police, who were wary of the gay culture emerging into daylight from the city's shadows. He struggled with decisions that felt like there was no ethically or morally right answer, and he probably should have honored his original feeling that political life wasn't right for him. But White later died by suicide, indicating that his severe depression was no copout.

Missing the Window on Missing Persons

The most insidious myths about law or policy are those that discourage people from seeking help when they need it. One of the worst of these is the idea that police don't want to hear about a missing person until 24 or 48 hours have passed.

✳   ✳   ✳   ✳

POLICE ARE DEPICTED as the heroes or the villains, in what seems like a 50/50 split. One of the most common villainous fictional police moves is to tell a frightened or panicked family member that they must wait 47 and a half more hours before they can report their missing sibling or spouse or in-law.

Certainly there are cases when police won't take immediate action about a missing person, because grown adults can take weekend trips or go off the grid when they aren't in danger. But in any situation where there's reason to suspect danger—missing work with no notice, leaving unattended animals, signs of home invasion, or other incongruous behaviors, or when the person is a child or a vulnerable adult, police can often start working right away.

More than that, acting quickly to find missing persons increases the odds of finding those people and finding them unharmed. If in doubt, call and ask anyway. If the police say no, you can always call Liam Neeson.

You're Gonna Need a Warrant for That. Or Probable Cause.

Jay Z isn't a lawyer, but he was right about the locked parts of his car being exempt from a search—well, mostly right.

❊   ❊   ❊   ❊

IN "99 PROBLEMS," JAY stops a cop who wants to "look around your car a little bit." In real life, police can only search your car if you consent to the search, and you can always say no to that request. But if the police officer has probable cause, they can search your car without your permission.

Car searches mostly come about because of suspicions of drugs. If police see drugs or drug paraphernalia out in the open in your car, that can count as probable cause to remove you from the vehicle and search the rest. If police smell smoke or other indicators, or if a drug dog scents on your car, that can also count as probable cause for a more comprehensive search.

Jay's response to the police is to say his glove compartment and trunk are locked and therefore off limits. For police to search any part of your car that isn't visible to the naked eye, they need probable cause, a warrant, or the driver's consent. Whether some parts are locked or not is immaterial—if an officer with probable cause asked you to open the trunk and you refused, that could be used against you as well.

But Jay is spot on that you should know your rights and be prepared. For some groups in the U.S., encounters as simple as traffic stops may quickly turn into serious threats of bodily harm.

Desperately Seeking Miranda

The reading of Miranda rights is one of fiction's favorite crime tropes. Detectives ask in hushed tones if their fellows have read the suspect their rights yet and it's very dramatic—will they have to let the suspect go? But you don't have to hear your Miranda rights until you're being interrogated.

✳   ✳   ✳   ✳

TELEVISION CRIMINAL SUSPECTS are always running out the door on a technicality, which isn't untrue to life, necessarily, although real-life suspects are often found not guilty in *court* based on technicalities rather than in the heat of the arrest moment. Crime shows help to perpetuate the myth that a suspect is as good as gone if the arresting officers did not read the Miranda rights. But this is only required before a suspect is interrogated, and failing to issue the Miranda warning doesn't mean the suspect is simply free to leave.

Any testimony using suspect comments from before they were Mirandized is just not usable in court, so detectives or officers must somehow get the suspect to repeat a damning confession or other piece of evidence again *after* they've been Mirandized. By then, the suspect's hackles are up.

These fictional officers make us feel like suspects have gotten away with a crime, because usually the officers are the good guys in the show. But Miranda rights are meant to protect civilians against overreaching by the law. Police can ask questions without Mirandizing if their goal is simply to learn more or get actionable information like the location of a kidnapped person or the loot from a robbery.

Of course, that information then forms the basis for evidence. Does that make it fruit of the poisoned tree? This is why people need attorneys. If in doubt, stay quiet.

Ocean's None

Glamorous bank robbers seem to live luxe lives of crime. Real bank robbers might be able to afford a used getaway car.

✳ ✳ ✳ ✳

REAL BANK ROBBERS are a sad bunch. Year-to-year average bank-robbery takes vary, but in the U.S. they're never more than about $10,000, which isn't enough to buy even the cheapest new car in *Car and Driver*'s list of 2017's cheapest new cars. (For the record, the stick shift Nissan Versa S is that car, and it's about $13,000.) In most years, the average is well below $10,000.

Exceptions to Prove the Rule

There are, of course, the more proverbial and wealthy bank robbers—Wall Street fatcats who make millions or billions of dollars by short-selling stocks or running hedge funds. But the age of the simple stick-'em-up bank robbery career is over. In the time between 1975's *Dog Day Afternoon* and 1994's *Trapped in Paradise*, bank robbery went from the center of a major dramatic movie plot to the symbolic act that begins a story of un-thought-out buffoonery. But Al Pacino's character in *Dog Day Afternoon* was also foiled by his robbery plans. The story unfolds as a tragedy.

Glamorous Heists

In 2001, the revived *Ocean's 11* followed the template of heist movies rather than simple bank robberies. The unique vault deep beneath Andy Garcia's casino offered a target much more like a rare diamond than a vanful of cash, and this reflects how consumer or even business banks were less and less appealing as targets in the new millennium. Today, tellers often can't open a cash drawer at all, instead using digital counting machines to dispense amounts of cash that are typed into a log. Banks have cameras everywhere and, usually, armed security. Even J.K. Rowling's *Harry Potter* books and the adapted movie series include a bank robbery with postmodern, wizardly twists to keep it fresh and interesting.

Boring Motives

Those who still rob banks in real life usually do it because they plan to get more cash than from a "consumer" robbery (meaning a convenience store or other business). But the takes are usually, on average, not very different—and bank robbers are apprehended by police at much higher rates because of the security measures in place at banks.

Prosaic Mosaic

Vice President Al Gore never said he invented the internet. He did play an influential role, though, which he may have overstated in the moment.

✳ ✳ ✳ ✳

Private and Public

BY THE EARLY 1990s, the internet had existed in some form for decades. The U.S. military led development of network technology, incentivized by how much a secure network could benefit them. The invention of Ethernet, in early forms of the same cables we use today, helped to revolutionize the *intra* net, meaning groups of connected machines at offices and other work sites. Computer scientists worked hard to find the best ways for data to travel on these lines.

But the burgeoning internet relied on connecting discrete and often faraway machines. These early connections via phone landlines simply couldn't carry much data at all, especially compared to the instant response time of local networks. (This difference persists: well into the oughts, gamers still gathered 'round for LAN parties, and many new games are released with "local multiplayer" modes.)

The Gore Bill

Gore, then a U.S. senator, created and introduced the High

Performance Computing Act of 1991, usually shortened to the Gore Bill. President George H.W. Bush expressed optimism about what the "Information Superhighway" (remember that?) would mean for life in America and around the world. In a way, the kind of infrastructure that Senator Gore had learned about and pushed among his colleagues is, in layman's terms, an extremely huge local network. Instead of one pipeline that runs down the center of the office building, one proverbial, enormous pipeline runs the breadth of the United States.

An Auspicious Beginning

This was an ambitious and astronomically large undertaking. Vice President Gore may have fumbled the catch when he spoke vaguely about his role in this legislation, but he has plenty to be proud of. The bill funded the project that became the Mosaic internet browser, one of the very first to place images into websites. The Mosaic browser, developed with government funding at the University of Illinois, represented a huge step forward in accessibility and availability of the internet to an average computer user. And it preceded, by just two years, the launch of Netscape Navigator—the first major consumer web browser, developed in part by a former Mosaic engineer.

The Aftermath

It's hard to imagine now, or even remember, that these early browsers were not free. Microsoft "disrupted" the browser industry by using parts of Mosaic to build Internet Explorer, which was first released in 1995 as a bundled free alternative that could wipe Netscape Navigator off the map. Strangely, Microsoft caused the entire browser industry to pivot to a freeware model, with some browsers going a step further by being open source. The internet we have today may not be the vision shared by Vice President Gore and President Bush at the time, but it is built on their forward-looking decisionmaking with the 1991 Gore Bill.

Radar Is In the Details

Police speed radar doesn't work in the rain or snow. An officer must show me the radar reading. In other words, some technicality will let me weasel out of this speeding ticket.

✳ ✳ ✳ ✳

MOST DRIVERS WHO regularly go over the speed limit know that their time will eventually come. It's just the law of averages. Over a long enough sample time, you have to expect any statistically likely outcome to happen. But that doesn't mean drivers don't contort themselves with rationalizations about how it won't happen to them.

Let's review some common speeding myths. If they make you sad, maybe you can cry to get out of a ticket.

1. **Radar doesn't work in the rain.:** Technology improves by leaps and bounds, and modern radar guns are very sensitive. That said, your gut feeling that police officers don't want to pull you over in the rain because it's cold and wet and a drag is probably right.

2. **If I'm in a group, I won't be pulled over.:** If a cop can get a reading on one of the cars in a group and can eyeball that all the cars are going around the same speed, they can pull over anyone they want from that group.

3. **Officers are working against a speeding-ticket quota.:** This is a sticky one, because police officers shouldn't be subjected to quotas and usually insist publicly that they aren't. But if you've had a job and felt the pressure to perform up to a certain standard, you know how consequences can be implied or held over your head. In any case, a police officer can't use you to fill their quota if you aren't speeding, talking on your handheld smartphone, or committing some other obvious offense, so it's still your fault at the end of the day.

4. **Police can't conceal themselves in order to use radar without my noticing.:** Officers can "hide" wherever they like, whether after a narrow overpass or down a sneaky runoff. It's funny to claim that this isn't fair, since speeding is optional, unless you're Sammy Hagar.

5. **An officer needs to show me the radar reading if I ask.:** This is wishful thinking. A police officer on the clock who's just doing their job isn't going to feel lenient toward you for arguing over technicalities. More importantly, if they show you the radar gun, there's no easy way for a layperson to tell if the speed on the screen is from five minutes or five hours ago.

6. **My radar detector will protect me.:** Radar detectors are a great idea, and if a cop is simply flashing continuous radar into interstate traffic or another situation that requires quantity like that, radar detectors do work. But a cop picking off individual cars can blink their radar gun on and off in as little as a second. No one's brakes work that quickly, and you'd wreak havoc if you tried. Now, in the era of the speed camera, one major advantage of radar detectors is that some models let users set up the areas where speed cameras are found. That alone can pay for the radar detector in automated ticket savings.

7. **Police have to lock in my speed for my ticket to be valid.:** The extensive training and ethical obligations of police officers mean that their word is almost always good. If they see a reading and then accidentally erase it, you don't magically have your honor restored.

Illinois's Little-Known Black Codes

Did Illinois ban the immigration of black people into the state in 1862?

✳   ✳   ✳   ✳

NOT ONLY THAT—ILLINOIS remained a slave state until the Emancipation Proclamation. In fact, the biggest myth of all in terms of Illinois's relationship to slavery is that it was a true-blue northern state. In reality, Illinois clung to severe laws that limited any free black traffic through the state, instead treating even casual travelers as though they must be someone's slaves by the very fact that they were black. It was actually illegal to free slaves in Illinois.

This kind of policy, and the length of time for which Illinois clung to it, puts the state in line more with Georgia than New York. So the rest of the nation was not surprised when Illinois residents easily voted to codify its anti-black laws in 1862, and the state kept these laws in place even as it ratified the thirteenth amendment in 1865.

Poorly Kept Secret

Undercover police don't have to identify themselves if asked.

✳   ✳   ✳   ✳

TELEVISION DETECTIVES ARE prone to blurting out information that's convenient for the plot. They get mixed up with the wrong people, or their bosses are corrupt and they must team up with the bad guys in order to find the *real* justice. There are all kinds of reasons it benefits a fictional character to look severe or concerned and ask an undercover law enforcement official, "Are you a cop?" The same applies to drug dealers and sex workers who ask the cursory question before going ahead with a transaction.

In reality, cops are able to lie in a variety of contexts in order to do their jobs well and safely. Some are more readily debatable, like the way cops can lie in order to arrange stings with drug dealers or sex workers. But for cops on undercover assignments that require temporary identities and effective cover, their lives may be in danger if they're found out. Police can also lie to you inside the interrogation room. Coerced confessions often come from scenarios where, for example, detectives tell an exhausted suspect that they can go home after they just write out this quick little confession.

Chapter 7

Presidents

Anyone Can Be President...Almost!

With hard work, reasonable intelligence, and a lot of money, anyone can be president, allegedly. But what if you weren't born in the United States? You still have a shot—if you have the right parents.

✳ ✳ ✳ ✳

WHEN JOHN MCCAIN ran for the presidency in 2000 and 2008, some argued that his being born in Panama made him ineligible for the highest office. The opposition had a field day, chiding McCain for defying the founding fathers' wishes—but they were wrong: It is possible to have been born on foreign soil and still be commander in chief.

According to the U.S. Constitution, Section 1, Article II, a "natural-born citizen, or a citizen of the United States...shall be eligible for the Office of President." So who is considered to be a natural-born citizen? In 1790, the first naturalization law stated that "the children of the citizens of the United States that may be born beyond sea, or out of the limits of the United States, shall be considered as natural-born citizens." McCain's parents were American citizens, so even though he was not born within the bounds of the United States, he qualifies as being "natural born."

However, it would require a change in the Constitution to allow former California governor Arnold Schwarzenegger to seek the presidency. Although he has been a naturalized U.S. citizen since 1983, he was born in Austria to Austrian citizens, which disqualifies him for the presidency. Schwarzenegger has said he supports a constitutional amendment that would allow him to run.

The Executive Office

One would assume there were precise rules about who might be president and vice president and who should succeed them. We asked around and learned it's not at all clear-cut.

Q: Who's in line to be president?

A: The vice president, of course, followed by the Speaker of the House of Representatives and the president pro tempore of the Senate. After that it goes to the Cabinet: secretary of state, secretary of the treasury, secretary of defense, attorney general, and on through the rest of the cabinet posts. The secretary of homeland security is last.

Q: Can an immigrant become president?

A: No. "No Person except a natural born Citizen, or a Citizen of the United States, at the time of the Adoption of this Constitution, shall be eligible to the Office of President." That's out of Article II of the Constitution. Because no one is still alive from 1788 (the year the Constitution was ratified), most legal scholars interpret this to say that one must be born to U.S. citizenship to be eligible for the presidency.

Q: How about vice president?

A: The 12th Amendment says that no one ineligible to be president can be elected vice president. However, that amendment mainly governs the meeting of the electoral college—an important distinction. If the president appoints you vice president, you aren't elected.

Q: Can a two-term president run for vice president?

A: There's debate about it. The 12th Amendment seems to rule it out. The 22nd Amendment says you can't be elected more than twice; it doesn't say you can't run, just that the electoral college electors cannot elect you. However, if the elected vice president died or resigned, the president could presumably appoint a former two-term president as vice president. Some argue that this means the former two-term president isn't constitutionally ineligible at all, and thus could actually be elected vice president. The Supreme Court prays it will never have to rule on the subject.

Q: What does it really mean when we "impeach" a president?

A: This caused a lot of confusion when it almost happened to President Richard Nixon. Everyone assumed "impeach" meant "remove." It doesn't. If you impeach someone, you have damaged that person's honesty or credibility. When Congress passes articles of impeachment against a president—which more or less translates to "The president has wronged"—it can then choose to vote to remove him or her. Andrew Johnson and Bill Clinton are the only U.S. presidents who have actually been impeached.

Sick Assumptions

An ill person can't be a good president.

✳ ✳ ✳ ✳

WE CAN SET aside bias toward the sick or disabled at first as we examine this myth, because those who believe it probably have good intentions. In an American culture that already values hard work to an extreme degree, which we joke is the "puritanical work ethic," the duties of a president seem strenuous in terms of physical hours and tasks *and* the emotional toll of countless different stresses. In fact, presidents with "too much downtime" are ridiculed for being ineffectual.

Many historians now believe President Abraham Lincoln, considered by most to be our greatest president, suffered from clinical depression and perhaps a glandular disorder that caused his exceptional height. These theories are not offered to undermine Lincoln's presidency but to explore his secret life as a human being. Our feelings toward presidential health are probably more motivated by fear of secrecy than a fear of actual physical health problems.

President John F. Kennedy suffered from a number of serious health problems that he worked hard to treat. President Dwight D. Eisenhower had both a heart attack and a stroke while in office. Both men had flaws and made decisions we may not agree with, but there's no reason to link these decisions with a physical health problem. After all, if a completely able-bodied president made a decision we didn't agree with, we would blame that president's judgment—not their health.

There are two extreme cases of presidential physical health, on opposite ends of the spectrum. President Woodrow Wilson suffered a debilitating series of strokes and his wife Edith basically acted as president in his place, which hindsight shows us was not the correct course of events. On the other hand,

President James Garfield was shot in the gut on July 2, 1881, which was only several months into his term. He survived for more than a month and a half despite the inept doctors who stuck their unwashed fingers into his wounded body, and he suffered unbelievable pain as infection slowly took his life. Garfield remained President until the moment he died.

The logical flipside of any suggestion that a sick person can't be a good president is that a healthy and able-bodied person is automatically a better candidate. Certainly this isn't true in the first place, but a healthy person can become a sick person in the blink of an eye. While president, Lyndon B. Johnson had his gallbladder and a stone from his ureter removed. During a post-surgery press conference, Johnson lifted his pajama top to show off his 12-inch scar.

In the Beginning

Presidents must swear the oath of office on the Holy Bible.

❋　❋　❋　❋

THE FIRST TEN amendments to the U.S. Constitution, and several of the next ten, are firmly and repeatedly taught in U.S. schools. But many of us grow cloudy on the amendments after the nineteenth. The twentieth amendment, in fact, is the constitutional guide to inauguration, declaring the day and time that power is handed over and providing for contingencies if elected officials are unable to serve.

Congress had realized over time that the staggering of elections, constitutionally required congressional sessions, and inauguration day for the president created dismayingly long lame duck times for many officials. But the twentieth amendment does not say anywhere, at any point, that anyone needs to swear on a Bible, nor does the original constitution.

So did anyone deviate from the tradition? President John Quincy Adams, a bit of a troublemaker in terms of tradition and etiquette, did not swear on a Bible but instead a book of constitutional law.

Some presidents have been sworn in privately—in 2009, a spoken error in President Obama's reinauguration meant they held a second ceremony the next day for formality's sake. Much is made of the heritage of the Bibles used by each president-elect, and this may account for our mistaken belief that the Bible must be involved. The Bible has been one of the bestselling books in the Christian world for as long as there have been books to buy. It was what motivated Johannes Gutenberg to complete his printing press in the first place. Since there has never been a non-Christian U.S. president, the Bible may be the one book that every single presidential household was sure to own.

A few presidents-elect, mostly early in the nation's history, have used whatever Bible was on hand. *The West Wing* makes light of this when President Jed Bartlet is unable to liberate his own historical family Bible from its place in a museum—they struggle to find another Bible on hand to replace it and threaten to fly his family Bible to Washington in its own airplane seat.

President George Washington used a Masonic copy of the Bible in his inauguration, a fact that has somehow escaped the mainstream of America's favorite pastime: conspiracy theorizing.

Awkward Inaugurals

Presidents are friendly when they pass power from one to the next on Inauguration Day.

✳   ✳   ✳   ✳

THERE'S NO RULE that says U.S. presidents need to be kind or even courteous to each other during the transition of power. This may be why the exceptions—kind letters from the previous First Lady to the next or from the President to his successor—usually make the news. President George H.W. Bush wrote a gracious, encouraging missive to President Bill Clinton, after famously saying, "My dog Millie knows more about foreign affairs than these two bozos." President Obama's letter to President Trump was bipartisan and hopeful in tone and spirit.

* President John Adams and his son President John Quincy Adams both chose not to attend the inauguration of their respective successors.

* President Herbert Hoover and President Franklin Delano Roosevelt looked like a hostile family Thanksgiving during Roosevelt's inauguration.

* President Harry Truman made a point to bring President Dwight D. Eisenhower's son home from combat in Korea, ostensibly to make a point. Eisenhower was furious at the disruptive special treatment.

TRUMAN

A Crazy Notion

Presidents cannot be mentally ill.

✳   ✳   ✳   ✳

As MORE AND more Americans are diagnosed with chronic but completely manageable mental illnesses like clinical depression, this myth cuts closer and closer to home. Why do we want to believe that a person with depression or another similar condition can't serve as president?

Historians who study the documents and behaviors of past presidents have found evidence that they believe indicates about half of the first 37 presidents had some kind of mental illness. Remember that alcoholism is a medical condition that counts in this category as well.

Some voters may say that past evidence of mental illness doesn't mean we can't suss out any mentally ill candidates today and prevent them from taking office. Certainly every voter is free to vote for whatever candidate they choose, but limiting the pool of candidates by filtering out recovering alcoholics, those with treatable depression, and the countless others whose conditions are well managed does not leave much of a variety.

Scholars have suggested in recent years that President Abraham Lincoln may have self medicated his depression or anxiety with a patent concoction (snake oil, in other words) with a high concentration of mercury, which may have contributed to mood swings and ill health prior to his tenure as president. He stopped taking the medicine during his presidency and was notably more even tempered, according to their research.

Lies My Teacher Told Me

Do presidents need to have a college education?

✳ ✳ ✳ ✳

NO ONE IN the United States is scrutinized so closely as its presidents, whose words—especially after the advent of radio, television, and internet—are often written down for posterity and safekeeping. Myths about the stupidity of George W. Bush, who often bumbled words in his public addresses, have grown larger than life. But there's no evidence that he is "stupider" than anyone else. He also has a law degree from Yale.

Modern politicians are more homogenized in terms of level of education and career (Aaron Sorkin's White House drama *The West Wing* jokes about its characters almost all having gone to law school), but earlier presidents were farmers and landholders. Some were classically educated and most were insatiably curious readers. President Thomas Jefferson sold his library of nearly 6,500 books to the Library of Congress after it was decimated by a fire. He said he'd accept "any price" for the books and noted that a Congressperson might need to refer to any subject under the sun.

The Private Thoughts of Presidents

What religion was [insert president here]?

✳ ✳ ✳ ✳

MUCH IS MADE of the relative religiosity—all on the Christian spectrum—of U.S. presidents. But each U.S. president to date is a professed believer in God. Some founding fathers famously were deists, but even these were still versed in the Bible and rejected organized religion or certain specific beliefs. Almost all presidential speeches conclude with a spin on "God bless America," and presidents have always evoked God and religious belief in both sincerity and gentle jest.

Who Elects the Electors? (We Do)

Is the Electoral College a conspiracy?

✳ ✳ ✳ ✳

Opaque Issues

IN THE AFTERMATH of any major election, a small percentage of roughly half the country's voting population takes to the internet or the airwaves to decry some part of the electoral process. Everything becomes a conspiracy—well, everything except the issues that may actually represent conspiracies, like jerrymandered districts or voter disenfranchisement. The Electoral College is a victim of such coping mechanisms. Is it a threat to our democracy?

Partisan Noise

This question grows very technical very quickly, and it's easy to see why this is durably fruitful ground for conspiracy theorists. There may be bipartisan or nonpartisan activism to eliminate or modify the Electoral College, but it's almost impossible to find amid the partisan protesting that their party did not win a particular election. In fact, the strongly partisan nature of reaction to the Electoral College is probably part of why it is never held up to scrutiny in a serious way.

In the Details

Most people's complaints about the Electoral College are mistakes of perception. The popular vote in a state may come down to tiny differences, but the electors in that state still vote for the candidate who won that popular election, whether in one large group that all votes the same or in a proportion that matches how the state's vote was divided. This can lead to an overall impression that the popular vote went one way and the Electoral College went another, when the vote is exactly right on a state-by-state basis.

A Huge Change

If voters really do want to abolish the Electoral College, that takes a step toward federalizing elections—meaning lumping the entire United States together—which may not make sense in a nation that has such strong state and local identities. But proponents argue that many states already have staunchly divided areas that resent each other for their influences on shared politics.

Regardless of where anyone falls on the issue of the Electoral College, it's a widely misunderstood institution that we could stand to reevaluate, if only to make the process more transparent to American voters.

They Sound More Like Tractor Tires

Was West Wing's Big Wheel of Cheese Day based on real events?

✳ ✳ ✳ ✳

PRESIDENTIAL CHEESE IS the stuff of legend. The term "big cheese" was inspired after a cheesemaker brought a 1,200-pound wheel of cheese to President Thomas Jefferson. Citizens declared it the "big cheese," referring to both the wheel and its important recipient.

But the cheese lore in question refers to President Andrew Jackson. In 1835, a different cheesemaker delivered a 1,400-pound wheel of cheddar to President Jackson. The appreciative president, whose love of cheese was well known, gave the cheesemaker a dozen bottles of wine and his hearty thanks. At the order of the president, the cheese was allowed to age for two years in the White House lobby. According to historians, Jackson served the cheese at a White House party.

No source is sure whether he encouraged passersby to stop in to sample his lobby cheese.

Big White Lies

Did the White House get its name after being painted white in 1814?

✳ ✳ ✳ ✳

THE FIRST PRESIDENTIAL residence was actually gray sandstone, and it was whitewashed periodically to prevent wear and tear to the stone. It was repainted white after the War of 1812 to cover smoke stains sustained when the building was burned by Canadian troops. But even then, the White House wasn't known as such. As with the First Lady and other president-adjacent people and objects, the presidential residence didn't have an official name and was referred to by various terms before one was generally settled on. This presidential domicile has also been called the "President's Palace," the "President's House," and the "Executive Mansion." In 1901, President Theodore Roosevelt officially gave the White House its current name.

Prince Arthur

Did President Chester A. Arthur replace the White House furniture because it wasn't good enough?

✳ ✳ ✳ ✳

NOT ONLY THAT—HE sold the old furniture to help raise the money. Known as "Prince Arthur" for his fine and fancy taste, President Arthur thought the White House needed a spruce when he took office after the death of President James Garfield. His love of comfortable accommodations and dining was well known to his partymates, and no one was very surprised. During Arthur's time as president, the issue of temperance began to grow in importance, especially with women activists, as embodied by legends like Carrie Nation. When asked about his drinking habits, President Arthur responded,

"Madam, I may be President of the United States, but my private life is nobody's damn business."

The White House was renovated a few other times to varying degrees, including by President Harry Truman, whose renovation was complete and more like a "gutting."

To Be Fair, He Wasn't Wrong

Did President Benjamin Harrison make his domestic staff turn the lights on for him?

✳ ✳ ✳ ✳

PRESIDENT HARRISON AND his wife were both afraid of the new electric lighting installed in the White House in 1891. At the time, even Thomas Edison's "safer" form of current, direct current, could easily electrocute someone; and Edison and Tesla were still embroiled in the Current Wars that inspired Edison to electrocute over a dozen animals using alternating current in front of audiences. So the president wasn't out of line, but it was unkind to press the risk on the White House workers instead.

Dark Times, Great Laughs

President Abraham Lincoln was one of the greatest presidents in U.S. history for his devoted, self-sacrificing leadership during the Civil War. But he was also a world-famous story- and joke-teller with a natural knack for comedy. Is this reputation legit?

✳ ✳ ✳ ✳

THE RELENTLESS STRESS of President Lincoln's political and personal life only increased the need for a sense of humor. Lincoln was a gifted writer and communicator whose talent for words lent itself to his dry wit. Lincoln's humor was rich and smart but never snobby, and his one-liners alone could fill a volume. He wanted to be liked and respected, and he practiced the Golden Rule. President Barack Obama cited Lincoln as one of his more special influences, visible in Obama's almost relentless use of analogies and other more "regular" language. Obama even held President Lincoln's Bible as he took the oath of office. From Lincoln this homespun wit and wisdom flowed naturally.

His life's correspondence—public remarks, letters, telegrams, and transcripts—fills seven volumes. Even in the darkest moments of the Civil War or his family tragedies, Lincoln was gracious and funny to all who crossed his path. He was sometimes less so to those who crossed him personally.

✳ "I have no speech to make to you; and no time to speak in. I appear before you that I may see you, and that you may see me; and I am willing to admit that so far as the ladies are concerned I have the best of the bargain, though I wish it to be understood that I do not make the same acknowledgment concerning the men."

✳ "MY DEAR SIR: —Herewith is the diplomatic address and my reply. To whom the reply should be addressed—that is, by what title or style—I do not quite understand, and therefore I have left it blank."

✳ "That part of the country is within itself as unpoetical as any spot on earth; but still seeing it and its objects and inhabitants aroused feelings in me which were certainly poetry; though whether my expression of these feelings is poetry, is quite another question."

✳ "I certainly know that if the war fails the administration fails, and that I will be blamed for it, whether I deserve it or not. And I ought to be blamed if I could do better. You think I could do better; therefore you blame me already. I think I could not do better; therefore I blame you for blaming me."

✳ "You don't know what you are talking about, my friend. I am quite willing to answer any gentleman in the crowd who asks an intelligent question."

* "I appreciate him certainly, as highly as you do; but you can never know until you have the trial, how difficult it is to find a place for an officer of so high rank when there is no place seeking him."

* "I think I can answer the Judge [Douglas] so long as he sticks to the premises; but when he flies from them, I cannot work any argument into the consistency of a mental gag and actually close his mouth with it."

* "Logan is worse beaten than any other man ever was since elections were invented."

* "I shall prefer emigrating to some country where they make no pretense of loving liberty,—to Russia, for instance, where despotism can be taken pure, and without the base alloy of hypocrisy."

* "This is not a long letter, but it contains the whole story."

* "We hold these truths to be self-evident, that all British subjects who were on this continent eighty-one years ago were created equal to all British subjects born and then residing in Great Britain."

* "Has it not got down as thin as the homeopathic soup that was made by boiling the shadow of a pigeon that had starved to death?"

* "I am rather inclined to silence, and whether that be wise or not, it is at least more unusual nowadays to find a man who can hold his tongue than to find one who cannot."

* "Men are not flattered by being shown that there has been a difference of purpose between the Almighty and them."

Lincoln's Repatriate Act

Did President Abraham Lincoln believe in repatriating freed slaves to Africa or Haiti? If so, did he later change his mind, or not?

✳ ✳ ✳ ✳

AH, ONE OF the stickiest wickets of them all: the relative racism or bigotry of our greatest president. We've always known that young Lincoln supported repatriating freed African Americans to colonies in Africa or Haiti. In fact, he tried one disastrous experiment with free black people sent to Haiti, where they died of starvation or disease until the survivors eventually had to be rescued. But historians disagree about his perspective later in his political career. After the Emancipation Proclamation, some insist that President Lincoln still believed in repatriation. And they claim that this new insight should cast President Lincoln's legacy in a whole new light.

It doesn't need to. Lincoln pushed for and signed the Emancipation Proclamation. He acted in the cause of abolition and made enormous sacrifices toward that cause. Whatever President Lincoln believed privately about African Americans, he publicly crusaded for their right to be free and to stay in the United States if they wished. No comment, writing, or any other record ever shows Lincoln to suggest African Americans should be *required* to repatriate anywhere. That difference is critical.

Repatriation had its roots in the idea that there were slaves in America whose living relations were still in Africa. Instead of repatriation, it was a kind of reunion. Of course, racial attitudes were bewildering at the time and white repatriatists were relieved to have an option that simply removed black people from America. The fact that repatriation made sense to some African American people at the time does not excuse the racism of the white people who campaigned for it.

President Lincoln's public legacy is one of liberation, period. We can never know what Lincoln believed in the deep recesses of his heart, and for him to be a true proponent of racial equality would have made him a needle in a haystack at the time. But his policies and his efforts following the Emancipation Proclamation all planned to enforce the freeing of every slave in the United States, and he never said publicly that he believed freed slaves should be forced elsewhere.

The failed colony of freed slaves in Haiti is a complicated story all by itself. The Union had crafted a clever loophole to avoid returning escaped slaves to the Confederacy by declaring these free people to be spoils of war, basically. They were known as "contrabands" because of the technical definition that allowed them to stay in the North. But northerners at the time were not much less racist than their southern counterparts and didn't make any notable effort to help contraband people to settle or find employment. In the North, abolitionists had long featured lighter-skinned African-Americans as a way to make them seem more "palatable" to fellow white people—a specific form of racism perpetuated by white people, usually called colorism, that continues today.

This ambivalent climate made many contraband people jump at the chance to volunteer for an exploratory trip to Haiti to establish a colony of freed American slaves. The idea of a new life in a historically black nation, albeit one with grave political upheavals of its own, was an unknown quantity that could turn out to be good. Soon, competing expeditions began a kind of war for the public's goodwill, and no one won, least of all the free black people who simply wanted to start a new life. For these people, there was no freedom to be found in America, at least not yet.

"Wars produce many stories of fiction, some of which are told until they are believed to be true."

— ULYSSES S. GRANT

Outré House

Did President Abraham Lincoln really tell the crass story depicted in the 2012 film Lincoln?

❋ ❋ ❋ ❋

OUR GREATEST AND most human president was a raconteur at heart. His varied and challenging life gave him a wealth of rich material, and he had realized early in his career as a river boat worker, let alone later as an attorney and politician, how much a good story could win people over.

After President Lincoln's shocking death, the public swarmed to meet a train that traveled with the slain president's body. Lincoln's onetime legal partner and friend, William Herndon, set about chronicling his friend's life and times in a way that honored his memory. Among these stories and anecdotes was, of course, an infamous joke about Ethan Allen finding a portrait of President George Washington hanging in a bathroom. The punchline is:

"There is nothing that will make an Englishman —— so quick as the sight of General Washington."

Advance Notice

Did President Abraham Lincoln write the Gettysburg Address on an envelope on his way to the battlefield?

❋ ❋ ❋ ❋

OUR AMBIVALENT AMERICAN values emerge again in this myth. We cherish hard work and the great results we believe it can produce, but something is so charming and charismatic about a speech dashed off at the last minute. Any college student with a major paper due in the morning can relate.

President Lincoln was a careful and meticulous writer. He made drafts and we still have several of these drafts. But

Lincoln did not write the final draft, the text that he delivered on the battlefield that day, until after he arrived in Gettysburg. It was not written on the train.

No word on the many thousands of tourists who may have written the Gettysburg address, and maybe even directions, on the backs of *their* envelopes. Zing! President Lincoln might even have enjoyed that joke.

In Dentures

President George Washington had wooden teeth.

✳ ✳ ✳ ✳

THIS EXTREMELY POPULAR and durable myth is a bit baffling. Sure, it isn't true, but it's also not clear why Americans are so interested in it after more than 225 years. And historians can't find evidence of anyone at all having wooden teeth in the United States. Unless you used a super hard wood, you'd feel about the same as if you gummed your food instead.

President Washington had high oral hygiene standards by all measures for his time, but by nearly 60 when he became the first U.S. president, he had lost all his teeth.

Today, we expect to keep our own teeth for our entire lives if we're able, but that wasn't true for many of our grandparents or even parents. At some points, dentists encouraged people to simply have the rest of their teeth pulled and jump ahead to the denture phase. President Washington kept his teeth for a long time by the standard of his time.

Washington's dentures were made by placing ivory, animal teeth, and human teeth on a metal base. At the time, it was fairly common (for wealthy people like President Washington) to use human teeth from the deceased or that were lost by living people. In fact, the wealthy aristocrats of Europe had a field day making dentures from the healthy teeth of thousands of soldiers who died at Waterloo 1815 during the Napoleonic Wars, giving rise to the term "Waterloo teeth." You could argue that a patriot like President Washington would choose wood over the teeth of those who fell in combat. But really, we'll never know.

Expense Account

Was General George Washington really a spendthrift?

✳ ✳ ✳ ✳

WHEN WASHINGTON TOOK over the Continental Army in 1775, he refused to accept a salary. Perhaps he did so to demonstrate sacrifice and solidarity with the "have-nots," a group that included soldiers under his command. Many praised Washington without knowing that he had carte blanche to use government funds.

From September 1775 to March 1776, Washington spent more than $6,000 on alcohol alone. And during the harsh Valley Forge winter of 1777–78, while his troops died of hunger and exposure, Washington indulged his appetite. An expense-account entry included "geese, mutton, fowls, turkey, veal, butter, turnips, potatoes, carrots, and cabbage."

By 1783, Washington had spent almost $450,000 on food, saddles, clothing, accommodations, and sundries. In today's dollars, that's $5 million. When he became president, Washington again offered to waive his salary in favor of an expense account. The offer was politely refused, and he was paid a $25,000 stipend. It seems America could no longer afford the general's brand of sacrifice.

Originally the title of the leader of the United States was supposed to be "His Highness the President of the United States of America and Protector of the Rights of the Same." Washington, however, disliked the use of "His Highness" and settled upon simply "Mr. President." Fortunately, Washington's humility about his title suited the end of his king's-ransom expense account. There's no related term "president's ransom," though abuse of public funds for lavish meals and other personal use is still a prominent part of political life in these United States.

Take My Job, Please

Did John Adams really hate being George Washington's vice president?

✳ ✳ ✳ ✳

A DAMS HIMSELF IS known to have said:

"My country has in its wisdom contrived for me the most insignificant office that ever the invention of man contrived or his imagination conceived."

Certainly he earned himself a reputation when he suggested President George Washington should be honored as "His Majesty," and maybe this got Adams off on the wrong foot with Congress, who began referring to Adams as "His Rotundity."

After his own term as president, Adams didn't attend the inauguration of President Thomas Jefferson. He had strong feelings in general, and spoke out against Jefferson.

"The Declaration of Independence I always considered as a Theatrical Show. Jefferson ran away with all the stage effect of that; i.e. all the Glory of it."

But President Adams may have had his own reasons for doing so. As he said:

"No man who ever held the office of president would congratulate a friend on obtaining it. He will make one man ungrateful, and a hundred men his enemies, for every office he can bestow."

I Cannot Tell a Lie, Except This One

The cherry-tree myth is well known, but how did it begin?

✳ ✳ ✳ ✳

PRESIDENT GEORGE WASHINGTON was a world-renowned war hero and leader. But the only anecdote most people know about the first president, besides another whopper about his wooden teeth, is the infamous cherry tree legend, fabricated by a "biographer" who was concerned that Washington seemed too dull. Perhaps he was right: Washington's inaugural address was 31 pages long, and the original pages were later given away by a bored historian.

Illusions of Grandeur

President George Washington was not the first president.

✳ ✳ ✳ ✳

THIS "GOTCHA!" IS a favorite of contrarians or sticklers, because someone served as president of the Continental Congress. That man's name is John Hanson, and it's clear he hasn't remained much in the public imagination since his time in the job. But his job was different from "president of the United States" as written into the U.S. constitution, a job which George Washington fortuitously decided to accept.

Soused in Session

Did Vice President Andrew Johnson open a Congressional session while drunk?

✳ ✳ ✳ ✳

HE DID! DESPITE his legacy as the tough, stalwart military governor of his home state of Tennessee, Johnson infamously relied on booze to steel himself for the beginning of his term as vice president.

Lincoln supported and advised Johnson, then Tennessee's military governor but previously both a congressman and a senator, as he beat back rebel insurrection and held his state's government together with scant and hard-won shoestrings. Some in Johnson's state even accused him of being Lincoln's puppet.

"The movement set on foot by the convention and Governor Johnson does not, as seems to be assumed by you, emanate from the National Executive."

—ABRAHAM LINCOLN

Though he held views we now find repugnant—he opposed rights for liberated African Americans and struggled with public, very racist beliefs—those views had evolved quickly and were often set aside in Johnson's service for his nation. By all measures, he was a brave patriot through and through.

But public speaking rattles even the bravest people. The morning he took the oath as vice president, he drank too much whiskey (arguably any amount is too much in the morning on a work day) and went on an anti-Southern rant. Johnson was too intoxicated to swear in the new senators; a Senate clerk had to handle it.

"The inauguration went off very well except that the Vice President Elect was too drunk to perform his duties and disgraced himself and the Senate by making a drunken foolish speech. I was never so mortified in my life, had I been able to find a hole I would have dropped through it out of sight."

—SENATOR ZACHARIAH T. CHANDLER

Lincoln defended Johnson, who was not only a tried-and-tested friend to Lincoln and the Union but also an ideal complement for the Republican ticket: Johnson was a pro-Union Democrat. And Johnson became more of an introvert, let's say, after his very public run-in with Liquid Courage.

"I have known Andy for many years . . . he made a bad slip the other day, but you need not be scared. Andy ain't a drunkard."

— ABRAHAM LINCOLN

In the Morning Nudes-Paper

Was John Quincy Adams caught skinnydipping by reporter Anne Royall?

✳   ✳   ✳   ✳

O H, THERE ARE few myths we want to be true as badly as this one. First, the good news: President John Q. Adams did swim naked in the Potomac River. The nudity sounds scandalous, and it may have been; but if the alternative were a "bathing costume" made of cotton or wool, we'd all be tempted to ditch our kit for the skinny. The legend says that President Adams took these swims in the very early morning and continued until age 79.

Reporter Anne Royall was an exceptional woman. Like brave and lovely Margaret Fuller a few decades afterward, Royall traveled and wrote about her journeys and experiences. She was not a proto-papparazzo staking out the president's swimming hole. In fact, she and President Adams were friends, and there would be no need to "catch" him to get an interview.

But it was Royall's grit and determination that led evangelical Christians to create the scandalous rumor. She had joined the workforce in late middle age as a widow with no income, and she quickly found herself the subject of a great deal of unflattering attention from traditionalists who believed women shouldn't work in such a public field. She was even arrested and convicted of "scolding," which is like hysteria . . . except louder.

A couple of factually inaccurate plaques helped to legitimize the rumor of Royall's alleged riverbank exclusive with the president. Multiple monuments to Royall perpetuated these myths and misinformation about her life, and interested parties—descendants of the same zealots who had convicted Royall of being a "scold"—protested when the fallacious plaques were removed decades later.

Stretching the Truth

Did noted dark novelist Nathaniel Hawthorne write a fawning biography of President Franklin Pierce? The bromance is strong in this true story. Hawthorne, most famous for his novel The Scarlet Letter, *wrote an 1852 biography of Franklin Pierce that didn't exactly tell the whole truth and nothing but the truth—his book practically defines misinformation. Pierce was an otherwise un-noteworthy president.*

✳   ✳   ✳   ✳

ANY STUDENT IN the United States who was ever made to read Nathaniel Hawthorne's *The Scarlet Letter*—or who watched a movie version instead—knows the writer to be a purveyor of dark moral warnings. But Hawthorne did a nigh unrecognizable about-face when he wrote a loving, maybe even fawning, biography of his friend Franklin Pierce.

The two men were born the same year and met as teens, and the lifelong friendship between them was real. Less real was the version of Pierce presented in Hawthorne's biography, which was timed to coincide with the 1852 presidential election.

"This frankness, this democracy of good feeling, has not been chilled by the society of politicians," Hawthorne wrote, in one of many rosy depictions of Pierce's general lack of having distinguished himself in almost any way—besides being anti-abolition.

Hawthorne himself admits he's out of his comfort zone writing nonfiction (ahem) about an old friend. Of course, money talks, and Hawthorne was richly rewarded with a lucrative foreign position in the Pierce administration. In the twenty-first century parlance, we might call this biography "sponsored content."

It's a Trap

How many battles made up 1858's Utah War?

✳ ✳ ✳ ✳

THIS IS A trick question. President James Buchanan sent a
federal army to assert authority over the unruly Utah territory. The war was immensely unpopular with the American
public, who considered the entire expedition unnecessary
and expensive. Buchanan was happy to resolve it in 1858.
Aside from destroyed property, the Utah War, or "Buchanan's
Blunder" as it was called, ended without a single pitched battle.

A Superior Summer

*President Calvin Coolidge spent the summer of 1928 fishing in
Wisconsin and working out of a nearby high school.*

✳ ✳ ✳ ✳

IN THE LONG summer days before air conditioning,
Washington, D.C. must have been unbearable. With temperatures that easily reach the high 90s and a lot of sunshine,
the gaggles of governing men in suits must have jumped at the
chance to spend a summer in northern Wisconsin at the invitation of a senator. They shut down the local high school and
turned it into the presidential office building during their stay.
Superior High School has since been demolished, but a plaque
remains at the site to memorialize its onetime use as a summer
home. President Coolidge even invited his opponent Herbert
Hoover to visit. He might not have done so if he'd known
Hoover was going to beat him.

President Coolidge wasn't the only one to escape the summer
heat of the White House. President Abraham Lincoln and
his family spent much of each year at nearby Soldier's Home,
which was one of the highest points in Washington, a bit like
the high-altitude summer capital the British established during

their colonization of India. High elevation meant cooler temperatures and more breezes.

Try Again

Did President Calvin "Silent Cal" Coolidge silence a White House guest with his austere wit?

❋　❋　❋　❋

THIS STORY SEEMS too good not to be a myth, but it comes from President Coolidge's own First Lady and appears as canon on the White House website. Grace Goodhue Coolidge may have remembered the story from a time before they occupied the White House. Even if she or President Coolidge himself thought it up, it's a great standalone joke that helps to illustrate his nature. We'll never know for sure, but the anecdote goes that a young woman sitting next to President Coolidge at the dinner table said she bet she could get him to say "at least three words" to her. He apparently answered, "You lose."

Old Rip

Did President Calvin Coolidge meet a famously long-lived toad?

❋　❋　❋　❋

THIS LEGEND WILL never be definitively proven or disproven, but the toad did in fact meet with President Coolidge. A living horned toad was once placed into the cornerstone of a building in Texas as an informal experiment. Thirty-one years later, more than 3,000 people gathered. When the old cornerstone was opened and the dusty and apparently lifeless horned toad was held up, it began kicking a leg and looking for breakfast. Dubbed Old Rip after Rip Van Winkle, the horned toad allegedly lived another year, during which it toured the United States and received a formal audience with President Coolidge.

Somewhat Unpleasant

Did President Grover Cleveland really claim a 9-year-old girl as his future wife?

❋ ❋ ❋ ❋

Reader, he married her.

President Cleveland was one of very few bachelors to ever be elected U.S. president. In the 1870s, already almost middle aged, he was asked about his continued bachelorhood. He dibsed the young girl who would eventually become his wife, although at the time she was just 9. He was reported to say: "I'm only waiting for my wife to grow up."

True to his word, he wed Frances Folsom in the Blue Room of the White House on June 2, 1886, an event that turned Folsom into the youngest first lady in our nation's history: Cleveland was 49 years old, and Folsom was just 21.

The Best Possible Fact

Was President Gerald Ford really a male model in his youth?

❋ ❋ ❋ ❋

The presidential hits just keep on coming. Young Gerald Ford worked as a male model through his 20s and was even a cover model on *Cosmopolitan* magazine. The young, handsome, athletic Ford had an all-American image that was highly prized during his youth, and he even met his future wife while he was working as a model.

Un-Filtered Oration

Did President Jimmy Carter really claim to have seen a UFO?

✳ ✳ ✳ ✳

ALTHOUGH HIS ONE term in office is the stuff of wisecracks and failed expectations, President Carter's extensive, tireless humanitarian work since then may make him our greatest living president. But it's true that he claims he once saw an unidentified flying object. "It was the darndest thing I've ever seen," he said publicly about the incident, where he claims he and a group of others watched a mysterious, inexplicable light for about ten minutes. Of course, President Carter was a model citizen in the Jimmy Stewart vein, and he filed a report about his sighting. That was the only reason it eventually came out in the press.

We'll Take His Word Anyway

Did President Theodore Roosevelt touch off the myth that piranhas are vicious mob predators?

✳ ✳ ✳ ✳

HE DID! YOU can thank President Roosevelt for his help in spreading the myth of the piranha as a relentless, bloodthirsty carnivore. During a trip through Brazil in 1913, Roosevelt witnessed a piranha feeding frenzy that caused him to label the fish "the embodiment of evil ferocity."

But according to historians, Roosevelt was the victim of a setup. A local ichthyologist blocked off a section of river with nets and stocked it with thousands of pole-caught piranha, which were left unfed for several days.

When Roosevelt and his entourage arrived by boat, they were warned not to stick their hands in the water because of the vicious fish that lived there. Skeptical, Roosevelt and the journalists who were with him demanded proof, so an ailing cow was driven into the water, where it was immediately devoured by the starving piranha.

Roosevelt was awestruck and he went home with a tale of terror that remains popular to this day, inspiring countless movies, documentaries, and campfire tales.

It's definitely a myth. Go ahead, take a swim. At least a shark won't mistake you for a dolphin ... allegedly.

Frost Nixin'

Was poet Robert Frost hindered in his reading by the sunshine at President John F. Kennedy's inauguration?

✳ ✳ ✳ ✳

THERE ARE DEMONSTRABLE facts in this claim, and there are conjectures. Robert Frost did perform a poem at President Kennedy's inauguration, and he did opt to recite a poem from 1942 that he had memorized, instead of the newly written poem he brought to the inauguration. Was he discouraged by the bright sunshine, the glare off of the January snow, or his own typewriter's faded ink? We can never know for sure. It could have been all three. Frost was 86 years old at the time, and he was one of few people at the inauguration to die before President Kennedy's horrible and untimely death. Frost was 88 when he passed away in January of 1963.

That Princeton Bite

Bookish, mercurial President Woodrow Wilson had a biting wit that rivaled President Abraham Lincoln's.

✻ ✻ ✻ ✻

PRESIDENT WILSON WAS backward-looking in some ways, like his published writings on racial purity, his strong push for segregation, or and his screening of the *Birth of a Nation* in the White House. His term has been looked at askance because of the way his wife Edith was the de facto president after Wilson's catastrophic stroke in 1919. In 1912, it took 46 rounds of ballots before he was chosen as the Democratic nominee for president.

But he was a former Princeton University president with several published books and a reputation for a razor-sharp tongue. He also believed in women's suffrage after the strong role women were willing and able to play in World War I. Wilson's administration oversaw the crafting and passage of the nineteenth amendment to the U.S. constitution.

President Wilson is divisive but was a brilliant thinker. His *bon mots* are less funny than those of President Abraham Lincoln, but reading them gives the impression Wilson might be scrappier in a no-holds-barred war of words.

✻ "A boss is a much more formidable master than a king, because a king is an obvious master, whereas the hands of the boss are always where you least expect them to be."

✻ "A conservative is a man who just sits and thinks; mostly sits."

✻ "Business underlies everything in our national life, including our spiritual life. Witness the fact that in the Lord's Prayer, the first petition is for daily bread. No one can worship God or love his neighbor on an empty stomach."

* "The purpose of a university should be to make a son as unlike his father as possible. By the time a man has grown old enough to have a son in college he has specialized."

* "If you think too much about being re-elected, it is very difficult to be worth re-electing."

* "If you were on the desert of Sahara, you would feel that you might permit yourself,—well, say, some slight latitude in conduct; but if you saw one of your immediate neighbors coming the other way on a camel,—you would behave yourself until he got out of sight."

* "The way to stop financial joy-riding is to arrest the chauffeur, not the automobile."

* "There are blessed intervals when I forget by one means or another that I am President of the United States."

* "Conservatism is the policy of making no changes and consulting your grandmother when in doubt."

* "It is certainly human to mind your neighbor's business as well as your own. Gossips are only sociologists upon a mean and petty scale."

* "No man is genuine who is forever trying to pattern his life after the lives of other people, —unless indeed he be a genuine dolt."

* "Uncompromising thought is the luxury of the closeted recluse."

* "I would not for the world discredit any sort of philanthropy except the small and churlish sort which seeks to reform by nagging. [...] Are we to allow the poor personal habits of other people to absorb and quite use up all our fine indignation?"

* "A mob is a body of men in hot contact with one another, moved by ungovernable passion to do a hasty thing that they will regret the next day."

Hoo Boy

Was Hoover Dam named, unnamed, and renamed for President Herbert Hoover?

✳ ✳ ✳ ✳

PRESIDENT HOOVER WAS a divisive figure, to say the least. It's possible that no course of action could have spared the United States from the Great Depression, but Hoover became a stand-in for failed efforts to spend the Depression away. When a cabinet member suggested the incipient Boulder Dam be named for President Hoover, his idea was met with derision and controversy, but the name stuck for a while. After Hoover lost his reelection bid to President Franklin Delano Roosevelt, the name was changed back to Boulder Dam.

But the dam flip-flopping caused confusion with average citizens and cartographers alike. In 1947, Congress passed a resolution to name the dam Hoover Dam once and for all. After its star turn in *National Lampoon's Vacation*, the Hoover Dam is here to stay, in name and in fact.

Ambidextrous Vehicle

Did oft-overlooked President Gerald Ford throw two first pitches at the 1976 All-Star Game?

✳ ✳ ✳ ✳

AT THE 1976 ALL-STAR Game, the athletic and ambidextrous Gerald Ford thrilled fans by throwing one pitch right-handed to Johnny Bench of the Cincinnati Reds and a second pitch left-handed to Carlton Fisk of the Boston Red Sox. He could write with either hand and did some athletic moves with one versus the other. His first-pitch overachievement helped create the contrast between himself and President Jimmy Carter: one an all-American athlete and father figure, the other a country scholar with an eye on environmentalism.

Of course, President James Garfield could write Latin with one hand and Greek with the other — at the same time. But that will never earn you a $72 million contract.

Not a Sports Fan

Did President Jimmy Carter refuse to throw out a first pitch during his term?

✳ ✳ ✳ ✳

PRESIDENT CARTER MADE no secret of the fact that he wasn't much of a sports fan, and he only went to one baseball game during his time in office. Of course they offered him the opportunity to throw out the first pitch, and millions of people are salivating at the idea of throwing out *any* first pitch, let alone at game 7 of the World Series.

But Carter passed up the chance. Certainly if he couldn't throw a ball well, a badly thrown first pitch could be worse than not doing it at all. Maybe he simply didn't want the attention or to disrupt the fans' excitement over the last game in the series. The rejected offer helped to cement his reputation as something of an untraditional president. Contrast with President Dwight D. Eisenhower, who once said, "I wanted to be a real major league baseball player, a genuine professional like Honus Wagner." Or President Richard Nixon, who's considered the most avid baseball fan to ever serve as president.

After just one term, President Carter chose not to run for reelection. "My name is Jimmy Carter, and I'm not running for president," he famously said in a speech, trying to poke fun at his own unconventional place at a convention. Years later, he added, "I can't deny I'm a better ex-president than I was a president."

Hats Wracked

Did President John F. Kennedy kill hats?

✳ ✳ ✳ ✳

YOUNG, CHARISMATIC, AND bold, President Kennedy spoke in sweeping sea-to-shining-sea-isms that helped propel postwar America into a time of great prosperity, advancement of knowledge, and power. His legacy is debated with great energy: Was he a good president or is he famous for his good looks and shocking assassination? But one thing is for certain: Kennedy had a lasting impact on hats.

President Kennedy sparked a surprisingly durable rumor when he did not wear a hat to his inauguration. His choice coincided with the continued decline of the hat, which shrank in the 20th century from *de rigueur* to baseball caps in restaurants. Was Kennedy's slight indeed one small step for hats, one giant leap for hatkind?

The truth is that Kennedy wasn't wearing a hat when he took the pledge, but he wore a fine silk hat for much of the rest of the day both before and after. Kennedy didn't like hats and avoided wearing them when he could. He felt they made him look too old, and as the youngest-ever U.S. president and strong mobilizer of the liberal youth vote, he wanted to keep his image young and vital.

President Dwight D. Eisenhower didn't wear a hat for the majority of his first inauguration ceremony, and it didn't seem to cause any kind of a fracas. If politicians had that sort of influence on fashion, President Barack Obama could have ruined the tie industry with his love of an open top shirt button. President Donald Trump may start a trend for candyfloss hairstyles previously only seen in the *Hunger Games* series.

There's an entire book dedicated to debunking the myth that President Kennedy caused the downfall of the derby. In his book *Hatless Jack*, journalist Neil Steinberg confirms that fashion is indeed fickle. Of course, books upon books are written about the clothing choices of first ladies and women politicians, so it's about time a gent joined the ranks of the scrutinized.

Fishing Term

President Grover Cleveland used his one-term presidential sabbatical, the only one in U.S. history, to write a collection of his reflections and essays about fishing and the outdoors.

✳ ✳ ✳ ✳

GROVER CLEVELAND'S POLITICAL career had a unique respite: the four years between his discrete terms as president. His young wife Frances bore the first two of the family's five children during this time, and Cleveland discovered a fanatical love of fishing. His hobby reached a zenith when he published a book of his thoughts about the outdoor arts.

There aren't many common threads to pull between Cleveland and his contemporary Theodore Roosevelt, but they shared an earnest love of sport and a belief in its curative, educational powers. Cleveland throws in a lot of prescriptive sass, too. Both great men could be called haughty transcendentalists at heart.

"Thus, when short fishing excursions have been denounced in a mendacious newspaper as dishonest devices to cover scandalous revelry, I have been able to enjoy a sort of pleasurable contempt for the author of this accusation, while congratulating myself

on the mental and physical restoration I had derived from these
excursions."

— GROVER CLEVELAND

A Tall Yalta Tale

*Did President Franklin Delano Roosevelt's health jeopardize the
U.S. during the leadup to the Cold War?*

✳ ✳ ✳ ✳

THERE'S NO DOUBT that President Roosevelt was in poor
physical health by the time negotiations took place after
the end of World War II. Famously, the British physician
accompanying apparent *paragon of health* Prime Minister
Winston Churchill made a comment that President Roosevelt
did not seem fit to attend. But Roosevelt's health issues were
all physical.

He had congestive heart failure, meaning a then-terminal
accumulation of fluid in the lungs, and dangerously high blood
pressure. Certainly he was in rough shape and had to work
hard to attend these negotiations, but his mind was clear and
sharp. Conflating physical health with mental wellness is a
slippery slope to biased thinking toward people with physical
disabilities or limitations—something we in the twenty-first
century know is a fallacy.

Chapter 8

Wellness

Warts

Can you roll the tape to clear up a plantar wart? What about vitamin C?

✳　✳　✳　✳

MOST PEOPLE HAVE one of these ugly bumps at one point or another. Warts are caused by the human papilloma virus (HPV) and are contagious. That's why an initial wart can create a host of others. Common warts are the rough-looking lesions most often found on the hands and fingers. The much smaller, smoother flat warts can also be found on the hands but might show up on the face, too. Warts that occur on the soles of the feet are called plantar warts and can sometimes be as large as a quarter. Genital warts, which have become a more common problem, develop in the genital and anal areas. If you suspect that you have a genital wart, see your doctor; do not try the remedies suggested here.

No one knows why warts occur and disappear and later recur in what appears to be a spontaneous fashion. For example, some women say they develop warts when they become pregnant, but the gnarly lumps disappear soon after they have their babies. A medical mystery also surrounds the fact that researchers have yet to find a way to get rid of warts for good. The solution may lie in developing a wart vaccine, but an approved, safe vaccine has yet to be created. That leaves the wart sufferer with two options: Having a dermatologist treat the warts or trying a few methods on their own. As for home remedies, some people swear by certain tactics, while others will never have any success with them. And it seems that in some cases, prevention may be the best medicine. Here are some tips to help you be wart-free.

Be sure it's a wart. First and foremost, before you try any type of treatment, know whether your skin eruption is a wart or another condition. Warts (except the small, smooth flat wart) commonly have a broken surface filled with tiny red dots. Moles, on the other hand, are usually smooth, regularly shaped bumps that are not flesh colored (as flat warts can be). A rough and tough patch that has the lines of the skin running through it may be a corn or a callus. There is also a chance that the lesion is skin cancer. You may be able to recognize skin cancer by its irregular borders and colors. But if you have any doubt, ask your doctor. In addition, if you have diabetes, circulation problems, or impaired immunity, do not try any home therapy for wart removal; see your doctor.

Don't touch. The wart virus can spread from you to others, and you can also keep reinfecting yourself. The virus develops into a wart by first finding its way into a scratch in the skin's surface—a cut or a hangnail, for instance. Even shaving can spread the flat warts on the face. Inadvertently cutting a wart as you trim your cuticles can cause an infection. So keep viral travels to a minimum by not touching your warts at all, if possible. If you do come in contact with the lesions, thoroughly wash your hands with soap and hot water.

Stick to it. An effective treatment for warts that's cheap and doesn't leave scars is adhesive tape. In fact, a 2002 study found that tape therapy eliminated warts about 85 percent of the time, compared to a standard medical treatment using liquid nitrogen, which was only successful on 60 percent of warts. Wrap the wart with four layers of tape. Be sure the wrap is snug but not too tight. Leave the tape on for six-and-a-half days, and then remove the tape for half a day. You may need to repeat the procedure for about three to four weeks before the wart disappears. You can try this on a plantar wart, but be sure to use strips of tape that are long enough to be properly secured.

Try castor oil. The acid in castor oil probably does the trick by irritating the wart. It works best on small, flat warts on the face and on the back of the hands. Apply castor oil to the wart with a cotton swab twice a day.

"C" what you can do. Vitamin C is mildly acidic, so it may irritate the wart enough to make it go away. Apply a paste made of crushed vitamin C tablets and water. Apply the paste only to the wart, not to the surrounding skin. Then cover the area with gauze and tape.

Heat it up. One study found that having patients soak their plantar warts in very hot water was helpful because it softens the wart and may kill the virus. Be sure the water is not hot enough to cause burns, however.

Don't go barefoot. Warts shed viral particles by the millions, so going shoeless puts you at risk for acquiring a plantar wart. The best protection is footwear. Locker rooms, pools, public or shared showers, even the carpets in hotel rooms harbor a host of germs—not just wart viruses. You can catch any of a number of infections, from scabies to herpes simplex. Never go barefoot; at the very least, wear a pair of flip-flops.

Keep dry. Warts tend to flourish in an environment that's damp, especially in the case of plantar warts. That's why people who walk or exercise extensively may be more prone to foot warts, says the American Academy of Dermatology. So change your socks any time your feet get sweaty, and use a medicated foot powder to help keep them dry.

Take precautions with over-the-counter preparations. The Food and Drug Administration (FDA) has approved wart-removal medications made with 60 percent salicylic acid, but most common over-the-counter remedies contain 17 percent. While the stronger formulas may work well for adults (except for those who have sensitive skin), they are not recommended for children. Salicylic acid works because it is an irritant, so no matter which strength of solution you use, try to keep it from irritating the surrounding skin. If you are using a liquid medication, do this by smearing a ring of petroleum jelly around the wart before using the medication. If you're applying a medicated wart pad or patch, cut it to the exact size and shape of the wart. Apply over-the-counter liquid medications before bed and leave the area uncovered.

Cover your cuts and scrapes. The wart virus loves finding a good scratch so it can make its way under your skin. By keeping your cuts and scrapes covered, you'll help keep the wart virus out.

Organic Food

Organic food is not more nutritious than conventional food. But you may still have good reasons to purchase it.

FARMERS HAVE USED natural substances that repel bugs or weeds for thousands of years. The USDA has national standards for "safe" amounts of both natural and synthetic pesticides and herbicides, and both conventional and organic foods fall into the safe zone by these standards.

In thousands of studies, scientists have found that organic food can have equivalent "chemical" content with no nutritional advantage over conventionally grown food. For people whose interest in organic food was based on the myth that these foods are more wholesome and nutritious, the news was staggering.

There are still reasons to seek out organic foods if you choose to. Some consumers like the idea of a simpler approach to farming where organic protocols are followed. They may fear genetically modified crops (which scientists also do not find to be dangerous or nutritionally compromised) or appreciate bolstering a farming system that avoids the involvement of major international farming conglomerates and their patented chemical blends.

Some kinds of produce tend to absorb more surface chemicals than others, and you can find guides to these fruits and vegetables online. You may find that you want to seek out organic grapes or apples but don't mind buying conventional bananas. And, of course, you may find that conventional produce is the right choice for you and your family—and your budget.

What a Pill

Am I healthier because I take a daily vitamin?

✳ ✳ ✳ ✳

ALMOST ALL PHYSICIANS recommend that people try to get their recommended daily amounts of vitamins and trace minerals from food. Supplements are costly and often they're made of forms of vitamins or minerals that are less understood. Something about the way vitamins are carried into our bodies as they naturally occur in food makes them absorb into our systems and be more effective.

Usually, you'll be told that it probably doesn't hurt to take a vitamin. That's true if you stick with a typical consumer vitamin, although research is examining the role of vitamins all the time and our understanding could change. The known danger now is for vitamins that offer very high doses, like B vitamin supplements, which seem like the sky is the limit with the daily recommended value percentage they offer. Can taking 10,000% of anything really be good for you?

Sunburns

The discomfort of sunburn can lead us to try outlandish things, but the effective methods are surprisingly simple, and they don't include that neon-colored aloe gel.

✳ ✳ ✳ ✳

PEOPLE HAVE WORSHIPPED the sun for thousands of years, but only in the past century have humans worshipped the sun by intentionally baking themselves to a golden tan or, as may be more often the case, an angry red burn beneath it. Although few things can penetrate the skin's outer layer (*stratum corneum*), the sun's ultraviolet rays easily pass through this protective envelope and damage the cells and structures found beneath.

A tan develops because pigment-producing cells called melanocytes produce brown pigment (melanin) to protect the skin from invading rays and prevent further damage to the skin's structures. Dark-skinned people more readily produce melanin, while light-skinned individuals don't produce it well or produce it in blotches that appear as freckles. This latter group burn easily, even with mild sun exposure.

Despite the dangers the sun poses, many of us are lax about protecting our skin. If you end up with a painful sunburn, the following remedies can help ease the pain. Keep in mind, though, that these remedies cannot reverse the damage caused by unprotected exposure to the sun's rays, damage that can lead to skin cancer. The best protection is to stay out of the sun.

Apply cool compresses. Soak a washcloth in cool water and apply it directly to the burned areas (do not put ice or an ice pack on sunburned skin) for several minutes, rewetting the cloth often to keep it cool. You can also add a soothing ingredient, such as baking soda or oatmeal, to the compress water. Simply shake a bit of baking soda into the water before soaking the cloth. Or wrap dry oatmeal in cheesecloth or a piece of gauze and run water through it. Then toss out the oatmeal and soak the compress in the oatmeal-water solution.

Take a soak. Slipping into a tub of chilly water is a good way to cool the burn and ease the sting, especially if the burn is widespread or on a hard-to-reach area (such as your back). Avoid soap, which can irritate and dry the skin. If you feel you must use soap, use a mild one, such as Dove or Aveeno, and rinse it off well. Definitely skip the washcloth, bath sponge, and loofah. Afterward, pat your skin gently with a soft towel. If you're usually tempted to linger in the tub for hours, take a shower instead. Soaking too long can cause or aggravate dry skin, which can increase itching and peeling.

Toss in some oatmeal. Adding oatmeal or baking soda to bathwater may help soothe skin even more than applying a compress or just soaking in plain water. Prepare the oatmeal as you would for an oatmeal compress, holding the bundle under the faucet as the tub fills, or buy Aveeno oatmeal powder at your local pharmacy or health-food store and follow the package directions. If you use baking soda, sprinkle it liberally into the water. Soak no longer than 15 to 20 minutes to avoid overdrying the skin.

Drink up. You can easily become dehydrated when you are sunburned. Drink plenty of fluids, especially water, like you would if you had a fever. You can determine whether you're hydrated enough with a quick check in the bathroom: If your urine is relatively clear, you're doing fine. If it's dark, you need to drink more water.

Apples and Oranges

Does an apple a day keep the doctor away?

✳ ✳ ✳ ✳

YES AND NO. Certainly apples, which are especially good for you if you eat them with the skin on, are part of a healthy diet that can help prevent disease and support your health. People who regularly eat apple are also more likely to have other good health indicators. But the old folk-saying may date from a time when apples were the only fresh fruit many people had access to.

Apples were actually one of the major staple foods in the English colonies of the 1600s, when frightened settlers were too afraid to try the local foods they saw the "scary" native Americans eating, so they brought apple trees by the shipload. Apple pie is almost unheard of in Britain but it was one of the only celebration foods in the early colonies. Centuries later, it's the go-to dessert for any true-blue American potluck.

Insect Stings

You hear the buzz, you see the bee, but before you can act— Oweee! You've been stung. Almost all of us have had this experience at least once, and it's no fun. But you can take the ouch out of being stung with simple household materials, and there are other often-repeated things you shouldn't try.

✳ ✳ ✳ ✳

FOR MORE THAN 2 million people in the United States who are allergic to the venom of stinging insects, however, the consequences can be much worse than a little pain. Their symptoms can include hives, wheezing, dizziness, and nausea and require emergency medical treatment. In the worst cases, shock, unconsciousness, and cardiac arrest can occur. Those who don't have such serious reactions can try the following tips to take the soreness out of a sting.

Apply meat tenderizer. Simply applying a teaspoon of unseasoned meat tenderizer mixed with a few drops of water to a sting can bring quick relief. An enzyme in the tenderizer, either papain or bromelain, dissolves the toxins the insect just shot into you. Carry a bottle filled with the solution with you when you know you're going to be in an area with bees, because it only works when you immediately apply it to a sting.

Try a baking-soda paste. Think of this as "plan B" if you don't have any meat tenderizer. Although baking soda can't neutralize insect venom, it will help relieve itching and swelling.

Scrape out the stinger. Bees and some yellow jackets have barbed stingers that anchor in your skin after you're stung. (Other stinging insects have smooth stingers that remain intact on the bug.) You should get the stinger out as soon as possible because it will continue to release venom into your skin for several minutes after the initial sting. Resist the urge to squeeze, grab, or press the stinger, however. This will just make matters worse by pumping more venom into your skin. Try this instead: Using a clean knife blade, or even a fingernail, lift the stinger up and gently scrape it away.

Put it on ice. Rub ice over the sting site. This may help reduce some of the inflammation and swelling.

A Sweet Lie

Does sugar contribute to hyperactivity in children or adults?

✳ ✳ ✳ ✳

THIS MAY BE a myth and may not be a myth, but it was probably caused by ambiguity between saying a child is "acting hyper" and saying a child "probably has attention deficit hyperactivity disorder." Sugar can spike any person's blood sugar and give them a brief little thrill, but that's a far cry from a psychiatric diagnosis.

It also doesn't make intuitive sense in the body that any amount of sugar in a child could alter their brain chemistry to induce a lifelong condition. Most *chemical medications* can't even cross the blood-brain barrier.

Blisters

Someone told me I'm getting blisters because I'm wearing the wrong socks, but I get them without socks sometimes too.

✳ ✳ ✳ ✳

BLISTERS ARE TENDER spots that fill up with fluid released by tiny blood vessels in an area where delicate skin tissues have been burned, pinched, or just plain irritated. The feet are extremely susceptible to these small, yet painful problems. Virtually everyone has experienced friction blisters, the kind caused by hot, sweaty feet, or ill-fitting shoes.

If you're tiptoeing around a blister right now, read on to learn how to take care of it. Some of these tips will surprise you.

Make a tent. Instead of simply placing an adhesive bandage right on top of the blister, "tent" the bandage by bringing in its sides so the padding in the middle of the bandage raises up a bit. A tented bandage will help protect the blister while exposing it to air, which will speed healing.

Or, just let it breathe. Some physicians believe a blister needs as much exposure to air as possible and should never be covered. You may want to give your blister a chance to "breathe" occasionally by going without a bandage, especially when you're at home and your blister is less likely to need protection from bumps and debris.

Put it up. Elevating the blistered area can help relieve pressure and temporarily ease discomfort.

Drain it. Although some doctors believe a blister should never be popped because of the risk of infection, most agree that a blister causing extreme discomfort—such as one on a toe or under a nail—is a candidate for draining. However, you should never open a blister that was caused by a burn, and you should allow a doctor to treat a large blister that might open on its own through normal activity. If you want to pop a blister, first wipe the blister and a sewing needle with rubbing alcohol. Prick the blister once or twice near its edge, then slowly and gently press out its fluid.

Keep the roof on. Once you have popped the blister and drained the fluid, do not remove the deflated top skin. This skin, called the blister's roof, protects the blister from infection and forms a "bridge" across which new cells can migrate on their journey to heal the site.

Soak first. It will be much easier to drain a blister on a tough-skinned area, such as the sole of the foot, if you spend a day or two softening it up. Soak the blister for 15 minutes three or four times a day in Burow's solution, which is available at most pharmacies (follow package directions).

Watch for signs of infection. Visit your doctor if you see redness, red streaks, or pus around a blister.

Be patient. It usually takes about a week to ten days for the body to reabsorb the blister's fluid.

A-Positive It's a Lie

Does blood only turn red when it hits oxygenated air?

✳ ✳ ✳ ✳

THIS IS A well known perceptory myth. How can our blood look blue inside our bodies and red when it comes out? As children, we might talk with our friends about how blood flowing in one direction is blue and the other direction is red, based on whether it's gone through the lungs yet.

The idea that oxygenated blood is a different color or that oxygen in the air changes the color of blood is fun to think about but no less outlandish. If that were the case, people who bled out underwater would bleed a different color than those on air. In space, our blood might not have any color at all.

In reality, our blood looks blue beneath our skin because it's further down than it looks and altered in appearance of color by the soft tissue in between.

Snoring

I've heard that I can sew a tennis ball to the back of my snoring spouse's pajamas. That can't really work, can it?

✳ ✳ ✳ ✳

SNORING (MAKING A raspy, rattling, snorting sound while you breathe during sleep) is a fairly common affliction, affecting 40 percent of men and 25 percent of women. Older people are particularly prone to snoring: About one-third of people aged 55 to 84 snore.

Snoring is a breathing and sleep disorder that can have serious medical consequences and may be a result of sleep apnea, a serious condition where breathing stops repeatedly during sleep. Sleep apnea also raises the risk of cardiovascular disease (if you or your partner is prone to snoring, visit the National

Sleep Foundation website or speak with your doctor for more information).

Because of the frustration of trying to treat snoring, there are dozens of ineffectual remedies that don't address the root causes of snoring. They offer false hope instead of proven help. The tips that follow may help you—and your bed partner— sleep more peacefully.

Sleep on your side. You're more likely to snore if you're lying on your back, and sleeping on your stomach is stressful for your neck.

Use tennis balls. Not to shove in your mouth, but to keep you from rolling onto your back during sleep. Sew a long, tight pocket onto the back of your pajama top, and put two or three tennis balls into it. (Don't sew? Put the tennis balls in a sock and then use a safety pin to both close the sock and attach it to the back of your pajama top.)

Avoid alcohol and tranquilizers. Both alcohol and sleeping pills can depress your central nervous system and relax the muscles of your throat and jaw, making snoring more likely. These substances are also known to contribute to sleep apnea. (You should never, of course, drink alcohol and take tranquilizers at the same time.)

Lose weight. Excess body weight, especially around the neck, puts pressure on the airway, causing it to partially collapse.

Treat your allergies. Chronic respiratory allergies may cause snoring by forcing sufferers to breathe through their mouths while they sleep. Taking an antihistamine just before bedtime may help. If your nose is stuffed up, try using an over-the-counter saline spray or a humidifier.

Buy a mouth guard. Your dentist or doctor may be able to prescribe an antisnoring mouth guard that holds the teeth together and keeps the lower jaw muscles from becoming too lax.

See a doctor if you are pregnant and snoring. Sometimes, being pregnant will cause women to snore. The snoring may begin because of the increased body weight and because the hormonal changes of pregnancy cause muscles to relax. Whatever the reason, snoring during pregnancy can rob your baby of oxygen. Talk with your doctor about it.

Elevate your head. Sleeping with your head raised may take some of the pressure off the airway, making breathing easier. Raise the head of the bed by putting blocks under the bedposts, or prop up your upper body (not just your head, which can actually inhibit breathing) with pillows.

Riding the Waves

Will my microwave give me cancer?

❋ ❋ ❋ ❋

INSIDIOUS MYTHS SURROUND the microwave, maybe because it still seems like an incongruous miracle product. The internet is filled with message boards where people claim they watered one plant with regular water and one with microwaved water and one plant has died. People claim that microwaved food is less safe to eat or that it's somehow chemically altered. None of this is true.

Yes, your microwave works by using radiation, but no, that radiation is not the kind that can give you cancer. The radiation from the sun does, though, as does the radiation produced by nuclear chemicals and reactions. The fact that all these things are called "radiation" doesn't mean that they all, as a rule, cause cancer.

Microwaves are just up the spectrum from radio waves, which we are all walking through all the time. Radio waves even pass through our walls! Sunlight can't do that. But no one claims that radio waves cause cancer—at least, no one without a tin-foil hat.

Sinusitis

If you have regular, chronic sinus pain, there are surprising and simple ways to try to minimize the discomfort.

✳   ✳   ✳   ✳

INSIDE YOUR NOSE is an intricate system of narrow passages and eight hollow, air-containing spaces that enable you to inhale air from the environment and process it along to your lungs. The hollow spaces, known as the paranasal sinuses, are located in pairs behind the eyebrows, in each cheekbone, behind the nose, and between the eyes.

The main function of your sinuses is as a "conditioner" for inhaled air on its way to your lungs. Normally, the membranes lining the nose and sinuses produce between a pint and a quart of mucus and secretions a day. This discharge passes through the nose, sweeping and washing the membranes and picking up dust particles, bacteria, and other air pollutants along the way. The mucus is then swept backward into the throat by tiny undulating hairs called cilia. From there, it is swallowed into the stomach, where acids destroy dangerous bacteria.

But when those nasal passages become irritated or inflamed by an allergy attack, air pollution, smoke, or a viral infection such as a cold or the flu, the nose and sinus membranes secrete more than the normal amount of mucus. They also swell, blocking the openings and preventing an easy flow of mucus and air. This sets the stage for bacteria to flourish. If your sinuses make your life miserable, you don't have to live with the discomfort.

Take good care of yourself. Maintaining a healthy immune system will bolster your resistance to germs, leaving you less likely to catch a cold or come down with the flu and making the symptoms more manageable if you do get sick. Shore up your body's defenses by eating right, staying in shape, and getting plenty of rest.

Live the sanitary life. You don't have to move into a sterile, germ-proof bubble or walk around wearing a surgical mask. Just use common sense: If the guy next to you at the bus stop is coughing his brains out, move away. And if someone in your family has a cold or the flu, avoid unnecessary contact with his or her germs.

Hydrate. Keeping yourself well-hydrated helps ensure your sinuses are in top shape. So drink plenty of fluids—eight tall glasses of water a day is a good goal.

Clear the air. Avoid pollutants in the air, stay indoors if the air quality is poor, and above all, avoid anyone who is smoking (and you should definitely not smoke).

Control allergies. Because allergies can cause sinusitis, know your allergy triggers and do your best to avoid them. You can also see an allergist to investigate desensitization treatments designed to help the body develop immunity to the offending substance.

Vaccines Don't Cause Autism

Do vaccines cause autism? This has become one of the most pernicious and destructive myths of modern times. Imagine the horrified faces of historical people whose children died of scarlet fever when they find out childhood diseases have reemerged, especially affecting the children whose weakened immune systems mean they can't be vaccinated at all.

❄   ❄   ❄   ❄

No Link at All

STUDY AFTER STUDY has shown that there is no link *at all* between vaccines of any kind and autism. For those who rely on celebrities for their parenting advice, there are plenty of unqualified actors who are paid to play pretend as a job who are on board with all kinds of conspiracy theories. Most Americans are not very scientifically literate in the first place, but groups with higher numbers of fine-arts degrees may be even less so, and certainly aren't *more* qualified to speak to our health concerns. A registered nurse, with at least a bachelor's degree in science and healthcare and a standardized qualification, isn't allowed to prescribe medication—some internet celebrity should not tell you that colloid silver and powdered mushrooms will prevent cancer, or that a pendant will ease your back pain.

Rolling the Medical Clock Backward

The vaccine conspiracy began with a radically misguided and mistaken physician who was stripped of his license over the sheer dangerous incorrectness of his terrible work. His study was not statistically significant or rigorous, it isn't duplicable, and it's been disproven thousands of times since.

He has doubled down on his claims, and he maintains a business which seems to just be his followers giving him money directly. And he has created a confirmation-bias echo chamber where the fact that he's shunned by the medical industry means he must "really be onto something." His fearmongering has resonated with modern parents who are in the center of a terrible Venn diagram where everything they choose is judged by other parents, every media outlet harps on how allegedly dangerous chemicals are coating our entire lives, and every decision they make feels like a moment when they can permanently damage their children.

Limits of Skepticism

It's completely understandable to be bewildered and feel skeptical and look for answers. The best source for those answers is the world of trained, educated, and certified medical professionals. Even a staggered immunization schedule, which many anti-vaccine activists choose as a "compromise," can leave their and other children vulnerable to diseases. As herd immunity falls in communities where anti-vaccine activists gather, immune-compromised children are the first to suffer.

You Are Filled with Poisons

A juice cleanse detoxifies your body.

✳ ✳ ✳ ✳

IF ONLY SOMEONE could start the rumor that detox cleanses cause autism, two of the most inexcusably baseless myths in modern life could cancel each other out.

A juice cleanse is a brief program where users consume only juice, or sometimes juice plus certain fruits and vegetables, for some number of days. The most responsible form of a juice cleanse is just a day or two with enough fatty "juices" made from nuts or coconut to at least replace some of the nutrients the detoxers are missing.

The biggest lie involved in juice cleanses, though, is that they detoxify your body. There are actually not just one but several organs in your body that already do this job. Juice-cleanse advertising makes it sound like everyone is a little bit poisoned all the time and they don't know it. Like the idea that we don't know when we're dehydrated, this is simply not true in any sense.

The juice cleanse probably began as the crash diet master cleanse, in which users drink a scary cayenne lemonade and eat no food for basically as long as they can manage. If you're getting heartburn just thinking about it, you're not alone. And while the master cleanse has proponents who lie about its ability to freshen up your insides, it is really still a crash diet.

How coincidental that juice or master cleanses all cause you to lose many pounds in no days while they're clearing out all your pretend toxins! Celebrities feel a lot of need to detox in the two weeks before the Oscars or Emmys. Brides who already feel pressured by the beauty industrial complex can even force their bridesmaids to do a synchronized detox cleanse just before their weddings.

Even healthy forms of changing your diet to lose weight have a very, very high long-term failure rate. Crash diets are the for-profit University of Phoenix Online to the sensible-weight-loss industry's Ivy League.

Bronchitis

Every illness is different, and bronchitis has its own signature set of symptoms. But it is often confused with strep or other respiratory bugs.

✳ ✳ ✳ ✳

BRONCHITIS IS AN often-painful infection in the major bronchial tubes (airways) that lead to the lungs. A persistent virus, frequently the same one that causes colds or the flu, is most often the cause of acute bronchitis (rarely, bronchitis can be traced to a bacterium or fungus).

Bronchitis causes the walls that line the inside of the bronchial tubes to swell and produce greatly increased amounts of thick yellow or green mucus. The lung irritation and mucus trigger a throaty, persistent, productive hacking, and the throat gets irritated from coughing.

Other symptoms include a burning or aching pain just beneath the breastbone, a feeling of tightness in the chest, wheezing or shortness of breath, and/or a "rattling" sensation in the lungs and chest. A low-grade fever, chills, and achiness may also occur. The irritation caused by the virus in turn leaves the respiratory tract vulnerable to other complications, such as pneumonia.

Fortunately, acute bronchitis generally goes away on its own within a few days or a week, although the cough can sometimes linger for weeks or even months. Until your body has shaken the infection, however, there are some things you can do to decrease discomfort and help your body heal.

Humidify your environment. Believe it or not, coughing is actually good for you. It's the body's way of eliminating the infection that causes bronchitis. Help it along by using a warm- or cool-mist humidifier to add moisture to the air. The added humidity will help bring the sputum up and out of the body. Standing in a steamy shower with the bathroom door closed or keeping a pan of water at a slow boil on the stove (never leave it unattended!) can also help loosen and bring up phlegm.

Drink plenty of liquids. Taking in extra liquids helps keep the sputum more fluid and therefore easier to expel. It doesn't really matter what type of liquid you take in, although tea, soup, and other warm liquids may feel better than cold ones. As a bonus, warm fluids can also soothe the irritated throat that might result from all that coughing.

Gargle with warm salt water. Gargling with salt water may provide a double dose of relief by soothing the inflammation in the throat and by cutting through some of the gunky mucus that might be coating and irritating the sensitive throat membranes. However, watch your measurements. It only takes one teaspoon of salt in a glass of warm water; too much salt causes burning in the throat, and too little is ineffective. Gargle as often as you need to, but be sure to spit out the salty water after gargling.

Take aspirin or ibuprofen to relieve the chest pain. If a bout with bronchitis produces muscle pain in the chest, these anti-inflammatory medications may provide some relief. Aceta minophen does not have an anti-inflammatory effect and so may be less helpful. However, because of the risk of deadly reaction called Reye's syndrome, don't give aspirin to children younger than 19; use acetaminophen instead.

Brain Gains

Crossword puzzles help to keep my brain in shape.

✳ ✳ ✳ ✳

RECORD NUMBERS OF
Americans are diagnosed
with Alzheimer's disease as
the baby boomers continue
to age, and "brain health"
advice has flooded in from all
sides to help assuage people's
fear of this sad and little-
understood disease. But most
of that advice is not fully
formed or is delivered in an
ambiguous way.

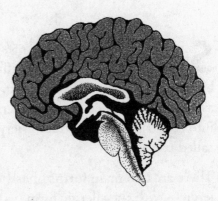

Crossword puzzles are great for specific kinds of thinking and
for checking up on your level of memory in general. But cognitive scientists recommend that people who wish to help their
brains stay fresh and alert do a broad mix of activities that
involve as many different skills and forms of thinking
as possible.

Enjoy the daily crossword puzzle for what it is: a fun, challenging puzzle. Doing it regularly can help you gauge your memory
over time, and consistently completing crosswords is good for
your word skills like fluency. But the puzzle itself won't help
improve your memory or cognitive skills overall. Maybe if you
completed the crossword in an unfamiliar language instead?
Actually, that sounds really fun.

Asthma

Asthma is on the rise. Taking some surprising small steps can help an asthma sufferer to stay calm and manage their condition a little better. And allergies can cause or worsen asthma.

✳   ✳   ✳   ✳

SOME 20 MILLION AMERICANS have asthma, a condition in which breathing becomes difficult because of narrowing or blockage of the airways in the lungs. The lungs of people with asthma are inflamed and supersensitive; they're easily provoked into constriction by a wide variety of outside factors that are called triggers.

There are two main forms of asthma—allergic and nonallergic—with the allergic form being more common. Allergic asthma develops in people who have allergies, and the same substances (called allergens) that provoke their allergy symptoms also trigger their asthma symptoms. Both the allergy and asthma symptoms are the product of an overreaction by the immune system. Common triggers include dust mites, pollen, mold, and pet dander.

With nonallergic asthma, on the other hand, the triggers that irritate the lungs and bring on asthma symptoms have nothing to do with allergies or the immune system. This type of asthma can be sparked by dry air, cold weather, exercise, smoke, strong perfume, stressful situations, intense emotions, even laughing.

Although there is no cure for asthma, it can be managed. In addition to working with your doctor, you can take measures to help control the condition. The key is to track down your triggers and, as completely as possible, eliminate them from your life. In short, you can often help counter an asthma attack before it happens.

Smite the mite. Dust mites—or rather the feces and dead bodies of these microscopic bugs—are one of the most common allergic asthma triggers. They're everywhere in your home, although they love the bedroom because they feed on the dead skin cells we constantly shed, and we spend a great deal of time there. Reducing the number of dust mites will help ease symptoms if you have allergic asthma triggered by these little critters. Here are some tips:

* Enclose your mattress in an airtight cover, and then cover it with a washable mattress pad.

* Wash your sheets in hot water every week, and wash your mattress pads and synthetic blankets every two weeks.

* Use polyester or Dacron pillows, not those made of kapok or feathers, and enclose them in airtight dust covers.

* Wear a mask over your mouth and nose while cleaning, and leave the room when you have finished the job.

Minimize mold. No matter how vigilantly you clean, mold and other forms of fungi are probably lurking somewhere in your house. To keep this stuff out, shut your windows, because mold spores can come right in, even if the windows have screens. In addition, stay out of attics, basements, and other dank, musty places; put on a face mask and check your bathroom (especially under the sink and in the backs of cabinets) and closet (especially unused shoes) for mold; and have someone else investigate the inner workings of air conditioners, humidifiers, and vaporizers for mold.

Make peace with pollen. Because it's just about impossible to escape pollen, learn how to control your exposure to the powdery allergen instead. Avoid cutting grass or even being outside while grass is being mowed. Keep your windows closed as much as possible and use an air conditioner to cool your home in warm weather. Room air purifiers are also available that can purify recirculated air, removing particles of all sorts. After being outside in the midst of pollen, take off your clothes and wash them, if possible, or run a vacuum over those that can't be washed.

Wash yourself, too, including your hair.

Don't pet a pet. Taking a few commonsense measures may allow you to coexist with a beloved animal companion and its dander—the dead, dry skin that flakes off and triggers asthma symptoms. Never allow your pet into the bedroom: If the animal is in the bedroom at any time during the day, the dander will remain for hours. Leave the pet home if you are going for a car ride, and if you do have direct contact with your pet (or any animal), wash your hands right away. In addition, try bathing your dog or cat once every other week in warm water with no soap. Bathing the animal in this way significantly reduces the amount of allergen on your pet's fur.

Watch the weather. Pay attention to how changes in the weather affect your asthma. You might even keep an asthma journal by recording the temperature, wind velocity, barometric pressure, and humidity on days when you suffer attacks. Knowing what types of weather conditions can leave you gasping for air may help you avoid problems. For instance, people with asthma should stay indoors when it is very cold outside, because a rush of cold air can cause a spasm in the bronchial tubes.

Exercise your options. For years, people with asthma were told to avoid exercise because it would induce attacks. Research has shown, however, that getting regular aerobic exercise increases the amount of huffing and puffing an asthmatic can tolerate. Begin with short workouts and gradually increase their duration. Keep a bronchodilator with you, at least at first. If you feel tightness in your chest and can't work through it, use the device. If one type of exercise still brings on attacks, try another form of exercise. You may not be able to tolerate running, for example, but you may be able to swim regularly. Talk with your doctor about what will work best for you.

Avoid aspirin. Aspirin can trigger asthma attacks in certain people. Play it safe and avoid aspirin and products that contain it if you have asthma, even if you've never experienced a related flare-up. Check the labels on every over-the-counter drug you purchase. Avoid those that list "aspirin" and those that contain the initials "ASA," "APC," or "PAC"; ask the pharmacist if you are unsure whether the medication you want to buy contains aspirin.

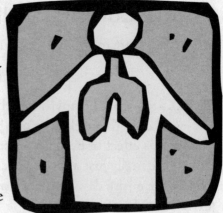

According to a report from the National Asthma Education Program, people with asthma should also stay away from certain nonsteroidal anti-inflammatory agents (ibuprofen is one such medication) that have effects similar to aspirin's. Opt instead for such "usually safe alternatives" as acetaminophen, sodium salicylate, or disalcid, but check with your doctor to be sure. You may also need to avoid tartrazine (yellow food dye No. 5), which is found in a number of soft drinks, cake mixes, candies, and some medications, if it aggravates your asthma.

Mind your mind. The notion that asthma is "all in your head" has gone the way of many medical myths. However, doctors believe that asthma is an illness with both physical and emotional aspects. For example, asthma attacks can be triggered by emotional changes, such as laughing or crying, or by stress. Although you may not be able to "think away" an asthma attack, keeping your mind at ease may prevent you from panicking at the onset of an asthma attack, which will make a bout with breathing trouble less scary. A positive attitude works wonders to enhance your other coping methods.

A Ten-Calorie Grain of Truth

After a workout, my body keeps burning more calories all day.

✳ ✳ ✳ ✳

YES AND NO. This myth is technically true. But as with workouts themselves or our food intake, we vastly overestimate this effect of exercise on our metabolism, the result of which is usually just a few extra calories burned throughout the rest of the entire day. If you're really bean-counting, have a few extra M&Ms.

More people who regularly workout report feeling hungry after a workout, and usually they're hungry for more than a few extra calories. Remember that protein and fiber in particular help you feel nourished and satisfied after a workout, but ultimately you should eat whatever snack you want. And drink plenty of water to replace your lost fluids!

Nausea & Vomiting

What we call the "stomach flu" is probably a brief food-borne illness in reality.

✳ ✳ ✳ ✳

WE'VE ALL BEEN there, and it's no fun. Perhaps it's the "24-hour flu" bug, or maybe it was something you ate. Whatever the cause, now you're feeling queasy and sick. The tips that follow are designed to reduce your discomfort and help relieve symptoms as quickly as possible, but if vomiting is violent or persists for more than 24 hours, or if your vomit contains blood or looks like coffee grounds, see a physician right away.

Let it run its course. The best cure for the 24-hour "stomach flu" (it isn't truly influenza; that's an upper respiratory infection caused by specific viruses) is bed rest and time. The more rest you get, the more energy your body will have to devote to fighting the invader.

Stick to clear liquids. If your stomach is upset, it probably doesn't need the additional burden of digesting food. Stick to fluids until you feel a little better and have stopped vomiting. Clear, room-temperature liquids, such as water or diluted noncitrus fruit juices, are easier to digest, and they are also necessary to prevent the dehydration that may result from vomiting or diarrhea.

Don't drink alcohol. Alcohol can be very irritating to the stomach, so if your tummy is turning over, now is certainly not the time to imbibe. You'll also want to avoid fatty foods, highly seasoned foods, beverages containing caffeine, and cigarettes.

Eat easy-to-digest foods. When you are ready to start eating again, start with soft, plain foods, such as bread, unbuttered toast, steamed fish, or bananas. Avoid fatty foods and foods that are high in fiber. Another tip is to start with tiny amounts of food and slowly build up to full meals.

Let it flow. The worst thing you can do for vomiting is fight it, because vomiting is your body's way of getting rid of something that is causing harm to your stomach. Plus, trying to hold back the urge can actually tear your esophagus.

Try a cold compress. A cold compress on your head can be very comforting when you are vomiting. It won't stop you from spewing, but it might help you feel a little better.

Balance those electrolytes. Along with replacing the fluids you lose through vomiting, it is also important to maintain the balance of sodium and potassium (the electrolytes) in your system. If you spend more than a day or two vomiting, have a sports drink, such as Gatorade, which is easy on the stomach and is designed to replace electrolytes. Try diluting it with water if drinking it straight bothers your stomach.

Yoga Joints

Yoga can relieve my joint pain.

✳ ✳ ✳ ✳

THE COOPTING OF yoga from its roots as a spiritual practice could fill a thousand doctoral theses. But it has retained a sheen of holistic goodness that isn't really earned by those who do yoga as a casual form of exercise.

Yoga can help to ease joint pain by building strength and stretching muscles to help your body support itself and be more flexible. At the same time, yoga, especially the more rigorous forms, is strenuous and can put more pressure on your joints than they're used to. Holding poses requires strength we may not have yet, and when the intended muscles begin to tire, other muscles can pick up the slack and may be strained.

Trying to do too much can cause you to wobble or lose your balance in unfamiliar poses, and that can tweak or strain your muscles as well. If you're a beginner, instructors usually say to take it slow and listen to your body as you try new things. A good instructor will also watch you closely and correct your form to make sure your body is aligned and supported. Almost any yoga pose can be modified, not just for beginners but for people with different levels of bodily control or ability.

Body Building

Weightlifting makes women bulky.

✳   ✳   ✳   ✳

FIRST AND FOREMOST, anyone can be buff and strong, and you should aim to look however you want. Strength training burns proportionally more fat than cardiovascular exercise, and stronger muscles can help to support your body to prevent injury and facilitate further progress.

But this myth also misunderstands the difference between the sexes in terms of musculature. Women and men have varying levels of hormones like testosterone, which allows men's bodies to gain visible muscle in a way most women's bodies do not. Most women would need to supplement their testosterone in order to "bulk up."

Lactose Intolerance

Humans are the only animals to continue to drink milk as adults, and many ethnic groups have rates of lactose intolerance of half or even 90% or more. Could this affect you?

✳   ✳   ✳   ✳

EATING DAIRY PRODUCTS has unpleasant consequences for 30 million to 50 million Americans because they're lactose intolerant. That means they don't properly digest lactose, the sugar found in all milk products. This problem is usually due to a shortage of the enzyme lactase, which breaks down milk sugar in the small intestine into simple parts that can be absorbed into the bloodstream. The end result of this lactase deficiency may be gas, stomach pains, bloating, and diarrhea. If you're lactose intolerant, you may want to try these helpful tips to ease your symptoms.

Determine your level of lactose intolerance. The best way to assess your tolerance is to first get all lactose out of your system by avoiding lactose-containing foods for three to four weeks. Then start with very small quantities of milk or cheese. Monitor your symptoms to see how much or how little dairy food you can handle without experiencing discomfort. Once you know your limits, management becomes easier.

Stick with small servings. Although you may not be able to tolerate an eight-ounce glass of milk all at once, you may have no discomfort from drinking a third of it in the morning, a third of it in the afternoon, and a third of it at night.

Pair your dairy. If you eat some cheese or drink a little milk, plan to do so with a meal or a snack. Eating dairy on an empty stomach can worsen your symptoms.

Try yogurt. Yogurt with active cultures doesn't cause problems for many lactose-intolerant people, but you may have to buy it at a health-food store. Yogurt is a great source of calcium, if you can tolerate it.

Choose hard cheeses. If you can't pull yourself away from the cheese aisle, pick hard, aged cheeses, such as Swiss, cheddar, or Colby. They contain less lactose than soft cheeses.

Get calcium from other foods. Lactose-intolerant people, especially women and children, should be sure their calcium intake doesn't plunge. Green leafy vegetables, such as collard greens, kale, turnip greens, and Chinese cabbage (bok choy), as well as oysters, sardines, canned salmon with the bones, and tofu provide lots of calcium, as does calcium-fortified orange juice and soy milk. You may also want to take calcium supplements; talk with your doctor about the dosage that is right for you.

Watch out for medications. Lactose is used as filler in more than 20 percent of prescription drugs (including many types of birth control pills) and in about 6 percent of over-the-counter medicines. If you take such a medication every day, it could cause symptoms. Complicating matters is the fact that lactose may not be listed under the inactive ingredients on the label. Ask your doctor or pharmacist, or contact the drug's manufacturer to find out if what you're taking contains lactose.

How Dairy You

Milk is good for you, but the milk lobby has exaggerated its goodness.

✳   ✳   ✳   ✳

FOR MOST AMERICANS, milk is a dietary staple that provides much of their naturally occurring calcium—meaning not from supplements. But so far, science hasn't shown that more calcium means better health, fewer broken bones, or anything else. Added calcium like that in nondairy milks can actually irritate your stomach and impair absorption.

Milk has protein, which is the latest milk-lobby ad tactic. But milk also has a surprising amount of sugar and fat, making it more caloric than most people realize. Especially if you drink whole milk, moderation may be the best bet. But cheese is the true secret villain of the dairy story, with an enormous amount of sodium.

No food is "good" or "bad" on its own, but it's a problem when the nutrients people try to avoid or have in moderation are minimized by an ad campaign.

Pros and Cons

Will yogurt help my digestive tract? Is it because of probiotics?

✳ ✳ ✳ ✳

SOMETHING IS VERY American about the idea that you can fix indigestion by adding more of a different kind of food to the mix. Probiotic yogurt is all over the airwaves, and it makes sense as a market, because more people than ever are sharing their experiences with chronic indigestion as represented by irritable bowel syndrome and other digestive disorders.

But yogurt isn't any more special or effective than anything else. Moreover, boutique yogurt brands marketed as notably probiotic usually say in the fine print that you're supposed to eat them three times a day for them to work. This is a costly habit to get into in exchange for unproven medical benefits.

Most physicians say probiotic supplements probably won't hurt you so why not try them? Digestive disorders can respond to the placebo effect like anything else, so even if the supplements themselves don't help you, you may feel better anyway. Conditions like IBS and even migraine are simply not well understood, and specialists rely on patient trial and error to identify anything unusual in their diet that may help or worsen their symptoms.

One exception when probiotics may actively help is if you're experiencing all-the-time indigestion after a round of antibiotics, which are infamously rough on the natural gut flora we rely on to keep us comfortable. A physician may suggest you take probiotic supplements after you finish the course of antibiotics—but not before, as the antibiotics will, of course, only kill the probiotics.

Heartburn

For decades, the cause of painful ulcers was misunderstood, but heartburn is still a mystery. Some surprising foods or beverages, like mint, can exacerbate heartburn despite reputations as stomach soothers.

✳ ✳ ✳ ✳

YOUR ESOPHAGUS, THE tube that carries what you swallow down to your stomach, can literally be burned by the industrial-strength acids your stomach releases to digest food. Those acids are meant to stay where the tough stomach lining can handle them. Unfortunately, we can experience something called reflux. That's when some of the stomach contents, including the acid, slip back up through the esophageal sphincter, the valve that's supposed to prevent the stomach's contents from reversing course. The reflux causes that burning sensation between the stomach and the neck. Here are some ways to put out that fire and keep it from flaring up again.

Keep your head up. One way to protect your esophagus while you sleep is to elevate the head of your bed. That way, you'll be sleeping on a slope, and gravity will keep your stomach contents where they belong. Put wooden blocks under the legs at the head of your bed to raise it about six inches.

Say no to a postdinner snooze. People who lie down with a full stomach are asking for trouble. Wait at least an hour before you lie down.

Loosen your belt. Tight clothing can push on your stomach and contribute to reflux.

Lose the fat. Abdominal fat pressing against the stomach can force the contents back up.

Get in shape. Even mild exercise done on a regular basis, such as a daily walk around the neighborhood, may help ease digestive woes. However, avoid working out strenuously immediately after a meal; wait a couple of hours.

Don't smoke. Nicotine from cigarette smoke irritates the stomach lining, as well as the valve between the stomach and the esophagus, so smokers tend to get heartburn more often.

Be careful of coffee. The caffeine in coffee relaxes the esophageal sphincter, which can lead to reflux. But even decaffeinated coffee may cause reflux problems: Research suggests the oils contained in both regular and decaffeinated java may play a role in heartburn.

Be wary of peppermint. For some people, peppermint seems to cause heartburn. Try avoiding the after-dinner mints.

Skip the cocktail. Alcohol can relax the sphincter and irritate the stomach, which can lead to reflux.

Slow down on soda. The carbon dioxide in soda pop and other bubbly drinks can cause stomach distention, which can push the contents of the stomach up into the esophagus.

De Hydration Myth

Do I need to drink eight glasses of water a day? Am I dehydrated and I don't know it?

✳   ✳   ✳   ✳

THIS BEWILDERING MYTH is, nonetheless, entrenched in our lives. But unless you feel thirsty, you don't need to drink any more water than you naturally would. The only demonstrable way more water can potentially help your health—and everyone is different, so this isn't a blanket rule—is that drinking water instead of caloric beverages like soda means you likely consume fewer calories overall.

Many weight-loss programs strongly incentivize drinking a lot of water, because it can help you feel fuller and eat less overall.

Digestion can feel easier when we're hydrated, and it's easy to picture a slice of pizza becoming a gluey mess inside our stomachs. Certainly it doesn't hurt to drink more water if that's what you want to do, as long as you stay moderate. Overhydrating can actually poison your body if taken to extremes like drinking a gallon of water in a short time.

People who don't have kids or spend much time with kids may also not know that babies *can't* drink water. This is one reason it's very important to keep babies cool, covered, and comfortable when they're outside on hot days. Options to rehydrate babies are simply very limited because of their tiny, growing systems.

As for dehydration, the symptoms of this condition are noticeable and alarming. Feeling thirsty does not mean you're "already a little dehydrated"—a frightening headache, dizziness, weakness, blacking out, and other nightmare symptoms mean that you're dehydrated. Feeling thirsty means you should just drink some water.

Loose Stools

If you're running to the restroom, some surprising food tips may help soothe your savage insides.

✳   ✳   ✳   ✳

DIARRHEA IS UNCOMFORTABLE and unpleasant, but generally no big deal in otherwise healthy adults. However, if diarrhea becomes a chronic condition, the situation changes. Or if it affects the very young, the elderly, or the chronically ill, it can be dangerous. And if you don't drink enough fluids, you could find yourself complicating what should have been a simple situation.

Unless diarrhea persists—which can signal a more serious problem—you usually don't find out its cause. Treatment for a temporary bout is aimed at easing the symptoms and at preventing dehydration, the most serious consequence of diarrhea.

Keep hydrated. You can lose a lot of liquid in diarrhea, but you also lose electrolytes, which are minerals such as sodium and potassium that are critical in the running of your body. Drink two quarts (8 cups) of fluids a day, three quarts (12 cups) if you have a fever. Plain water lacks electrolytes, but it's a good, gentle-on-the-tummy option that can help you replace lost fluid. Other choices include weak tea with a little sugar; sports drinks, such as Gatorade; flat soda pop (decaffeinated flavors like ginger ale are best); and fruit juices other than apple and prune, which have a laxative effect. Another option is to buy an over-the-counter electrolyte-replacement formula, such as Pedialyte, Rehydralyte, or Ricelyte. These formulas contain fluids and minerals in the proper proportion. Whatever you choose to drink, keep it cool, not ice cold. And sip, don't guzzle—small amounts at a time will be easier on your insides.

Sip some broth. Any broth flavor will do, but drink it lukewarm instead of hot, and add a little salt to it if it's not already salty.

Put a heating pad on your belly. It may help relieve abdominal cramps.

Try yogurt. Choose a brand that contains live lactobacillus cultures, which are friendly bugs that normally live in the gut. (Even people with lactose intolerance can usually handle this type of yogurt.)

Eat easy-to-digest foods. Good choices include soup, gelatin, rice, noodles, bananas, potatoes, toast, cooked carrots, soda crackers, and skinless white-meat chicken.

Don't do dairy. Avoid milk, cheese, and other dairy products (except yogurt, unless you don't usually tolerate it well) while you have diarrhea, as well as for one to three weeks after it stops. The small intestine, where milk is digested, is affected by diarrhea and simply won't work as well for a while.

Cut out caffeine. Just as it stimulates your nervous system, caffeine jump-starts your intestines. And that's the last thing you need when you have diarrhea.

Say no to sweet treats. High concentrations of sugar can increase diarrhea. The sugar in fruit can do the same.

Steer clear of greasy or high-fiber foods. These are harder for your gut to handle when you have diarrhea.

Gain What Exactly?

No pain, no gain.

✳ ✳ ✳ ✳

THIS IS THE single worst exercise myth. Yes, your muscles may feel tired while you work out, and weightlifting may give you a *gentle* sensation of "feeling the burn." You'll feel sore the next day. But any kind of muscle or joint pain, sensations of tearing, or other surprising feelings during your workout should cause you to stop what you're doing. If you can't find another form of exercise that does not cause the same feeling, stop your workout altogether and speak with a doctor before you try again.

Constipation

Discomfort and pain make us want to sit down and rest, but the best way to get moving is to, well, get moving.

✳ ✳ ✳ ✳

IRREGULARITY IS ONE of those things that no one likes to talk about. It's personal and, well, a little awkward. But if you have ever been constipated, you know it can put a real damper on your day. A sudden change in bowel habits requires a visit to your doctor to rule out more serious underlying problems. But for the occasional bout of constipation, here are some tips to put you back on track.

Get moving. When you are active, so are your bowels—and the more sedentary you are, the more slowly your bowels move. That may partially explain why older people—who tend to be less active—and those who are bedridden are prone to becoming constipated. You don't have to run a marathon; a simple walking workout will do.

Raise your glass. Drinking an adequate amount of liquid may help alleviate constipation or prevent it from happening in the first place. The reason for this is simple: If you are dehydrated, your stool will become dry and difficult to pass. A good rule of thumb is to drink a total of six to eight cups of fluid throughout the day, and perhaps a bit more when you're perspiring heavily during exercise or hot weather. (This general guide doesn't apply, however, if you have a kidney or liver problem or any other medical condition that restricts your intake of fluid. In that case, your doctor will need to advise you on how much fluid is appropriate.)

The caffeine in a cup of coffee can stimulate the bowels, so a cup or two of java (or tea) in the morning might help get things moving. But because caffeine is also a diuretic that pulls fluid out of your body, be sure to fill most of your fluid needs with water, seltzer, juice, milk, or decaffeinated beverages.

Bulk up. Sometimes, a little extra dietary fiber is all you need to ensure regularity. Fiber, the indigestible parts of plant foods, adds mass to the stool and stimulates the colon to push things along. Fiber is found naturally in fruits, vegetables, grains, and beans (although refining and processing can significantly decrease their fiber content). The current recommendations for daily dietary fiber intake are 20 to 35 grams, but most people eat only 10 to 15 grams a day.

Eat at least five servings of fruits and vegetables daily. Select a variety of fruits and vegetables, and opt for the fresh produce over juice as much as possible. A glass of orange juice, for instance, provides 0.1 gram of fiber, while eating an orange gives you 2.9 grams.

Eat six ounces of grain products each day. That's in addition to the five servings of fruits and vegetables just mentioned. Grain products include cereals, breads, and starchy vegetables (such as corn, green peas, potatoes, and lima beans). Whenever possible, choose whole grains such as whole-wheat bread and whole-grain cereal. Check the labels on cereal boxes; anything with more than five or six grams of fiber per serving qualifies as high fiber. The best bread has at least two grams of fiber per slice and is labeled "whole-grain" or "whole-wheat" (the word "wheat" alone or a brown color does not guarantee that the product includes the whole grain). And don't forget beans. Dried beans and legumes are excellent sources of fiber.

Reject refined foods. Bump up your fiber intake by switching from refined foods to less-refined foods whenever possible. Switch from a highly processed cereal to a whole-grain cereal, move from heavily cooked vegetables to less-cooked vegetables, and choose whole-grain products over products made with white flour. A half-cup serving of white rice has 0.3 gram of fiber; a half-cup serving of brown rice contains 1.75 grams. And while a one-ounce serving of potato chips has 1.2 grams of fiber, a one-ounce serving of popcorn supplies 4.1 grams.

Wake Up!

Why does turkey make you sleepy?

✳ ✳ ✳ ✳

IT DOESN'T. THINK about your average lunchtime turkey sandwich, which probably doesn't make you feel sleepy. On Thanksgiving, when most Americans eat their peak amount of turkey for the year, we also surround the turkey with literal piles of different delicious and buttery side dishes and bread, with bonus points for the snacking that usually happens through Thanksgiving days spent with family.

Tryptophan is found in many foods besides turkey, and you probably can't think of any other single one. Maybe it's making you sleepy instead, but probably not! Next Thanksgiving, if you have a vegetarian at your gathering, ask them nicely if they get sleepy after dinner. Then you'll know to blame the mashed potatoes.

Repeat As Needed

Can weekend warriors have the same health benefits as those who exercise more regularly?

✳ ✳ ✳ ✳

WE WANT TO believe this because life feels too hectic to fit in the number of exercise sessions or amount of physical activity physicians recommend. But one or two workouts a week just isn't as good for you as a more regular and structured program of three or more times a week.

The silver lining is that even a ten-minute walk every day can improve your health outcomes. And taking breaks to stand up, stretch, and move around also helps to avoid eye strain from computer usage. If you have access to a gym or health center, a brief session of cardiovascular exercise like rowing or using the elliptical machine can mix up your routine and increase your energy levels without disrupting your schedule too much.

Muscle Pain

After a muscle strain, a hard workout, or doing an unusual task, you can have muscle fatigue and soreness. Should you use ice or heat? Should you rest or try to stretch it out? What's the real deal?

✳ ✳ ✳ ✳

MUSCLE SORENESS AND cramps aren't generally life threatening, but they can be uncomfortable and painful. They can also dim your enthusiasm for physical activity, which in turn can negatively affect your overall health and well-being. Here are some tips to ease the pain and prevent the problem from recurring.

Stop. If your muscle cramps up while you're exercising, stop. Don't try to "run through" a cramp. Doing so increases your chance of seriously injuring the muscle.

Give it a stretch and squeeze. When you get a cramp, stretch the cramped muscle with one hand while you gently knead and squeeze the center of the muscle with the fingers of the other hand. Try to feel how it's contracted, and stretch it in the opposite direction.

Walk it out. Once an acute cramp passes, don't start exercising heavily right away. Instead, walk for a few minutes to get the blood flowing back into the muscles.

Try quinine. Many competitive swimmers drink tonic water, which gets its flavor from a small amount of quinine, to prevent cramps. Although there isn't much in the way of scientific research to support drinking tonic water for muscle cramps, you might want to try it.

Chill out. If you know you've overworked your muscles, immediately take a cold shower or a cold bath to reduce the trauma to them. World-class Australian runner Jack Foster used to hose off his legs with cold water after a hard run. He told skeptics if it was good enough for racehorses, it was good enough for him! If an icy dip seems too much for you, ice packs work well, too. Apply cold packs for 20 to 30 minutes at a time every hour for the first 24 to 72 hours after the activity (just place a thin cloth between the ice pack and your skin). Cold helps prevent muscle soreness by constricting the blood vessels, which reduces blood flow and thus inflammation.

Go bananas. Muscle cramps can sometimes be caused by a lack of potassium. Try eating a banana a day—the potassium-rich fruit might help keep cramps away.

Avoid heat. Using heat may feel good, but it's the worst thing for sore muscles because it dilates blood vessels and increases circulation to the area, which in turn leads to more swelling. Heat can actually increase muscle soreness and stiffness, especially if applied during the first 24 hours after the strenuous activity.

Drink plenty of fluids. One cause of acute cramps, especially when you're exercising intensely during hot weather for an hour or longer, is dehydration. Be sure to drink enough fluids before, during, and after exercising. If you're running, aim to drink about a cup per hour. Don't overdo it, however, because drinking too much water can cause a dangerous imbalance in the body's mineral stores. What about those sports drinks? You really don't need them unless you're exercising intensely for longer than an hour at a time. Water is better.

Take a Jog

Running on a treadmill is less stressful for your joints than running on pavement.

❋ ❋ ❋ ❋

YOUR BODY WEIGHT and gait are the same on the treadmill or on the sidewalk. Most people wear supportive, cushioned shoes when they run, so any minor difference in firmness between the surfaces is negated. Trainers recommend a variety of exercise to avoid joint strain. You can also use strength training to build the muscles that help to support your joins, which can lessen your risk of injury or the stress on joints that have been injured in the past. Runners, especially distance runners, are more likely to injure themselves in any given time frame of exercise than almost any other group.

Headaches

I get regular headaches but I don't think they're migraines. I know I should drink a glass of water to see if that helps. I've heard smoking can make headaches worse. Is that true?

❋ ❋ ❋ ❋

IF YOU SUFFER from frequent, severe headaches that put you out of commission several times a month, you need to seek medical attention. Likewise, if your headaches are associated with physical exertion; changes in vision; or weakness, numbness, or paralysis of the limbs, skip the urge to self-treat and see a doctor. If you're already seeing a physician and aren't getting relief, think about getting a referral to a headache specialist or headache clinic. However, if you get only the occasional headache, read on.

Quit smoking. Smoking may bring on or worsen a headache, especially if you suffer from cluster headaches—extremely painful headaches that last from 5 to 20 minutes and come in groups.

Lie down. Lying down and closing your eyes for 30 minutes or more might be one of the best treatments for a bad headache. For some types of headaches, such as migraines, rest may be the only way to interrupt the pain cycle.

Don't let the sun shine in. Resting in a darkened room may alleviate the pain, especially if your symptoms resemble those of a migraine (severe pain on one side of the head, nausea, blurred vision, and extreme sensitivity to light). Bright light may also cause headaches. Even staring at a glowing computer screen may be enough to trigger brain pain. Wearing tinted glasses or using other means to filter bright light and minimize glare might keep away headaches.

Use a cold compress. A washcloth dipped in ice-cold water and placed over the eyes or an ice pack placed on the site of the pain are other good ways of relieving a headache. Whatever you use, keep in mind that speed is critical: Using ice as soon as possible after the onset of the headache will relieve the pain within 20 minutes for most people.

Try heat. If ice feels uncomfortable to you, or if it doesn't help your headache, try placing a warm washcloth over your eyes or on the site of the pain. Leave the compress on for half an hour, rewarming it as necessary.

Don't drink. Drinking more alcohol than you're used to often causes a pounding headache. But even a single serving of some alcoholic beverages can trigger head aches in certain people. For example, dark alcoholic beverages, such as red wines, sherry, brandy, scotch, vermouth, and some beers, contain large amounts of tyramine, an amino acid that can spark headaches in people who are sensitive to it.

Get moving. Regular exercise helps release the physical and emotional tension that may lead to headaches. Walking, jogging, and other aerobic activities help boost the body's production of endorphins (natural pain-relieving substances).

Cut down on caffeine. The same chemical in coffee and tea that perks you up in the morning can also make your muscles tense and raise your anxiety level. Consuming too much caffeine can also cause insomnia, which can trigger headaches. Another problem is that many people drink several cups of coffee a day during their workweek but cut their consumption on Saturdays and Sundays. This pattern can lead to weekend caffeine-withdrawal headaches.

Myth Blaster

You can "target" areas for weight loss.

❋ ❋ ❋ ❋

THE DECISION TO lose weight is between people and their physicians based on their own criteria for health. But if you do have this goal and you've done even cursory research about exercise or nutrition, you've probably found suggestions to "blast your core," reshape your hindquarters, or get thinner arms. It's just not true that you can determine where your body loses fat.

You can target muscle groups for strength training or certain exercises, but this will tone and shape your *musculature*, not burn fat in the same area. Body fat cells are pretty much equally distributed around our bodies, and the way they deflate and change is out of our control. Even the same person making efforts to lose body fat ten or twenty years apart will notice different results in the way their body changes.

Back Pain

Almost every American suffers from back pain at some point in his or her life, with many citing chronic back pain. The good news is that by following some simple steps, you can be feeling better in just a few days. With care and medical attention you may find that your back pain isn't chronic after all, or at least more manageable.

✳ ✳ ✳ ✳

Easing the Pain

THE FOLLOWING REMEDIES are appropriate for anyone who is suffering from back pain due to tight, aching muscles or a strain. However, if you are experiencing pain, weakness, or numbness in the legs, or a loss of bowel or bladder control, see a doctor right away.

Don't take it lying down. Mounting research shows that lying down for an extended period not only fails to speed up relief of lower back pain but it also may make it even worse. If you feel you must rest your aching back, the best position is lying flat on your back with two pillows underneath your knees. Never lie facedown, because this position forces you to twist your head to breathe and might cause neck pain. Any more than three days of bed rest could weaken the muscles and make them more prone to strain.

Ice it. Applying an ice pack to the painful area within 24 hours of an injury can help keep inflammation to a minimum and ease discomfort by decreasing the ability of nerves to send pain signals to the brain. Place a thin towel on the painful area, then apply the ice pack on top of the towel. Leave the pack on for 20 minutes, take it off for 30 minutes, and then replace it for another 20 minutes.

Take a hot bath. If more than 24 hours have passed since the injury occurred, ice will not help reduce inflammation or pain.

After that first day, heat may help increase the elasticity of the muscles somewhat, so try soaking in a tub of hot water for 20 minutes or more. Pregnant women, however, should not sit in a hot bath or hot tub for too long, because raising the body temperature over 100 degrees Fahrenheit for long periods may cause birth defects or miscarriage. If you are pregnant, contact your doctor for advice before trying a hot soak.

Invest in a new mattress. A soft, sagging mattress may contribute to the development of back problems or worsen an existing problem. If a new mattress is not in your budget, however, a three-quarter-inch-thick piece of plywood placed between the mattress and box spring can help a little. In addition, try to sleep on your back with two pillows propping up your knees.

Relax. Much back pain is the result of muscles made tight by emotional tension. Learn and practice a relaxation technique, such as meditation, or try a deep-breathing exercise, such as closing your eyes, breathing slowly and deeply, and counting backward from 100.

Preventing Future Pain

Many of the activities you engage in each day, such as sitting, lifting, bending, and carrying, can put a strain on your back. You can help prevent pain and ensure the health of your back for years to come by learning new ways of doing these things.

Use a cushion. Most seats in cars and trucks are not designed to support the small of your back, although some newer vehicles do provide adjustable lumbar support, at least for the driver. If the seat in your vehicle doesn't, buy a small cushion that can be fitted to provide the missing support. Despite what your mother told you about sitting up straight, leaning back at an angle of about 110 degrees is ideal for the back.

If you sit for long hours, get up and walk around periodically to increase blood flow and decrease stiffness.

Put your arm behind your back. If you get stuck sitting for a long period in a seat that doesn't support your lower back and you don't have a cushion, try rolling up a towel or sweater so it has about the same circumference as your forearm. Then slide the rolled-up cloth between your lower back and the back of the seat. In a pinch, you can simply slide your forearm between your lower back and the seat back to ease the strain on your back. Try to make small adjustments in the curvature of your lower back every few minutes or so.

Swim. Many experts agree that swimming is the best aerobic exercise for a bad back. Doing laps in the pool can help tone and strengthen the muscles of the back and abdomen, which help support the spine, while buoyancy temporarily relieves them of the job of holding up your weight. Walking is the next best choice for a low impact.

Lift with your knees bent. The large muscles of your legs and buttocks are better equipped to bear heavy weight than your back muscles are. Keep your back straight and bend only your knees, rather than bending at the waist, as you squat to pick up something. Then, as you rise, concentrate on using your leg muscles to push your upper body and the object back up into a standing position, again without bending at the waist.

Carry objects close to your body.
When picking up and carrying heavy objects, pull in your elbows and hold the object close to your body. When reaching for a bulky item on a shelf, stand beneath it and rest the object on your head. That way your erect spine carries the weight, placing less burden on your back muscles.

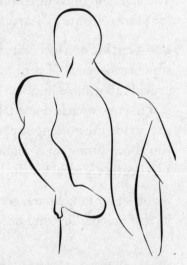

Arthritis

Baby boomers have brought arthritis numbers in the U.S. soaring to new highs. But the best ways to soothe your joint pain can be counterintuitive.

✳   ✳   ✳   ✳

ACCORDING TO THE Arthritis Foundation, an estimated 46 million Americans are caught in the grip of some form of arthritis or joint problem. And few of us will make it to a ripe old age without joining the fold. If one of these diseases has a painful hold on you, read on. Although there are no cures, there are steps you can take to ease discomfort and get back more control over your life.

Easing Stiffness and Discomfort

Here are some tips to help relieve discomfort and get you back into the swing of things.

Keep moving. Be as active as you can to keep your joints functioning as long as possible. Even everyday activities, such as walking, gardening, and housecleaning, can help your joints, as can range-of-motion, aerobic, and resistance exercises. Talk with your doctor or physical therapist about the best exercises for you.

Play in a pool. A heated pool or whirlpool may be the perfect environment for exercise (unless you are pregnant, in which case you should avoid heated whirlpools and hot tubs, or have other chronic health problems, in which case you should get your doctor's approval first). Try a few simple exercises while in the water. The buoyancy will help reduce the strain on your joints. Warm water helps loosen joints and makes muscles more pliable. In a pinch, a hot shower may do: Running the stream of water down your back, for instance, may help relieve back stiffness and discomfort.

Get "down." Goose down blankets warm up the joints and help ease pain. If you're allergic to down, try an electric blanket.

Put on a scarf. Not around your neck, but around the elbow or knee joint when it aches. The added warmth may bring some relief, but be careful not to wrap it too tightly.

Pull on a pair of stretch gloves. The tightness may help reduce the swelling in arthritic fingers, and the warmth created by covered hands may make the joints feel better. Wearing thermal underwear may help, too.

Watch your weight. Being overweight puts more stress on the joints. In fact, a weight gain of 10 pounds puts the equivalent of 40 extra pounds of stress on the knees.

Protecting Your Joints

In addition to easing discomfort, you can learn to live well with arthritis by protecting your joints. Here are some helpful tips from the Arthritis Foundation.

Spread the strain. As a general rule, you want to avoid activities that involve a tight grip or that put too much pressure on your fingers. For example, use the palms of both hands to lift and hold cups, plates, pots, and pans, rather than gripping them with your fingers or with only one hand.

Avoid holding one position for a long time. Keeping joints "locked" in the same position for any length of time will only add to your stiffness and discomfort. Relax and stretch your joints as often as possible.

"Arm" yourself. Whenever possible, use your arm instead of your hand to carry out an activity. For example, push open a heavy door with the side of your arm rather than with your hand and outstretched arm.

Replace doorknobs and round faucet handles with long handles. They require a looser, less stressful grip (or no grip at all) to operate, so you'll put less strain on your joints.

Build up the handles on your tools. For a more comfortable grip, look for household tools, utensils, and writing implements that have chunky, padded handles. Or tape a layer or two of thin foam rubber, or a foam rubber hair curler, around the handles of brooms, mops, rakes, spatulas, knives, pens, and pencils.

Let automatic appliances do the work for you. Electric can openers and knives, for instance, are easier to operate than manual versions. An electric toothbrush has a wider handle than a regular toothbrush.

Let loose with loops. You won't need quite as tight a grip if you put loops around door handles, such as those on the refrigerator and oven. Have loops sewn on your socks, too, and then use a long-handled hook to help you pull them up.

Contact the Arthritis Foundation. Learn about all kinds of joint-friendly or energy-saving items specially made for people with arthritis by contacting the Arthritis Foundation. Visit the organization's Web site at www.arthritis.org.

Beta Keep Guessing

Do carrots help you see in the dark?

✳ ✳ ✳ ✳

BETA CAROTENE, OR vitamin A, is important to your vision and your optical health. But not even vitamin A can help a human's eyes see in the dark. We're simply not able to, and it makes sense from the way our eyes are shaped and how they function.

All eyes evolved beginning as patches that responded to light, and light remains the fundamental ingredient in almost every creature's form of vision. Some, like bees or butterflies, can see outside the spectrum of what humans consider to be visible light. Some animals can see in the dark, although this is often more like infrared vision.

Carrots taste good and they're good for you, but they won't give you superpowers. The myth began as a piece of gossip spread by the British during World War II, both to frighten the Germans and to demonstrate whether the Germans would begin to eat a lot of carrots to gain their own nightvision.

Under Pressure

Stress causes high blood pressure.

✳   ✳   ✳   ✳

THIS MYTH, MORE of an outdated belief, warrants a trip to the dictionary. Hypertension is the medical term for high blood pressure, from Latin *tensio*. Literally the term means something like "stretched super tight." Tension has accumulated a bunch of meanings.

* High-tension cables or wires are specially made for use in engines, where they connect the spark plugs to the distributor and other ignition-related parts. Tension means voltage in this context.

* Tension headache is by far the most common kind of headache, enough so that almost all everyday headaches are basically synonymous with tension headache. There are many contributing causes or triggers for tension headache, and one of them is stress.

* In knitting, physics, exercise, and more, tension refers to tautness, competing opposite forces, and more.

* Tense situations refer to stressful quiet, disagreements, or other awkward scenarios. Tension between colleagues or friends is a way to describe a negative feeling that people usually feel pressured to resolve.

The Nitty Gritty

Hypertension is named literally for the high pressure created in the blood vessels, but the use of tension in figurative ways leads to conflation with stress—another word used in figurative and literal ways. Stressing a piece of hardware means to apply more force than it's made for. So hypertension does literally stress your blood vessels, which are some of our bodies's most important "hardware."

Real Causes and Confusion

But emotional stress is not linked to hypertension. For some people, factors include obesity, high sodium consumption, sedentary lifestyle, and a host of other suspected factors that are being investigated by doctors and researchers. Some diseases cause hypertension, and identifying these cases can be frustrating as doctors try to treat hypertension before they notice the underlying disease.

Although emotional stress doesn't play a part as far as scientists can tell, this idea makes intuitive sense, which may be why the idea persists. When people get angry or emotional and their heart rates speed up, the connection between stress and our hearts feels clearer than ever. And emotional stress does contribute to or exacerbate a bunch of other physical health problems, including some that affect the heart.

Sore Throat

My throat hurts, but these lozenges I bought aren't making any difference. Do I have strep throat?

✳ ✳ ✳ ✳

A SORE THROAT CAN be a minor, but annoying, ailment, or it can be a symptom of a serious illness. Causes range from a stuffy nose or a cold to strep throat.

Because untreated strep throat can lead to rheumatic fever and scarlet fever, it's important to get medical help as early as possible. Along with producing severe soreness in your gullet, strep throat may be accompanied by fever, body aches and pains, and malaise.

If you have these symptoms, or if you have a sore throat that lasts more than two or three days, see a doctor. For mild sore throats that accompany a cold or allergy, the tips below may help ease your discomfort.

Gargle with warm salt water. Make a saline solution by adding $1/2$ teaspoon salt to a cup of very warm water. Gargling with this fluid can help soothe a sore throat.

Gargle with Listerine. Another good gargling fluid is the mouthwash Listerine. If you share the product with anyone else in your household, don't drink straight from the bottle; instead, pour a small amount into a cup.

Drink hot liquids. Coating the tissue in your throat with warm liquid, such as coffee, tea, or hot lemonade. Hot liquids soothe the inflamed membranes in the thoat that are the source of your pain.

Take it easy. Common sense dictates staying in bed or at least resting when a sore throat has you down. You'll have more energy to fight the infection.

Suck on hard candy. Some doctors say sugar can help soothe a sore throat and the ticklish cough that may come with it. If nothing else, sucking on hard candy, even the sugar-free kind, can help keep your mouth and throat moist, which will make you feel more comfortable.

Steam it out. One old-fashioned remedy for a cold or sore throat is a steam tent—sitting with your face over a bowl of steaming hot water and your head covered with a towel to keep in the steam. Several scientific studies have shown that steaming can shorten the duration of a throat infection.

Keep the fluids coming. Drink as much fluid as you can—at least eight to ten 8-ounce glasses per day. Keeping your throat well-lubricated with soothing liquids can prevent it from becoming dry and irritated and may even help banish the infection faster.

It Does Sound Gross

Does cracking your knuckles give you arthritis?

✳   ✳   ✳   ✳

THIS MYTH MAY have been started by friends of knuckle-crackers who think knuckle-cracking is gross. They aren't wrong about that, but there's no evidence that cracking your knuckles gives you arthritis.

Floating around on the internet somewhere is a slow-motion X-ray view of a knuckle being cracked, and you can see a pocket of gas moving quickly from one place to another within the knuckle. This is a simple mechanism that doesn't seem to cause any harm to the knuckles themselves or the tissue around them.

Lifelong knuckle crackers may show off their chronically swollen knuckles and claim that this is the result of cracking them for years, but this has also not been studied. Swelling is usually reserved for fluid-filled, temporary inflation of tissue because of an injury, not simply that a body part may change over time. If the knuckles don't feel painful or stiff, there's probably nothing to worry about.

Influenza

Everyone says they have the "stomach flu" or a "flu bug." What is the flu really, and what can be done about it?

✳   ✳   ✳   ✳

ALTHOUGH "THE FLU" has become a catchall term for any affliction of the upper respiratory tract (and is also often improperly used for infections of the gastvrointestinal tract), the condition it refers to—influenza—is a specific viral infection that strikes every year, typically between October and April. Your best defense against the flu is to be vaccinated, but because flu strains change every year, no vaccination is going to be 100 percent effective. Vulnerable children and the elderly can experience serious flu complications or related illnesses.

Regardless of the strain, the symptoms are generally the same: high fever, sore throat, dry cough, severe muscle aches and pains, fatigue, and loss of appetite. Some people even experience pain and stiffness in the joints. If you don't manage to avoid this relentless bug, you can do a few things to ease some of the discomforts and help your body fight back.

Rest up. Plan on sleeping and relaxing for a few days. Consider the flu a good excuse to take a needed break from the daily stresses of life. If you absolutely must continue to work, at least get to bed earlier than usual and try to go into the office a little later in the morning.

Drink, drink, drink. Drinking plenty of nonalcoholic, decaffeinated liquid (alcohol and caffeine both act as diuretics, which increase fluid loss) will help keep you hydrated and will also keep any mucous secretions you have more liquid. The flu can cause a loss of appetite, but patients often find warm, salty broth agreeable. If you're not eating much, juices are a good choice, too, because they provide nutrients you may be missing.

Humidify your home in winter. Part of the reason the flu tends to strike in the colder months is your furnace. Artificial heat lowers humidity, and a dry environment allows the influenza virus to thrive. (Colder outside air also pushes people together in confined indoor spaces, making it easier for the flu bug to spread.) Adding some moisture to the air in your home with a warm- or cool-mist humidifier during the winter may not only help prevent the spread of flu, it may also make you feel more comfortable if you do get it.

Suppress a dry cough. You can reach for over-the-counter relief for a dry, hacking cough that's keeping you from getting the rest you need. When shopping for a cough remedy, look for a product that contains the cough suppressant dextromethorphan.

Encourage a "productive" cough. A cough that brings up mucus, on the other hand, is considered productive and should generally not be suppressed with cough medicines. Drinking fluids will help bring up the mucus of a productive cough and will ease the cough a little, as well.

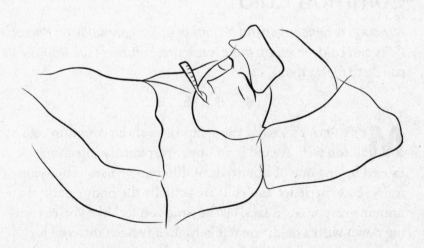

Sugar Rush

Sports drinks are a better way to rehydrate after exercise.

✳ ✳ ✳ ✳

RECOMMENDATIONS VARY ABOUT whether or not you should have a simple carbohydrate like sugar before a workout in order to have so-called fast energy to burn. But no one recommends sugary foods or drinks *after* a workout. Sugar doesn't support muscle recovery the way that, say, protein does. So your best bet is to drink water and have some protein to help your muscles recover and get stronger.

Sports drinks or rehydrating drinks like Pedialyte are great if you've been sick and feel dehydrated or out of wack, though. You can also try watering a sports drink down with some water. Many workout enthusiasts use sugar-free energy mixes and recommend them, but a lot of these products are just caffeine, which may make some people agitated or jittery rather than energized and productive.

Common Cold

Although Americans spend billions of dollars annually on doctor visits and cold remedies, there is no cure. Still, there are things you can do to feel better.

✳ ✳ ✳ ✳

MOST PEOPLE KNOW the symptoms of the common cold all too well. A cold is an upper respiratory infection caused by any one of hundreds of different viruses. The symptoms you experience as a cold are actually the body's natural immune response. In fact, by the time you feel like you're coming down with a cold, you've likely already been infected for a day and a half. Unproven homeopathic remedies make false promises, but many time-tested home treatments can relieve some of your symptoms.

Rest. First and foremost, you should take it easy because your body is spending a lot of energy fighting off the cold virus. Staying away from work is probably a good idea too, from a prevention standpoint; coworkers will appreciate your not spreading the cold virus around the workplace.

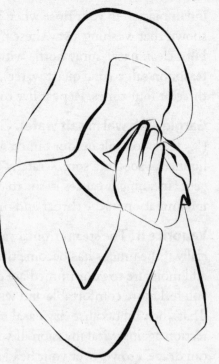

Drink up. Nonalcoholic fluids may help thin the mucus, thus keeping it flowing freely and making it easier for the body to expel. When mucus is ousted, so are the viral particles making you sick that are trapped within it. Water and other liquids also combat dehydration. Drink at least eight ounces of fluid every two hours.

Cook up some chicken soup. One of the most beneficial hot fluids you can consume when you have a cold is chicken soup. Moses Maimonides, a physician and rabbi, first prescribed chicken soup for the common cold in twelfth-century Egypt and it has been a favorite folk remedy ever since. In 1978, Marvin Sackner, M.D., of Mount Sinai Hospital in Miami Beach, Florida, included chicken soup in a test of the effects of sipping hot and cold water on the clearance of mucus. To the doctor's surprise, chicken soup placed first, hot water second, and cold water a distant third. Physicians aren't sure exactly why chicken soup helps clear nasal passages, but many agree "it's just what the doctor ordered."

Use a saltwater wash. Molecules your body makes to fight infection called cytokines, or lymphokines, cause the swelling and inflammation in your nose when you have a cold. Research has shown that washing away these molecules can reduce swelling. Fill a clean nasal-spray bottle with diluted salt water (one level teaspoon salt to one quart water), and spray into each nostril three or four times. Repeat five to six times per day.

Gargle with warm salt water. Gargling with warm salt water (¹/₄ teaspoon salt in four ounces warm water) every one to two hours can soothe a sore, scratchy throat. Salt water is an astringent (meaning it causes tissue to contract), which can soothe inflammation in the throat and may help loosen mucus.

Vaporize it. The steam from a vaporizer can loosen mucus, especially if the mucus has become thick and gunky. A humidifier will add moisture to your immediate environment, which may make you feel more comfortable and will keep your nasal tissues moist. That's helpful because dry nasal membranes provide poor protection against viral invasion. If you don't have a vaporizer, you can drape a towel over your head and bend over a pot of boiled water—just be careful not to burn yourself.

Identity Swap

Fat can turn into muscle.

✳ ✳ ✳ ✳

THIS MYTH IS confounding because it doesn't make any sense. If you worked really hard, could you turn your appendix into a pancreas? Body cells generally become and remain what they are. People who say this may be using the expression figuratively, because they envision shedding fat and building muscle in the same visual spot on the body. In any case, your body is permeated with muscles, including many muscles that are deep inside your internal organs. Fat is a superficial layer around the very outside beneath your skin.

The Mighty Brains and Bods of Chess Masters

Chess is seen as the territory of the nerdy genius, but its masters come in all shapes, sizes, ages, raw intellects, and styles of play. And its challenges are physical as well as mental.

✳ ✳ ✳ ✳

Can the best chess players "see" dozens of moves ahead?

PLANNING AND FORECASTING moves is a critical part of the strategy of chess, incentivizing players who can see multiple paths of progress and optimize their choices. Chess masters might be able to telegraph that many moves with chess novices or when most of the pieces are off the board, although even that still seems staggering to an average person. But chess insiders guess the real number is "only" 10 or 15 moves ahead.

This level of planning and forecasting makes chess an ideal field for game theoreticians to study. Branching decisionmaking and choosing the best from a set of options is also of great interest to computer scientists who are busy studying ways to improve computing using the thinking skills of the human brain.

Does getting older make you better at chess?

This is the age-old question of experience versus raw talent. But those who play and study chess point out that savants like Bobby Fischer, who became the then-youngest grandmaster at age 15, have become more and more common. Computerized chess makes it simple to practice on your own and sharpen skills at an early age that took older generations a lifetime.

None of that is to say younger players are inherently better or have an edge. But the game of chess is changing logistically in a way few would have predicted 30 years ago. And it's all the more staggering that Fischer accumulated the level of skill that he had by age 15 before the personal computer was developed.

The best chess players can still beat computers.

This is a sad myth to debunk, but no, computers have far surpassed human players by now. There are limits to human thinking capacity that computers continue to pass or even lap as the capacity of hardware goes up and the cost keeps falling. The math of this is simple to think about. Ten options for this move, then ten options for each of those first options, and so forth. The numbers quickly grow far too large for the human mind to comprehend, let alone meaningfully work into our strategy.

Computing is, at the end of the day, an enormous number of math problems done extremely fast. And really, that's what chess always has been. Much of human strategy at any game is learning when to guess that certain moves are unadvisable— we're rarely 100% certain that our opponent will or won't take a certain action. A computer doesn't even need to fudge this value because it can all be calculated. The best computers beat the best human players in almost every game.

Experts at games like chess are probably physically weak.

This myth cuts both ways, as many believe world-class athletes can't also be smart. A Baltimore Ravens player earning a Ph.D. in mathematics from the Massachusetts Institute of Technology made headlines when he retired from the NFL after just four years. He explained that the increase in findings that football could damage his brain helped to inform his decision, because his career in mathematics could suffer.

Chess players must not only sit still but focus intensely for hours at a time, and anyone with an achy back or even a hangnail knows how these niggling issues can jeopardize someone's ability to concentrate. Most chess masters keep up regular exercise routines. And physical activities like tai chi or yoga can help to increase your sustained focus if you keep up a regular practice.

Allergies

A large number of people suffer from seasonal allergies, and the changing world climate can create new sufferers each season. Here are some surprising home remedies that can help—without any dubious medical claims.

❋ ❋ ❋ ❋

Hidden Severity

For many people, each change of season brings its own brand of allergy triggers and irritants. In cases of common hay fever and allergies, these pollutants can bring on symptoms that range from a continuous, annoying postnasal drip to a full-scale, coughing-sneezing-itchy-eyed allergy attack. Other allergy sufferers, such as those with allergic asthma or an allergy to bee stings, can die from attacks. The following tips are designed to help reduce the discomfort caused by the most common allergies. They may be used in combination with an allergist's treatment or, if your allergies are mild, by themselves.

Rinse your eyes. If your eyes are itchy and irritated and you have no access to allergy medicine, rinsing them with cool, clean water can be soothing. Although not as effective as an antihistamine, this remedy certainly can't do any harm.

Try a warm washcloth. Do your sinus passages feel congested and painful? A washcloth soaked in warm water may make things flow a little easier. Place the washcloth over the nose and upper-cheek area, and relax for a bit.

Say hello to saline. Irrigating the nose with saline solution (salt water) may help soothe upper respiratory allergies by removing irritants that become lodged in the nose and cause inflammation. In fact, saline solution may even wash away some of the inflammatory cells themselves. You can buy saline solution at your local drugstore, or you can make your own fresh solution daily by mixing a teaspoon of salt and a pinch of baking soda in a pint of warm, distilled water. Bend over a sink and sniff a bit of solution into one nostril at a time, allowing it to drain back out through the nose or mouth; do this once or twice a day. (If you also have asthma, however, check with your doctor before trying this remedy.)

Wash your hair. If you've spent long hours outdoors during the pollen season, wash your hair to remove pollen after you come inside. The sticky yellow stuff tends to collect on the hair, making it more likely to fall into your eyes.

Take a shower. If you wake up in the middle of the night with a coughing, sneezing allergy attack, a hot shower may help by removing any pollen residues you've collected on your body throughout the day. (You might want to change your pillowcase, too.) There's also a good chance your sinuses will open up, at least for a while, making breathing a little easier. The warm water may even help you relax and go back to sleep.

Protect your eyes. On a windy day during pollen season, a pair of sunglasses (or your regular prescription eyeglasses, if you wear them) can help shield your eyes from airborne allergens. For extra protection, try a pair of sunglasses with side shields or even a pair of goggles.

Shut the windows. A fresh breeze blowing through an open window on a spring day may sound inviting, but it's bad news for an allergy sufferer, because pollen can fill the house. Keep windows closed at all times to minimize contact with the powdery stuff.

Go bare. Carpets are a notorious haven for dust mites, which are microscopic bugs that feed on the dead skin cells we constantly shed; dust-mite droppings spur allergies in millions of people. Bare floors that are vacuumed and damp-mopped frequently will help keep down your home's dust-mite population (you can't get rid of them all). If you can't remove all the carpeting in your home, at least opt for bare floors in your bedroom. Studies show the bedroom harbors more dust mites than any other room in the home, and you probably spend about a third of every day there.

Filter your vacuum. When you can't remove carpets, keeping them as clean as possible will help you breathe a bit easier. But beware: Many vacuums blast small particles of dust back into the air, leaving behind plenty of allergens to keep you sneezing and wheezing. Use a vacuum that has a built-in HEPA (high-efficiency particulate air) filter or attach a filter to the exhaust port of your canister vacuum (uprights usually don't have an exhaust port). If dust really bothers you and you have the money, consider investing in an industrial-strength vacuuming system. Speak with your allergist to find out whether such products are appropriate for you and where you can purchase them.

Dust with a damp cloth. Dusting at least once a week is important, but if done improperly, it may aggravate respiratory allergies. Avoid using feather dusters, which tend to spread dust around; instead, control dust with a damp cloth. Dusting sprays may give off odors that can worsen allergies. If dusting really bothers you, don't do it. Ask a spouse or family member to do the dirty work, or hire a housekeeper, if possible.

Dehumidify. Dust mites love a humid environment because it allows them to reproduce like crazy. Invest in a dehumidifier or use an air conditioner, which works equally well. A dehumidifier can also help prevent mold, another allergen, from growing (just be sure to follow the manufacturer's maintenance instructions). And use the exhaust fan when cooking or showering to keep humidity to a minimum.

Wash your pet. Fido and Fifi produce allergy-causing substances in their sweat and saliva that get on their fur. Fortunately, these allergens dissolve in water, so a warm bath can rinse away the problem. If you're a cat owner and can't imagine bathing your beloved feline for fear of nearly being scratched to death, take heart: Some cats (though a minority, to be sure) purr when bathed. If you start bathing your feline regularly when it's a kitten, chances are better that clean-up time will be a harmonious experience. Wash your cat in warm water, with no soap, once every other week. In addition, try to wash your hands soon after you've had direct contact with your furry friend.

And Umami

The five senses are sight, hearing, taste, touch, and and smell.

✳ ✳ ✳ ✳

THOSE ARE THE major five senses, but humans have almost limitless senses, like our senses of motion, of time passing, and of space around us. Humans detect (or senses) an amazing amount of information at virtually all times, and our complex world is constantly serving up amazing *new* amounts for us.

One major overlooked sense is our spacial relationship, which allows us to "mindlessly" walk, sit, and do countless other things without needing to see them up close or watch and monitor ourselves while we do them. It's miraculous when you really think about it. Thank you, stereo vision!

Fever

Knowing when a fever is serious or life-threatening could make the difference between an average day and an appalling tragedy. But clashing information can create confusion over what constitutes an emergency. What is a fever really, and when is it serious?

✳   ✳   ✳   ✳

FEVER IS NOT a disease in itself but simply a symptom of some other condition, usually an infection caused by a bacterium or virus. When such an enemy invades, white blood cells attack, releasing a substance called pyrogen. When pyrogen reaches the brain, it signals the hypothalamus, a tiny structure at the base of the brain that regulates the body's temperature, to set itself at a higher point. If that new set point is higher than 100 degrees Fahrenheit, you have a fever. When a fever develops, what should you do? Try the advice that follows.

Don't force yourself under cover. Shivers are your body's way of creating heat to boost your temperature, so if your teeth are chattering or you feel chilled, by all means, cover up to make yourself more comfortable. However, once your fever is established and you start feeling hot, bundling yourself under a pile of blankets will only hold in the heat and likely make you feel worse. You can't "sweat out a fever," or get a fever to break by forcing your body temperature up even higher. So if you feel as though you're burning up, toss off those covers or use a single, light sheet.

Undress. With your body exposed as much

as possible, your sweat glands will be better able to release moisture, which will make you feel more comfortable. Strip down to your skivvies—that means a diaper for an infant and underpants and thin undershirt for an older child or adult.

Dip. Sponge yourself with tepid water or, better yet, sit in a tub of cool water (though definitely not ice-cold water, because that can induce shock) for half an hour. If you put a feverish child in a tub or sink of water, be sure to hold him or her. Don't apply an alcohol rub, because it can be absorbed into the skin and cause alcohol poisoning.

Sip. Fever, especially one accompanied by vomiting or diarrhea, can lead to fluid loss and an electrolyte imbalance, so it's important to keep drinking. Cool water is best, but unsweetened juices are okay if that's what tastes good. Getting a child to drink plenty of water is sometimes difficult, so try Popsicles or flavored ices that are made primarily of water.

Let it run. Bear in mind that fever-reducing drugs (antipyretics) are designed to make you feel more comfortable during the course of a fever. The fact is, however, that fever may do an ailing body some good by making it less hospitable to the infecting organism, so you may want to let it run its course rather than rushing to bring it down with medications. An untreated fever in an adult or a child older than six months of age tends to be self-limited, relatively benign, and unlikely to escalate to the point that it causes harm. Letting a fever run its course is not the best idea for everyone, however. Seek medical advice immediately for:

* An infant younger than two months of age with a rectal temperature of 100.2 degrees Fahrenheit or higher (or lower than 95 degrees)

* A child two months of age or older with a rectal temperature of at least 102 (or, in an older child, an oral temperature of at least 101)

* A child two months of age or older with a rectal temperature between 100 and 102 (or, in an older child, an oral temperature between 99 and 101) that is accompanied by unexplained irritability; listlessness or lethargy; repeated vomiting; severe headache, stomachache, or earache; croupy "barking" cough; or difficulty breathing

* Any fever that lasts more than one day in a child younger than two years of age or more than three days in a child two years old or older

* A pregnant woman with any above-normal body temperature (generally 100 degrees or higher)

* An otherwise healthy adult with a temperature higher than 104 (oral); a temperature of 102 (oral) or higher accompanied by a serious underlying illness, such as heart arrhythmia or lung disease; or a temperature of 100 or higher that lasts for more than three days or is accompanied by severe headache, neck pain or stiffness, chest or abdominal pain, swelling of the throat or difficulty breathing, skin rash, sensitivity to bright light, confusion or unexplained irritability, listlessness, repeated vomiting, pain during urination, or redness or swelling of the skin

If a fever is making you or your child very uncomfortable, you can use a nonprescription antipyretic. Aspirin, ibuprofen, and acetaminophen are all antipyretics. Aspirin and ibuprofen also have an anti-inflammatory action, which can be an advantage in certain conditions, such as an abscess, that may cause fever. However, do not give aspirin products to children younger than 19 years of age because of the risk of a potentially fatal condition known as Reye's syndrome; stick with acetaminophen for children. Follow all package directions carefully.

Exercise Myth

The best way to lose weight is to exercise.

✳ ✳ ✳ ✳

AMERICANS NOTORIOUSLY UNDERESTIMATE the number of calories they eat, both in terms of individual foods and servings and overall daily intake. Athletes training for marathons or triathlons often find that they *gain* weight during their training because of the appetite increase that can accompany changes in exercise routines.

If your goal is to lose weight, the single best way is to examine your calorie intake. Most people are surprised by the reality of the situation after just a few days of keeping a food diary or using a tracking app. No one ever needs to restrictively diet or decide certain foods are "bad" or "off limits" unless they have a medical reason to need to do that. But thinking about what you're eating and making some simple changes can lead to positive results for your health.

Chapter 9

Plant Life

Changes in Latitude,
Changes in Attitude

Planting trees helps to fight global warming.

✳ ✳ ✳ ✳

DEFORESTATION HAS CONTRIBUTED to global warming, but in a more complicated way than this myth purports. Most of what we think of as deforestation is of the massive, unspoiled rainforests and other tropical forests near the equator. These wild areas help to trap carbon dioxide and turn it back into oxygen through photosynthesis.

They also literally absorb the heat of the sun and prevent it from further warming the planet's surface, the same way sitting under a shady tree helps us stay cooler. And water that evaporates from the leaves of trees and other plants helps to cool the air in a mechanism much like how humans perspire.

On the other hand, forests in northernmost latitudes actually warm the planet more. Like the greenhouse effect, these leafy canopies create a barrier that traps heat from reflecting back out into space. It's much more pronounced than any similar effect in equatorial areas that already have very warm climates.

All that is to say: Planting trees in deforested equatorial areas definitely does help to fight global warming. These trees have a direct and statistically significant effect on reducing carbon dioxide and overall temperature. But organizations that plant trees further from the equator are not helping, and may in fact make global warming worse.

Protective Custody

National forests are protected from destructive commercial activities like drilling.

✳ ✳ ✳ ✳

PRESIDENT THEODORE ROOSEVELT is usually imagined to be the creator of the U.S. National Park Service, but Yellowstone was designated in 1872, long before President Roosevelt got involved. The National Park Service (NPS) itself was signed into existence by President Woodrow Wilson in 1916, and the national system of parks, protected areas, and wildernesses has continued to grow since.

But *only* the national parks themselves are under the protection of the NPS. Conservation areas, wilderness areas, national scenic trails, and many other categories of national lands are under the jurisdiction of the Bureau of Land Management, which is actually the largest of all the land-protecting government agencies: the Bureau of Land management (BLM) oversees 40% of the nation's protected acreage.

The BLM can conduct commercial business on its lands in many ways. Ranchers can pay to graze cattle on BLM land, and there are over 60,000 petroleum wells on these lands. At the same time, the BLM is a huge frontier in renewable energy because of its huge holdings in western states with ideal settings for wind and solar energy collection.

There are different rules for protected lands whose purpose is to protect and foster wildlife, since any intrusion into animal habitats can have far-reaching and unpredictable consequences. Debate over use of the Arctic National Wildlife Refuge in Alaska, for example, has raged for decades. Technology makes it increasingly viable to drill for oil in this inhospitable region.

Grassy "No"s

Grass lawns are bad for the environment.

✳ ✳ ✳ ✳

Is Grass Drying Up?

INCREASING DROUGHT CONDITIONS in the western United States have brought gravel, moss, and other "lawn alternatives" to the forefront—but what about areas where water use isn't regulated, or isn't regulated *yet*? There are notable benefits for everyone who reconsiders a traditional grass lawn.

Most grasses used for lawns in the United States are from Europe, which is why they can require so much additional work when planted on American land. Kentucky bluegrass was imported at some point, probably as an animal-feed grass. It thrives in cooler climates, so grows most and looks best during the spring and fall. And because it has shallow roots, it fries easily in summer heat and must be heavily watered.

Looking Forward

In the perfect suburban landscapes of the postwar United States, the extra work of a cool-weather lawn was worth it. But the environmental impact and even the reduction of available water have pressed people to look to alternatives. Lower-maintenance grasses like Bermuda or zoysia can stand up to drought and heat, but they have shorter overall growing seasons and need sun. The lawn of the future may simply not be grass at all.

More Reasons to Change

Even if you live in a climate where grass is easy to grow, there are reasons to think twice about your lawn. Close-trimmed grass is usually environmentally neutral at best, and you may decide that it makes sense for your home and family to make a change to support the planet, especially if your lawn requires a lot of watering, chemicals, or other intervention in order to thrive. You may simply be tired of dedicating time and money to all this maintenance.

Wild Decisions

Landscape architects—different from landscapers or landscape designers—have led the way in analyzing natural resources and choosing the least impactful plants and structures to introduce in outdoor spaces. Making thoughtful choices with your lawn, like planting wildflowers or allowing native plants to "reclaim" your space, can help the local soil and water supply alike.

If no news is good news, choosing an alternative to a grass lawn is the least disruptive and therefore best news for your local environment. With lower maintenance costs, fewer chemicals, and less overall labor, the alternatives can make sense even to those who aren't concerned by environmentalism.

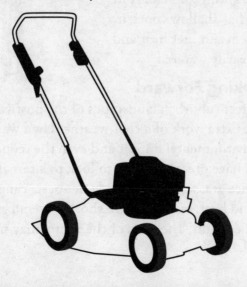

Blue Over Genes

Genetically modified crops are unhealthy.

❋ ❋ ❋ ❋

Too Soon to Tell

AS WITH THE debate over organic food, this question gets very complicated very fast. Scientists mostly agree that the simple mechanism of modifying food is not inherently dangerous as far as they know. Already, that's a lot of caveats, and there aren't very good long-term studies about the kind of specific genetic modification we're doing.

The Legacy of Better Plants

Humans have grafted and bred hybrids of plants for thousands of years using simple methods. How did growers start to physically cut branches from one tree and attach them to another? It's easy to imagine a desperate situation where a dead fruit tree threatened the food supply of a family or village enough to warrant a Hail Mary pass.

Hybrids are usually made using trial and error with different plant species. Growers can mix pollen from one plant with another, introducing the genetic material from a different species in order to make a plant with qualities of both. And by experimenting over time, they can choose a blend that combines the qualities they want: a bigger tomato, a juicier apple, or a seedless cucumber.

Modern Risks

Direct genetic modification of crops is, its proponents argue, simply a modern version of these age-old forms of agricultural science. No one is scrappier or more resourceful than a food grower, and their dedicated and thoughtful work over thousands of years is why we have so many delicious fruits and vegetables today.

But industrial capitalism throws a wrench into this argument. Companies like Monsanto have vast empires built on their designer seeds and fertilizers, and they've fought massive legal battles to keep these formulae top secret. Farmers

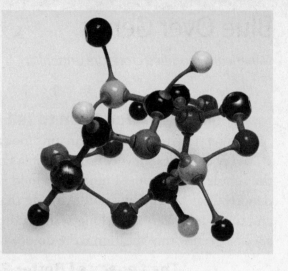

must buy a fresh supply of bespoke seed corn every year because it's illegal to reuse these crops.

The Sharp Cutting Edge

Should you be able to trademark a plant? These sticky questions are being asked and answered daily in the twenty-first century. But what if an agribusiness conglomerate made a form of crop that could be "switched" to fail in the fields if its growers didn't comply with some corporate standard? Or what if an entire year's worth of corn or soy were deemed unsafe for human consumption because of some late-breaking news about the effect of a particular genetic modification?

The technology itself is not unsafe, but the relationship between modern farming and territorial intellectual property can't be undone enough to study genetic modification as some abstract idea. So the argument is murky and warrants a lot more study and scrutiny.

All Ground Up

Coffee grounds are a great fertilizer.

✳   ✳   ✳   ✳

THIS OLD WIVES' tale offers a perfect storm of repeatability: it uses a waste product, makes a surprising claim, and would be difficult to disprove. But there are some immediate red flags about the idea, and they turn out to be valid as well. Overall, this myth is a big question mark. Another myth claims that dairy is good for growing moss, when in reality, gardening with dairy is just good for attracting mold. Maybe we can combine these myths into one big cappuccino of deception.

Percolating Objections

Coffee is caustic enough that plenty of people either forgo it altogether or mellow it out using insulating dairy. The grounds are still very acidic and contain caffeine, both qualities that are generally harmful to plants. For these reasons, coffee grounds don't make sense as part of a blanket rule shared with all gardeners or plant owners.

Guardian reporter James Wong wrote about an experiment he did in his own garden in 2016, where two identical vegetable patches could be compared. He followed the folk wisdom of sprinkling coffee grounds onto one vegetable patch each day and kept the other one coffee-free as he usually would. The results, where the coffee-treated plants became visibly sick or died, caused him to think again.

Wong found reasons why this happened, including the acidity and caffeine. The best insight from his experiment is the idea that caffeine is a way for the plants that produce it is to kill off their competition. Psychoactive alkaloids—nicotine and opium are also in this category—are great ways for plants to defend themselves. The ways they alter the human mind aren't the same ways they work on plants, or at least plants don't have minds to alter. But the chemical ways these substances affect our brains and body chemistry speaks to how they can equally or more severely impact plant life.

A Cup by Cup Basis

Experts say you can use coffee grounds to accomplish good things in your garden, but they should be applied carefully, sparingly, and never in direct contact with the stems or roots of your plants. Some plants love acidity enough that you might use coffee grounds, in small quantities, to make the soil more acidic. But too much and the caffeine will still slow down these plants in both growing and flowering.

It's wonderful to think you might turn many people's most regular source of garbage into a secret dynamo of plant nutrition. But proponents are coffee cherry-picking and offering a variety of competing pretend facts and anecdata. If this all makes you think again about coffee grounds in your garden, maybe you can use those grounds in a compost pile instead.

Mass Extinction

The decline in Earth's biodiversity isn't really that bad.

✳   ✳   ✳   ✳

A LITTLE BIT OF information can go a long way in the wrong direction, as climate-change deniers show us. The human mind finds it easier to look at its local conditions and draw conclusions than to think abstractly and extrapolate about the whole planet and faraway habitats. If we have a very cold summer day, how can there be global warming?

That same logical flaw applies to the massive species loss on Earth in the last century or more. Individual backyards may have the same variety of species as they always did, and we hear in the news when an exotic animal is found roaming wild in a city or other incongruous place. Doesn't that show species diversity is fine?

Humans pay closer attention to animals than plants, but plant loss has been enormous as we continue to deforest and otherwise change plant habitats. Animals, too, have been displaced by human encroachment. When wild animals are found in cities and other unusual places, it's because their natural habitats are not right anymore.

Scientists call the modern era a sixth mass extinction event, in the same series as the mass extinction that killed most of the dinosaurs. Despite that, biodiversity has stayed the same or increased in some zones, and habitats continue to shift among temperature zones because of climate change.

A Watched Pot

You should replant your indoor plant in a bigger pot so it can grow bigger.

✳ ✳ ✳ ✳

I**N OUR RUSH** to ensure that plants have plenty of space for their roots, it seems that many of us also overestimate how much space their roots should take up. As with planting trees outdoors, giving an indoor plant too much space in a pot can be counterproductive.

More importantly, a bigger pot doesn't correspond with a bigger plant every time. Some plants prefer to have compact roots, and they can thrive from a smaller pot. Especially if this trade-off means you can fit more sun-loving plants into the sunniest parts of your windows, it may be worth it.

In an overlarge pot, the soil can stay damp because there aren't enough roots to absorb the moisture. This can lead to root rot, bacterial growth, and other problems. If that's a concern, you can investigate ways to help your soil drain more rapidly or methods to water more gradually.

Local Dilemma

Buying "local crops" is more sustainable.

✳ ✳ ✳ ✳

The Best of All Possible Worlds

P**HILOSOPHER GOTTFRIED LEIBNIZ**, most famous for his calculus beef with Sir Isaac Newton, wrote extensively about theoretical Earths. In his book *Theodicy* he related a myth about the Roman god Jupiter, who was the major creator figure in the Roman Empire before the advent of Christianity.

Jupiter had his pick of infinite different versions of the world, and he used his godly wisdom to choose the best one. From time to time, Leibniz explained, Jupiter revisited those other Earths to continue to make sure he'd chosen correctly. He was always pleased to find that he had.

Unfortunately, the Real World

There is some perfect theoretical Earth where local crops are plentiful for everyone. But in the real world where we all live, most people simply could not survive on what grows locally anymore. The level of attention, number of agricultural workers, and amount of land required are just all beyond the capacity of our available resources.

Local food has become something of a euphemism for a form of shopping and eating that only niche markets with money can support. For most American consumers, choosing the conventional produce they prefer at a local supermarket means spending less, but it can also cost less for the environment. Conventional produce can be shipped in gigantic, relatively efficient quantities that cost less energy per piece than the special resources that may be required to grow a crop locally.

Avocados and Don'ts

When it comes to the environment and sustainability, very few issues are at all clear cut. Every choice involves thought, context, and compromise. There are factors that are beyond anyone's control at this point in Earth's history, and we must answer to those factors even though we didn't cause them ourselves.

Is it practical to argue that everyone in the U.S. should choose local foods when there isn't enough local food, by a factor of *many times*, to feed us all? The cost of remaking the U.S. workforce, landscape, and soil or greenhouse makeup to support this change would be far more than the purported environmental savings of making the switch.

Deep Roots

A hole for a tree should be twice as wide and twice as deep as the roots.

✳   ✳   ✳   ✳

WHEN YOU PLANT a tree, the top of its roots should be flush with the surface of the soil. We think of trees as having gigantic, deep roots, but most trees like to keep their roots relatively shallow and quite spread out horizontally. Tree roots may work their way deeper into the soil after the tree has settled and grown bigger and needs more nutrients, but the roots will be firmly anchored in their preferred place before that happens.

This makes sense if you think about it. Deeper soil is more compacted, with less air and therefore less oxygen. It's cold because it's buried and insulated from the sun. The organic matter and other biological changes that work nutrients into the soil barely reach the deeper soil. Anyone who's ever seen a cross-section of their local soil knows it probably sits in discrete layers with very little intermingling.

So trees prefer to reach out into the shallower soil that has more nutrients, warmth, and oxygen. It's also easier to push roots through soil with a bit more aeration. You can also encourage your tree's roots to spread and grow by filling the planting hole with the same dirt you just took out. If the soil right next to the tree's roots is more rich and nourishing, the roots will never branch out from the planting hole.

High Stakes

Baby trees must be staked in order to be supported as they grow.

❋   ❋   ❋   ❋

TREE PEOPLE (THE human kind, not like Treebeard and the Ents) have their work cut out for them in trying to correct this myth. It was likely begun by landscaping workers who felt that tiny saplings just looked too vulnerable to be left without some kind of support. There are some cases when you should stake a tree, but these are exceptions rather than the rule. If you plant a tree on a slope or in really challenging soil, staking might be a good idea.

Otherwise, trees do well when they find their own way. Bending and swaying in the wind and weather help a tree's roots to become strong, flexible, and resilient. Staking, especially when tied too restrictively or kept up for too long, is like keeping a splint on an already weak limb that needs to be able to accumulate its own strength instead.

A Watertight Case

Painting, varnishing, or otherwise "sealing" a freshly cut tree branch can keep out infection.

❋   ❋   ❋   ❋

TREES ARE INCREDIBLY tough and resilient, and they've been surviving fallen branches and other serious "wounds" for millions of years. If a tree has a dead section that needs to be pruned, many people cover the exposed wood with a watertight coating of sealant or even tar. The goal of this is to keep out any icky little stuff that can infect a tree the same way a person's exposed injury can become infected.

This analogy also helps us understand why the sealant myth is wrong. Watertight bandage products like "liquid bandage" are only useful for specific instances of very shallow cuts, and for people like cooks or swimmers who spend a lot of time getting their hands wet. Otherwise, any covering that doesn't breathe can end up sealing germs *into* the injury, and any incipient infection can't be flushed out.

Instead, let the newly exposed wood breathe freely and use its natural defenses against infection. There's no evidence that sealing the wood helps the tree, and there *is* evidence that it can accelerate or even encourage decay.

Waterless Plants

I researched and bought plants that don't need to be watered.

* * * *

SOMETIMES GARDENING OR landscaping can seem like trying to match on a dating site. Filter out plants that need too much sunlight. Filter out plants that need too much attention. Filter out plants that are poisonous to dogs. The options narrow down until we find our soulmate in plant form, but as with dating sites, looks can be deceiving.

When we see thriving plants in specialized natural environments, there's some selection bias at work. Yes, the plants we see are healthy, but we don't see the dozen others of the same plant that weren't so lucky. Plants for "drought conditions" don't require a lot of regular attention once they're settled and mature, but they do need to be watered and cared for until that happens. There's no need to enact "survival of the fittest" in the privacy of your own yard.

A plant you never water does have a vaguely sitcom feeling about it, though, like in a few months you realize your neighbor has been watering your "waterless" plant all along. Don't be a person who makes their neighbors pity their dry plants.

Too Much of a Good Thing

You can never add too much pesticide or fertilizer.

✳ ✳ ✳ ✳

FERTILIZER COMPONENTS LIKE potash and nitrogen are all tested at similar amounts to what the manufacturer or seller instructs you to use. These components can have adverse effects at higher levels, and they're not even the more synthetic or bug-killing ingredients. You may be willy nilly when you pour laundry detergent into the washer or add cayenne to a pot of chili, but you'd think twice before taking four or six aspirin at a time—hopefully.

If the instructed amount of a particular product isn't getting the result you want, don't add more and assume it will work better. Try a different product, a different application time, or an adjustment to some other variable. It's hard watching struggling plants day after day, but patience will eventually pay off. If you'd killed the plants by overfertilizing, there'd be no such luck. And pay close attention to whether or not a product is meant to be diluted before you apply it!

Concrete Thinking

Adding sand to clay soil will loosen it up.

✳ ✳ ✳ ✳

MIXING SAND AND clay is actually how you make a rough form of cement, which you may have found out the hard way after your garden dried and firmed up into a patio. In order to effectively add sand to your clay, you'd need to use so much sand that you had nearly replaced all the soil, which isn't a solution either. The best way to break up clay is to use a light, absorbent, nutritious soil. Clay is a very dense suspension of water in dust, almost a very thick paste instead of a powder.

When it has an opportunity to dry out a bit, it can be crushed back into powder instead of heavy clods. (And at that point, you might try adding some sand.)

Shady Claims

Can sunshine burn leaves that have water droplets on them?

✳ ✳ ✳ ✳

THIS MYTH IS cited as a reason to water in the morning or at night, but in reality those are just the most convenient and prudent times to water plants. There's less evaporation in the cooler temperatures and without the sun shining, and most water utilities prefer customers water their yards or plants during the off-peak hours. The hypothetical science is that sunshine is focused by water droplets the same way a magnifying class can burn something on the sidewalk below.

But using a magnifying glass still takes a long time and is something of a myth in itself. Water droplets are much smaller and have inherent insulation—think about how quickly the air around your stove burner gets *very* hot compared with the time it takes for a pot of water to get up to the same temperature. Even on the small scale of a water droplet, water can hold more energy than air because of its four-times-higher heat capacity.

Negligent Herbicide

Organic pesticides are safer than manmade pesticides.

✳ ✳ ✳ ✳

IN JUDD APATOW's cult TV series *Freaks and Geeks*, one main character tries to convince another to smoke marijuana by saying, "It's from the earth." She snaps back, "Dog poop is from the earth." We tend to think of synthetic products as a separate and often sinister category, but naturally occurring poisons are *everywhere* around us. Think about all the common plants that are toxic to humans or animals, cause allergic reactions or rashes, or live as parasites.

There's a joke that circulates on the internet in response to people who are avidly "anti-chemical," since everything we ever touch or use is a chemical or made of chemicals in some way. In the joke, a narrator pretends to be alarmed by "hydrogen dioxide" which, of course, is just water. Synthetic pesticides can be chemically simpler than organic pesticides, since scientists can engineer them to have just what we need and nothing we don't. Any consumer product should be evaluated on a case-by-case basis before you choose what's best for your yard or garden.

Adding Injury to Injury

You should use fertilizer to help a sick garden plant.

✳   ✳   ✳   ✳

GENERALLY, A PLANT is happy in decent soil with adequate watering. Plants have specific ways to show that they lack certain nutrients, but otherwise, a plant that already looks sick is past the point when fertilizer is going to help—at least until the plant is healthy again. Adding fertilizer to plants that are distressed can take the plant's "attention" away from continuing to grow and heal itself, kind of the same way a big meal draws our blood flow to our stomachs and can make us feel tired.

Choosing the wrong fertilizer can also tilt bad soil even further out of balance in terms of nutrient content. There's no one right answer for all situations, so do your research before you reach for whatever fertilizer you have around.

Going, Going, Gone

A yellowing plant is already dead.

✻   ✻   ✻   ✻

A YELLOW PLANT CAN be interpreted like a yellow light in traffic: proceed with caution. There's no reason a yellowing plant necessarily *needs* to die, but you should think carefully about how much water, fertilizer, and light the plant is getting compared to what it might need.

Depending on the plant, you may find that pruning a yellow leaf helps the rest of the plant continue to thrive. If in doubt, keep trying and do your research. Your suspected "black thumb" may just be an impatient, unenlightened thumb.

Plant Fatalities

Indoor and outdoor plants all die in the winter.

✻   ✻   ✻   ✻

H UMANS LOVE TO bond over complaining about the weather, especially in the winter. But we're much more temperature resilient and flexible than we imagine, especially because we can layer on sweaters and warm socks and have hot beverages.

If your indoor plants seem to be suffering in the winter, think about trying to place them closer to a heat source, or at least definitely a little further from a potentially poorly insulated window. There's no reason an otherwise healthy indoor plant should automatically die when it's cold outside. Winter is the time when we need the brightness and good cheer of plants the most!

Misting the Point

Misting indoor plants can make them think they're in a humid environment.

✳ ✳ ✳ ✳

WATER MIST FROM a spray bottle hangs in the air for just a second before it settles. This is a fine way to get your plant's leaves wet, and plants like misting, but a plant that really calls for a humid environment should be kept near a humidifier.

Humidifiers are designed to place tinier "bits" of air into a much broader and more homogeneous pattern in the air. Basically, imagine trying to make mud out of sand and water, and then using soil and water instead. Smaller particles create a smoother solution.

Fearmongering in the Microwave

Does microwaved water kill plants?

✳ ✳ ✳ ✳

THIS BIZARRE MYTH is repeated by people who misunderstand how microwaves work or fear, in general, things they do not understand. When the story circulates, it's often accompanied by even stranger hand-waving scientific explanations of how microwaves, the harmlessly low radiation used by the microwave oven, corrupt the very nature of life itself.

Water is water is water. If anything were different about it after it came out of the microwave, you'd see this in the cup, where something new had replaced the water.

At the same time, microwaved water technically can explode. If a smooth-surfaced cup of water is microwaved for a very long time, it can become superheated, meaning boiling without the presence of the telltale bubbles that accompany boiling. Moving a cup of superheated water can shift the tension and cause it to immediately, rapidly boil and explode. However, this will probably never happen to you or anyone you know, unless you take a time machine and become friends with Howard Hughes.

Even then, it will only work if he uses a perfect, brand-new coffee cup every time—and if you remember to bring your microwave.

Fuzzy Moss Ideas

Moss isn't really a plant, it's a fungus or... something else.

THERE ARE SOME lifeforms that boggle our minds. Some are obvious, like the fish who live deep beneath the ocean and create their own light, or animals that live in such dark places that they've evolved past needing eyes. But others are much less glamorous. Many people with fish tanks have had to scoop algae out from between their swimming goldfish. Tiny mushrooms spring up overnight in our yards. Moss grows on rocks, trees, the ground, and everywhere else.

Mysterious Ways

Moss, which is soft and low to the ground and looks like nothing else in nature, is often touted as the yard of the future for those in drought climates. It's easy to see why people don't believe moss is a plant. It really doesn't look like our mental catalog of plants. It thrives in conditions that seem pretty un-plant-friendly. And although it definitely is a plant, its unique qualities have led scientists to conclude that it belongs in its own group of over 10,000 species of mosses.

In Elizabeth Gilbert's 2013 novel *The Signature of All Things*, a woman botanist who studies moss is inspired by the work of Charles Darwin to try to understand moss's place in the plant kingdom. Her journey to understand this unique organism parallels the real shifts in thinking about moss over time. Originally grouped with some other oddball plants, moss was given its own group only after additional careful study and understanding.

Taking Cover

There's a Cree origin story that shares elements with the Christian origin story of Noah's Ark. After a flood that covered the entire planet, a trickster had to somehow re-seed the solid ground. The trickster's raft grew moss that eventually formed the new land on the planet, creating the hills and forests that appear mossy from far away.

Today, some see moss as the form of greenery that could help salvage the bare earth in places affected by drought. Saving water is an important part of the appeal of moss instead of grass, but it's also critical that the ground *be* covered by something to prevent erosion of nutritious soil over time.

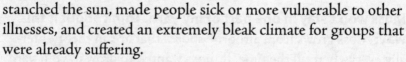

The Dust Bowl that contributed to and exacerbated the Great Depression was a result of drought conditions that began to self perpetuate. Swirling dust stanched the sun, made people sick or more vulnerable to other illnesses, and created an extremely bleak climate for groups that were already suffering.

Groups around the world have worked to farm in dry climates for thousands of years, so there's hope even if new areas of the world become more arid as a result of climate change. And alongside the specialized farming already used in parts of America today, moss offers a way for homeowners to do their part to keep the soil in place.

The Tiny Truth

Moss isn't well understood, and there are many myths about its nature, habitat, and behaviors. It helps to think of moss as a cluster of *tiny* plants. Some moss leaves are just one cell thick! Even the very outermost layer of human skin has half a dozen or more layers of cells. Our capillaries are one cell thick in order to freely exchange nutrients. If you ever played with making slides in a school science class, you may have gently scraped invisible cells from the inside of your cheek before dying them for visibility.

The major way mosses contrast with other plants is that they aren't "vascular," meaning mosses don't have the series of plant capillaries that draw moisture and nutrients up from a plant's roots. They can make nutrients through photosynthesis, and they absorb nutrients through their leaves because they don't have traditional roots.

Let's debunk a bunch of moss myths!

Moss only grows on the north side of trees. Sun exposure is what decides where the moss grows on a tree. Mosses like shady, moist spots with just enough ambient sunlight to whip up a good photosynthesis.

Moss needs shade. There are more than 10,000 mosses, and most of them do strongly prefer shade. Many mosses won't grow at all in direct sun. But there are some species that love the sun.

Moss won't stay in one part of my yard. Think about it this way: Moss grows from airborne spores that are, in theory, literally everywhere all the time. If moss wanted to grow in your yard or garden, it would already be there.

Moss needs to be kept moist. Mosses don't even always need water in order to survive, and they're very resilient. Some species are more drought tolerant than others, and an expert on drought lawns or gardens can help in choosing one.

Spanish moss is a true moss. Because of the confusion over time between moss and other idiosyncratic ground-cover plants, many plants named "moss" are not mosses.

Moss attracts pests. Mosses are better at thwarting pests than a lot of other plants. They're so dense and low to the ground that they don't provide cover or a comfortable perch for tiny monsters like mosquitos and fleas.

Moss comes with mold. Some mold can kind of visually resemble moss, and maybe that's why they're so often linked, but mold has no relationship at all to moss except when moss is visibly sick because of a mold attack.

Moss is a parasite. Moss doesn't live off of a host organism or actively harm anything, although its density of cover and moisture can sometimes affect porous surfaces like wood.

You can't walk on moss. Moss is springy and bouncy as long as you walk on it in a pretty chill way without dragging your feet or stomping.

Moss is a seasonal allergen. People can be allergic to moss, but this is really unusual, and definitely not nearly the large number who are allergic to ragwood or other seasonal allergens.

You can fertilize moss. Many ideas for fertilizing moss are more like ways to fertilize mold, if that's what you aim to do, but moss can't absorb traditional fertilizing at all.

Moss prefers "bad" soil. Mosses do love to grow where other plants aren't able to, but moss doesn't always even need soil—although you could argue that surfaces like rocks are pretty bad soil too.

Grass is the ground cover that most Americans know best, but a grass lawn is still a bed of dirt, full of bugs, with some soft greenery on top. A moss lawn doesn't have to be a shock or a compromise for those who live in areas that aren't grass friendly. And best of all, it never needs to be mowed.

Let's Take This Outside

It's safe to use outdoor garden chemicals on indoor plants.

✳ ✳ ✳ ✳

THERE ARE SO many reasons to debunk this unpleasant
myth! Outdoor chemicals may technically be safe for your
particular plant, and there's nothing inherently unsafe about a
product designed for your garden. But indoor spaces have pets,
kids, confined air, and all kinds of other things that may not
benefit from a chemical meant to be used outdoors. The same
is true of, say, spraypainting in the house or failing to ventilate
when you're using boxed hair dye.

As far as the compatibility of indoor and outdoor plants,
garden chemicals may be overkill. Your indoor plants hopefully don't have the level of pests and germs that outdoor plants
need to tolerate. A good rule of thumb is to use the least serious product to accomplish what you want, and for most indoor
plants, you may only need a fragrant essential oil or mild
household detergent to keep the bugs away.

Deadly Nightshades

*Do nightshade vegetables like tomatoes and eggplant contain a
toxic acid? Or a toxic alkaloid?*

✳ ✳ ✳ ✳

THE NIGHTSHADE FAMILY goes far beyond tomatoes and
eggplants, including potatoes, bell and chile peppers, and
tobacco. There's also deadly nightshade, petunias, and the real-
life mandrakes featured as shrieking nuisances in the Harry
Potter series.

Nightshades can get a bad rap, but is it deserved? That depends
who you ask, although evidence suggests nightshades are fine.

Supermodel Gisele Bundchen and New England Patriots quarterback Tom Brady, a celebrity married couple, made news in 2016 with their radically healthy private-chef diet. Their self-imposed limitations are extensive, including no fruit, nightshade vegetables, gluten, caffeine, "fungus," dairy, or MSG.

This long, mystifying list might register with some readers as bordering on orthorexia, an eating disorder in which the pursuit of a so-called healthy diet leads to obsessive tracking, avoiding, and phobic reactions to allegedly unhealthy foods.

But Bundchen and Brady have a dedicated private chef who offers up tailored meals to fit their purported needs, which definitely must make it easier not to choose foods that aren't part of your plan. Strangely, despite their laundry list of no-nos, Bundchen and Brady do still eat meat.

Their chef's shoutout to nightshades drew attention to this whole family of vegetables. Are they the new gluten, another food that is not harmful at all for about 99% of people? Should we take the word of someone who swaps a gluten-containing whole grain for trendy quinoa that actually doesn't have any more protein or less carbs than that comparable whole grain? Let's address some claims.

Nightshades cause migraines. Migraines are enigmatic and individual sufferers should choose for themselves when it comes to avoiding trigger foods. But there isn't a demonstrable link between nightshades and migraine. Other common triggers like chocolate or garlic have longer paper trails to back them up.

Nightshades contain a toxic alkaline. Certain specific nightshades, like potatoes that have turned green and need to be thrown away, do contain solanine. But almost all other vegetable nightshades are fine.

Nightshades contain a toxic acid. Nightshades have oxalic acid in small quantities, while the herbs parsley and chives contain much more of the acid by volume. Oxalic acid can stop your body from absorbing calcium but only if you consume very little calcium to begin with—and a *lot* of nightshades and other vegetables with oxalic acid.

Nightshades make arthritis worse. Arthritis is a frustrating condition that can lead sufferers to grasp for possible triggers, very similar to migraine. There's no evidence that nightshades worsen arthritis inflammation or pain. But again, individual sufferers can do their due diligence to find if they experience discomfort around any kind of food or substance.

Nightshades cause general inflammation. Inflammation has become a health buzzword without a clear definition. Acetaminophen is an anti-inflammatory drug; does that mean it cancels out a nightshade? In any case, there's no evidence that nightshades cause inflammation in people without an allergy to them. Chiles may make your mouth feel inflamed, but you can douse that with milk, unless you're Gisele.

Nightshades can upset your stomach. Certainly you may find that specific nightshades, like starchy fried potatoes or hot chiles, upset your stomach. And everyone's digestive system is different. If you find that you feel sick or bloated after meals where you've eaten these foods, you can try avoiding them for a couple of weeks to see if you notice an improvement.

Nightshades aren't worth eating. The nightshade vegetables represent a huge portion of the human diet during the agricultural age. For a surprising number of Americans, the slice of tomato they get on a sandwich embodies one of their most consumed vegetable groups—after lettuce. This huge family of very nutritious vegetables should be part of the diet of everyone who doesn't have an explicit health reason to avoid it.

It's interesting to find the "unhealthy" potato among the eggplants, tomatoes, and peppers. Potatoes may be caloric, but they contain many nutrients, and they were even carried onto ships to help prevent scurvy because of their high levels of vitamin C. The alkaline substance that green potatoes produce is a natural defense against predators, which is what the spiciness of peppers and the other nightshade idiosyncrasies are probably for. It may be part of why this family of plants is so robust and durable.

The danger with drawing a circle around an entire family of foods and declaring them off limits for no reason, as many people have done with gluten as well, is that all humans must always eat every day. Placing restrictions on foods that are good for us only makes choosing foods feel even more frustrating overall, and that feeling of confusion and helplessness can create a bad feeling around eating. Food nourishes us and keeps us going, even nightshades.

In 2017, Tom Brady released a book that forms the cornerstone of his new pyramid scheme of wellness products. In between complete common-sense nonstarters like how people should eat more vegetables and get enough sleep, he throws in plugs for his Tom Brady brand of Tom Brady supplements. We can only hope one of them contains some nightshades to mix things up a little.

He's Actually a Cartoon

Spinach has a ton of iron.

✱ ✱ ✱ ✱

IF YOU WANTED proof that cartoons are more memorable
than school, this myth is Exhibit A. Television's Popeye the
Sailor Man lived for spinach—canned spinach, in fact. (When
you really think about the idea of eating undrained, room-temperature spinach straight from the can...)

And from this, it seems that everyone in America learned the
same lesson about spinach being high in iron and really good
for you. The thing is, spinach has no more iron than any other
dark leafy green. It has iron and it is good for you but we don't
actually get much of the iron in a usable form.

Next time, think twice about health role modeling from someone who smokes a pipe.

Who's Afraid of Chamomile?

Chamomile tea can cause allergy symptoms.

✱ ✱ ✱ ✱

DID YOU KNOW chamomile is a daisy? Ragweed is also in
the daisy family, and many people are allergic to the plants
of this family. The association has led some people to wonder
if or claim that chamomile tea can cause an allergic reaction.
Usually the answer is no, because the allergen part of these
plants is their pollen, which is the reason spring is the primary
hay fever season.

If someone had a severe enough allergy to the daisy family, they
could hypothetically have a reaction from an herbal infusion
made of dried leaves and flowers in hot water. That level of
allergy is very rare. If you have mild, manageable allergies but
have avoided chamomile for this reason, it may be worth a try
after all.

Blanket Rules

Fresh herbs taste better than dry herbs and are more potent.

✳ ✳ ✳ ✳

ANY BLANKET STATEMENT about how something tastes is probably a myth. For every ten people who prefer fresh parsley, there are ten more who swear by dried. What you like depends on how you plan to use it, what your taste is, and what you're comfortable with. In terms of flavor, there's often not a noticeable difference, and people who are snobby about fresh herbs seem a bit gauche. Plenty of people can't reasonably buy fresh herbs for a variety of reasons, and dried herbs have been a staple of every world cuisine for a very, very long time. If you'd like to suggest to someone's grandparents that you're sure fresh rosemary would taste better, you're welcome to try.

Some fresh herbs are poisonous and they need to be carefully prepared and completely dried out before they're safe to use. If you insult someone's grandma's cooking, you may find out firsthand. And if you do love fresh herbs, especially the ones like basil that *are* so delicious right off the plant, consider growing your own.

Efficacy of Medical Herbs

Medical herbs are not effective at treating symptoms or illnesses.

✳ ✳ ✳ ✳

I'T'S VERY FOOLISH to place your trust in herbal remedies instead of consulting with a doctor. But it's also foolish to insist that herbs don't have any medicinal value. Aspirin is derived from plants. The entire opioid family, which includes codeine, vicodin, and most of our most effective painkillers for people with debilitating chronic pain, is derived from the poppy plant. Digitalis has become many different cardiovascular treatments. Menthol and camphor are used to spot-treat minor pain. Ephedrine and pseudoephedrine (the active ingredient in Sudafed) were derived from the ma huang plant.

Now there's also medical marijuana to contend with, and thousands of baby boomers suffering migraines or the side effects of brutal chemotherapy regimens are discovering classy-looking edibles. But prescription drugs derived from cannabis have been prescribed to cancer patients for years to aid with nausea and other side effects.

Scammy supplements are what tend to make the news, when herbs have low-key improved humans's quality of life for all of human history. A careful and thoughtfully chosen herbal treatment plan won't cure your strep throat but it may help you feel more comfortable and have more energy. A good doctor can discuss this with you while keeping an open mind, so don't be afraid to ask.

Factual Supplement

Herbal supplements are safer than drugs because they have no side effects and do not interact with drugs.

✳ ✳ ✳ ✳

THIS MYTH IS a dangerous one. Many herbal supplements have a mild effect on symptoms, if they have any at all. But some that are more consistently effective can both have side effects and interact with other drugs. This is especially true for drugs that are derived from herbs, like how willow bark is the natural ancestor of aspirin.

Even if the side effect or drug interaction is mild and merely a little unpleasant, it's always better to know what exactly you're taking and how it's affecting both your symptoms and your overall well being. One of the most common drug interactions is with plain old grapefruit, which doesn't even purport to be a medicine itself but can impair major and serious medications.

Herbal Remedy

All herbs are safe to eat.

✳ ✳ ✳ ✳

ANYONE WHO THINKS this way hasn't read enough stories about witches. But, of course, there are real counterparts to the sorceresses and local "wise women" of fiction. These women passed down books or oral accounts of recipes for tinctures and herbal blends that purported to treat diseases, relieve symptoms, and yes, even poison someone. (Poison had humane uses for people who kept livestock.)

If you narrow the field down to only those herbs we think of as culinary, there are still exceptions. Essential oils and other concentrated forms of certain herbs can be poisonous, like peppermint and mustard oils. And products made from herbs are generally not regulated by the FDA because they're labeled as "dietary supplements."

In 2015, major retailers were forced to stop selling herbal supplements that often contained little or none of the labeled herbs: saw palmetto, echinacea, ginseng, garlic, gingko biloba, and St. John's Wort. Some were simple placebos with no plant material at all. At that point, you might as well buy homeopathic medicine products instead—or just drink some water.

Naturally Preserved

Dried herbs last basically forever.

✳ ✳ ✳ ✳

DRIED HERBS MAY not visibly deteriorate or grow extra bacterial or fungal friends, but that doesn't mean a five-year-old bay leaf is good to cook with. Most of the compounds that add flavor to our favorite herbs and spices are contained in the "wet" ingredients like water or oil, so the longer a dried herb or spice is kept, the more that flavor continues to mellow and eventually disappear almost completely.

But these products do last a good long time. If you keep your dried herbs in airtight containers in a cool, dry pantry or cabinet, you may find that you need to use a little bit more to get the same flavor after a while, but they'll be fine at least until the expiration date on the package.

Pick a Pepper

Pink peppercorns are the same as any other kind of pepper.

✳ ✳ ✳ ✳

PEPPERCORNS HAVE GONE haute. First, grocery stores began stocking disposable pepper grinders so we can all recreate that Olive Garden feeling at home. Then pepper became peppercorn *blends* with many colors. Recipes for light-colored foods call for white pepper instead of black, so your vichyssoise doesn't look like meatless sausage gravy instead. The most common blend is white, black, green, and pink peppercorns together in one grinder.

Black and green peppercorns are basically the same thing but differently prepared for use. They're baby drupes (a peach is its tree's drupe) that grow on the pepper plant. White peppercorns are prepared by boiling mature drupes and stripping off the outsides. There is a red peppercorn, but it's different from the red pepper flakes you get at pizza places.

Pink peppercorns aren't peppercorns at all—they're not even drupes! They're fruits from a totally different plant, related neither to peppercorns nor to the family that includes bell peppers and chiles. In fact, they're related enough to cashews that they can trigger a tree nut allergy. And since a dried fruit is pulpier and less woody than a drupe, pink pepper can get gunky in your grinder.

We use plenty of different plants as pepper-like seasonings, but pink pepper is the only one to have a clear misnomer of "pepper." Horseradish, Chinese mustard, and the whole oeuvre of chili and cayenne powders add heat to many world cuisines. Horseradish and wasabi are both part of the mustard family, which also includes cauliflower, cabbage, and turnips. Mustard oil is thought to be toxic in large enough quantities, and is illegal to import into the United States as a cooking product.

Raw Nerves

Raw vegetables have more nutrients. Therefore, a raw diet is more nutritious.

✳ ✳ ✳ ✳

Case Study: the Panda Diet

YOU MAY BE familiar with the plight of the giant panda, a beautiful and incongruous animal on the endangered species list. These pandas only live in China or in captivity around the world. They spend virtually all their waking hours eating bamboo, because over the years, they evolved from carnivores to not just herbivores but bamboo-vores. Bamboo is hard to chew, hard to digest, and not very nutritions, like a tougher celery that you have to eat constantly in order to get enough calories.

A Legacy of Cooking

The panda is a good case in point about an exclusively raw diet or exclusively raw vegetables. Raw foods are great in moderation, like any other nutritious foods. But to rely only on raw foods is to draw a large limitation around both your diet and your life in general. Cooking changes the nutritional profile of your vegetables, although usually not by much in terms of vitamins and minerals; more importantly, it makes vegetables easier to digest and absorb.

Learning to cook our food was one major factor that allowed our prehistoric ancestors to have the time, resources, and energy to change their lives into the "human lifestyle" we recognize today. They learned to talk and created language. They began to draw and eventually to write in pictographs, characters, and words. They invented agriculture and were able to settle into groups that became communities.

Tread Lightly

There's an element of classism that factors into the raw diet craze. No known culture in the history of the world has relied on an uncooked food as any of its staple crops. This is simply too unpredictable for most climates where humans live, where learning to preserve and eventually to can foods safely helped everyone to survive through each long winter. But someone with the luxury of a grocery store and a generous food budget can always stock up on imported avocados.

Any Way Is a Good Way

Nutritionists and nutritional activists usually say that a fruit or vegetable in almost any form is preferable to not eating a fruit or vegetable, and most Americans eat far below the recommended number of servings of these foods. If roasting your broccoli causes you to eat a healthy amount of broccoli, definitely do it. If raw broccoli floats your boat and your digestive system can tolerate it, eat that instead! Every day is a new chance to cook, not cook, and eventually eat whatever you choose. But an all-raw diet is not inherently better than anything else.

Dried Beans

You shouldn't pick green beans when they're wet.

✳   ✳   ✳   ✳

LIKE CUTTING FLOWERS underwater, the wet green beans rule sounds mythical because of how fussy it seems. Why does it matter if we pick green beans when they're wet? We wash them before we eat them anyway.

But *many* fruits and vegetables perform most admirably when you pick them off of dry plants. Garlic is best picked when it's dry, which makes sense because you store it dry and often keep it at room temperature. Wet garlic has all kinds of layers and nooks and crannies to trap moisture that can cause the garlic to molder and rot.

Raspberries are prone to the same problem, which is why they're often dry inside their packaging when we buy them.

Other berries and some softer fruits are less delicate than raspberries but can still turn bad in a wet environment. Even if you pick them and then promptly hand-dry each piece of fruit, this is less effective than just waiting for the fruits to dry on the vine, so to speak.

Green beans have the most severe reaction to being picked wet, which is why it's the version of this advice that most people have heard. Green beans are susceptible to a specific fungal disease that can be spread by handling and picking from the wet plants, which is heartbreaking after tending the plants all season. The disease affects not just the beans themselves but the entire plant.

There are plants that benefit from picking in the cooler and damper parts of the day, like lettuce, which you can imagine behaving more like a flower than like a squash. A cool, wet environment keeps a lettuce perky and crisp. And if in doubt about any other plant, do your research. But definitely let your green beans dry before you pick them.

They're Not the Only Crushed Ones

Is "natural" food coloring made of crushed bugs?

✳ ✳ ✳ ✳

RED FOOD COLORING known as carmine or cochineal is made from crushed scale bugs. The dye is prepared by grinding the bodies of insects into a fine powder and then boiling it in ammonia or baking soda. That doesn't sound fun, but it could be worse: Some carmine preparations involve isinglass, a glue made from the swim bladders of fish.

People can be allergic to carmine, and it's difficult to avoid because of its place as the category killer in red dyes. In ingredient lists, dyes like carmine are listed with descriptors like "lake"—which refers to the chemical makeup of the dye used—and sometimes a number that refers to the additive that renders the dye for a particular use.

This dye is often dismissed as natural, like that means something is harmless in the first place, but it's even stranger that crushing dead bugs and then boiling them in ammonia still counts as natural. To describe carmine in language that sounds almost hippie-ish is misleading. It's a very old pigment and a very good one, and industrial chemical processes have only made it better.

There's a similar red dye that's made from a residue left by insects rather than their decimated shells. This insect and its resin are both called lac, and it's the namesake of both shellac and lacquer. Both substances are applied to give a shiny coating:

* Shellac is still used for food industry purposes, but it was supplanted in many home sealant applications by synthetic resins, which are plastics. (Records were made of shellac before vinyl was invented!)

* Lacquer can be made from resin from lac bugs or from trees. But almost all modern lacquers are synthetic resins. Lacquer is more waterproof and durable than shellac.

Guano Guano Everywhere

Bird and bat droppings were once a major part of the world economy.

✳   ✳   ✳   ✳

IN OUR MYSTERIOUS world, people's "nonsense detectors" operate in a donut shape. We tend to believe mild-sounding myths and rumors because they can seem too small and harmless for anyone to bother lying or exaggerating about. And we tend to believe *the most outrageous* things we hear because they're too strange not to be true. In the middle are a lot of things we disbelieve more or less correctly.

Guano, the local and industry term for bat and bird droppings, fall into the category of too ludicrous to disbelieve. The enormous value of such a gross-sounding product lies in its chemical makeup, and to explain why, we need to briefly dive into some agricultural backstory.

Why Do We Farm?

Imagine the first person, or the first several people who were all in different areas, deciding to try to plant a seed in order to grow food. (This thought exercise works with almost everything we eat. Imagine the first person to eat the wedge of old milk that had solidified and begun to smell a little like feet. Imagine the first person to bring an oyster into the house and say, "Nah, I don't think we need to cook it first.")

This event likely took place in the Fertile Crescent, the collective term for an area that includes much of the Arabian Peninsula, the Nile Delta, and parts of the Mediterranean coast. About 12,000 years ago, these ancient and ingenious people dropped barley and other seeds into the ground. Maybe it happened by accident in a sort of Isaac Newton apple-on-the-head moment and someone noticed that there were tiny plants growing out of some discarded old food. But it's hard to imagine food being thrown away by hunter-gatherer groups. They also began keeping animals around, eventually domesticating them. These weren't the first domesticated animals *period*, because dogs have been found buried alongside their people at sites that predate the advent of agriculture. But having meat and dairy animals and a more reliable source of food crops changed the course of human history.

The ancient (but way less ancient) Egyptians and others experimented with soil, ash, manure, and other substances they thought might improve their crops. But it wasn't until the explosion of industrial farming that the commercial fertilizer industry took off. In the meantime, ideas like crop rotation also helped to boost productivity on farms around the world.

The Big 3

In the 1800s, scientists began experimenting in earnest to find why some substances helped plants to grow better while others did not. They used the scientific method, designing experiments and using both control and experimental groups to measure their results accurately.

One by one, these pioneering scientists uncovered three ingredients that are vital to fertilizing plants: nitrogen, phosphate, and potassium. Plants leech these three nutrients from soil in larger quantities than any other nutrients, and scientists realized that stripped nutrients were one reason why crop rotation had improved outcomes for farmers. Different crops require different nutrient profiles from the soil.

The Bat (and Bird) Signal

The element phosphorus doesn't show up anywhere in nature in its pure form. It readily combines with other elements to form phosphates, meaning compounds with one phosphorus atom and four oxygen atoms. In turn, phosphates form crystals with other molecules, and these are known as phosphate minerals. Turquoise is an example of a phosphate mineral.

One major source of phosphates is bird and bat droppings, or guano. Over many thousands of years, these droppings form phosphate rock. But even as fresh droppings, guano contains all three major fertilizer elements. Sea birds make more valuable guano but bat guano is also valued. By the time imperialist European explorers discovered the value of guano, it had been used for a millennium by the Quechua people whose language gave it its name.

Nauru'd Awakening

At the turn of the nineteenth century, the first foreign explorer found his way to the tiny island nation of Nauru. He gave it an English name but that didn't last long, and the island has been Nauru for two hundred years. The Nauruan people were and remain a mix of descendants from other Pacific island groups, and beginning in the 1800s, some Europeans joined the genealogy.

This tiny island has just eight square miles of surface area, most of which was taken up by huge deposits of phosphate rock: thousands of years worth of being the local hangout for Pacific sea birds. Nauru and a couple of fellow tiny Pacific islands almost singlehandedly floated the phosphate, and therefore fertilizer, industry for decades.

But brutal, aggressive strip mining has left Nauru bare. The phosphate is gone, leaving barren, spiky expanses of rock behind. Runoff from the mines has killed much of the surrounding marine life. Nauru has almost no arable land and can't support a seaport. The same birds who once thrived in their own paradise aren't interested in returning to a bleak expanse of rock. Mining operations abandoned Nauru to its fate and the island became independent in the 1960s.

The Industrial Aftermath

Companies began researching and manufacturing fertilizers long before Nauru was strip mined, but discovery of these rich natural sources of readymade fertilizer derailed the synthetic fertilizer industry for a while. Eventually, when the Pacific island supply ran out, these fertilizer companies reclaimed the market.

Today, the chemical makeup of guano is still the same basic profile used by major fertilizers. Scientists have worked to craft seeds that use fewer nutrients and fertilizers that have added benefits beyond the Big 3 nutrients. But as with the guano boom of the early twentieth century, several gigantic companies dominate the world fertilizer market.

Agribusiness and agricultural research science also contributed to the development of new strains and varieties of world staple crops, making them part of a portfolio of cutting-edge technologies to help every development level of farming to produce better, stronger, more productive crops.

What Ever Happened to Nauru?

Newly independent Nauru became a democracy without political parties, probably because there are only about ten thousand people in the entire nation. It has scrambled to attract any kind of industry, and mistakes have been made in that scramble. In 2003, *This American Life* ran a long feature by Jack Hitt about Nauru's brush with tax-haven greatness and other attempts to create a new economic base, including a failed musical about Leonardo da Vinci.

Global climate change will affect low-lying islands like Nauru more than almost anyplace else, because a matter of just several feet of water could cover almost all the inhabitable land on Nauru and others like Kiribati. Imperialist powers destroyed most of their island, and climate change will likely destroy the rest—all because of the saga of guano.

Gua-No Fun

Do they really use bat droppings in mascara?

✳ ✳ ✳ ✳

GUANO—THE INDUSTRY TERM for bat droppings—may be useful, but not for this. The confusion seems to come from an ingredient called guanine. But all of our high-school biology teachers have all gotten together to cry about the perpetuation of this myth, because guanine is one of the four building blocks of human DNA. Is human DNA made from bat droppings too?

But the truth about cosmetic guanine isn't very great either. In cosmetics, guanine, sometimes called "pearl essence," is usually made from ground fish scales. Pearl essence is what gives your shampoo its pleasing, gentle, glittery quality. And it turns out that some people do use guano in beauty products.

In Japan, the guano from a specific bird has been used as a facial treatment for a thousand years. It's called *uguisu no fun*, and yes, it's hard to imagine a more "no fun" thing than applying bird droppings to your face. But the guano is sterilized and dried thoroughly so it can be sold in a safe and uniform powder. It was used as a cleanser by geishas who spent much of their lives in heavy, chemical makeup that damaged their skin.

Both guano and fish scales are resources that biodegrade and are reabsorbed into the ecosystem. The birds of Japan that are raised for their guano eat a normal bird diet of seeds, bugs, and whatever they find around. These products may make us queasy on first blush, but they're preferable to an oceanful of plastic microbeads that cause fish to choke. Everything is relative in the pursuit of beauty.

Mistaken bystanders also sometimes claim that a food additive ingredient called guanylate is also a form of guano. It seems that we as a species may need to review some principles of language. There's even a term for this phenomenon: *false friends* are words that may have a similar root etymology but mean completely different things. (And in real life, your false friends are the ones who try to frighten you with hearsay about guano.)

A Cut Below

Do I really need to cut flowers underwater? That seems silly.

❋ ❋ ❋ ❋

WE ALL WANT this to be a myth because it's annoying to have to cut flowers underwater. There's good news and bad news about it. First the bad: Cutting flowers underwater is the right way, and it does extend the life of the cut flowers. On the other hand: Experts say it only increases the life of the flowers by about a quarter, so you may find that that isn't worth fussing with underwater cutting.

Behind the Stems

Flowering plants are fed and nourished through tiny channels that run up the length of their stems and leaves—these plants are vascular, the same root (Latin for "vessel") as the human cardiovascular system. And plants can suffer an injury exactly like one that happens to humans when air is introduced into their circulatory system. Cutting a stem cuts off the water and nutrient supply from the roots, but it can also let air into the channels the flower needs in order to feed itself.

Cutting a flower underwater helps the flower keep its natural channels free and working to allow water and nutrients in. This is how underwater cutting extends the life of your flowers. Florists also suggest that you can repeat this process every few days to keep flowers fresh and healthy for as long as possible.

Pick a Mix

There are some surprising extra ways to extend the life of your bouquet, some of which should be mixed and matched for best results.

Add a few drops of vodka. Alcohol slows flowers down as they ripen, but too much can impair them—just like humans.

Add a tiny bit of bleach. Bleach kills bacteria, and a very small amount won't smell bad in the big scheme of things.

Put a penny in the vase. President Lincoln is the luckiest charm of all. But actually, it's the copper in pennies that helps to keep gross fungus out.

Drop an aspirin in the vase. The salicylic acid in aspirin helps to prevent growth of bacteria. Crush one up and mix the powder into your vase.

Add a few drops of vinegar. Vinegar is an effective acid and can help keep mold away. Using a milder vinegar can mitigate any smell factor.

Add a little sugar or soda. Flowers need nutrients. A little goes a very long way, though, because sugar is also a good source of food for bacteria.

Seal the stems in warm water. After you cut flowers, you can submerse them briefly in warm water to help the cut ends become more resilient.

Refrigerate overnight. Think of flowers like a much prettier, inedible lettuce—would you leave lettuce out for days and expect good results?

The envelope of powder that comes with floral arrangements is usually a mix of plant food *and* an antibacterial agent. It's always a good idea to throw that in with anything else you try.

Remember that every action needs an equal and opposite reaction (Newton's third law of floral longevity), so a nutrient must be paired with a bacterial inhibitor. Aspirin plus sugar. Bleach plus soda. But again, use a *very light hand* with any of these, and don't expect any miracles.

Just Orchids

Orchids are fussy and challenging to care for.

✳   ✳   ✳   ✳

THE ORCHID FAMILY is the biggest group of flowering plants in the world, with over 25,000 species. Some even have beautiful foliage in lieu of beautiful flowers; all are striking and find devoted collectors around the world. But capricious shoppers may grab potted orchids from the floral section at a local grocery store and be dismayed when they die shortly thereafter.

Is it orchids that are the problem, or is it us?

Fussing or Overfussing?

Caring for orchids *can be* challenging. They require regular attention and feeding, although not any moreso than other common plants can. But many orchids are killed by overwatering and other forms of fussing. The attention orchids need is more like monitoring than a regular routine of automatic watering, and they should be looked at every day if possible. If that sounds like too much thinking for a houseplant, honor that instinct and choose a different plant.

Orchids have two interesting roles besides the keeping and displaying of the plants themselves. First, although orchids come in virtually every color and pattern and variegation imaginable, "orchid," the official named color, is a pretty boring shade of purple. Maybe you remember orchid as the neon purple shade in the very first palate of Microsoft Paintbrush colors. And second, vanilla comes from an orchid. The seed pods made into vanilla are from a species of orchid that's actually a climbing vine. These pods are called "vanilla bean," but that's a misnomer.

Myth-Understood

Any plant as mysterious, exotic, and challenging as the orchid has naturally spawned a great many myths.

Orchids are too hard to grow. The baseline to keep an orchid alive and healthy enough to bloom is really pretty average—don't be afraid to buy an orchid and try it out, especially if you get a hardy hybrid.

You can water orchids with ice. This is a source of a lot of confusion, because there are hybrid orchids that tolerate ice as a way to water slowly and evenly, but almost all other orchids do not tolerate this.

Orchids bloom forever. How could anything bloom forever? But orchids can bloom repeatedly in close succession if you're an especially careful tender capable of next-level moves.

Orchids die after they stop blooming. This is somewhat true for some species of salmon but definitely not for orchids.

Orchids need special soil. Some don't and some do—some orchids grow as vines or cling to rocks!

Orchids don't need to be watered. For an optimal orchid experience, orchids should be watered on an as-needed basis; that said, some can go weeks or months without added water and don't suffer too much.

You can't water orchids at night. In theory you can, although the cool darkness of nighttime can let critters start to grow in the freshly watered environment.

Orchids can't grow outside of hot, humid places. Although many orchids love the warmth of the equator, with 25,000 naturally occurring orchid species, there's almost no place orchids don't grow in nature.

Orchids are parasites. Parasitic plants are ones that leech nutrients from a host plant, and no "domesticated" orchid does that, although some species feed with the help of a fungus.

Orchids are expensive. This was true when international botanists had to travel for months on a ship in order to try to bring back a few surviving orchid plants, and rare orchids can be costly, but most are in line with any perennial houseplant.

I need a greenhouse to grow an orchid. If you wanted to grow a tropical orchid in a temperate climate, you might need a greenhouse, but otherwise there are varieties and levels of care to suit all indoor temperatures.

Orchids have healing qualities. Unless you mean the healing quality of having a beautiful living thing in your home, probably not.

Think of the enormous number of available "house orchids" as a personality test whose results will pair you with a great fit for your level of attention, temperature, and more. There's no shame in deciding a plant is too needy for what you're willing to give, and there's no shame in picking up an orchid to give it a try, especially when most orchids prefer *less* watering than more.

Chapter 10

Leisure Time

The Power of Radio

"To all newspapers and radio stations—all those who reach the eyes and ears of the American people—I say this: You have a most grave responsibility to the Nation now and for the duration of this war."

—President Roosevelt, Fireside Chat, December 9, 1941

✳   ✳   ✳   ✳

THOUGH MOST AMERICAN citizens were thousands of miles from the front lines, the advent of radio allowed them to experience World War II in an intimate way. More than 90 percent of American families owned at least one radio and listened, on average, for about four hours daily.

World Leaders Connect with Their Citizens

Allied and Axis leaders used radio to beam messages of hope, determination, and steadfastness, as well as patriotic messages that encouraged and spurred citizens to action.

On December 8, 1941, at 12:30 P.M., President Roosevelt addressed a joint session of Congress and the nation on radio, requesting that war be declared against Japan. When he spoke, Roosevelt changed his opening sentence, which was written as "a date which will live in world history," to the now famous "a date which will live in infamy."

Roosevelt used radio to deliver State of the Union speeches and his so-called Fireside Chats to Americans across the nation. Some of his more famous broadcasts included the December 1940 speech "Arsenal of Democracy," which outlined American support for Britain, China, and Russia; the January 1941 "Four Freedoms" speech that made the case for American protection of basic human rights around the world; the April 1942 speech that addressed sacrifice and American resolve; and his December 1943 address which hinted at the approaching invasion of France.

British Prime Minister Winston Churchill was one of the war's most powerful orators. Britain had been at war for six months when Churchill broadcast his famous "No Surrender" speech in June 1940. In a rousing discourse, Churchill told his listeners the British would, "Go on to the end. We shall defend our island, whatever the cost may be...we shall never surrender."

Churchill won the admiration of his countrymen through his honesty. In one broadcast he acknowledged the British defeat on the beaches of Dunkirk, France, where almost 340,000 British and French soldiers had been evacuated. Churchill used the event to spur his nation to action. "I expect the Battle of Britain is about to begin. Upon this battle depends the survival of... our own British life and the continuity of our institutions. Hitler knows that he will have to break us...or lose the war. If we can stand up to him, all Europe may be free...but if we fail, then the whole world...will sink into the abyss of a new Dark Age."

State-Sponsored Propaganda

Governments around the world were quick to grasp the role radio could play in molding public opinion. All of the war's major combatants organized propaganda and information ministries, and radio became one of the most important tools in their arsenal.

The United States Office of War Information (OWI) was established in June 1942. This federal government agency coordinated the domestic release of war news and operated an overseas branch, which administered a propaganda campaign. The radio arm of the OWI was known as the Voice of America (VOA). VOA began broadcasting news programs about America's war efforts into German occupied countries in February 1942. The U.S. government hoped that by doing so, they could counteract the propaganda being espoused by the Nazis. The department initially used short-wave radios loaned by NBC and CBS.

The American Forces Network was established by the U.S. War Department in 1942 to help counter enemy radio broadcasts, which could often be picked up by servicemen in the field. The first broadcast to American troops occurred on July 4, 1943. Broadcasts included entertainment shows, newscasts, and sports reports.

The Nazis were masters of propaganda. Joseph Goebbels quickly rose through the ranks of the Nazi party, and in 1933 assumed the title of Reich Minister of Popular Enlightenment and Propaganda.

Goebbels realized the power of radio from the outset. In remarks given at the opening of the German Radio Exhibition in August 1933, the Nazi Propaganda Minister said, "It would not have been possible for us to take power or to use it in the ways we have without the radio."

When the Nazis began their invasion and occupation of neighboring countries, Goebbels kept a European map in his office displaying radio transmitters captured by the Nazis, as well as a world map indicating the global reach of various short-wave transmitters under his control. To distribute the Nazi's anti-Semitic message, Goebbels ordered production of an inexpensive Volksempfanger, or "People's Radio Receiver." By 1939, Germany was second only to the United States in the number of radios owned by citizens.

The Voices of Treason

The German and Japanese propaganda machines used several American- and British-born men and women to broadcast their messages of doubt and mistrust to Allied soldiers serving overseas.

William Joyce, an American raised in Ireland, was a senior member of the British Union of Fascists. Facing the prospect of arrest, Joyce fled England for Germany on the eve of the war. In October 1939, Joyce became Germany's main English-speaking radio personality, and although it was illegal for Britons to listen to his broadcasts, Joyce had almost as many listeners as the British Broadcasting Corporation.

Joyce was given the nickname "Lord Haw-Haw" by a London newspaper journalist. He began his broadcasts with the phrase, "Germany calling, Germany calling." He created anxiety amongst the British population with tales of a German Fifth Column operating on the island nation. Joyce was captured shortly after Germany's surrender and was eventually hanged for treason.

The Germans also utilized the talents of Mildred Gillars, a 29-year old aspiring stage actress dubbed "Axis Sally." Gillars broadcast a show called "Home Sweet Home" from Berlin. She conducted interviews with Allied Prisoners of War while disguised as a Red Cross worker, which she then combined with propaganda clips for use on her radio broadcasts.

Gillars was convicted on one count of treason after the war and spent 16 years in prison. The charge was based on just one broadcast—a radio drama titled "Vision of Invasion," which told the story of a mother who dreamt of her dead son, killed when his ship was destroyed during the invasion of France.

The Japanese employed several English-speaking women, collectively nicknamed "Tokyo Rose," to broadcast propaganda messages of cheating wives and girlfriends to servicemen in the Pacific. One of the women, Iva Toguri D'Aquino, was initially cleared of wrongdoing by both the FBI and the Army's Counter Intelligence Corps. When she returned to the United States, gossip columnist Walter Winchell lobbied for her prosecution. D'Aquino was eventually convicted on one count of treason in 1949 and served six years in jail, but was later pardoned by President Gerald Ford.

A New Brand of Journalism

As war consumed Europe, Americans were informed of overseas events by daily radio news updates. While newspapers reported current news events, their stories were sometimes delayed for several days before appearing in print. Radio, on the other hand, was immediate: What happened on a given day was in many instances relayed to audiences the same day.

In the spring of 1936, a Columbia Broadcasting System (CBS) rookie reporter named Edward R. Murrow moved to London, as CBS's European news director. Murrow assembled the war's finest ensemble of radio reporters, who subsequently became known as "the Murrow Boys." The small group of men and one woman defined the role of the broadcast correspondent.

Murrow made his first broadcast from Vienna, where he covered Hitler's entry into Austria. Over the course of the war, Murrow and his team transmitted thousands of stories to the CBS studio in New York City, which were then transmitted to affiliated stations.

Murrow and his staff often took risks to bring stories to his listeners. In one instance, Murrow accompanied a British bomber crew on their raid over Berlin. The account, titled "Orchestrated Hell," won the reporter a Peabody Award.

Besides witnessing the bomb runs, Murrow was also given permission to fly on a paratroop drop. As the sound of wind blew in through the open door of the cargo plane, Murrow counted off the men as the soldiers jumped from the plane. He then told the tragic story of two men who plummeted to their deaths when their parachute lines became entangled.

During the D-Day invasion of Normandy, CBS reporter Richard Hottelet flew in a B-26 Marauder along the shores of Utah Beach, while down below him coworker Charles Collingwood used the first portable tape recorder, a 55-pound behemoth, to record events occurring in the landing zone.

One of the war's most riveting broadcasts came after Murrow and Collingwood traveled to the Buchenwald, Germany, concentration camp at war's end. Murrow was traumatized by the experience and broke down in tears. In his broadcast three days later, Murrow told his listeners what he had witnessed, saying, "The tragedy of it simply overwhelmed me." Murrow and his team made the events in Europe real for Americans listening back home, relaying the sights and sounds of a world at war.

Shortly after its invention, radio quickly became the dominant form of home entertainment. Radio was the link to the world, and over the course of the war, the new medium evolved into an effective platform for disseminating news and propaganda.

Cleveland Rocks!

Thanks to one plucky disc jockey, Cleveland's claim to fame is being the city where rock 'n' roll was born.

✳ ✳ ✳ ✳

IN JULY 1951, a new radio show hit the airwaves on Cleveland's WJW radio. The show was the brainchild of Leo Mintz, owner of Cleveland's popular Record Rendezvous, who spotted a new sales trend in his store: More and more white teenagers were buying so-called "race music"—rhythm-and-blues records cut by African American artists.

Mintz bought a block of late-night air time and convinced Alan Freed, a newcomer to the Cleveland broadcasting scene, to host a show devoted to playing R & B music. On July 11, the show made its debut.

Cleveland was a town that record industry executives always kept their eyes on. The city was known for its ear-to-the-ground music scene and as a place where new music trends and tastes took root before spreading to the rest of the country. Now, as Freed spun R & B records in the wee hours past midnight on WJW, the Forest City began introducing the world to a powerful new music phenomenon that would come to be called *rock 'n' roll*.

Rock 'n' Roll, Baby!

Looking to create a unique identity for the show (and for himself), Freed unveiled an on-air shtick inspired by New York musician Louis "Moondog" Hardin. Freed opened the show with Hardin's instrumental recording that would become the show's theme, "Moondog Symphony," announced to listeners they were tuned in to the "Moondog Radio Show," and introduced himself as the self-anointed "King of the Moondoggers." His high-energy persona spoke directly to listeners, with a hip lingo that borrowed from the street vernacular of the African American community.

Freed's show also pushed the envelope with respect to race and music. It wasn't the first program to feature R & B music, but his insistence on playing only original recordings by the original black artists broke racial barriers. Freed was careful though; he refrained from playing the rowdier R & B numbers until after 1:00 A.M., when WJW's station manager went to bed.

Freed's show resonated with young listeners, black and white alike, developing a following of fans dubbed "Moondoggers." They loved the music Freed would famously coin *rock 'n' roll;* a phrase he lifted from R & B lyrics, unaware that African American musicians used the term as code for good sex.

More Rock 'n' Roll Firsts for Cleveland

On March 21, 1952, Freed took his rock 'n' roll to the streets with the staging of the Moondog Coronation Ball at the 10,000-seat Cleveland Arena. A raucous congregation of black and white kids turned out to watch several big-name African American artists perform live in what is now recognized as history's first rock 'n' roll concert. Along with ticket holders came upwards of 20,000 other fans looking to crash the sold-out show. As the unruly throng tried to bust its way in, fire department officials shut the concert down after one song by opening performer Paul "Hucklebuck" Williams. The first ever rock 'n' roll concert became the first ever rock 'n' roll concert riot.

With that, Freed and his rock 'n' roll radio show became an overnight sensation. Recordings of Freed's show began airing in New York City. In September 1954, Freed took his show and trademark catchphrase to the Big Apple, where he promoted rock 'n' roll artists and shows. Shortly after, the music industry began advertising rock 'n' roll records. A music phenomenon born in Cleveland was about to rock the rest of the world.

"The police don't want you to have any fun."

—ALAN FREED, IN FRONT OF A CONCERT CROWD IN BOSTON, 1958

One-Channel Wondering

How come there wasn't a channel one on your television?

❋   ❋   ❋   ❋

HAVE YOU EVER wondered which programs Bruce Springsteen saw in 1992 as he surfed the channels available on his newly installed cable? Was it the smarmy cast of *L.A. Law* that so repulsed him? Or was it the predictable mystery of *Matlock* that pushed him over the edge? Or perhaps the vampiric visage of Ron Popeil? This is a question for philosophers to debate; we'll probably never know the answer. But there's one thing that we can say for sure: In all of his channel flipping, the Boss never took a look at channel one—he couldn't have. Channels start at two and go up from there.

It wasn't always this way. The American television industry took off in April 1941, when two stations began to broadcast from New York: WNBT (later NBC) and WCBW (later CBS); they used channels one and two, respectively. Within a year, the nation had four television stations that reached more than ten thousand households—and channel one was a going concern.

But World War II brought the fledgling medium to a grinding halt. For the next several years, the country devoted its resources to more pressing needs. By the time commercial broadcasting was ready to resume in 1946, new technological developments had changed both radio and television. Competition for the airwaves was fierce—stations could broadcast farther, faster, and on higher frequencies than ever before.

Everyone wanted a piece of the big pie in the sky. A series of congressional hearings were held to apportion the broadcast spectrum, and by 1947, the Federal Communications Commission (FCC) had awarded a total of thirteen channels to the television networks. Channel one was designated as a community channel for stations with limited broadcasting range because it had the lowest frequency.

But there was trouble in this television paradise. As the number of broadcasters increased, the airwaves began to get crowded, especially in larger metropolitan areas. Frequencies started to overlap, causing chaos and complaints when viewers found their quiz shows scrambled with the nightly news, or vice versa.

The FCC took steps to reduce this interference. In 1948, the organization decided to free up space by disallowing broadcasts on the lowest frequency—channel one. That bandwidth would instead be devoted to mobile land services—operations like two-way radio communication in taxicabs. Commercial television retained channels two through twelve. When the FCC's plan went into effect, television manufacturers simply dispensed with the one on the tuning dial; the millions of people who bought their first television sets in the 1950s barely even noticed its absence.

Since then, our options for televised entertainment have multiplied at a staggering rate. Bruce Springsteen's fifty-seven-channel cable package sounds quaint to today's subscribers who have hundreds of stations and a DVR to record them all. Even customers who "cut the cord" have limitless options online. But even with this nearly unlimited number of channels available in our living rooms, we'll never again have a channel one.

12 Useful Rules of Etiquette that Most People Seem to Have Forgotten

Emily Post spent her life sorting out the vagaries of where to seat royalty at a dinner party, what was acceptable attire for a semi-formal wedding, and how much to tip the chambermaid. She would be appalled to learn that most of us have abandoned even the basic tenets of manners. But it isn't too late. Follow these tenets and make Emily proud!

✳   ✳   ✳   ✳

1. **Use the Magic Words** *Please, thank you, excuse me, sorry.* For things big and small, friends, family, coworkers, and even strangers deserve a sprinkling of the magic words.

2. **Write the Official Thank You** Some things deserve "the H"—a handwritten note. Thank yous—they aren't just for weddings.

3. **Learn Your French** "Répondez s'il vous plaît," aka RSVP, sounds confusing but it isn't. It means "Pick up the phone and tell me if you're coming or not. No changing your mind at the last minute. No assuming I know you're coming (or not coming). Call!"

4. **Make Introductions** Instead of letting a person lurk behind you, mute and uncomfortable, say: "Friend A, I'd like you to meet Friend B. Friend B, this is Friend A."

5. **Outlaw the Manners Police** Emily Post, the Queen of Manners, would never look down her nose at someone who used the wrong fork at dinner or (perish the thought) actually point out a manners gaffe. Why should you?

6. **Get Off Your Butt** We may all be equal but that doesn't absolve you from offering some people your seat on the bus: pregnant women, people with small children, the elderly, or a person with a medical condition that might make standing difficult. (Hint: crutches? Yes. Mechanical arm? No.)

7. **Don't Hijack Host Duties** Hosts specify on invitations who is invited. Anyone not mentioned—children, houseguests, teenager's boyfriend—isn't going. And don't *ask* if you can bring extra guests. Your host will say yes but will secretly complain that you were impolite enough to ask. There may be some wiggle room on this one though. An extra at an informal BBQ isn't as problematic as an extra at a formal affair like a wedding.

8. **Learn to Tell Time** No one thinks your perpetual lateness is cute. Plan ahead for traffic jams, phone calls, and wardrobe malfunctions.

9. **Forget Money Exists** Stop talking about money! Don't offer or ask for info about salary, purchases, or market losses.

10. **Remember Life Is Not Jerry Springer** Celebs and reality stars may routinely blab about their personal lives, but it isn't polite. "Did you have in vitro?" is not a conversation opener for a stranger in the elevator or your cousin Elaine! Neither is marriage, divorce, or sex.

11. **Stop Asking for Gifts** Nowhere on an invitation should gifts be mentioned—a move that indicates guests are being invited, not for their charming personalities, but for their gift potential. A few friends should have info about registry, preferences, or charities to tell guests *only* if they ask.

12. **Do Not Be Disruptive** In public, your every action should be measured against this motto. Drunk at the office party? Cell phone ringing at the movies? 30 items in the 10 items or less aisle at the grocery store? Insisting on a special lo-carb, vegan-organic meal at a dinner party? All disruptions. All bad manners.

"Good manners can replace morals. It may be years before anyone knows if what you are doing is right. But if what you are doing is nice, it will be immediately evident."

— P. J. O'ROURKE

18 Tips for Public Speaking

If this were a list of the human race's greatest fears, public speaking would be right at the top. Whether it's forgetting your lines or realizing you have a tail of toilet paper hanging out of your pants, fear of public speaking really boils down to fear of being ridiculed, rejected, and publicly humiliated. But don't worry—with the following tips, you'll be fine!

1. **Watch the Masters:** If you've got a speech or presentation in your future, start looking for what makes successful public speakers so successful. Note their styles and habits and keep them in mind as good examples.

2. **Fix Up, Look Sharp:** If you're in a position where public speaking is required, let's hope you've already got a handle on the importance of personal grooming. If not, take heed: The better you look, the more ready and professional you'll feel. A lot of people are going to be looking at you—make sure you look your best.

3. **Hello, Room. Nice to Meet You.:** If at all possible, check the specs of the room where you'll be speaking. Is it football stadium big or conference room big? What about the sound system? If you'll be using a microphone, it's a good idea to test it out beforehand. The more familiar you are with your environment, the more comfortable you'll be at the podium.

4. **Sober Up:** If your speaking engagement is at a social function (i.e. wedding, reunion), it might seem like a good idea to guzzle as much liquid courage as you can before your speech. But listening to a sincere speech from someone who's nervous is much better than listening to incoherent babble from someone who's loaded.

5. **Know Your Material:** Winging it is not a good idea when you've got a speech to make. While going with the flow and being flexible is smart, trusting yourself to be brilliant without any preparation is something even the pros don't attempt. Do your research. Know your topic and what you're going to say about it and how you'd like to say it. The more you know, the more confident you'll be up there.

6. **Practice, Practice, Practice:** Once you're prepared, go through the speech. Then read it again. Then again. And then once more. Practice in front of a mirror. Practice to your dog. Grab a friend or family member and practice in front of a real human being. Every time you go through your presentation, you're adding a layer of preparation.

7. **Visualize Yourself Being Fabulous:** Negative thinking will get you nowhere but down in the dumps. If you believe that you'll be great, you will be. If you think you're going to fail, you probably will. It's as simple as that.

8. **Know Your Audience:** To whom are you speaking? If they're colleagues, they probably want to learn something from you. If they're friends, they're likely looking to be entertained. If it's a judge, well, he or she wants to be convinced. Know who your audience is and tailor your speech and delivery to them. Give them what they want!

9. **Relax!:** We're usually our own worst critics. If you forget to read a sentence off your notes, it's doubtful anyone will know. If you skip forward to the next image on the projector by mistake, no one's going to run you out of town. Don't worry. It's not life or death, it's just a speech.

10. **Don't Give It Away:** If it really, truly makes you feel better to announce to the room that you're so nervous before you begin, go ahead. But your speech will have a lot more weight if you don't. Chances are good that you're the only one who knows you're shaking in your boots—why show

the cracks in your armor? Let them believe you have it under control, even if you don't feel like you do.

11. **Slow Your Roll:** One of the biggest indicators of nervousness is the lightning-fast talker. You might have the best speech ever written, but if no one can understand what you're saying, it doesn't matter. Pace yourself and remember to speak at a normal (or even slightly slower) pace when you're speaking publicly.

12. **The Eyes Have It:**   People trust people who look them in the eye, so look at your audience when you're speaking to them. Don't look at the floor—there's nothing down there. Don't look solely at your notes—the audience will think you haven't prepared. You appear more confident when your head is up, which puts your audience at ease and allows you to take command of the room.

13. **Go On, Be Funny!:** Who doesn't like to laugh a little? You don't have to be a comedian, but a few lighthearted comments can help humanize you to your audience. Win them over with a smile and a well-timed clever remark, if you can. But be advised, too many jokes can weaken your credibility.

14. **Your Errors Are Okay:** So you tripped on the microphone cord. So what? So you said macro when you meant micro somewhere in your speech. So you accidentally said the name of your sister's ex-boyfriend during your toast instead of the name of her new husband—so what! Everyone makes mistakes. Acknowledge them and move on.

15. **Keep It Short, Please:** Even the president's State of the Union Address is only around an hour. Know what's

expected of you and deliver that—and no more. We've all been tortured by a speaker who goes on and on, caring little for the audience's interest or comfort level. Don't be one of those speakers—always leave them wanting more.

16. **It's SO Not About You:** The more you can take the focus off yourself, the better. After all, it's not likely you're being asked to give a presentation of your life story. So concentrate on the message and find freedom in just being the messenger.

17. **Fake It 'Til You Make It:** The old saying "fake it 'til you make it" is actually pretty good advice. Even if you have zero confidence in yourself, try acting like you do. The longer you fake it, the more comfortable it will feel, until, voilà, you're a bona fide confidence machine.

18. **Be Yourself:** We're all human. We're all a little afraid of the podium, the microphone, or the boardroom. Despite what you may believe, people don't want you to fail. They ultimately want to see you succeed. Give them what they want by just being the best you you can be.

Scream Machines and Vomit Comets

Today's crop of thrill rides stagger the imagination. From a heart-stopper that shoots riders higher than the Eiffel Tower, to a mind-boggler that reaches 100 miles per hour faster than any production car, the following scream machines electrify the senses as they agitate the innards.

✳ ✳ ✳ ✳

Big Shot

RANKED AS THE highest thrill ride in the world, Big Shot, located at the Stratosphere Hotel and Casino in Las Vegas, has been scaring the tar out of adrenaline junkies since its debut in 1996. This compressed-air vertical "blast" ride launches riders 160 feet into the air. Seems rather tame until you consider that Big Shot's launch pad is 921 feet off the ground on the side of the Stratosphere Tower. Less than three seconds after blast-off, newly acrophobic riders find themselves an astounding 1,081 feet from terra firma.

Timber Tower

As its name suggests, Timber Tower, located at Dollywood in Pigeon Forge, Tennessee, gives riders the sensation that the 65-foot-tall cylindrical tower they are sitting atop has broken free from its base and tumbled over like a freshly chopped tree falling toward the ground. Add to the mix the fact that riders are spinning horizontally around that tower as it falls and then rights itself only to fall in the opposite direction over and over again, and what you get is a circumstance where riders see death rushing toward them and then they don't; then they do; then they don't, as if trapped in a continuous loop.

Kingda Ka

Officially the tallest and fastest roller coaster in the world, Kingda Ka, located at Six Flags Great Adventure in Jackson,

New Jersey, has effectively thrown down the gauntlet to its challengers. With an overall height of 456 feet and an actual drop of 418 feet, this monster is only beginning to puff its chest. But Kingda Ka's greatest strength lies in its blistering speed. Shot from ground-level into a 90-degree vertical spiral, riders accelerate from 0 to 128 miles per hour in just 3.5 seconds! In comparison, an aircraft carrier catapult launch excels planes from 0 to 150 miles per hour in roughly 2 seconds.

Mega Drop

Found at amusement parks and traveling carnivals, the Mega Drop's 115-foot-tall objective is simple: Twelve passengers sit around a ring that's slowly raised to the top of the tower. Then, without warning the vehicle is released and free-falls downward at 69 feet per second (approximately 47 miles per hour). A magnetic braking system decelerates the plummeting cab until it is stopped by four beefy shock absorbers.

Superman Ultimate Flight

If you've ever wanted to fly like a superhero, then head over to a Six Flags theme park in Georgia, Illinois, or New Jersey, where this ride's specially designed cars tilt passengers facedown into

a flying position, so that they're suspended horizontally from the track above. Riders get a bird's-eye view at the top of a 109-foot hill before sailing through the air at 60 miles per hour in a series of loops, spirals, turns, and rolls. This truly is a unique thrill ride.

Son of Beast

As wooden roller coasters go, this monster at Kings Island in Cincinnati, Ohio, is without peer. Built in 2000, it is currently the world's fastest wooden roller coaster at 78 miles per hour, the world's tallest at 218 feet, and features not only the world's loftiest first drop for a "woody" at 214 feet but the world's greatest second drop (164 feet) as well. Beyond these records there is one honor that no longer applies. When Son of Beast opened, it was the only "looping" wooden roller coaster in the world, but the loop was removed before the 2007 season. These days, the mighty "Son" carries on the grand tradition set forth by the original Beast, also at Kings Island.

The Screamer

The Screamer, a 168-foot-tall, 3.5 g-force-inducing swinging pendulum ride at Sacramento's Scandia Family Fun Center, lives up to its name with startling regularity, as do most thrill rides that rocket their riders toward the ground at 65 miles per hour. But the ride's name has proven prophetic in more ways than one. Fed up with listening to the banshee shrieks, area residents complained shortly after the ride opened in 2007. Since then, a rigidly enforced "no scream" policy has been in effect. If anyone is caught screaming on the ride, it is stopped and the offending party is sent to the back of the line. Ironically, the park's motto is, "It's a Scream!"

10 Classic Amusement Park Rides

Roller coasters get all the attention. But what about the tamer rides with shorter lines and more relaxed height restrictions? Read on to learn about the favorites among the lesser-known rides. Some are unique, some have been copied for decades, but all of them are vital to the atmosphere of the midway.

✳ ✳ ✳ ✳

1. **Tilt-A-Whirl:** In 1926, Herbert Sellner finished his design for the Tilt-A-Whirl and began building one in his backyard. Sellner's ride involved seven cars attached at various fixed pivot points on a rotating platform that raised and lowered itself. The cars themselves were free spinning, but when you added the centrifugal force and the platform's gravitational pull on the cars, they would wildly spin in countless directions at variable speeds. Calculated chaos ensued. Since then, Sellner Manufacturing Company has built more than 1,000 Tilt-A-Whirls and inspired hundreds of knockoffs. Those who look a little green or lose their lunch of hot dogs, cotton candy, and soda pop are probably just coming off a Tilt-A-Whirl.

2. **Ferris Wheel:** Ah, the mighty Ferris wheel—provider of a million romantic moments and breathtaking views. For the World's Columbian Exposition of 1893 in Chicago, engineer George Ferris presented fair organizers with his idea of a giant rotating wheel that would carry passengers in cars attached around the outer edge. He convinced organizers to allow him to build the structure, which would rival France's Eiffel Tower. Indeed, Ferris's wheel, which cost $380,000 and stood 264 feet tall with a wheel diameter of 250 feet, was a huge success. Each car held 60 people, and, at 50 cents a ride, the wheel was one of the most popular attractions at the World's Fair. The Ferris wheel is a must-have for any carnival.

3. **Insanity:** Built in 2005 at the top of the Stratosphere Hotel Tower in Las Vegas, this ride isn't kidding around. The second-highest thrill ride in the world at 906 feet above terra firma (second to its nearby Stratosphere brother, "Big Shot"), the Insanity arm extends 64 feet over the edge of the hotel tower, spinning passengers at top speeds. If that's not insane enough for you, hang on. Soon, the spinning gets even faster, and riders are propelled upwards at a 70-degree angle. Insanity creators claim that "riders will experience the thrill of being flung over the edge of the tower" as they look down for a couple of breathless seconds at a glittering Las Vegas far below.

4. **Scrambler:** There are many names for this ride and its variations, but Americans usually call it the Scrambler. Whatever name is emblazoned on its side, this ride is fast—really fast. Picture this: the ride has three arms. On the ends of each of those arms are clusters of individual cars, each on a smaller arm of its own. When the Scrambler starts, the main arm and the little arms all rotate. The outermost arms are slowed and the inner arms are accelerated, creating an illusion of frighteningly close collisions between the cars and their passengers. The Scrambler proves that you don't have to go on a roller coaster to lose your lunch or have the wits scared out of you.

5. **Bumper Cars:** If you've ever wanted to recreate the excitement and thrill of a fender bender, this is your ride! Bumper cars (or "dodgem cars"), which were introduced in the 1920s, feature a large ring or pen with a graphite floor designed to decrease friction. Riders climb into miniature electric cars that draw power from an overhead grid and proceed to slam into the other cars in the pen. Wide rubber bumpers keep things safe—as safe as you can get with no brakes! Still, bumper cars are so popular you'll find them in just about every theme park, county fair, or carnival you visit—just follow the crashing noises and laughter.

6. **"It's a Small World":** The theme song to "It's a Small World" is woven into American (and international) pop culture—even if you've never been to a Disney theme park, you probably know the chorus. In 1964, the World's Fair came to New York, and Walt Disney and team created animatronic children of the world that featured anthems from various countries around the globe. In order to streamline the ride, which takes guests on boats through the animated panoramas, composers Robert and Richard Sherman came up with the now famous tune.

   Many find the "small world" experience to be a little naive and simplistic, but that's what the creators were going for—people everywhere getting along so well they sing songs and hold hands. All day. For hours. The same song...over and over again.

7. **Log Rides:** If you were a lumberjack in America in the late 1800s, a "log ride" wasn't something you'd line up to do. Log flumes were handmade channels created by loggers to transport felled trees to the sawmill.

   Stories of lumberjacks riding logs down the flume inspired the many versions of the log rides we know today. The first one, called El Aserradero ("the sawmill" in Spanish), was located at Six Flags Over Texas back in 1963. Passengers boarded a hollowed out "log" and rushed down the flume, getting soaked in the process. The ride was so popular that the park added another log ride a few years later. Famous log rides include Disney's Splash Mountain and Perilous Plunge at Knott's Berry Farm in California, the tallest and steepest log ride with a 115-foot drop.

8. **The Haunted Mansion:** The "Happiest Place on Earth" gets a bit scary with the Haunted Mansion, another juggernaut of an amusement park attraction created by the fine folks at Disney. The ride opened in August 1969 in Disneyland and featured ghosts, murderous brides, blood-

spilling families, and a host of other specters designed to scare park-goers silly as they ride through in a "doom buggy." The Haunted Mansion is among the most popular Disney rides in history, and it even inspired a movie— *The Haunted Mansion*, starring Eddie Murphy, was released in 2003.

9. **The Rotor:** Quick! Get up and twirl around as fast as you can for three straight minutes, then jump as high as you can into the air! Feel that free-falling, vertigo sensation? If not, why not go on a rotor ride? Designed in the 1940s by engineer Ernst Hoffmeister, the Rotor has many versions in theme parks all over the world. The premise is pretty much a simple lesson in centrifugal force: Take a large barrel and revolve the walls of said barrel really fast. When it's going super fast, drop the bottom out of the barrel, and watch as all the people inside stick to the walls. Other names for this simple but popular ride include Gravitron and Vortex.

10. **Carousel:** The most elegant of all amusement park rides, the carousel dates back to around A.D. 500. Drawings from this time period show riders in baskets circling a post. The carousel, or merry-go-round, remains a carnival staple worldwide. The ride consists of a rotating platform with seats that move up and down. The seats are the really special part, made of wood, fiberglass, or plastic and shaped to look like decorated animals, such as deer, cats, fish, rabbits, giraffes, and, of course, horses.

Old carousels and carousel pieces can be worth lots of money these days depending on the level of artistry that went into their manufacture. Fun for young and old alike, even when the Triple-Threat-Xtreme-Screamer roller coaster is phased out, the carousel will still be turning round and round.

The Long Tradition of Wedding Drunkenness

Still steaming mad at Uncle Ralph for getting totally wasted and ruining your reception? Just comfort yourself with the knowledge that folks have been getting blotto at weddings for thousands of years.

✳ ✳ ✳ ✳

EVEN JESUS CHRIST seemed annoyed at the prospect of drunken revelers when his mother informed him that the wine had run out at the wedding at Cana. "Dear woman, why do you involve me?" he asked before giving in and working a miracle to keep everyone happy. Since then, weddings and liquor have gone together like Courtney Love and cosmetic surgery: It *should* make everything better, but does it, really?

Cog Stand

Though heavy drinking at weddings happened all over the world throughout history, the United Kingdom is really hard to top when it comes to nuptial boozing—plus they wrote everything down for our enjoyment. Communal cups added to the feeling of alliance and kinship, but they also made excessive drinking harder to avoid due to peer pressure. On the Orkney Islands, for example, it was traditional for two types of round, wooden drinking vessels—or *cogs* as they were known—to be passed around at every wedding celebration. The *cog-gilt-cogs* were kept at each table of 24 guests, while the *menye-cogs* were circulated throughout the entire dining hall. The menye-cogs themselves were broken down into three categories—the best man's cog, the priest's cog, and the bride's cog. See? These people took their wedding drinking seriously!

Driven to Drink

Even worse than a guest getting drunk at the reception is a groom being drunk at the ceremony. Perhaps the most famous historical example of this is George, the Prince of Wales, who arrived at his 1795 hitching loaded to the gills. The 32-year-old George didn't want to get married at all—he was perfectly happy with his mistress, the 42-year-old Lady Jersey—but his father, King George III, was often ill. The heir to the throne needed to step up and reassure the people that all would be well in case of his dad's death. He was thus forced to marry his cousin, 26-year-old Caroline of Brunswick, a woman who utterly repulsed him. George rebelled by showing up at the Chapel Royal at St. James Palace in a hopelessly inebriated state. He proceeded to pout, cry, screw up the vows, and repeatedly glance over at Lady Jersey, who must have been thrilled to be in attendance.

Death by Drunkenness

Two hundred years later, it's easy to laugh at the Prince's drunken antics, but we would do well to remember that excessive drinking can turn what should be a beautiful day into a horrible nightmare. Take the case of 35-year-old Wu Chengfeng. The Taiwanese insurance executive was so excited and happy about his wedding in the spring of 2009 that he invited every classmate he had known at Tamkang University to the reception at a ritzy Taipei restaurant. Following a Chinese custom that dates back to the 12th century, Wu drank more than he should have—one and half bottles of red wine and four beers. Technically, this should not have been enough to kill him, but combined with recent overwork and a preexisting asthma condition, the binge proved fatal.

Despite such cautionary tales, wedding drunkenness will no doubt go on for a very, very long time. A search of "drunk wedding" on YouTube turns up all kinds of embarrassing videos from all over the world—even places where drinking alcohol is prohibited by law or religion. While excessive drinking at weddings may never be abolished, brides can only hope that it can be somewhat controlled.

The Waxing and Waning of Honeymoons

The honeymoon is time alone with the one that you love. Or a much-needed rest after the stress of planning and attending your own wedding. The honeymoon is a wedding tradition that couples treasure. But it wasn't always that way.

2500 B.C. and earlier: In ancient Babylonia, it was tradition for the bride's father to give the groom honeyed mead (a type of wine). He drank this every night for 30 days after the wedding to promote fertility. Some consider this the origin of the word honeymoon.

A.D. 400: The earliest honeymoons were a period of function rather than fun. In the Scandinavian regions of Europe, during Viking times, the groom stole his new bride away for about a month or "moon." During this time, her family and friends searched for her. The hope was that the new bride would be pregnant with the couple's first child by the time she was "found."

16th century: For the first time, the honeymoon became a romantic vacation for the newlyweds. Fun at last. Another possible origin of the word honeymoon cropped up during this century when a man named Thomas Blount referred to the period just after the wedding by saying, "It is honey now, but will change as the moon."

1820s: Europeans—probably noticing that newly married Americans were taking vacations abroad—adopted the honeymoon for themselves. The French called them *les voyages à la façon anglaise* or English-style voyages.

1830s: American couples discovered Niagara Falls as a honeymoon destination. It was closer and less expensive than a European vacation—and every bit as beautiful.

Victorian era: In Victorian times, the honeymoon finally became a wedding tradition. Typically, the groom's family would pay for this romantic vacation after the wedding. The honeymoon—or bridal tour—was initially taken only by the wealthy, since it frequently lasted for weeks or even months. Wedding couples took these earliest honeymoons by train, with the best man accompanying the couple to the station. He was the only one who would know their destination, so they wouldn't be disturbed. The bad news: The bride and groom were kept apart during the engagement and used the honeymoon to get to know each other better. Italy was the most popular destination for English couples during Victorian times. Family members who couldn't attend the wedding often went with newlyweds on their honeymoon. There goes the romance!

20th century: At the turn of the century, the idea of taking a honeymoon spread through all classes of people in the United States and into Canada, as well.

1940s: Wartime took its toll on the honeymoon tradition. Many grooms were already in the service or heading off to war. Weddings were often small affairs, and honeymoons frequently took place in a hometown hotel or within a few hours' drive. Sometimes the bride-to-be traveled to the military base, and the groom was able to get a few days furlough to get married and enjoy a night or two with his bride before the realties of war separated them again.

2000s: Now, many American couples are choosing exotic destinations for their getaways. Aruba, the Cayman Islands, Cancun, Greece, Spain, and England are among the most popular spots, perhaps gaining popularity because they are far away from the couple's hometown. Some locations are quiet, offering a chance to relax and regroup, while others have plenty of activities to keep the couple active. For couples choosing to stay in the United States, the most popular destinations are now Hawaii, Florida, and Las Vegas. For the newly married but young at heart: Disney World.

Scaring the Pants Off the Audience

Joy buzzers hidden under theater seats; insurance policies to ensure against "death by fright"; glowing skeletons hovering over the heads of audience members—these are just a few of the gimmicks that legendary movie producer and director William Castle unleashed on audiences in the 1950s and '60s.

✳   ✳   ✳   ✳

Death by Fright and Flying Skeletons

Castle's first gimmick was born out of necessity. Having sunk everything he owned into the making of *Macabre* (1958), Castle was worried that the movie would flop, so he decided he needed a unique way to get people into the theaters. In a stroke of genius, Castle invented Death by Fright Insurance. As people purchased tickets for *Macabre*, they were handed a certificate that claimed to be a $1,000 life insurance policy from Lloyd's of London, which could be redeemed should the filmgoer die of fright during the movie. Castle also hired women to pose as nurses and even parked hearses outside the venues. *Macabre* was a modest hit, and Castle was convinced that he was on to something.

So when the Vincent Price thriller *House on Haunted Hill* was released the next year, Castle claimed that it had been filmed using a process called *Emergo*, which caused the ghosts and ghouls in the movie to come off the screen and into the audience. Toward the end of the movie, a walking skeleton emerges from a vat of acid to "exact its revenge." At that precise moment, theater workers released a glowing skeleton that flew on wires above the heads of audience members. Arrrgh!

"The Tingler Is Loose in THIS Theater!"

Hot on the heels of the success of Emergo, Castle came up with a new gimmick for the release of *The Tingler* in 1960. According to Castle, the movie was filmed in *Percepto*, a unique process that allowed moviegoers to "feel every shocking sensation" of the film. Trailers for *The Tingler* carried a guarantee that "The Tingler will break loose in the theater while YOU are in the audience!"

The movie itself centered on a bizarre centipedelike creature—the Tingler—which supposedly lives in the human spinal cord. During the movie, the screen went dark and the characters yelled, "Watch out! The Tingler is loose in THIS theater!" That's when Percepto kicked in, with an image of the Tingler projected onto the screen as though it were crawling on the projector. Prior to the start of the movie, theater employees had rigged several seats with buzzers. Once activated, the buzzers gave those lucky (or unlucky) viewers a mild zap, although many people claimed that it only made them laugh. Either way, once word got out about the buzzers, children tried to be the first inside the theater so they could crawl under the seats to see which of them were "wired."

The Magic of Illusion-O

In 1960, prior to the release of *13 Ghosts*, Castle said that the movie was filmed in *Illusion-O*, which allowed patrons to see ghosts hidden in the movie. As people entered the theater, they were given a "ghost viewer/remover," which was a piece of cardboard with strips of red and blue cellophane. If you wanted to see the ghosts, you looked through the red viewer; if you didn't want to see the ghosts, then you looked through the blue part.

Since the viewers had a red side and a blue side similar to 3-D glasses, many believed the film was shot in 3-D. In reality, the film was shot in black and white with blue tints added to the scenes with the "ghosts," which made them visible when people looked through the red portion of the viewer.

Deciding the Fate of Mr. Sardonicus

For *Mr. Sardonicus* (1961), Castle decided to let his audience decide how the movie would end. As patrons entered the theater, they were all given pieces of cardboard bearing a drawing of a hand giving the "thumbs-up" signal. The film's main character, Mr. Sardonicus, does some dastardly deeds, but by the end, the movie appears to be heading toward a storybook ending. That's when Castle appeared on-screen to explain that the cards were part of the "punishment poll." Castle told the audience that if they felt Mr. Sardonicus deserved to be happy, they should hold their cards with the thumbs-up sign high in the air. If, however, the audience believed Mr. Sardonicus should be punished for his evil deeds, they were to hold their cards up with the thumb facing down. After these instructions, Castle pretended to count the votes, then he let the audience know the results, and the appropriate ending was played.

Castle believed that audiences would almost always vote for the punishment ending and therefore made that the original ending. He was right. The happy ending was never played.

A Turning Point

Most people believe that *Zotz!* (1962) signaled the beginning of the end for Castle's gimmicks. In the movie, Tom Poston plays a bumbling professor who finds a mysterious gold coin. If he exclaims "Zotz!" while holding the coin, mayhem ensues. Those purchasing tickets were each given a magic Zotz coin, which was nothing more than a piece of gold-colored plastic.

Number, Please

Castle wanted to promote *I Saw What You Did* (1965) with giant plastic telephones because the film centered on a pair of girls who accidentally prank-call a killer. But before the film was released, the telephone company received so many complaints about prank calls that they forbade Castle from promoting his film with phones or even mentioning the role telephones played in the movie. Instead, Castle decided to install seat belts on some of the seats in the back rows—the "shock sections" of the theater—to keep moviegoers from flying out of their seats from shock.

One Last Gimmick

Castle continued to try small gimmicks here and there for the next decade, but his final film to use a gimmick as a promotional tool came in 1975 with the release of his film *Bug*. The film itself was a throwback to the monster-type films that were so popular in the 1950s and '60s. For the film, Castle announced that because there were so many dangerous stunts performed, he had to take out a $1 million life insurance policy on the movie's star. Who was the star of the film? Hercules the cockroach.

Foodie Films

What could be better than sitting down to a movie with a big bucket of popcorn? How about sitting down to a movie with a buttery lobster, a juicy steak, or a piping hot wedge of lasagna? Here are a few films that are sure to get your stomach growling.

✳ ✳ ✳ ✳

Babette's Feast (1987)

Based on a story by Danish writer Isak Dineson, this French–Danish movie won the Oscar for Best Foreign Language Film. Two beautiful young sisters, who have been forbidden to marry by their strict, religious father, grow old and increasingly bitter. They hire a needy French woman named Babette to cook and clean for them, but when Babette wins the Parisian lottery, she decides to leave town. Before she goes, she cooks a sumptuous French meal for the sisters and their nearly forgotten suitors. The images of Babette's dinner are downright delectable, and the movie delicately stirs in themes of love, faith, and patience.

Fried Green Tomatoes (1991)

A movie about friendship, inspiration, and tasty home cookin', *Fried Green Tomatoes* gets labeled as a "chick flick" but truly has something for everyone. Based on the popular novel by Fannie Flagg, the movie follows a forty-something woman (Kathy Bates) as she tries to get her husband's attention. She meets an elderly woman (Jessica Tandy) in need of a friend and listens to her tale of friendship, mystery, and intrigue. In turn, the muddled middle-ager is inspired to seize the day and tend to what's truly important in life. You'll have to watch the film to learn the integral part the title dish plays in the stories of several generations of strong Southern women.

Like Water for Chocolate (1993)

It's Mexico. It's hot. It's 1910, and Tita is bound by tradition not to marry while she cares for her elderly mother, but of course, Tita falls in love with Pedro. To be close to Tita, Pedro marries her sister (gee, thanks honey), but of course, Tita and Pedro can't contain their passion for each other. In the film, which was adapted from a novel by Laura Esquivel and directed by her husband, Alfonso Arau, Tita shows her feelings through her cooking and the result is . . . well, *hot*. You can't miss the steamy, though sometimes heavy-handed, love scenes. Be warned: You'll probably have a craving for either hanky-panky, guacamole, or chocolate by the time the credits roll.

Big Night (1996)

Written by actor Stanley Tucci and codirected by Tucci and actor Campbell Scott, *Big Night* follows the trials, tribulations, and tiramisus of a pair of Italian brothers who are trying to make their New Jersey restaurant a success in the 1950s. The story is based on Tucci's own experiences and examines the conflict between art and commerce.

A rival restaurant nearby offers bigger portions of inferior food and terrible Chianti but continues to thrive, while the brothers' smaller restaurant struggles. A plan is hatched for a "big night" to honor singer Louis Prima at the restaurant, and the characters scramble to make everything perfect. The movie is stocked with great scenes around the table and in the kitchen and offers laughs, some Old World nostalgia, and a whole lotta pasta!

Chocolat (2000)

Nominated for five Academy Awards, this sensuous film is packed with exceptional actors and a lot of cocoa powder. Juliette Binoche plays Vianne, a chocolatier who opens up shop in a sleepy French village to find that her product inspires latent passions in the villagers. Not everyone is pleased about this, especially the town's stuffy mayor, played brilliantly by Alfred Molina. When heartthrob Johnny Depp comes to town, he and Vianne find their hearts melting like a couple of bonbons. The movie is languid and lighthearted—perfect for an after-dinner treat.

Ratatouille (2007)

The combination of food and rodents doesn't readily appeal to most, but somehow it works in Pixar's *Ratatouille*. This animated feature follows the adventures of Remy, a rat with culinary skills that lead him all the way to the kitchen of a famed Parisian restaurant. Director Brad Bird (*The Incredibles*, 2004) keeps *Ratatouille* sizzling with dazzling animation, hilarious details, and more than a few heartwarming moments.

Horse-ing Around

For decades, directors have been moved to make movies about horses. In fact, the subgenre of films about the majestic animals offers dozens of horse-centric movies to choose from. Most of the films have similar themes: nobility in the face of cruelty, loyalty between animal and human, and strength in times of adversity. So curl up with some oats, and check out some of the most famous horse movies in the stable.

✳   ✳   ✳   ✳

Black Beauty (1921–1994)

ANNA SEWELL'S 1877 NOVEL, narrated from the point of view of a horse, has been adapted for the silver screen at least five times. In addition to the films, several TV versions have been made, too. A favorite amongst fans seems to be the 1946 black-and-white film version starring Mona Freeman, but with so many adaptations to choose from, you can see the touching story of Beauty in a variety of styles from different eras.

My Friend Flicka (1943)

If you want the full story of the horse named Flicka, you should probably read the 1941 book by author Mary O'Hara. The film version tones down the story for younger audiences, but the basics are the same: A young boy, played by the talented Roddy McDowall, befriends a horse and the pair experience many joys, trials, and tribulations, which bring them closer together.

A television series based on the story aired in the late 1950s, and you can still catch it in reruns from time to time.

National Velvet (1944)

Before she was Cleopatra, Elizabeth Taylor was Velvet Brown, a young girl whose love for a horse named "The Pie" keeps it out of the glue factory. After Velvet saves the horse, she trains it to compete in the Grand National horse race, with the help of an embittered ex-jockey, played by Mickey Rooney. When the jockey hired to ride her beloved horse shows his lack of faith in the animal, Velvet decides to disguise herself as a boy and ride him herself. In 1978, a less beloved sequel, *International Velvet*, was released.

The Black Stallion (1979)

This film, produced by Francis Ford Coppola, is the classic "boy and his horse" story. A boy and an Arabian stallion are shipwrecked together on an island. The two keep their distance for a while, but a friendship blossoms—cue swelling music and stirring scenes of galloping on the beach. When the two are rescued, "The Black" is entered into a nail-bitingly close race. The boy is coached by a former jockey, played by Mickey Rooney in a nod to his role in *National Velvet*. Beautifully directed by Carroll Ballard, who was adept at handling nature-driven stories, *The Black Stallion* is high drama fit for the whole family.

The Horse Whisperer (1998)

This film, starring Robert Redford, Kristin Scott-Thomas, and a young Scarlett Johannson, tells the tale of a traumatized young girl and her equally troubled horse. A trainer seems to magically heal the horse, which helps to heal the girl. Featuring sweeping shots of the wide-open Montana landscape, a romantic spark between the trainer and the girl's mother, and lots of tear-jerking moments, *The Horse Whisperer* got mixed reviews, but it is a well-crafted adult drama directed by Redford.

Seabiscuit (2003)

During the Great Depression, stories about underdogs (or underhorses, for that matter) were eaten up by a public needing a shot of hope. Enter Seabiscuit, an undervalued, undersized thoroughbred whom no one thought could win any races. Seabiscuit proved them all wrong. His story was first turned into a best-selling book by Laura Hillenbrand before it became an acclaimed film starring Jeff Bridges, William H. Macy, and Tobey Maguire.

Hidalgo (2004)

Based on the life of Frank Hopkins, a cowboy who rode with Buffalo Bill's Wild West Show, *Hidalgo* tells the story of a man, his horse (that's Hidalgo), and a race that no one believed he could win. Set against the backdrop of the Arabian desert, *Hidalgo* follows Hopkins, played by a rugged Viggo Mortensen, as he dodges those who would have him lose the centuries-old Ocean of Fire race across the desert. A little love interest and a lot of white-knuckle moments with a steed that just won't quit make this movie a must-see for horse lovers.

Girls Gone Golfing

When encountering a female foursome on the links, many a male golfer has muttered that GOLF is an acronym for Gentlemen Only, Ladies Forbidden. Only in your dreams, guys!

✳ ✳ ✳ ✳

No one is completely sure about the origin of the name for the game that involves whacking a small orb across a manicured field. It is speculated that the sport's odd moniker comes from the Dutch words *kolf* and *kolve*, which mean "club." By the time those words had crossed the channel and entered the Scottish lexicon, they evolved into *golve*, *gowl*, and *gouf*.

Mary on the Links

Regarding the game's exclusion of ladies, history tells us that women have been playing almost as long as men have. Mary, Queen of Scots, was an avid golfer in the 16th century—before she was beheaded for treason, that is. Her fondness for the sport became evident when she squeezed in a quick 18 just days after the murder of her second husband.

This seemed to cause great consternation among her followers, who felt she should be praying instead of putting. In fact, Mary may have been responsible for introducing the term *caddy* into the vocabulary of golf. When she played the game growing up in France, military cadets often carried her clubs as she took "a good walk wasted." When she returned to Scotland in 1561, she introduced the practice to her subjects, and the club-touting cadets were dubbed "caddies."

Give Me an "H"!

There's widespread belief that the "H" in the center of the Montreal Canadiens' logo stands for Habitants. In fact, it stands for "hockey"—go figure.

✳   ✳   ✳   ✳

THE LOGO FOR the Montreal Canadiens consists of a stylized "C" with the letter "H" situated in its middle. The "CH" actually stands for *Club de Hockey Canadien* (Canadian Hockey Club). Yet, to this day, some of the most ardent Montreal Canadiens supporters believe that the "H" in the center of their favorite team's logo stands for Habitants.

This much is true: For the majority of its existence, the most successful hockey team in the history of the game has been known by its nickname, *Les Habitants*, or simply the Habs. Of course, the team has also been called *Les Glorieux* (the Glorious) and *Les Bleu, Blanc, et Rouge* (the Blue, White, and Red). Mostly the Canadiens have been called victorious—the club has won an astonishing 24 Stanley Cup championships since first hitting the ice on January 5, 1910.

The origin of the nickname *Les Habitants* comes from the earliest days of the franchise. Originally formed in 1909, the team was organized as an exclusive French hockey club that awarded negotiation rights to any French-speaking player born in the province of Quebec. Natives of the province were often referred to as *Habitants*, a French word that means settler or inhabitant. Since every member of the initial team was of French origin, the players and their team were called *Habitants* by their fanatic followers. Although the team has always been known as the Canadiens, the franchise was initially owned by an organization called the Canadian Athletic Club. The team's original club logo was a "C" interlocked with the letter "A." In 1917, the corporation became known by its present name and the "CH" logo was adopted for the first time.

Spanish Fly

Although dance is an essential element of the accomplished art of flamenco, it's by no means the most important. And unless they're performing for show, most dancers dress in black.

✳   ✳   ✳   ✳

✳ The flamenco is often thought of as just a dance, but it's actually a complex musical convolution composed of four harmonious parts: guitar, vocals, dance, and hand clapping.

✳ Don't be fooled into thinking that the dance is widely performed throughout Spain. The flamenco's origins are rooted in one specific area of the country—Andalusia, a region composed of eight provinces, including Cardoba and Granada. It is generally acknowledged that flamenco grew out of the unique uniting of native Andalusian, Islamic, Sephardic, and Romany cultures.

✳ The central component that gives the flamenco its flavor is the music, a percussive portfolio of rhythm, tempo, and time. It sets the pulse of the spectacle and generates the pace and emotional center that fuel the visual aspect of the performance. The music is propelled and augmented by sweeping strums and rhythmic finger taps on the guitar, accompanied by hand claps and foot stomps, all employed to create and caress the beat. The flamenco dance is an impassioned, powerful performance characterized by grand gesturing with the arms and intricate footwork.

✳ Many Spanish dancers who perform for crowds of tourists hold castanets or wear them on their fingers to further accent the cadence and tempo of the music; likewise, these dancers are more likely to don elaborate costumes. Women wear long dresses that are adjusted at the waist and complemented by an underskirt that may be colorful, plain, or adorned with polka dots. Flounces or strips of pleated material on the skirt and the sleeves provide the final visual effect.

Doubting the Big Dipper

There are folks who like to argue that NBA great Wilt Chamberlain built his statistics against inferior competition. In fact, he faced some of basketball's all-time greatest players.

✳ ✳ ✳ ✳

PROPONENTS OF THE myth argue that because of his overwhelming size, Wilt Chamberlain had an unfair advantage over his opponents. Although it's true that Wilt the Stilt stood more than seven feet tall and weighed nearly 275 pounds, he was still a smooth ball handler and a crisp and accurate passer. He possessed a deadly jump shot and was nimble on his feet, attributes not usually associated with an athlete of his size. And he played in an era before the dunk was a recognized offensive weapon, so the majority of his points were made the old-fashioned way—he earned them, often while being double- and even triple-teamed. Height alone is never enough. Just ask Rik Smits, Shawn Bradley, and Ralph Sampson, a trio of much-heralded seven-footers who couldn't manage to translate size and dominance at the college level into the big-league success that Chamberlain enjoyed.

Known as "The Big Dipper" (he often had to dip his head while walking through doorways) and "Chairman of the Boards" during his playing career, Chamberlain held a number of NBA records, including the unapproachable mark of 100 points in a game and 55 rebounds in a game. Chamberlain had to stand in the paint and go toe-to-toe with luminaries such as Bill Russell, Kareem Abdul-Jabbar, Nate Thurmond, and Bob Cousy, hard-nosed competitors whose talent was exceeded only by their determination. In fact, during his 14-year career on the hard court, Chamberlain faced more than half of the 50 players named to the NBA All-Time team in 1996.

Daily U.S. Consumption for 12 Items

Living in the United States has its perks. If you want to brush your teeth, you can buy a toothbrush. If you outgrow your pants, you can shop for a new pair. If you need a soy latte and a Twinkie, you can get those pretty easily, too. America is definitely "the land of plenty," and the statistics that follow offer a glimpse of how many goods U.S. consumers use every day and how much they spend on them. The numbers may surprise you...

✳   ✳   ✳   ✳

1. **Movie Tickets—3.8 million:** If the average cost of a movie is $7, Americans spend about $26.6 million a day at movie theaters. Take that number times 365, and the industry rakes in $9.7 billion annually, which doesn't include profits from popcorn, soda sales, or DVDs.

2. **Greeting Cards—19.2 million:** There's a card for every occasion—heck, there's a card for occasions you didn't even know existed! Between birthday, holiday, and "just because" cards, Americans show loved ones they care by spending $7.5 billion a year on greeting cards.

3. **Denim Jeans—641,000 pairs:** Since Levi Strauss invented blue jeans in 1873, Americans have loved the fashionable pants. Whether you're buying a pair of generic jeans at a discount store or plunking down $300 for designer denim, the blue-jeans industry is big business in the United States. Today, the average price of a pair of jeans comes to about $60, which means Americans spend about $38.5 million on denim pants every day, or $14 billion annually.

4. **Domestic Beer Kegs—975,000:** Where there's a big celebration, or a bar, there are kegs of beer. Kegs of premium beer can get into the $200 range, but we're talking about good ol' American macro-brews. These average $60 per

keg, so Americans spend about $58.5 million on them. Consumers down around 356 million kegs per year, which works out to more than $21 billion per year.

5. **Pampers—300,000 packs:** Pampers has the market cornered on the needs of new parents and sells its Jumbo pack (56 diapers) for around $13. Americans spend $3.9 million a day—$1.4 billion a year—keeping baby bottoms dry.

6. **Cosmetic Procedures—20,000:** Liposuction alone boasts about 1,000 procedures a day, and Botox injections have hit the 5,000-a-day mark. Whether you're going in for a tummy tuck or an eye lift, you can expect to pay an average of $1,700 for an appointment with a plastic surgeon. This means that the American cosmetic surgery industry makes about $34 million a day or $12.4 billion every year.

7. **Axe Body Spray—28,876 cans:** Priced around $5 per can, this deodorizer for frat boys and jocks pulls in approximately $145,000 every day. Guys are spending about $53 million a year to smell nice.

8. **Starbucks Coffee—153,424 pounds:** The little Seattle coffee shop that could is now an internationally recognized trademark that rivals McDonald's when it comes to brand identification and customer loyalty. Americans like their Starbucks so much that the company orders around 56 million pounds of coffee beans every year.

9. **Oreo Cookies—205,000 bags:** An 18-ounce package of the iconic chocolate cookie filled with vanilla frosting is going to set a person back about $3.99. That means Americans spend nearly $818,000 every day, or about $300 million each year, on their beloved Oreos.

10. **Cigarettes—1.1 billion:** With huge campaigns by antitobacco activists and health organizations across the country, Americans smoke a lot less than they did in the past. Still, the tobacco industry is a juggernaut, selling more than

400 billion smokes a year. With the average cost of a pack at $3.50, the U.S. spends $70 billion a year on cigarettes.

11. **Krispy Kreme Doughnuts—1.9 million:** This statistic refers to the Original Glazed variety of Krispy Kremes, served piping hot at various spots along the daily commute. If each doughnut costs 79 cents, Krispy Kreme businesses pull in more than $1.5 million a day on Original Glazed doughnuts alone. That's not including crullers, jelly-filled doughnuts, or coffee.

12. **iPods—88,163:** The iPod is essentially a portable hard drive with headphones. Apple CEO Steve Jobs and his team of savvy engineers revolutionized the entire music industry with the iPod. A 30-gigabyte iPod that holds 7,500 songs and 40 hours of video costs $249. The price goes up from there, depending on added features, or skip the video and the price goes down. Still, on average, that's about $18 million a day and more than $6.4 billion a year—music to Apple's ears.

The Bronzed Age

Who decided suntans are attractive?

✳ ✳ ✳ ✳

S UNTANS HAVE BEEN in and out of fashion throughout history. In many primitive societies, the sun was revered as the center of the spiritual universe, and a perpetual tan was a sign of religious fidelity. In our own slightly less primitive time, sun worship is still common, but the purpose isn't religious. We do it because, as Paris Hilton might put it, "it's hot."

How did it get that way? In the nineteenth century, debutantes and socialites—the Paris Hiltons of their day—would have been praised for their paleness. To compare a lady's skin to alabaster—a hard, white mineral used in sculpture—was to offer a high compliment indeed. But toward the end of the nineteenth century, doctors began to realize that sunlight is necessary for good health, as it promotes vitamin formation in the body. This didn't make suntans attractive overnight, but it helped dissolve the stigma against them. In the twentieth century, tans grew more and more popular from aesthetic and social perspectives, even as evidence that linked sun exposure to skin cancer mounted.

If one person deserves credit for really sparking the current suntan rage, it's famed fashion designer Coco Chanel. She was sunburned while on vacation one summer in the 1920s, and her resulting tan became all the rage. "The 1929 girl must be tanned," she would later say. "A golden tan is the index of chic." Coco was clearly on to something: As a society, we do think that tans are attractive.

Experts say that a suntan nowadays suggests someone who is rugged, athletic, and unafraid of things. It also suggests wealth, leisure, and the freedom to be outside while others are slaving away indoors. This represents a dramatic change from the nineteenth century, when tanned skin was more likely to indicate a life of manual labor in the fields—a sign of someone at the bottom of the social ladder rather than the top.

That's the sociological explanation. There's also a theory that centers on evolutionary psychology—it has to do with the "attractiveness of averageness." Studies have shown that when there is a heterogeneity (or range) of genes present in a person, the resulting face is more average—it is free of unusual quirks of size or shape. Over the millennia, humans have come to innately understand that such a person is also more robust physically, without the genetic weaknesses or flaws inherent in inbreeding.

When a fair-skinned person's face is tan, it appears to be closer to the overall human average, theoretical as this might be. If it seems far-fetched, consider that studies have shown that people of all skin colors tend to believe that the most attractive faces have hues that are between light and dark. In other words, the folks we find most alluring have suntans.

Charred, I'm Sure

Why do men like to barbecue?

✳   ✳   ✳   ✳

THINK ABOUT IT: Have you ever been to a barbeque where the lady of the house flipped the burgers and brats on the grill outside with a beer in hand? It's just a fact of life that when the barbeque's fired up, there's a man hunkered over it doing the cooking—even if the slob refuses even to make a can of soup in the kitchen under normal circumstances.

And yet the leading minds of our country can give no definitive explanation of the phenomenon. Even a scholarly book called *Why Do Men Barbeque?*—published by the Harvard University Press, no less—avoids the subject, despite the title. Nary a mention of why men do the barbequing. But we're pretty sure we know why, and the answer stems from two deep-rooted anthropological realities: (1) Men have traditionally done the hunting in the human clan, and (2) men have traditionally done the religious sacrifices. And barbequing evokes features of both.

First, the hunting. In the days before McDonald's and Arby's, men left the clan and went in search of food, ideally something huge and meaty. If they succeeded in bagging the beast, they might have roasted some of it on the spot to ensure that they had the energy to drag the rest of the carcass back home. And once the men got it home, they would probably still be in charge of the cooking—roasting an elk or a mammoth had to be a big, messy, hot, and fiery affair, requiring masculine strength and physical courage. Furthermore, when there was a beast being roasted, other hungry, cranky humanoids noticed it for miles, so it was best that the male hunters were there protecting the barbeque.

That's part of our educated guess. The other part has to do with sacrifice. Ancient literature is full of evocative scenes of men—it's always men—roasting meat on open fires. The first few wisps of smoke from the meat—which we still recognize with longing, even in our suburban backyards—were considered to be especially sacred, an offering to the gods for the meal that was about to be consumed. Once you see a barbeque as a reenactment of this prehistoric spiritual drama, it's easy to imagine how the decidedly un-politically correct gender roles of the ancient world would be replicated in our own backyards, for better or worse.

In general, barbequing is a different affair from cooking indoors. It harks back to the day of hunters facing dangers and making offerings to their gods, all while guarding their hard-won quarry. The women? They were indoors grinding meal for bread—no less important, but presumably safer.

But the times, they are a-changin'. So any woman reader who wants to strike a blow for a new millennium of gender enlightenment is encouraged to send her man back into the house to prepare the couscous salad and braised asparagus while she takes up the spatula and tongs, cold beer in hand.

Lily Dale, New York— U.S. Headquarters of the Spiritualism Movement

For centuries, the bereaved have sought ways to speak to their loved ones on the Other Side. In the 1840s, the Spiritualism movement swept across the United States. Spiritualists believe that an afterlife awaits us all, and that in it, ethereal beings retain many of the interests they had during their time on earth. They also believe that with the help of mediums—people who are able to see and communicate with the dead—the living can make contact with their deceased loved ones during formal sessions known as séances.

✳ ✳ ✳ ✳

The Awakening of the Spirits

IN THE MID-1870S, a group of committed Spiritualists began hosting summer meetings at Cassadaga Lake in southwestern New York. Believing that nothing is preordained or destined, the Spiritualists emphasized free will; they felt that it was up to the living to make choices based on guidance from the spirits.

To practice their religion, the Spiritualists purchased 20 acres of land near Cassadaga Lake and established the community of Lily Dale in 1879. In addition to offering the services of mediums, psychics, and other faith healers, the Lily Daleans also offered summer classes to followers of the Spiritualism movement. Lily Dale became so popular that a hotel was built in the town in 1880, and in 1883, a 1,200-seat auditorium was added.

Over the years, Lily Dale's freethinkers attracted many famous people: Susan B. Anthony spoke there frequently, Mae West visited the assembly, and, in 1916, the cottage of sisters Margaret and Kate Fox was moved to Lily Dale. (In 1848, the Fox sisters claimed that they had communicated with the spirit of a murdered peddler at their home in Hydesville, New York. This incident is often cited as the beginning of the Spiritualist movement.) Unfortunately, the Fox sisters' cottage burned down in a fire in 1955.

Haunting the Spiritualists

Given the presence of so many mediums, it is no surprise that ghosts are often seen in Lily Dale. The full spectrum of spirits—from full-bodied apparitions to shadows and orbs—regularly appear in photos taken around the town. The Maplewood Hotel's lobby is decorated entirely with "spirit precipitated art"—art that was created with the assistance of spirits. Sometimes during a séance, a medium will set out a bowl of paints and a blank canvas; when the session is over, a painting—usually a portrait of the spirit that has just made its presence known—will be complete. One of the paintings in the hotel's lobby depicts a figure with a white beard wearing a white robe; it is unknown who this man was in life, but several guests have seen his apparition in the building's hallways. A blind, mute, quadriplegic woman created a spirit-assisted tapestry over a period of nine years. While the woman was in a trance, the spirits guided her and helped her to embroider the tapestry using only her mouth.

Modern Spiritualist Living

These days, groups often gather around Inspiration Stump (a grove in the Leolyn Woods) during the summertime. At these meetings, a medium gives short messages to the people in attendance from the various spirits present. People sit quietly, barely moving, so as not to disturb the medium's work. Even those who do not receive a message from a spirit feel rejuvenated, and many find themselves more aware of spiritual energies while at Inspiration Stump. Afterward, audience members often book individual sessions with the dozens of certified mediums who live year-round in the Lily Dale community.

People who wish to plan a trip to Lily Dale will find an extensive guide to workshops, lectures, and classes online. Keep in mind that although the Spiritualists practice their religion year-round, Lily Dale's two hotels are closed from late September until June. During the off-season, those wishing to visit a medium or attend a workshop can arrange to stay at a private home through the Lily Dale Spiritualist Church or the Church of the Living Spirit. In order to live amongst the spirits full time, one must become a member of the Lily Dale community and apply to the Lily Dale Assembly Board of Directors to essentially earn the right to call this quaint, yet hauntingly beautiful town home.

Freaky Friends

Some people are drawn to cute and cuddly puppies or furry little kittens while others like the idea of owning a unique one-of-a-kind pet. It might surprise you to find that it's perfectly legal to keep some very unusual animals as pets (double-check before you buy one). But would you really want to?

✳   ✳   ✳   ✳

Serval—If you're a cat-lover, this might be the pet for you. Servals are larger than the average house cat, measuring three feet from head to tail and weighing anywhere between 15 and 40 pounds. They're regal animals but beware – they don't take to litter box training as well as most house cats.

Stick—No, we're not promoting a new Pet Rock fad here. A stick is a three- to four-inch-long insect that resembles, well, a stick. With proper care they can live for several years. Like the popular hermit crabs, their needs are simple and they're inexpensive to own. Sticks like company, so you if you've got the space, you might want to buy two.

Chinchilla—Chinchillas look like a cross between a rabbit and a squirrel and are known for their thick luxurious gray fur. Their coats are so thick and water-resistant that they clean themselves by rolling in dirt. While it may be legal to own a chinchilla, it is not legal to kill it to make its coat your own.

Wallaroo—Even the name is cute. If you want a pet the size of a 5th grader this may be the one for you. A cross between a kangaroo and a wallaby (in size and appearance) this Australian marsupial's typically lifespan is 15 to 20 years.

Kinkajou—At first glance, you might think this animal was a primate, but it's really a part of the raccoon family. Weighing in at a mere three to seven pounds, kinkajous love to hang by their tails. They have long and skinny tongues, which help them dine on honey and termites in the wild. And for a good parlor trick, kinkajous take the "moon walk" dance to a new level—they can turn their feet backwards to run in either direction.

Capybara—One look at this adorable animal (in a photo) and you'd probably be hooked. But would you feel differently if we told you the capybara is the world's largest rodent at four feet tall and 100+ pounds? Think twice before you get one, though—they prefer a home with a swimming pool, can be territorial and have very large teeth. And did we mention that it's a rodent?

Pygmy Goat—Social, and good-natured animals, pygmy goats are the goat family's answer to the popular pot-bellied pig. Sort of. Ranging from 50 to 85 pounds, these pets are best housed outside. The good news? When you own your own goat, you never run out of milk.

Horned Frog—At six to seven inches long (and wide) these frogs are quite a handful. Fortunately, that only describes their size—they are actually quite easy to care for. They eat and sleep a good share of the day and pose little risk of escape. They're known for their extra-large mouths, which earned them the nickname, "Pacman frogs" after the little video game.

Hedgehog—While cute to look at, these sharp-quilled animals may prove to be a pain to own. Ranging in size from 14 to 39 pounds, they are literally hard to handle. They would make a great pet for garden-owners, however, as they love to eat common garden pests such as insects, worms, mice, frogs and snakes. Yum.

Functional Art: The American Quilt

Whether you curl up for a nap under your grandmother's quilt or do a little quilting yourself, rest assured, your interest in this beloved bedding is steeped in tradition.

✳ ✳ ✳ ✳

The First Few Stitches

QUILTING IS THE process of sewing together layers of fabric and filler. The bottom layer is called the "backing," the middle layer is the filling or "batting," and the top layer is called, well, the "top." The layers are sewn together to create a piece of cozy bedding.

People have been quilting—but not necessarily making quilted blankets—for a long time. An ivory carving from around 3600 B.C. depicts a king in a quilted cloak. Excavation of a Mongolian cave revealed a quilted linen carpet, and a pair of quilted slippers found near the Russia/China border was probably from the eighth or ninth century.

Patchwork, the process of piecing together scraps of fabric to make a larger whole, was widely practiced in Europe through the 1600s because it was economical. Old clothes and blankets were often recycled into something entirely new.

Early Amish Influence

The roots of the traditional quilt began to take hold in Europe and the United States in the 18th century. The oldest existing piece is the Saltonstall quilt. It was made in Massachusetts in 1704 and, though tattered, provides a window to the quilt-making styles of the era.

Amish settlers arrived in Pennsylvania in the early 1700s, and their quilts, known for jewel-tone fabrics and striking geometric patterns, surfaced in the 1800s. Our concept of patchwork quilts, patterns, and blocks has been greatly influenced by Amish quilters.

An Industrial Revolution

By the end of the 18th century, the textile industry in England had been fully mechanized, and the French were coming up with better, faster, and cleaner ways to dye fabric. Large quantities of colorfast, printed cottons became readily available, much to the delight of people everywhere.

By the time the War of Independence rolled around, the vast English textile industry was exporting thousands of tons of cotton to America. These fabrics made up the majority of the clothes and quilts of the era.

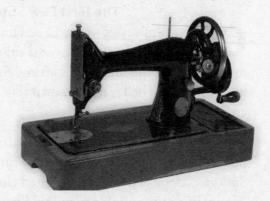

Social Hour

It's a misconception that people made quilts just for practical purposes. In fact, most quilters engaged in the hobby because they loved the craft—not because they needed a blanket. By 1820, sewing groups were widespread, allowing people to work together to sew quilts that were pulled across large frames.

Many of the close-knit community sewing bees (or "sewing circles") of yesterday still function as quilting guilds and clubs today.

Patterns and Designs

Though some quilters specialize in whole-cloth quilts, most of the quilts made today are of the patchwork variety. Pieces of fabric are sewn together to make a single block; multiple blocks are then stitched to each other, creating the quilt top.

One of the most admired quilt styles comes from Hawaii. These quilts incorporate just two colors—usually red and white—and one large cutout design sewn directly onto the quilt top. The striking geometric shapes and intricate stitching have made Hawaiian quilts popular among quilters and quilt admirers for two centuries.

Modern-Day Quilts

Quilting in the United States experienced a revival in the 1970s, largely due to the country's 200th birthday. As part of the celebration, women and men alike took a renewed interest in quilting and in folk art and crafts in general.

The surge in the popularity of quilting turned this humble pastime into the $3.3-billion-a-year industry it is today. The current movement toward more simple, eco-friendly lifestyles will likely keep quilting alive for years to come.

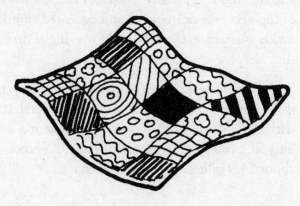

The Bermuda Dry-angle

What happens to those socks that get lost in the dryer?

✳ ✳ ✳ ✳

DOGS EAT THEM. Aliens abduct them. The heat and rapid spinning motions of the dryer transport them to an alternate space-time continuum. Or maybe they wind up in the Bermuda Triangle or on a giant sock dune on the planet Saturn.

Of course, there's always the possibility that they've simply departed this physical world for the great big sock drawer in the sky. May 9 is officially Lost Sock Memorial Day. Come to think of it, one of those TV news magazine shows should really investigate the possibility of a sock suicide pact. Hey, if you spent your days warming the sweaty toes of some smelly teenager, wouldn't you consider checking out early?

Short of sending Geraldo Rivera undercover as a 100 percent stretch nylon Gold Toe (we could spin him around in a Maytag to see what happens), is there any way to know where all the lost socks go? There's got to be a logical explanation, right?

Well, conspiracy theorists maintain it all has to do with a long-time clandestine concordat between America's sock weavers and the major appliance makers. Have they created some sort of top-secret sock material and patented tumbling action that makes our anklets, crews, and knee-highs disintegrate into thin air?

Strange how socks seem to go missing without leaving a single thread of evidence behind. You can sweep that laundry room with the precision of a forensic scientist at a crime scene. The only clue you'll uncover in this case: U.S. sock sales amount to about $4.9 billion annually. Hmm...

Reps from both sides adamantly deny any wrongdoing in the disappearance of perhaps millions of American socks over the years. In fact, executives at Michigan-based Whirlpool say it's not them, it's you. According to Whirlpool, your dirty socks often don't even make it to the machine. They fall out of the laundry basket in a trail behind you on the way to the washer. Or your kids shoot them around like basketballs so they end up under the bed. Research by Whirlpool's Institute of Fabric Science also reveals that static cling is a culprit. When socks do make it to the dryer, static can send one up a pant leg and another into the corner pocket of a fitted sheet.

What's the solution? Whirlpool recommends placing socks in mesh laundry bags, while Linda Cobb, a DIY Network host and the author of *Talking Dirty Laundry* with the Queen of Clean, advocates the use of sock clips. These are designed to keep single pairs of socks together as they wash and dry.

Of course, clipping each and every pair of socks in the family hamper is going to be time-consuming—and who knows if it'll even work? It would be a whole lot easier to just accept that all those lost socks were taken by the "little people." You do know that gnomes, leprechauns, and pixies turn stolen socks into cozy blankets for their wee offspring, right?

Monopolizing the Rules

When you run out of Monopoly houses or hotels, toss on some pennies or other markers instead.

✳ ✳ ✳ ✳

POOR MONOPOLY, ONE of the most misunderstood board games. Invented by an anticapitalist educator as a thought exercise about the downsides of the free market, it's been embraced for decades by the bossiest, worst winner in every American family. Not only do we miss the intended point of the game—most of us play it wrong by adding our own rules. And these rules, in turn, artificially stretch the game out, which leads to our additional complaint that it takes too long. The capitalist snake eats its own capitalist tail in a family ouroboredom.

The number of houses in the Monopoly box is limited by design, forcing players to choose wisely, in theory. Instead, many of us are lining up M&Ms on every property we own to create never-ending rent-gouging gauntlets. No wonder we're still playing twenty hours later.

But it's not us rule-breaking simpletons who've gotten it most wrong. In 1988, a San Francisco jeweler made a custom Monopoly set with houses and hotels made of solid gold. The board was encrusted with gemstones and even the dice had diamonds instead of dots. When you add in the ethical quandaries associated with gemstone mining, this is one hot international capitalism brouhaha.

Ultimately, our invented rules for Monopoly make the gameplay more fun in the moment for our groups of friends or family, and that's what really counts. Remember that the next time a Monopoly pedant starts to ask about your stance on Free Parking.

There are hundreds of special themed Monopoly games from

the last 80 years, along with special editions (like anniversaries) of the traditional game. Collectors covet the rarest games or the ones most relevant to their industries or interests. One landscape architect with a large collection of Monopoly games says her favorite is the National Parks Edition, released in collaboration with the National Parks Foundation.

One piquant themed Monopoly is for Fox's cult television show *Firefly*, aired in 2002 and beloved by nerds more and more in the years since. The show is set in a far future where there really *is* a monopoly over the planetary system, which the heroes move away from as they move toward a frontier that resembles the historical American west. In the game, you reclaim those planets one at a time.

Sore Loser

My game opponent won because they were lucky.

✳ ✳ ✳ ✳

SOMETIMES THIS IS true. In games where you spin or roll dice to move forward, everything is random. And some games randomize the events on purpose in order to make the game more spontaneous and challenging. But for games like Scrabble or chess, and even for card games where you're dealt a random hand, luck plays a smaller and smaller role as you go higher in the ranks of players.

In Scrabble, higher-level players know that how you manage the letters on your rack is as important as the words you play. They know tiny words and words that allow you to "dump" many vowels at once. They keep the letters most likely to form seven-letter words and cycle through the rest until they have a valuable seven-letter play in their hand.

In chess, players understand strategy and can put themselves in their opponent's shoes to estimate how the rest of the game is going. They can make moves while predicting with fairly high certainty what their opponent will do in return. They understand the ramifications of a move for all their other pieces.

For card games like canasta and hearts, there is strategy in choosing what to keep in your hand and what to pass or play. And in bidding games like euchre or bridge, there is also an element of risktaking that pays off for players who can correctly predict the value of the cards in their hand and their position around the table.

You can think of luck in these situations as it might apply to the competitors in the final round of the national spelling bee. Sure, you could call it luck if a child is given a word they've just recently studied and easily remember. But the competitors in the final round have a Swiss Army knife of skills to help them interpret and parse even the most unfamiliar word using its country of origin, the example sentence, and its meaning. They can even glean information from their competitors' failed attempts. There may be a modicum of luck in this, but they've worked extremely hard to earn that luck.

The Artistic "I"?

There are many myths that discourage people from learning to draw.

✳ ✳ ✳ ✳

AGING AMERICANS LOVE to complain that younger generations are part of a "participation trophy" culture, receiving pats on the head and accolades for even our most mediocre outings. But young people also feel a great deal of pressure to excel, and that can express itself as a fear of spending the time being bad at something that it may take in order to get good.

Some people probably really can't draw, but that percentage must be low. Looking at the selection of illustrations, webcomics, editorial cartoons, and many other pieces of line art that the average person sees in a day, we see that *technically* good drawing is not the major appeal of these works. The cartoonists and illustrators we love have style and individual flair. Their drawings are recognizable in an instant.

It's more socially acceptable to say you're learning a musical instrument than to say you're learning to draw; or at least it feels like it is. But why is that? There are drawersful of ugly or awkward drawings in the attics or desk drawers of everyone whose drawings you've ever loved. No one sits down with a pencil one day and begins an M.C. Escher tessellation.

When people say they can't sing or carry a tune or that they don't have rhythm, we believe them, because these skills are such a daily and routine part of life. We sing in the car together. We dance at parties. We trust other people to have realized they lack some piece of a skill that other people have. But drawing is more of a black box, and if you've never practiced, you don't know for sure. Don't let the following myths keep you from trying.

I wasn't born with artistic talent, so I'll never be very good.

Americans love a good "I wasn't a natural so I worked *really hard* and succeeded" story, but we don't seem to notice that almost all the people who tell these stories are in fields like the arts or sports. We think these industries are almost comically exclusive to some group of instant baby Mozarts who know from a young age that they're destined to succeed.

Certainly people with natural talent can have some advantages over those who must work much harder to keep up. But not only can those hard workers keep up after all, they may also find that their work eventually allows them to excel and express themselves with ease and confidence. They're no longer the hardest workers in the room; they've sharpened their skills into efficient and hard-won moves that they can now do with flair.

The best drawings are realistic.

Other visual arts have long embraced abstraction as not just an alternative to but often a bettering of realistic work. Even our love of the beautifully lifelike marble statues from ancient Greece and Rome is tempered by how those statues are not in their original brightly painted exteriors, may be missing parts, and have been coaxed, somehow, from solid blocks of marble. These complicating factors add context that heightens our appreciation and enjoyment.

But drawing is still strongly linked with realism. There were times when realism was critical to the intended goal of a drawing, like when courageous people explored the world and made detailed impressions of new plants and animals. Even so, the most skilled of these botanical artists somehow conveyed the idea of a plant in a stem or two and a handful of leaves or flowers, not the entire plant. They understood that editing the scope of their drawing gave it clarity and power.

A drawing doesn't need to closely resemble reality to be good, powerful, artistic, or otherwise significant. The Surrealists capitalized on realistic objects by distorting them or jumbling them into new contexts. Illustrators depict ideas using more figurative drawings that make logical and visual sense but use their styles to add to the material. Many who doodle find that they return to the same little patterns or motifs again and again—maybe your motifs are the beginning of your style.

Artist Chuck Close made his name with large-scale portraits so realistic that they're called hyperrealistic or photorealistic. In his case, the scale alone makes these works staggering and magnificent, but otherwise they are extremely faithful reproductions of how people look. After a debilitating stroke, Close changed gears and began making abstract portraits using canvasses divided into squares that he fills with concentric squares or circles. From far away they still look realistic. And they're still enormous. Close adapted to a new life after his major medical crisis and found a style just as specific to him as his photorealistic portraits had been before.

Only artistic people can draw.

This myth quickly grows out of its box and becomes a full-scale philosophical inquiry. Engineers who draw schematics have talent, style, and an eye for detail that they apply to specific tasks for clients or teams to use. Does that practical application and standardized overall look mean they aren't artistic? No one can answer that in a satisfying way.

But the point remains that drawing is a skill that can benefit people of all stripes and in all walks of life, many of whom wouldn't call themselves artistic.

Someone who's good at drawing can draw anything.

There are a few hilarious telltales in the work of artists you admire, if you look closely and know what you're looking for. Many artists who can and do draw excellent human faces and bodies all day every day end up drawing hairstyles on everyone that cover where their ears should be. Everyone's arms end "out of frame" or with hands hidden in pockets so no one has to have hands. Clothes look flat because the wrinkles and shading aren't the best.

For better or worse, no one can draw anything.

No Laughing Matter: Coulrophobia

It's a malady in which the sufferer has an abnormal or exaggerated fear of clowns, and experts estimate that it afflicts as many as one in seven people.

✳   ✳   ✳   ✳

Beware of the Man with the Red Nose

THE SYMPTOMS OF this strangely common affliction range from nausea and sweating to irregular heartbeat, shortness of breath, and an overall feeling of impending doom. Is the sight of Ronald McDonald more chilling than your Chocolate Triple Thick Shake? There could be a few reasons why.

The most common explanation for coulrophobia is that the sufferer had a bad experience with a clown at a young and impressionable age. Maybe the clown at Billy Schuster's fifth birthday party shot you in the eye with a squirting flower, doused your head with confetti, or accidentally popped the balloon animal he was making for you. Some of the most silly or mundane things can be petrifying when you are young. And though the incident may be long forgotten, a bright orange wig or bulbous red nose might be enough to throw you back into the irrational fears that plagued your younger days.

When Good Clowns Turn Bad

Who could blame you? If television and movies have taught us anything, it's that clowns often are creatures of pure evil. There's the Joker, Batman's murderously insane archenemy; the shape-shifting Pennywise from Stephen King's *It*; the human-eating alien clowns in *Killer Klowns from Outer Space*; and a possessed toy clown that comes to life and beats the bejesus out of a young Robbie Freeling in Steven Spielberg's *Poltergeist*.

Real-life serial killer John Wayne Gacy didn't do much for the clown cause, either. Before authorities found the bodies of 27 boys and young men in his basement crawl space, Gacy was known as a charming, sociable guy who enjoyed performing at children's parties dressed up as Pogo the Clown or Patches the Clown. That ended when his crimes were discovered, but even on death row, he still had an unwholesome interest in clowning—he took up oil painting, and clowns were his favorite subjects. The industry has never recovered.

Be Afraid—Be Very Afraid

It's enough to give anyone the heebie-jeebies. But some experts say there's more to coulrophobia than traumatic childhood events or pop-culture portrayals. Scholar Joseph Durwin points out that since ancient times, clowns, fools, and jesters have been given permission to mock, criticize, or act deviantly and unexpectedly. This freedom to behave outside of normal social boundaries is exactly what makes clowns so threatening.

A *Nursing Standard* magazine interview of 250 people ages four to sixteen revealed that clowns are indeed "universally scary." Researcher Penny Curtis reported some kids found clowns to be "quite frightening and unknowable." Seems it has a lot to do with that permanent grease-painted grin. Because the face of a clown never changes, you don't know if he's relentlessly gleeful or about to bite your face off. In the words of Bart Simpson: "Can't sleep; clown will eat me."

Don't Try This at Your Next Backyard Barbecue

Walking barefoot on hot coals isn't quite as perilous as it may seem, although amateurs are still advised to steer clear of the embers.

✻　✻　✻　✻

THERE WAS A time when the feat (pun most certainly intended) of walking on hot coals was the domain of mystical yogis who dedicated their lives to pushing the physical limits of the body by using the awesome power of the mind. Then along came reality television. Now on any given night, we can tune in to some pudgy actuary from Des Moines waltzing across a bed of glowing embers for the nation's amusement, seemingly unharmed. So what's the deal? Is walking on hot coals dangerous, or even difficult?

At the risk of prompting legions of idiots to inflict third-degree burns on themselves, the answer is no. Walking on hot coals is not as impressive as it seems—but please, please, read on before you try something stupid.

The secret to walking on hot coals has nothing to do with mental might and everything to do with the physical properties of what's involved. It comes down to how fast heat can move from one object to another. Some materials, like metal, conduct heat very well—they're good at transmitting thermal energy to whatever they touch. Think of your frying pan: You heat it up, slap a juicy steak down on it, and witness an instant sizzle—the metal easily passes its heat to an object of lower temperature. On the other hand, consider the bed of hot coals that's used for fire walks. It started out as chunks of wood—and wood is a terrible conductor of heat.

But don't go for a romp over hot coals just yet. It's also important that the hot coals are not, you know, on fire. If you've seen a fire-walking demonstration on TV, you may have noticed that there were no jumping flames, just smoldering embers—the coals probably had been burning for hours and had built up a layer of ash. And ash is another poor conductor of heat—sometimes it's used as insulation for this very reason.

Run, Don't Walk

All the ash in the world can't help you unless you keep one final thing in mind. Think about it: What sort of gait do you see when a person is traversing a bed of hot coals? A stroll? An amble? A saunter? No, no, and no—it's all about making a mad dash. As a result, the amount of time that any one foot is in contact with a coal might be less than a second. And the exposure is not continuous, as each foot gets a millisecond break from the heat with each step.

So if you take a poor heat conductor like wood, cover it with a layer of insulation, and have intermittent exposure to the heat, the likelihood of sustaining serious burns is low. Of course, we don't advise that you try this stunt at your next backyard get-together. What if you fall? Or even slip or stumble? You'll have a lot of explaining to do at your local ER.

I Know It When I See It

What makes something "art"?

✳   ✳   ✳   ✳

IF YOU WANT to see a name-calling, hair-pulling intellectual fight (and who doesn't?), just yell this question in a crowded coffee shop. After centuries of debate and goatee-stroking, it's still a hot-button issue.

Before the fourteenth century, the Western world grouped painting, sculpture, and architecture with decorative crafts such as pottery, weaving, and the like. During the Renaissance, Michelangelo and the gang elevated the artist to the level of the poet—a genius who was touched by divine inspiration.

Now, with God as a collaborator, art had to be beautiful, which meant that artists had to recreate reality in a way that transcended earthly experience.

In the nineteenth and twentieth centuries, artists rejected these standards of beauty; they claimed that art didn't need to fit set requirements. This idea is now widely accepted, though people still disagree over what is and isn't art.

A common modern view is that art is anything that is created for its own aesthetic value—beautiful or not—rather than to serve some other function. So, according to this theory, defining art comes down to the creator's intention. If you build a chair to have something to sit on, the chair isn't a piece of art. But if you build an identical chair to express yourself, that chair *is* a piece of art. Marcel Duchamp demonstrated this in 1917, when he turned a urinal upside down and called it "Fountain." He was only interested in the object's aesthetic value. And just as simply as that: art.

This may seem arbitrary, but to the creator, there is a difference. If you build something for a specific purpose, you measure success by how well your creation serves that function. If you make pure art, your accomplishment is exclusively determined by how the creation makes you feel. Artists say that they follow their hearts, their muses, or God, depending on their beliefs. A craftsperson also follows a creative spirit, but his or her desire for artistic fulfillment is secondary to the obligation to make something that is functional.

Many objects involve both kinds of creativity. For example, a big-budget filmmaker follows his or her muse but generally bends to studio demands to try to make the movie profitable. (For instance, the movie might be trimmed to ninety minutes.) Unless the director has full creative control, the primary function of the film is to get people to buy tickets. There's nothing wrong with making money from your art, but purists say that financial concerns should never influence the true artist.

By a purist's definition, a book illustration isn't art, since its function is to support the text and please the client—even if the text is a work of art. The counter view is that the illustration *is* art, since the illustrator follows his or her creative instincts to create it; the illustrator is as much an artistic collaborator as the writer.

Obviously, it gets pretty murky. But until someone invents a handheld art detector, the question of what makes something art will continue to spark spirited arguments in coffee shops the world over.

Casino Dealer

For those who pine for the bright lights of Vegas, dealing blackjack or baccarat might be a dream. One roulette dealer on the Vegas Strip told us a little more about his work.

Q: Why do some people call you a "croupier"?

A: That's a title more often used among pretentious characters, of whom there are many in Las Vegas. But in my book, "croup" refers to a bad cough, and I don't think I'd enjoy a job as a professional cougher.

Q: No offense, but your job doesn't look much more difficult than coughing. Spin a wheel, wait for a ball to stop, figure out winnings. There has to be more to it than that.

A: If you want to make your car payment, there is. Casino dealing is the ultimate people job. The game itself, whether it's roulette or blackjack, isn't very hard. People are winning or losing money, and they react to that—that's what requires me to have good social skills. People will keep playing a table partly because of the environment the dealer creates.

Q: A fortune flows across your table every workday. How much of it do you get to keep?

A: I won't tell you what I get, but if it weren't for tips, I could do just as well in retail sales. The more players I have and the more winners who come through, the more tips I make—thanks to the tradition of "winners tip."

Q: Is it hard to break into your field?

A: Easy to break in, hard to stay. You can find gambling nearly anywhere in the country, though some training helps you get hired. People don't realize how many jobs there are on a casino staff: cashiers, dealers for all the games, pit clerk, pit boss, hosting, and security—a lot of security. Most casino employees don't deal cards or craps or roulette. Some don't know how to play, and you'd be surprised how many never gamble a nickel.

Q: How's it possible to cheat at roulette?

A: I watch for that very carefully. Some people will try to manipulate the ball. People used to have an accomplice create a distraction, then blow at the wheel through a straw. Casinos ended that by putting clear shields around the wheels. Other people try bumping the table at the right time. I

keep my hand on the table at all times while the wheel's going, so if someone bumps the table I'll feel it. The first time I'll use my instincts; maybe it was an accident. The second time is no accident, and we'll ask the person to leave. All casinos work diligently to spot cheaters.

Q: How easy is it for the house to cheat? The most cynical view of the gambling industry is that it's run and rigged by organized crime.

A: The house has a natural statistical advantage, with no need or reason to cheat. In theory, if the house wanted to cheat, it'd use electromagnets. I can think of quite a few ways, but if I were asked to involve myself in actually doing them—or if I knew they were going on—I'd resign without notice. I don't want to go to jail. We get inspected; I think our gambling equipment is subject to much tougher scrutiny than those new voting machines. I'm not sure this will comfort you any, but the casino business is very corporate. We get lectures on how to reduce liability. We even get retirement benefits. It isn't *The Sopranos* by a long shot.

Grape Expectations

The world of wine can be intimidating for beginners, but a little bit of information can help you ease your way into any educated wine discussion.

✳ ✳ ✳ ✳

Expensive wine is the best wine.

THESE BLANKET STATEMENTS are fun because they're wrong in different ways that allow for a lot of exploration. Cost of wine doesn't always correlate with quality, especially for extremely rare and old wines that may have turned. Sometimes brand hype or excitement over a novel varietal can inflate the cost of a bottle that hangs in the middle of the pack otherwise.

More importantly, an expensive bottle of a wine you don't *love* is never going to be the best wine for you. When you know the kinds of wine you like best and have enough experiences buying or ordering them, you'll learn which expensive bottles are worth it for you and which are not.

The rule of thumb often given to more casual wine drinkers is to order the second-cheapest bottle on the menu. By the same stroke, the third- or fourth-most expensive bottle might be the best combination of quality and value.

Big corporate brands can't make great wine.

Upscale or luxury products can be absorbed into conglomerates that harm the brands, like the Luxottica company in the glasses and sunglasses sphere. One corporate Pac-Man travels the game board eating dots: Ray-Ban, Oakley, Persol, licenses for Dolce & Gabbana and other designer labels, and eventually there's one company left standing.

Large corporate winemakers usually own a lot of different labels and use their quantity of scale to offer consistent wines. There don't tend to be shortages or empty shelves at any time. No haute cuisine is going to be rocketed to the moon by a predictably good corporate bottle, but there's definitely something to be said for a product you can buy again and again and know you'll enjoy it.

Critics say these wines are too closely monitored and normalized to have individual character the same way smaller wines do, and that's indubitably true for the big brands' varieties you see in every liquor store in the nation. Not every day has to be a special occasion with a challenging wine. If a good corporate wine is a nice value and enjoyable for your group, go for it.

Small wineries are more authentic.

Authenticity is a buzzword with little real meaning. Smaller wineries may use more traditional winemaking processes, because they don't have the bulk quantities that usually lead to modernization. Moreover, smaller wineries tend to rely on customers who are willing to pay a premium for good wine from a small winery.

For geographically protected wine varieties, the idea of authenticity has the highest stakes, because a deviation from a type of grape or area of production could lose them a particular label altogether. And for wine drinkers who cherish the oak flavor of a barrel-aged wine, it may be important to ensure you're buying wine that really *is* aged in a barrel rather than mixed with oak chips or other flavorings.

If "authentic" can stand in for the idea of an unadulterated wine, meaning without the addition of unnecessary stuff like Mega Purple, then there may be valid reasons of quality to stick with authentic wines. But this idea simply doesn't correspond to the size of a winery. Poor viticulture practices can bring down the quality of a batch of wine made in a five-gallon bucket as well as a thousand-gallon steel vat.

And what's Mega Purple? This "kosher additive" from the makers of Manischewitz and Mad Dog is a grape juice concentrate used to sweeten and deepen the color of red wine. Wine purists correctly call this an adulteration, and Mega Purple helps to round out the purported flavor profile of super cheap wines. Well, and plenty of mid-market wines, too.

Mega Purple is at least a *food-based* food additive. In the 1980s, many wineries were found to be adding a chemical called diethylene glycol to their wines to boost sweetness. You may recognize diethylene glycol from such hits as "The Reason Your Antifreeze Puddle Smells Sweet" and "Tastes Good as It Poisons Your Pet."

The antifreeze phenomenon was so far into the zeitgeist that it forms the plot of the eleventh-ever episode of *The Simpsons*. Bart is sent to France as an exchange student, where he's made to sleep on the floor, stomp grapes with his bare feet, and safety-taste wine treated with antifreeze.

Some experts point out that small wineries offer a more personal experience if you deal with them directly, and this can create an authentic feeling that keeps you coming back. The owners themselves may be on hand to recommend a vintage or varietal to you based on your likes and dislikes. You may feel more personally valued as a customer if you're one of a hundred instead of thousands. If this sounds good to you, maybe you should plan a trip to Napa Valley.

You should keep trying until you learn to like "good" wine.

Wine experts and connoisseurs disagree about one major element of the process by which beginners start drinking wine. Should people stick with *very* cheap, dimensionless wine if that's what they find they like? Or should they start with the most reasonably priced complex wines that give them something to swirl and sniff?

If you've decided that you're getting into wine as a hobby that you plan to take seriously, it may be best to bypass the cheapest wines altogether, since of course something sweet that eventually gets you drunk is going to seem pretty much fine. If a sweet wine is your likeliest gateway to the rest of wine culture, pick an interesting and good-quality sweet wine like a Sauternes. Just don't ask too many questions about how it's made.

Wines with screwtops shouldn't be taken seriously.

Cork was a matter of utility when it first came into wide use. Winemakers realized that well sealed wine had better results, and in a more utilitarian sense, barrels needed to be sealed in order to travel and be stored safely. For a long time, wine was kept in barrels and dispensed directly from them into mugs, flasks or flagons.

Winemakers and publicans used whatever they had on hand to seal or reseal wine containers. Imagine if your kitchen had containers with holes punched in them without lids or stoppers. What would you use? You might twist a cloth to use as a stopper. If you needed an airtight seal, you might use candlewax to insulate the cloth. With waxed cloth, you could cover the end of a bottle or flask and tie string around it.

But if you knew a number of people were going to buy wine each day and they'd all have bottles that were the same size and shape, you could make or ask a craftsman to make a bunch of lids or stoppers for you. And as wine bottles moved toward a standard size, bottlers began to use cork.

Cork is a layer of the bark of a certain tree, the cork oak, which grows in areas around the Mediterranean Sea. Portugal grows and harvests the most cork in the world, and cork is a completely renewable resource. New cork grows back.

Like the papyrus sedge, the cork oak's unique composition led to the creation of an entire technology. Cork was squashable but watertight, making it ideal to seal almost anything. Slabs of cork are cut into pieces that are used "whole cloth," so to speak, but cork can also be made from little bits that are recomposed.

Standardized wine bottles and cork stoppers, used together, are three or four hundred years old. Almost nothing has changed in the world of wine packaging materials since then. Some wine drinkers really dislike wine sealed with a cork, which can be baffling to those who don't notice any difference between a cork and a screwtop wine.

The secret is that cork isn't truly airtight. Water is much thicker than air, meaning a watertight seal isn't necessarily airtight. (An airtight seal is necessarily always waterproof, though.) A tiny amount of air gets through the cork into a bottle of wine, and this minuscule stream can change the taste of the wine.

Sometimes this change is for the worse, which is referred to as "cork taint." Cork lobbyists (literally everything has a lobbyist!) protest against the use of this term and claim that the occurrence of cork taint is super low. But taste tests conducted by third parties have found different and much higher rates of cork-tainted bottles.

Because of this, plenty of high-end vineyards have switched to other forms of closure. **Synthetic cork** is a plastic blend designed to pass as cork, with similar qualities of "bounciness" and characteristic popping. Of course, plastic products have their own smells and behaviors.

Screwtops for glass wine bottles made of aluminum with a gasket or "wad" made of soft plastic or rubber. These are popular in markets outside of Europe where makers and consumers may be more likely to take chances by breaking with tradition.

There are **glass stoppers** that fit into the neck of the bottle and seal using a soft o-ring as the gasket. Other solutions are being developed and tested as quickly as people can think of new ideas and wonder how they perform over time. Alternative closures usually still allow air in after some time period, but the idea is that different materials don't change the taste of the wine to the extent that cork can.

Since natural cork is a unique and renewable resource, there's little adverse effect on the environment and no economic incentive to switch from cork. The issue of cork taint is the primary and often only reason. Because of this, the natural cork industry in Europe is working overtime to thwart the growth of alternative corks.

The winery that produces Trader Joe's famous "two-buck Chuck" (or is it three bucks now?) uses a composite of natural cork to keep an air of high-class quality around its bottles. The composite is kind of a plywood of cork: pieces that are glued and pressed together into shape, with a thin layer of cork veneer to make the ends presentable. Doesn't that make you feel classier?

Only casual drinkers like sweet wine.

Sweet wines are like animated TV shows and movies. There's instant appeal in a really palatable and simple-looking package. But that first impression gives both sweet wine and animation an ideal springboard to make more sophisticated offerings.

Think of ice wine, which is an expensive, niche product with a high return on investment for vintners. These grapes must be grown in a narrow belt of land that circles the world, in climates where grapes can grow but the weather still gets cold enough to freeze.

Vintners must risk leaving grapes on the vine for long enough that they could go bad before there's a freeze. When the grapes finally do freeze, they must be harvested and pressed within a tiny span of time. Laura Dave's novel *Eight Hundred Grapes* includes a harvest like this, when everyone in the protagonist's family and all their available friends must crowd into one small vineyard to grab every grape before the time window closes. In real life, and with employees, that means extra wages or overtime.

All that is to say, ice wines are expensive because of the high risk, and the results are complex and worthwhile partly as a result of the novel way in which this wine is made. And ice wine is *very sweet*.

Complicated things can appear simple. If you grew up watching *Rocky & Bullwinkle* or *The Simpsons*, you spent your childhood realizing how many different layers these shows contained. The art looked simple and the dialogue was funny. And later, there were references to political events, history, pop culture, and other works of art. And later still, there were sharp-edged satirical comments. You kept watching those shows well into adulthood, perhaps while sipping a nice sweet wine.

Some years are just bad for all wine.

Much hacky joking is made every day out of the inaccuracy of the weather reports we read online or see on the news. The overall average swoop of yearly temperatures and precipitation forms the climate, while weather is how things go from day to day on a more local level.

The factors that lead to a "bad vintage" are myriad, but no single factor can affect the entire combined winemaking area of the world. Germany is in far northern Europe, and even Burgundy, France is parallel with Lake Superior in terms of latitude. Napa Valley is the same latitude as southern Italy and Greece.

Ocean and air currents create completely different climates in these regions, and the sheer number of different wine grapes and styles add another layer of likelihood that something, somewhere, must turn out right in any given year. That idea makes intuitive sense, too. So how did the myth of the big bad vintage get started?

Wine is a very, *very* part of human culture. We'll likely never know its true origins, but archaeologists find wine presses carved into the bedrock of the sites of ancient civilizations. Like any other foods, perishable fruits had to be preserved in some way or they wouldn't last more than a couple of days. Discovery of fermentation was almost definitely an accident that someone realized turned out for the best.

For many centuries in burgeoning urban cultures around the world, wine and beer were much safer to drink than water. Even in rural settings, microbes in local water made people really sick. These people didn't yet have germ theory and didn't understand that boiling might kill the cause of the disease. Fermented beverages had a far better track record, especially with vulnerable groups like kids and the elderly.

But at some point, wine fell into the hands of the very wealthy, and it became the exclusive provenance of the French. Haute cuisine itself began and ended in France, and classical chefs are still taught French technique above all else. There are hundreds of legally defined and limited French regional wines. The infamous wine "battle of the regions" depicted in the movie *Bottle Shock* didn't happen until 1976.

For these reasons, vintages are often discussed solely as they affect not just France but even specific winemaking regions of France. We know now that the broadening of winemaking to many more areas of the world is an inherent insurance against the effects of a so-called bad vintage. And sometimes a bad vintage mellows into a good one further down the road.

An unbalanced wine will balance out with age.

Lack of balance comes in many varieties, and only some of these unbalanced wines will end up becoming good wines. Certainly if you're not sure about a particular vintage, don't rely on a hopeful guess in order to make an investment. Sometimes a bargain buy is worth what you pay for it rather than some kind of hidden treasure. Tannic wines will notably mellow with age, but this isn't a miracle either. Keep your expectations realistic when you buy a bottle you don't already like.

Some experts remind wine drinkers that their ability to suss out a good bottle for aging will itself only improve with time. So at first you may rely a lot on industry advice to decide where to invest your cellar dollars, but as you get better at tasting, you'll be able to find more hidden gems on your own. Especially because each palate is so different, what you like may differ radically from what those experts have recommended over the years.

Only red wines are worth keeping for a long time.

White wines and rosés are having a renaissance, or perhaps their first moment as the subject of serious thought and collecting in the modern age of oenophilia. Reds are the most well known "serious" old vintages now, but that doesn't mean they have a monopoly on your wine cellar today or far into the future.

A wine's "legs" are a measure of its quality.

Once a bottle of wine is opened, the exposure to air allows the wine to begin evaporating. After pouring, evaporation leads to a phenomenon called *wine legs*, where drops gather and drip down the inside of the wine glass. But the presence of wine legs doesn't mean that a wine is a higher quality—it just means the wine has a higher alcohol content, which increases the rate of evaporation. Alcohol, in the chemical sense, evaporates more quickly than water as a general rule.

White wine only pairs with chicken or fish. Red wine only pairs with beef or other red meat.

Choosing wines by color alone can already be a risk, since the profile of one varietal versus another can be drastically different in acidity, balance, and bouquet. But any blanket rules of pairing are leaving out a number of important factors.

Many dishes are balanced enough themselves to be open to pairing with an appropriate wine of any color. Sometimes, a heavy protein is served with a light, vibrant sauce that calls for a white wine. Fish can be served with a heavy and intense sauce that should be matched against a sturdy red. Even beyond the sauce or protein, how food is cooked can make a difference in your choice. Grilled food has a different sensory experience than sautéed or baked food. And if you're a vegetarian, that opens up a whole different set of questions and answers.

Wine is healthier than beer.

The issue of health in any alcoholic beverage is a bit of a non-starter, because any alcoholic beverage is a mild poison with a lot of empty calories. Wine has the sheen of health because of an antioxidant purported to turn back the hands of time in a variety of ways.

The discovery of this antioxidant was huge news, mostly because it gave people a reason to claim wine and chocolate were actually healthy, which falls under the category of "probably too good to be true at all."

There's a joke about how scientists alternate between claiming that meat is bad for you and then good for you, that low fat is good and that high fat is good, and so forth. But there are rules of thumb for food and nutrition that *do* stand the test of time.

The diets of many Mediterranean and eastern Asian cultures are found to include many fruits and vegetables, seafood, relatively little meat, and a general attitude of moderation. They eat whole grains and other carbs. Unless you're allergic or have an autoimmune disorder or other medical limitation, any diet that promises results when you remove one or more entire food groups is nothing more than a fad.

Lager, Stout, Pale Ale, Oh My!

Whether you're a connoisseur or an aspiring homebrewer, beer is a booming hobby industry unto itself. Some very old myths can hinder your enjoyment.

✳ ✳ ✳ ✳

If water tastes good, it will make good beer.

PERHAPS WE BELIEVE this because of the mythical New York bagel boiled in the mythical New York tap water. Bagels are briefly boiled, in plain water or with baking soda or another chemical "soda" added. This is also how soft pretzels are prepared!

In any case, there are reasons the attributes of good tap water don't apply to beer. The naturally occurring or added chemicals in our tap water can interfere with how yeast and hops and barley react in the slurry of a baby beer. Especially if you have hard water, meaning the water has a lot of naturally occurring minerals that you'll find accumulating on your shower sprayer or faucets, these can impair the development of your beer.

Water softeners add different chemical compounds that help to neutralize the other minerals, so soft water isn't necessarily better for making beer. The best way is to use distilled or filtered water to avoid any impurities that can hinder the brew.

Beer tastes best when it's cold.

Oh, pernicious American myth! Americans who've traveled to Europe know that our love of frosty beverages in general is not shared by those on the continent. Beer is a room-temperature art form in many European countries, and in Germany in particular, where you may be offered a beer *warming device*.

But very few foods or beverages, period, taste best when they're ice cold. Coldness hits our palate and dulls it, and cold can inhibit the compounds and other good stuff that gives food its flavor. Beer is no different. Letting it sit for a few minutes at room temperature will help the flavor to develop. The beer will smell more aromatic and be more inviting.

Bottled beer is better and classier than canned beer.

There's no speaking to class, really, because even craft beers come in cans now with little discrimination between cans and bottles. But as with soda in a plastic bottle versus a can, people form strong opinions about the different flavors of different vessels. When it comes to beer, cans simply do a better job keeping the taste fresh. Beer is light sensitive and responds badly to oxygen. A bottle with a twist-top allows light *and* oxygen in, even through the dark brown glass. An aluminum can is like a blackout curtain over an airlock—nothing is getting in there, period.

Draft beer is better than bottled beer.

In the best of all possible worlds imagined by Gottfried Leibniz, draft beer is better than bottled beer. It's fresher, in theory. But there's a lot standing between the keg and your glass, and each step can go badly wrong if your bar isn't on top of it. Bacteria wait to jump in at every stage of the draft setup, from the connection to the keg to the tap gun.

At a real dive, this means a can or bottle is your best bet, like choosing bottled water when you're traveling in an area without reliable tap water. Bacteria in a draft line will probably just make your beer taste a little funky, but you never know.

It's fine to leave beer at room temperature if that's how you bought it.

Experts say selling beer at room temperature is almost definitely a cooler-space issue rather than an intentional decision. Beer turns over fast on the shelf, so there isn't a lot of time for it to go skunky at the store, but you should put the beer in the fridge as soon as you can to slow down inevitable oxidation. The same science explains why apples turn less brown in the fridge than at room temperature.

Dark beer has higher alcohol by volume than light beer.

If you're a beer nerd or have a beer-nerd friend, you already know this is a myth. Beer bars with expansive menus usually list the alcohol by volume (ABV) of each beer, and craft IPAs are often one and a half to two times higher in alcohol than more traditional dark beers. Don't judge a book by its cover, or its color in this case.

I just don't like beer.

There are two very different answers to this sort of statement. If you're in the industry, you have incentive and implicit permission to try to introduce a customer to something new. But if you're meeting a friend or date at a neighborhood bar to hang out, don't try to talk them into anything. People like what they like and that's inappropriate to attempt to "fix."

But sometimes customers mention that they don't usually like beer in order to solicit expert feedback. Every newspaper and magazine food section is filled with coverage of the huge boom in craft-beer variety in the United States in the last ten years, and consumers accustomed to a steady bar diet of Budweiser realize there's much more out there to explore.

There are a million reasons for anyone to say they don't like beer, and unless they're opting in to a suggestion or some advice, it's best to keep our advice to ourselves. But if this statement is part of a challenge to find something they really might like, that's a skill every wine or beer lover should have on tap.

Chapter 11

Books

The Hitler Diaries Hoax

In 1983, Germany's popular magazine Stern *dropped a bomb: It now had access to Adolf Hitler's secret diaries. Experts soon revealed them as phonies authored by a modern crook, leaving prominent historians and major media looking ridiculous.*

✳ ✳ ✳ ✳

Counterfeit Collectibles

THE CROOK WAS Konrad Kujau, a man of numerous aliases and lies. He was born in 1938, and after World War II he lived in East Germany. He moved to West Germany in 1957 and began a life of petty crime, quickly specializing in forgery.

A lifetime Hitler fan, Kujau became a noted Nazi memorabilia "collector." Naturally, he manufactured most of his collection, including authentication documents. He built a favorable reputation as a dealer specializing in ostensibly authentic Hitler stuff: signatures, writing, poetry, and art.

The public display of Nazi anything is illegal in Germany,

as is Holocaust denial. Even WWII games sold in modern Germany cannot use the swastika. Nazi memorabilia collections remain strictly on the down low. Modern Germans overwhelmingly repudiate Nazism, and those born post-war also dislike association with a horror they didn't perpetrate. It's a painful subject.

Still, every country has closet Hitler admirers, and Germany is no exception. *Stern* journalist Gerd Heidemann was one—he even bought Hermann Goering's old yacht. In 1979, a collector (Kujau under an alias) invited Heidemann to check out his Nazi collection, including a bound copy of a diary supposedly authored by Hitler. The diary, which covered a period from January to June 1935, had been salvaged from a late-war plane crash in East Germany. The collector also claimed that there were 26 other volumes, each covering a six-month period.

Faulty Fact-Checking

Using his journalistic training, Heidemann went to East Germany and found a backstory that verified a plane crash. Although he didn't dig much deeper, he had a good excuse. At the time, the world thought in terms of East and West Germany. In East Germany, a socialist police state, no one nosed around except where the state approved. Heidemann and *Stern*'s West German homeland was the mainstay of NATO, and the border between East and West Germany bristled with a surprising percentage of the world's military power. *Stern* lacked an easy way to verify anything in East Germany.

So Heidemann basically pitched what he had to *Stern*, and the magazine swung from its heels. Salivating at the "find of a generation," *Stern* authorized Heidemann to offer an advance of $1 million (approximate U.S. equivalent) for the diaries. Kujau played coy, explaining that the other 26 volumes hadn't yet been smuggled out of East Germany. In reality, he needed time to forge them. He finally finished in 1981 and handed over the first volume to Heidemann.

At this point, everyone was too excited to bother with that tedious step called "authentication." *Stern* hadn't even learned Kujau's identity; it was too busy counting its future profit from serialization rights. Anyone who voiced worries about fraud was hushed. Some surprisingly big names entered bids, including *Newsweek*, *Paris Match*, and the *London Times*.

Stretching the Truth

The diaries themselves purported to reveal a kinder, gentler Hitler, a generally okay guy who wasn't even fully aware of the Holocaust. This Hitler is what modern Nazi sympathizers like to imagine existed, not the weird megalomaniac of actual history. But its improbability also spurred skeptics into gear.

In an attempt to deal with the naysayers, *Stern* got a bit hysterical, even insisting that noted British historian Hugh Trevor-Roper had pronounced the diaries authentic. But skeptics faulted the diaries' paper, handwriting, and style. After some controversy, West German authorities ran forensics. The testing proved that the paper, ink, and even glue were of post-WWII manufacture. *Stern* had been bamboozled.

Because *Stern* is to Germany what *Time* and *Newsweek* are to the United States, it had a significant amount of credibility to lose. Several *Stern* editors were soon looking for new jobs. To say that the West German government was "annoyed" is an understatement. After *Stern* fired Heidemann, the police charged him with fraud. Heidemann, in his smartest move in a long time, implicated Kujau. When this news was made public in the media, Kujau went into hiding. In May

1983, he decided to turn himself into the police, who were anxiously waiting to arrest him. After several days of intense questioning, the authorities learned that Kujau was a reflexive, perpetual liar who invented falsehoods to cover his fictions.

The High Price of Greed

Kujau and Heidemann were each sentenced to several years in jail. The judge said *Stern* had "acted with such naiveté and negligence that it was virtually an accomplice in the fraud." The roughly $5 million the magazine ultimately gave Heidemann to pay Kujau was never recovered. Heidemann's increasingly lavish lifestyle during the forgeries and subsequent investigations suggests that he spent the majority of the money offshore.

After his release, Kujau tried his hand at politics, replica painting, and (again) forgery. He died of complications from cancer in 2000, but his crime is considered one of the most bold and successful hoaxes of the century.

Declassified East German files later showed that Heidemann had been an East German spy, though it's uncertain whether that had anything to do with the hoax. He claims he was actually a double agent working for West German authorities. With his career prospects impaired, he now keeps a low profile. For its part, *Stern* would like to forget the whole thing.

Don't Believe Everything You Read!

Howard Hughes's autobiography, the Amityville Horror, the astounding story of a young Holocaust survivor who lived with a pack of wolves—great stories, but none of them are true.

✳ ✳ ✳ ✳

IN 2006, THE literary world reeled when it learned that writer James Frey's heart-wrenching memoir, *A Million Little Pieces*, was more fiction than fact. But literary hoaxes are nothing new. Over the years, dozens of books published as nonfiction have turned out to be nothing more than literary lies. Here are some of the most famous.

The Autobiography of Howard Hughes: Con artists Clifford Irving and Richard Suskind almost hit the big time in 1971 when they penned the "memoirs" of the world's most famous recluse, allegedly based on interviews between Howard Hughes and Irving. Just months before the book's release, Hughes came out of hiding to denounce the work as a fraud.

Misha: A Mémoire of the Holocaust Years: Belgian writer Misha Defonseca (real name: Monique de Wael) alleged in her 1997 best-selling autobiography that as a child she had escaped the horrors of the Holocaust by trekking across Europe, protected by a pack of wolves. In 2008, she admitted that neither that story, nor her claim of being Jewish, was true.

The Amityville Horror: A True Story: In 1977, George and Kathy Lutz fast-talked writer Jay Anson into penning this book about their terrifying experiences while living in a supposedly haunted house in the Long Island town of Amityville. Brimming with all manner of evil goings-on, the Lutz's story continues to be debated: Was it a clever hoax or a terrifying truth? Nevertheless, the experience was the subject of nine Amityville movies.

Angel at the Fence: The True Story of a Love That Survived: Herman and Roma Rosenblat convinced the world that they met and fell in love while Herman was a prisoner in a German concentration camp during World War II. Oprah Winfrey twice had the couple on her talk show and called their tale "the single greatest love story" that was ever told on her show. But, in 2008, Berkley Books cancelled *Angel at the Fence* at the last minute when it was revealed that their love story was pure fiction. In truth, the Rosenblats met on a blind date in New York after the war.

The Heart Is Deceitful Above All Things: This 2001 book spun the troubled life of author JT LeRoy, an HIV-positive former drug addict and two-bit hustler. Its popularity even led to a 2004 movie based on the book. In reality, "LeRoy" was New York writer Laura Albert. After the ruse was discovered, in 2007, Albert was convicted of fraud and ordered to pay reparations.

I, Libertine: Some literary hoaxes are done not so much to scam as to make a point. In this case, humorist Jean Shepherd wanted to prove that bestseller lists were compiled based not only on actual sales figures but also on requests at bookstores. In 1956, Shepherd encouraged his radio show listeners to visit their local bookshops and request the nonexistent book *I, Libertine* by Frederick R. Ewing. When shops actually became interested in carrying copies of *I, Libertine*, publisher Ian Ballantine hired science fiction author Theodore Sturgeon to write the book based on Shepherd's outline. Sturgeon churned out the manuscript in one exhausting session, with Ballantine's wife, Betty, penning the final chapter after Sturgeon fell asleep. Proceeds from the book were donated to charity.

Inspiration Station

Was Utopia a Utopia?

❋ ❋ ❋ ❋

IN 1516, SIR Thomas More wrote his most famous work: *Utopia*. Though the book portrayed the manners, religious habits, and political intrigues of the citizens of a fictional island called Utopia, More did not intend it to be read as some sort of far-flung fantasy. He was inspired to write the story by events that were happening in England and Europe at the time.

Today, "utopia" is most often used to refer to a place of harmony and perfection, but More's story is anything but. In the book, slavery and euthanasia are both permitted by the Utopian government, and private property is forbidden. Modern readers often confuse More's interests and intellectual curiosity for advocacy, when in fact he was simply trying to spark debate on issues he felt would inevitably confront humans in the real world, like whether the church should have female priests. It was one of these issues that brought about More's grisly end: After refusing to acknowledge the Church of England, Thomas More was beheaded by King Henry VIII in 1535.

In the twenty-first century, our taste runs strongly toward *dystopia* rather than utopia. Especially for the young adult (YA) market, series like *The Hunger Games* use themes of apocalypse and collapse of society to speak to the fears and anxieties of growing up. In this way, dystopian writers are directly in line with Sir Thomas More's use of so-called utopia to draw our attention to what faced us in the future.

When Poe Scooped Dickens

Edgar Allan Poe wrote many classic tales of the macabre. As it turns out, he also proved himself adept at completing the work of another famous writer of his day.

✳ ✳ ✳ ✳

IN MARCH OF 1841, the first part of Charles Dickens's new novel, *Barnaby Rudge*, was published in the United States. A few years before, The *Pickwick Papers* had made him one of the most famous authors in the world; something like 80% of all people who could read owned a copy of it, and for a good century it would be considered the funniest book ever written.

Barnaby Rudge, though, was not a particularly funny book. It was a grim tale of the anti-Catholic riots that swept through England in 1780, and it is probably the least-read of all Dickens novels today. Unlike most of his other books, there isn't even a movie version, unless you count a silent one from 1915. But *Barnaby* was fairly popular in its day, and the murder mystery introduced in the first chapter kept readers all over the world guessing as the book was published, one part at a time, over the course of a year.

Number One Fan Edgar Allan Poe

Poe was then an up-and-coming writer in Baltimore, and he began writing reviews of *Barnaby Rudge* after the very first chapters were published. In a review that appeared in the May, 1841, edition of *The Saturday Evening Post*, he described the murder mystery that had been laid out: A few years before the opening of the story, a local man who lived near the Maypole Inn, a tavern, was found murdered, and his gardener and steward had vanished. A body was later found and identified by clothes and jewelry as being that of the steward, but the gardener had escaped.

Having described the mystery, Poe then proceeded to solve it.

He laid out, in great detail, the identity of the murderer, the true identity of the body that had been found, and the precise method in which the crime had been carried out.

Poe was *almost* exactly right in his solution. Indeed, many believe that Poe's solution was a bit more elegant than the one Dickens ended up using. Some scholars have speculated that Poe's solution may have been precisely what Dickens had in mind when he started writing the book, but he changed it just a bit when he heard about Poe's review.

Some have doubted the story over the years, and scholars have tried to gather evidence proving—or disproving—the theory that Poe had seen more chapters than he let on when he wrote his review. Scholars are still fairly divided.

Pet Peeve

After the whole book had been published, Poe criticized Dickens for not making better use of Grip the raven, Barnaby Rudge's pet (who was named after a pet raven Dickens himself owned). Dickens had only really written the raven in because his children had asked him to, but Poe believed it could have been used to great symbolic effect; some say it was a determination to show how this could be done that inspired him to write "The Raven," Poe's most famous poem.

Poe never came right out and *said* that Grip inspired his famous poem, but it's hard not to notice a line in the fifth chapter of *Barnaby Rudge*, when Grip is first heard to make noise, and someone asks: "What was that — him tapping at the door?" And the reply is, "'Tis someone knocking softly at the shutter."

The similarity to the opening stanza of Poe's classic poem is hard to miss:

While I nodded, nearly napping, suddenly there came a tapping

As of someone gently rapping, rapping at my chamber door.

> "'Tis some visitor,' I muttered, "tapping at my chamber door—
> Only this, and nothing more."

The stuffed body of the real Grip is now a part of the Edgar Allan Poe collection at the Free Library of Philadelphia, where it sits: voiceless there, forevermore.

Pen Names and Pulp

As Vin Packer, Ann Aldrich, M. E. Kerr, and Mary James, this author has sold millions of books. Will the real Marijane Meaker please stand up?

✳ ✳ ✳ ✳

Vin Packer and the Paperback Revolution

IN THE EARLY 1950s, young college graduate Marijane Meaker was doing entry-level work as a proofreader for Fawcett Publishing's new paperback line, Gold Medal Books. Although Meaker had literary aspirations, she never imagined that her work would sell millions of books.

Before World War II, most books published in the United States were hardcover and were sold mainly in urban bookstores and department stores. But after the war, readers embraced the value and convenience of 25- and 35-cent paperbacks. The little books found success on spinner racks in bus stations, newsstands, supermarkets, candy stores, drugstores, and other nontraditional book outlets.

The paperback revolution produced a new literary genre: lesbian pulp. Ironically, these novels were originally written by and for straight males. Yet with paperbacks widely available outside of big cities, small-town women—many of whom could barely believe there were others out there who felt as they did—avidly consumed the lesbian pulps as well. Gold Medal caught on more quickly than other publishers; in 1952, Meaker was invited to write a lesbian-plot paperback original. Whether or not Gold Medal knew that she happened to be a real-life lesbian is unclear. At any rate, Meaker and the publisher agreed on the (faintly androgynous) pen name "Vin Packer." A publishing star was born.

Introducing Ann Archer

The first Packer novel, *Spring Fire*, sold nearly 1.5 million copies over the course of three wildly successful printings. And, sensational theme aside, it turned out Packer could really write! *Spring Fire* is propelled by complex, believable female characters whose longings and emotions are sensitively portrayed. Although federal and local censorship boards prevented the books from offering a happy ending that might validate lesbianism, Packer did suggest that the lifestyle had as much potential for joy as the straight life.

After Meaker retired the pseudonym in the early 1960s, she redebuted as "Ann Archer," whose nonfiction books about lesbianism are as unblushingly bold as their titles: *We Walk Alone*, *We Too Must Love*, and *Take a Lesbian to Lunch*. The Archer books naturally attracted the interest of lesbian and general readers, as well as feminists. By about 1970, Meaker/Archer was well respected within the burgeoning women's movement.

Meet M. E. Kerr

In 1972, Meaker reinvented herself yet again, this time as "M. E. Kerr," author of thoughtful teen novels. As is the case with the Packer titles, not every Kerr book includes homosexual characters (like 1994's *Deliver Us from Evie*), but the stories' central figures are psychologically complex and often at odds with "polite" society. More importantly, Kerr wrote about issues that were typically absent in teen books, such as serious illness, gay romance, divorce, death, and social-class tensions. Kerr often trafficked in endings that were less than completely happy—something teenagers could relate to. Meaker has said that whatever the genre or pen name she uses, she seeks to "write about people who struggle, who try to overcome obstacles, who usually do, but sometimes not. People who have all the answers and few problems have never interested me." For her boldness and quality of prose in books for young adults, Meaker was given a lifetime achievement award by Young Adult Library Services in 1993.

Meaker Moving Onward

While some observers have speculated that Meaker's pen names are part of an attempt to hide her own lesbian identity, the author has never denied her sexual orientation. And Meaker's fans can't be pigeonholed, either: young, old; male, female; straight, gay. Meaker understands the importance she holds for many readers, and the significance of her pen names to various groups of readers.

Tales from the Spinning Rack

Nine comic books helped to make the art form what it is today.

✳ ✳ ✳ ✳

COMIC BOOKS ARE an integral part of popular culture, and even those who don't read them (or won't admit to it) are familiar with the medium's most famous characters. Hundreds of titles and thousands of stories have been published since the very first comic books were created in the 1930s, but only a handful have actually advanced the art form. We've listed some of the most influential comics here.

1. **Funnies on Parade (1933):** Most historians consider this Procter & Gamble promotional giveaway the progenitor of comic books as we know them today. Inside were reprints of popular Sunday comics, including Mutt & Jeff and Joe Palooka. The first commercial comics soon followed, selling for ten cents a copy.

2. **Action Comics #1 (1938):** This comic's cover image has become a national icon. This issue heralded the debut of Superman, one of the best-known fictional characters in the world and the first popular costumed superhero (there are those who would argue that either Mandrake the Magician [1934] or The Clock [1936] is the actual *first* costumed superhero). Extremely rare and quite collectable, a mint copy sold at auction in March 2010 for $1 million.

3. **Detective Comics #27 (1939):** It's here that The Batman made his debut, beginning a franchise that would almost equal that of Superman. Though he possessed no super-powers, the Dark Knight caught readers' attention from the start and never let go.

4. **Sensation Comics #1 (1942):** Wonder Woman, one of the comics' first female superheroes, was introduced in *All-Star Comics #8*, but she found a permanent home in *Sensation Comics*. Created by psychologist William Moulton Marston and first illustrated by Harry G. Peters, the Amazon Princess would evolve into a feminist icon.

5. **MAD #1 (1952):** The brainchild of satirist Harvey Kurtzman, *MAD* was the first comic book to poke serious fun at popular culture. It became a huge hit and spawned a host of imitators, few of which lasted more than a couple of issues. *MAD* soon converted to a magazine format to avoid censorship by the newly formed Comics Code Authority.

6. **Amazing Fantasy #15 (1962):** This Marvel comic book featured the first appearance of Spider-Man and introduced the concept of the troubled superhero. Though Spider-Man possessed an array of remarkable super-powers, his teenage alter ego, Peter Parker, was beset by the same problems that afflicted most young people, including girl trouble and difficulties in school.

7. **Zap Comics #1 (1967):** Robert Crumb's *Zap Comics* wasn't the first underground comic book, but most historians consider it the official vanguard of the underground "comix" movement. In later issues, Crumb gave space to some of underground comics's most influential artists, including S. Clay Wilson, Rick Griffin, Spain Rodriguez, and Gilbert Shelton. Crumb, creator of the characters Fritz the Cat and Mr. Natural, among other characters, is still revered as a counter-culture icon.

8. **Raw Magazine #2 (1980):** Though not a comic book in the traditional sense, *Raw Magazine #2* is historically significant for presenting the first installment of *Maus*, Art Spiegelman's graphic adaptation of his father's life, particularly his time as a prisoner in a Nazi concentration camp. Rather than tell the story with people, Spiegelman depicted the Jews as mice and the Nazis as cats. The saga was later published as a graphic novel and went on to win a Pulitzer Prize Special Award in 1992.

9. **Watchmen (1986):** No comic series in the past 30 years has so dramatically affected both the medium and popular culture like *Watchmen*. With penetrating character psychology and layers of metaphoric imagery, Alan Moore and Dave Gibbons didn't reinvent the superhero genre—they made it seem as if it hadn't existed until that point.

15 Must-Read Books

Throughout time, literary appetites have been sated with a slew of masterpieces that have brought readers to the depths of despair and the heights of elation, opened a world of possibilities, and challenged them to contemplate the meaning of life. As Ralph Waldo Emerson said of books, "They are for nothing but to inspire." Here are 15 that everyone should read at least once.

✳ ✳ ✳ ✳

1. ***The Diary of a Young Girl* by Anne Frank:** First published in 1947, *The Diary of a Young Girl* chronicles the life of a Jewish girl while she and her family hide from the Nazis during World War II. The diary is the work of a deep, insightful mind, and the reader cannot help but be deeply affected by its poignancy. A few months after penning the last line of the diary, Anne died of typhus at age 15 while a prisoner at the Bergen-Belsen camp. The camp was liberated by Allied troops just a few weeks later.

2. ***Crime and Punishment* by Fyodor Dostoevsky:** *Crime and Punishment*, a psychological thriller first published in 1866, depicts the story of a murder from the killer's point of view. The novel illustrates the killer's fiendish game of cat and mouse with an implacable detective, but the real genius lies in the description of the inner turmoil that eats away at the murderer. As a bonus, the reader gets a history lesson on prerevolutionary Russia.

3. ***The Adventures of Huckleberry Finn* by Mark Twain:** According to Ernest Hemingway, *The Adventures of Huckleberry Finn* is the book that spawned all modern American literature. First published in 1884, it is the tale of a young rascal who teams up with a runaway slave. Together they travel down the Mississippi River, becoming embroiled in a series of adventures that expose them to the harsh realities of the American South. Despite the

antiracist tenor of the book, it has repeatedly been banned as racist—it uses the "n-word" 212 times. Nevertheless, the book reveals the hypocrisy of racism like few books since.

4. *Cujo* by Stephen King: *Cujo* shows master horror writer King at the top of his game. First published in 1981, it tells the story of the middle-class Trenton family, whose domestic problems are dwarfed when a rabid St. Bernard goes a-huntin'. The novel occasionally allows the reader to see things from the perspective of the canine killer, especially during the three-day onslaught of Donna Trenton and her young son as they remain cooped up in a stalled Ford Pinto.

5. *Charlotte's Web* by E. B. White: First published in 1952, *Charlotte's Web* is a simple tale that has delighted millions of readers for decades. What would happen if a spider could weave words into her webs? The answer provides the plot for one of the best-selling children's books of all time. But don't be fooled—this story has plenty for adults, too. The struggle to save Wilbur the pig's life provides the canvas on which important themes such as the meaning of friendship, the cycle of life and death, and the power of loyalty are explored.

6. *The Great Gatsby* by F. Scott Fitzgerald: Written in the 1920s, *The Great Gatsby* studies the loss of the American Dream in an era of material excess. Set during the period of unrestrained prosperity that Fitzgerald dubbed "the Jazz Age," the story revolves around the sordid deeds of wealthy young Jay Gatsby and his inner circle of flunkies, led by Nick Carraway. Carraway, representing the reader's conscience, exposes the hypocrisy and futility of the materialistic lifestyle—an urgent message especially today.

7. *The Grapes of Wrath* by John Steinbeck: An American classic first published in 1939, *The Grapes of Wrath* is a story of survival and human dignity, courage and hope. It chronicles the life of the Joad family, poor Oklahoma farm-

ers who set out at the height of the Great Depression for greener pastures in California. They ultimately discover, however, that promises of the good life are empty. The novel emphasizes the need for cooperative, rather than individual, solutions to the challenges facing society.

8. ***Animal Farm* by George Orwell:** Animals on a farm overthrow their human oppressors and establish a socialist state in George Orwell's *Animal Farm*. This modern fable, first published in 1945, is an allegory of the Soviet way of life. What starts out as an egalitarian society quickly degenerates into a state of terror where the pigs rule with an iron fist. The dangers the book warns about are not limited to socialism, reminding readers that absolute power leads to complete corruption.

9. ***All Quiet on the Western Front* by Erich Maria Remarque:** *All Quiet on the Western Front* was first published in 1929 and within 18 months had sold 2.5 million copies. Remarque, a German veteran of World War I, tells the story of Paul Bäumer, a German soldier who arrives on the battlefield with an idealistic vision of war. His illusions are quickly shattered as he is inexorably led to the conclusion that all war is pointless. No other novel so graphically portrays the horror and futility of war—a message that still needs to be heard today.

10. ***To Kill a Mockingbird* by Harper Lee:** Published in 1960, *To Kill a Mockingbird* is the only novel that Harper Lee has ever written, and it garnered her a Pulitzer Prize for Fiction. Set in a sleepy southern town during the Great Depression, the book is the first person account of a year in the life of young Scout Finch. During the year, two important things happen: Scout, her brother, and a friend try to out Boo Radley, a spooky recluse who lives next door; and Scout's father, the town lawyer, defends a black man against a rape charge. These two story lines are brilliantly woven

together and ultimately combine to reveal a powerful and moving message.

11. *Fahrenheit 451* **by Ray Bradbury:** In the world of Bradbury's *Fahrenheit 451*, firemen don't put out fires, they start them—to burn books. As relevant today as when it was published in 1953, the novel shows what life would be like under a totalitarian regime in which all critical thought is suppressed. The main character is Guy Montag, a fire-man (i.e. book burner) who sees his work as noble and beneficial to society. His confidence takes a hammering with the death of his wife and a subsequent relationship with a teenage girl who is full of curiosity about the world. Her disappearance is the catalyst that gradually transforms Montag into an advocate of free thought—he even starts to read books.

12. *The Lord of the Rings* **by J.R.R. Tolkien:** *The Lord of the Rings* by J.R.R. Tolkien was first published in three volumes between 1954 and 1955. The book is a sequel to Tolkien's earlier work *The Hobbit*, published in 1937. The central character is Frodo, a hobbit entrusted with a magical ring that is the source of power for the evil Sauron. The fate of Middle Earth ebbs and flows through page after page of spectacular fantasy, epic battles, and, ultimately, the triumph of good over evil. Perhaps the most powerful message of the book is its conclusion, which shows that although good has triumphed, evil has left a permanent mark in the world.

13. *Oliver Twist* **by Charles Dickens:** "Please sir, I want some more." This famous line was spoken by the orphan Oliver Twist in Charles Dickens's book of the same name. First published in 1838, *Oliver Twist* is a social novel, revealing the stark reality of 19th-century workhouses and the treatment of poor and underprivileged children. Oliver spends his first nine years on a baby farm—a place where orphans

were sold to the highest bidder—then he transfers to the workhouse. After six months of drudgery, he loses a bet and faces up to the cook with his famous request. The fallout has him parceled off to various brutes before setting off for London. On the way he meets a colorful character known as the Artful Dodger. It's a great adventure as well as an important reminder to protect society's most innocent and vulnerable members.

14. **_The Lord of the Flies_ by William Golding:** In _The Lord of the Flies_, a group of young boys are stranded on a deserted island and forced to govern themselves. The results are chaotic and deadly. Golding's story presents an allegory about human nature, individual welfare, and the value of communal living. The book was first published in 1954 and, although it sold only 3,000 copies in its first year, it had become a best seller by 1960.

15. **The Bible:** The Bible, made up of 66 separate books, is the most influential collection of books in human history and, by far, the best-selling book of all time. It has influenced some of the world's greatest art, literature, and music and has had a significant impact on law. Esteemed by scholars and extolled for its literary style, the Bible's effect on the lives of people in all strata of society has been particularly profound, inspiring a remarkable degree of loyalty in many of its readers. Some have even risked death just to read it. The Bible is the most translated, most quoted, and most respected book in Western society and probably the most controversial book in the world, surviving bans, burnings, and violent opposition.

Somewhere Over the Rainbow

We've put in some serious detective work to try to discover the true location of Oz.

✳ ✳ ✳ ✳

We Know It's Not in Kansas

I**S THERE A** soul in the civilized world who hasn't traveled with Dorothy and Toto to the magical kingdom of Oz, which was brought to life in the 1939 classic *The Wizard of Oz?* The young Dorothy (Judy Garland) and her beloved dog are whisked off their Kansas chicken ranch by that tornado and ultimately follow the Yellow Brick Road to Oz, where they meet the mighty wizard.

Beyond the fantasy, though, why not pin down the actual physical location of Oz? Impossible, you say? No, indeed. First of all, we can rule out one state because Dorothy utters the famous line, "Toto, I've a feeling we're not in Kansas anymore."

So where could the tornado have tossed Dorothy and her pooch? Well, even assuming this was one of the most devastating twisters of all time—an F5 on the Fujita scale used by meteorologists—there's a limit to how far a human being can be carried by a tornado.

According to researchers at the Tornado Project in St. Johnsbury, Vermont, small objects have whooshed great distances, but the farthest a human being has been thrown is about one mile.

How About Missouri?

So Dorothy couldn't have gone far—let's say a mile and a half because she was smaller than a full-grown adult. Therefore, Dorothy must have lived right on the Kansas border. And not out in the middle of nowhere, either, because at the start of the film, farm worker Hickory makes this statement: "But someday, they're going to erect a statue to me in this town."

So liftoff was near some kind of city or village right at the edge of Kansas. And you have to assume that Oz itself couldn't have been in an empty cornfield, either, because there would have needed to be some sort of population where Dorothy and Toto landed. Only the northern and eastern borders of Kansas provide search points, because most tornadoes move from southwest to northeast. A twister on either of the state's other two borders would have carried Dorothy and Toto farther into Kansas.

There is only one location that fits the description provided in the movie. Dorothy's Uncle Henry and Aunt Em must have lived just outside of Atchison, Kansas—east of Highway 7 near the Missouri River—and the infamous tornado carried girl and dog little more than a mile to the outskirts of Rushville, Missouri. Oz.

Before you scoff, consider some curious coincidences. Tornado activity in the Rushville area is 143 percent greater than the overall U.S. average. Oh, and Atchison is the birthplace of Amelia Earhart. The gallant aviatrix, Atchison's most famous daughter if you aren't counting Dorothy, vanished on her flight around the world in 1937 but was declared dead in 1939—the same year *The Wizard of Oz* was released. Perhaps Amelia can be found over the rainbow.

The Wreck of the *Titan*

*A book that eerily foreshadowed the Titanic tragedy fourteen
years before it occurred? You bet your iceberg!*

✳ ✳ ✳ ✳

Doomed Voyage

AS THE WORLD'S greatest steamship moved across the
North Atlantic darkness, an unseen foe lay in wait. The
ship dubbed "virtually unsinkable" by its creators would suffer
a fatal collision with an iceberg spotted too late. The staggering loss of life associated with the craft's sinking would deliver
a blow to man's hubris and act as a cautionary tale never to
underestimate the forces of nature. The story of the RMS
Titanic has become the stuff of legend. But this isn't that story.

Life Imitates Art

This is the story of another ship, the imaginary creation of
author Morgan Robertson. Robertson had a great love for the
sea. He wrote many tales of adventure on the ocean and his
stories were regarded as some of the most accurate and vivid of
his day. He told of the ill-fated passage of his fictional ship, the
implausibly named *Titan*, in the book, *Futility, or the Wreck of
the Titan.*

Had this tome been written after the 1912 sinking of the
Titanic, some might have accused Robertson of sensationalism
and cashing in after the fact. As it happened, however, this was
far from the case. Robertson wrote his sixty-nine page novella
in 1898, fourteen years *before* the Titanic slipped beneath
the waves. Its similarities to that tragedy run the gamut from
uncanny to eerie.

Titan vs. Titanic

How uncanny? The fictional *Titan* and the very real *Titanic*
both sank in April in the icy North Atlantic. Both vessels
used three propellers for propulsion and were traveling at over

22 knots per hour. Even the ships' dimensions were close, with the *Titan* stretching out to 800 feet and the *Titanic* to 882 feet.

But these similarities, while intriguing, only represent the tip of the iceberg—pun fully intended. Both ships met their end around midnight compliments of the aforementioned icebergs, after taking a hit on the starboard side. The *Titan* was described as "practically unsinkable" in the book, while the *Titanic* was described in newspaper articles as "virtually unsinkable." Each vessel was the largest afloat for its day, and each operated with an insufficient number of lifeboats, an oversight that would result in an appalling loss of life in both instances.

That last factoid is where things get really interesting. The *Titan* carried 24 lifeboats, less than half needed for her 3,000 passenger capacity. Likewise, the *Titanic* carried a total of 20 lifeboats, less than half needed for her 3,000 passenger limit. Both ships satisfied legal requirements in this area, but only just. When the *Titan* went down, more than half of her 2,500 passengers died as a result. Records show that more than 1,500 perished when the *Titanic* sank, more than half of the 2,200 passengers onboard!

Explaining the Inexplicable

Many of Robertson's contemporaries felt that he had a sixth sense. Since Robertson was known to have an interest in the occult, parapsychologists believed that the writer had experienced a paranormal vision. Others, grounded in religion, believed that the Robertson had been granted a gift of prophecy and used as a conduit. Naysayers, however, felt that the similarities between the *Titan* and the *Titanic* could be chalked up to little more than a grand coincidence.

But Robertson's story gets better still. In 1914 he released *Beyond the Spectrum*. The book told of a Japanese sneak attack on American ships docked in Hawaii. The aggressive action leads to a war between Japan and the United States. Coincidence? Precognition? Divine intervention?

15 Films Based on Stephen King Short Stories

Stephen King sold numerous short stories to magazines before Doubleday published his full-length novel Carrie *in 1973, launching a career that has spanned decades. As King churned out hit books like* Christine *and* The Green Mile, *Hollywood clamored for the opportunity to turn his prose into box office gold. More than 50 King stories have been filmed for the big screen or TV so far, and there's no sign of stopping.*

1. ***Carrie*** (1976): This story about a young girl named Carrie (Sissy Spacek) has a spot in the hallowed halls of classic horror movies. Carrie's over-protective mother shelters her so much that when she gets taunted mercilessly by her classmates, they learn that teasing Carrie is a bad idea—the girl's got a few nasty tricks up her sleeve. The movie, which also stars Piper Laurie and John Travolta, grossed more than $33 million. This was the first film adaptation of a King novel and years later, the first Broadway adaptation, too. *Carrie* the musical was one of the biggest flops ever, closing after just five performances and losing $7 million.

2. ***Children of the Corn*** (1984): This tale of terror came from a book of short stories entitled *Night Shift*, which also included future adaptations such as "The Lawnmower Man" and "Graveyard Shift." The children of Gatlin, a little town in Nebraska, are called to murder by a preacher-boy named Isaac. A young couple gets in the way of their plans. Peter Horton and Linda Hamilton star as the doomed couple Burt and Vicky. In one scene, a copy of *Night Shift* can be seen on the dashboard of their car. The movie was panned, but that didn't stop it from spawning seven sequels. Most of them are as weak as the original, but the seventh film, released in 2001, is reportedly the best of the bunch.

3. **Christine** (1983): Stephen King was so popular in the early 1980s that *Christine* the book wasn't even published before preproduction began on the movie version. Producers took a chance on his latest story about a boy and his car. That's right—Christine is a car, not a girl. Arnie Cunningham, who might have been played by Kevin Bacon if he hadn't chosen *Footloose* instead, is a high-school nerd who falls in love with a 1958 Plymouth Fury. The car is possessed and threatens to kill anyone who tries to get in its way. The story and the film are well known but not regarded as King's best. The author has the uncanny ability to tap into people's basic fears (rejection, clowns, ghosts, etc.), but his portrayal of a fearsome car didn't terrorize audiences as much as some of his other menaces.

4. **Cujo** (1983): Here, doggie-doggie! Here, doggie— AAAAGGGGH! That pretty much sums up the plot behind this King adaptation. Dee Wallace plays Donna Trenton, a mom with marital problems, and a young Danny Pintauro (of *Who's the Boss?* fame) stars as her son Tad. The two find themselves in big trouble when their car breaks down miles from town and the family dog appears to be very, very ill. Cujo, a Saint Bernard, has been bitten by a rat and is none too friendly for most of the film. It took five different dogs, a mechanical head, and a guy in a dog suit to get the shots of Cujo's raging—perhaps that's why this film has a slight cheese factor. The movie might not have nabbed any awards, but it remains a horrifying tale.

5. **The Dead Zone** (1983): A talented cast including Christopher Walken, Tom Skerritt, and Martin Sheen plays out this story of a schoolteacher involved in an auto accident that puts him in a coma for five years. When he awakens, he's got a knack for seeing the future, which is not as fun as it sounds. The story is loosely based on the life of famous psychic Peter Hurkos. Although this film hasn't reached the cult status of some other King adaptations, the

Academy of Science Fiction, Fantasy & Horror named it the Best Picture of the year.

6. **Dolores Claiborne** (1995): This psychological thriller tells the story of Dolores, a maid who works for a wealthy woman in Maine, the setting for many of King's stories. When the rich woman is murdered, Dolores's daughter comes in from New York to sort out all the details. Lots of flashbacks about the family's domestic problems ensue and a cast that includes Kathy Bates and Jennifer Jason Leigh plays out the vivid drama with engaging results and a suspenseful ending with a twist. The movie received excellent reviews, especially for the performances by the leading ladies. It did well at the box office, earning $25 million.

7. **Firestarter** (1984): College students beware: Those medical tests you participate in to earn money for rent could result in serious trouble later in life. So it goes with Andy and Vicky McGee, who were given doses of a nasty chemical in college that would adversely affect their future daughter, played by a cute but dangerous Drew Barrymore. A TV miniseries called *Firestarter: Rekindled* was produced in 2002, possibly because King is rumored to have hated the original, something filmmakers have to be wary of when working with him.

8. **The Green Mile** (1999): *The Green Mile* was based on King's series of six short books of the same name. In one of King's most successful movie adaptations, Tom Hanks stars as Paul Edgecomb, a cynical death row prison guard. Michael Clarke Duncan, Oscar-nominated for his role in the film, plays John Coffey, a prisoner accused of murdering two children. The movie grossed $136 million at the box office and DVD sales are still strong. King reportedly came to the set and asked to sit in the electric chair being used in the film. He didn't like how "Old Sparky" felt and asked to be released right away.

9. **Misery** (1990): King often centers his stories on a protagonist who bears a striking resemblance to himself. *Misery* is one of these. Novelist Paul Sheldon finds himself being nursed back to health by Annie Wilkes after crashing his car in the Colorado mountains. Annie is Paul's self-proclaimed number one fan and relishes the opportunity to help her favorite author. Kathy Bates won an Oscar for her role as Annie—she's terrifyingly good as the obsessed woman. If you pay attention, you'll catch a reference to another King book, *The Shining*. At one point, the odd couple discusses the "guy who went mad in a hotel nearby."

10. **Needful Things** (1993): This adaptation was a bit of a clunker, collecting more negative reviews than ticket sales. The movie didn't make much more than $15 million at the box office, which isn't too hot in terms of movie sales. The Faustian story, however, based on the King novel of the same name, is a strong one. Satan has a shop in a small New England town and gladly sells his customers whatever they need—for a price. The best-known actor in the movie is Ed Harris, who plays doomed Sheriff Alan Pangborn.

11. **Pet Sematary** (1989): When the Creed family's cat gets smooshed on the highway, an elderly neighbor instructs Mr. Creed to bury the cat in the "pet sematary" and watch what happens. The cat comes back, but he's a little different this time around. When Mr. Creed's son dies, guess what bright idea daddy has? Watch for a King cameo in the funeral scene. This campy, but intensely creepy, movie did well at the box office and got decent reviews for a horror movie. It also generated a sequel three years later, but it didn't do as well as the original.

12. **The Running Man** (1987): What other Stephen King screen adaptation can boast a cast that included not one but two future U.S. governors? Only *The Running Man*, which stars Arnold Schwarzenegger as the lead and Jesse

Ventura in a smaller role. The story, based on the novel of the same name written under King's nom de plume Richard Bachman, is set in the year 2017. America is a police state where criminals have the opportunity to run for their freedom on a weirdly ahead-of-its-time reality show. The movie did well when it was released, earning almost $40 million, and reviews were decent, especially for a story that King reportedly penned in less than three days.

13. **The Shawshank Redemption** (1994): Taken from King's *Different Seasons* short story collection, *The Shawshank Redemption* may be King's most critically acclaimed adaptation, garnering seven Oscar nods and grossing nearly $30 million at the box office. Morgan Freeman and Tim Robbins star as Red and Andy, two prison inmates who strive to reconcile their fates in different ways. This story is effectively frightening not because of supernatural events but because of the terror of watching one's life pass by.

14. **The Shining** (1980): The term cult classic doesn't really cover what *The Shining* is to American pop culture. Starring Jack Nicholson and Shelley Duvall and directed by Stanley Kubrick, *The Shining* is essentially a story about cabin fever—really, really, bad cabin fever in a haunted cabin where tidal waves of blood occur from time to time and a force called "the shining" possesses little kids. There is an element of camp that can't be denied about this particular adaptation, but King hated what Kubrick did to the story. The movie spawned a dozen catchphrases, including, "Heeeeere's Johnny!" and "Redrum! Redrum!"

15. **Stand By Me** (1986): The *Different Seasons* collection also included a story called "Fall from Innocence: The Body." *Stand By Me*, one of King's greatest movie successes, was based on this story. A group of preteen boys go on an adventure to find the body of a classmate who is missing and presumed dead. They are tailed by bullies and must

make very grown-up decisions throughout the course of the film, which garnered an Oscar nod for Best Adapted Screenplay. A critical and box office success, *Stand By Me* starred teen heartthrobs River Phoenix, Wil Wheaton, and Corey Feldman and is one of the most widely enjoyed King films to date, perhaps due to the focus on tension among humans rather than killer clowns or deadly cars.

Lore of the Lorax

Who was Dr. Seuss, and did he ever practice medicine?

✳   ✳   ✳   ✳

WRITTEN WITH JUST fifty different words, Dr. Seuss's *Green Eggs and Ham* is so succinct that it could have been scrawled on a prescription pad. But the only medicine that this "doctor" ever prescribed was humor, whimsy, and perhaps a side of one fish two fish red fish blue fish.

Born on March 2, 1904, in Springfield, Massachusetts, Dr. Seuss was the son of a brewmaster father and a pie-baker mother. His given name was Theodor Seuss Geisel. (Seuss was

his mother's maiden name.) So how did Theodor go from being a simple "Ted" to the world's most famous "doctor" of children's art and literature?

The story begins when Ted was a student at Dartmouth College. In the spring of 1925, he was the editor-in-chief of the university's humor magazine, *Jack-O-Lantern*. Unfortunately, his editorial tenure was cut short after he and his friends got caught throwing a party that featured gin. These, remember, were the days of Prohibition.

But getting fired didn't stop Ted from dispensing his occasional dose of drollery—he continued to write for and contribute cartoons to *Jack-O-Lantern*. To elude punishment, he signed his work with clever pseudonyms like "L. Pasteur," "L. Burbank," "D. G. Rossetti," and his middle name: "Seuss."

Seuss took on the self-appointed title of "doctor" several years later when he published his first children's book, *And to Think That I Saw It on Mulberry Street*, in 1937. It's said that he added the mock-scholarly "Dr." to his name as a joke. You see, Seuss's father had always wanted him to earn a doctorate and become a professor—and that didn't exactly happen. Seuss did go on to study at Oxford University in England after graduating from Dartmouth, but he became bored with academics and ditched his studies for a tour of Europe instead.

But back to that very first book: Though it's hard to imagine now, success as an author and illustrator did not come easy for the young doc. *Mulberry Street* was rejected by twenty-seven different publishers before it was finally released by Vanguard Press. Of course, once printed, the book won much praise for its unique illustrations. After that, a string of wildly popular works followed.

At the time of his death in 1991, Dr. Seuss had published nearly fifty books—including the classics *Horton Hears a Who* (1954), *The Cat in the Hat* (1957), *Fox in Socks* (1965), *The*

Lorax (1971), and *Oh, the Places You'll Go!* (1990)—and he's sold more books than any other American children's author. He's also won two Academy Awards, two Emmy Awards, a Peabody Award, and the Pulitzer Prize.

But guess what? According to Theodor's widow, Audrey Geisel, Seuss didn't much like to spend time with children. He never had any of his own and, in fact, was "afraid of children to a degree." Good thing the doctor didn't become a pediatrician!

Bible Translations You've Probably Never Heard Of

From historical to hip, they don't get read much today.

❋   ❋   ❋   ❋

1. **The Great Bible (1539)** This was the first authorized edition of the Bible in English. Though William Tyndale and John Wycliffe had already been flouting church law by translating scripture for the common folk, it was King Henry VIII who approved this version for his new Anglican church. It was prepared by a Tyndale crony, Miles Coverdale, commissioned by Thomas Cromwell. This was sometimes called the "Chained Bible," because churches

would make it available to parishioners (as ordered by Cromwell), but chain it down for safekeeping.

2. **The Geneva Bible (1560)** For a half-century before the King James Version, this was the standard; it was mass-produced and widely used. When Milton or Shakespeare quoted scripture, it was from this version. The language was vigorous, edgy for its day, a clear improvement over previous translations. Amazingly, this was what modern publishers would call a "study Bible," with an assortment of study guides, introductions, maps, and woodcut illustrations.

3. **The Primitive New Testament (1745)** Bible translators have always tried to work from the best Hebrew and Greek originals, but archaeologists keep finding new manuscripts, which continually shed new light on the text. Eighteenth-century scholar William Whiston sought to improve on the King James Version by working from some very early ("primitive") Greek manuscripts. A mathematician and scientist, Whiston suggested that Noah's flood had been caused by a comet.

4. **A Liberal Translation of the New Testament (1768)** A prolific writer and creative thinker, Edward Harwood brought the flowery language of 18th-century English prose to his free (liberal) paraphrase of the New Testament—as we can see in his 77-word subtitle (something about "the True Signification and Force of the Original . . . transfused into our Language"). His rendering of "Thy kingdom come"? "May the glory of thy moral government be advanced, and the great laws of it be more generally obeyed."

5. **The Twentieth Century New Testament (1898–1901)** A flood of new Bible translations came along in the 20th century, and this was the first, published in three parts, with a final collection offered in 1904. A team of about 20 Britons composed this version, but they weren't professional

scholars—they were teachers, home-makers, ministers, and even railroad workers who had studied ancient Greek and wanted to bring the Bible to life in the modern age.

6. **Fenton's Bible (1903)** In 1853, a young London business-man began work on a personal project, translating the Bible into modern English. Fifty years later he published the complete work: *The Holy Bible in Modern English.* Farrar Fenton wanted to capture the essence of the original, so he treated the psalms as the songs they were. Painstakingly, he fit other poetic books (including Job) into poetic meter. He also tried to put the books of the Bible into chronological order.

7. **The Bible in Basic English (1941, 1949)** For people just learning to read English, how can they understand the Bible, with its big concepts and massive vocabulary? That was the challenge taken by Samuel Henry Hooke, a British scholar. Using only 850 basic English words (defined by literacy experts), adding 100 words necessary for poetry and 50 distinctly Bible words, Hooke composed this easy-to-read version.

8. **The Amplified Bible (1958, 1962)** Where the BBE (see above) used fewer words, the Amplified Bible used more. Hebrew and Greek words seldom have direct parallels with English words. Instead, there might be multiple pos-sible translations, nuances, or cultural associations. The Amplified Bible provides alternate readings and explana-tory phrases in parentheses and brackets, just to make sure the full sense of the original is honored. It's hard to read out loud, but great for study. This was the first Bible project of the Lockman Foundation, which later sponsored the *New American Standard Bible.*

9. **The Berkeley Bible (1945, 1959, 1969)** English wasn't the native language of Dutch-born Gerrit Verkuyl, but as an undergrad in the United States, he began to see the need

for a modern translation to supersede the KJV. He didn't have much time to work on it for the 40 years after he made the decision, though. As a retiree, he tackled the project, naming it after his new hometown, Berkeley, California. His *New Testament*, published in 1945, met such critical acclaim that many wanted a complete Bible. Since Old Testament Hebrew was not Verkuyl's specialty, his publisher assembled an all-star team of scholars to finish *The Berkeley Version of the Bible in Modern English* in 1959. (This was revised in 1969as The Modern Language Bible.)

10. The New Testament in the Language of Today (1963)
As a pastor in Iowa during the 1930s and '40s, William F. Beck found that even his Sunday school teachers were having trouble understanding the stately KJV language. He began translating New Testament passages from the original Greek into language that made sense to them. After getting a doctorate in New Testament studies, he completed his translation of the NT, stating in his introduction that he wanted to "let God speak the language of today," the kind of language people use over "coffee and doughnuts."

Why Isn't the Bible in Chronological Order?

If you've ever tried to read the Bible like a novel, you've probably been frustrated or disappointed.

✳   ✳   ✳   ✳

What's Up with That?

A LOT OF PEOPLE who set out to read the Bible from cover to cover don't complete their goal. Why? Well, for one, the story keeps getting interrupted by long genealogical lists and ceremonial descriptions. And then there's the whole problem with one book not always picking up where the last one left off. What's up with that?

One simple answer is that the entire Bible is made up of 66 separate books, 39 of which comprise the Old (or Hebrew) Testament and 27 that make up the New (or Christian) Testament. It's not meant to be read as a novel, but as a collection of different types of literature with one overarching theme tying them together: God's interaction with humanity and his unfolding plan to bring his estranged creation back into fellowship with himself.

Outline of the Old Testament

This set of 39 books, which record much of Israel's early history, can be divided into 4 sections:

The first five books of the Bible—Genesis through Deuteronomy—make up this section. The word Pentateuch is made up of two Greek words: *penta* meaning "five," and *teuchos* meaning "volume" or "book." A lot of content—the Creation, the Flood, the Patriarchs, and Israel's earliest history—is included in these "volumes." They also contain the covenant law God gave to Israel when Moses led them from Egypt into the wilderness and finally to the doorstep of the Promised Land.

While there's plenty of history recorded in the first five books of the Old Testament, the next 12 books—Joshua through Esther—record about 700 years' worth of Israel's history, once they began settling in the Promised Land. This section covers the leadership of a series of judges and priests and then the nation's transition to monarch rule. Ultimately the kingdom breaks apart and the people are carried into exile. First, inhabitants of the northern kingdom are hauled up to Assyria. Later, the southern kingdom is conquered by Babylon until the people are allowed to return home once the Medo-Persians are in charge.

The books of Job, Psalms, Proverbs, Ecclesiastes, and Song of Solomon make up this section that lies roughly at the middle of the Bible. Like a refreshing pause, they intervene between the hard facts of history and the powerful ministry of the prophets.

In fact, the Bible contains some of the most exquisite poetry ever written.

Job, the title character of the book, inspires faith in the face of pain. Want encouragement and comfort? Check out the Psalms. For guiding principles in life, read through Proverbs: There are 31 chapters that can be read one at a time for a monthlong course in wisdom. Philosophers find Ecclesiastes an interesting read. Lovers might be surprised at how eloquent and explicit Song of Songs (or Song of Solomon) is in matters of romance. It's a rich section, especially for poetry lovers.

This section is made up of 17 books. Isaiah, Jeremiah, Ezekiel, and Daniel account for the first five books (Jeremiah also wrote Lamentations), and these are called the "major prophets." Following these are 12 other books—Hosea through Malachi—written by what are called the "minor prophets," for a total of 17 books.

Throughout Israel's history, God gave prophets—messengers to his people—to remind them of his Word and his ways and to denounced idolatry while calling them to undivided devotion to himself. Having a timeline handy as you read the prophets (good study Bibles usually include them) can help you understand them in the correct historical setting.

Outline of the New Testament

What about the New Testament? It repeats itself! Well, yes, indeed it does . . . at first, but that also has to do with sections within the 27 books this smaller Testament contains.

Let's start with the gospels. The first three Gospels are called the "synoptic Gospels," meaning they're coming from similar perspectives. They are three accounts of Jesus' ministry, recorded by three different authors. Their overlap has to do with their collection of data from eyewitnesses, some of which came from the same sources or from sources who witnessed the same events. John's Gospel is different and stands out in a number of ways. If you read one of the first three Gospels and then read John's, you won't have the sense of reading the same material twice. (Note: Even the synoptic Gospels have unique content, though, so it may worthwhile to read them all.)

The book of Acts, written by the Gospel writer Luke, gives an action-packed account of the start of Christianity and its growth. In this book, we discover how the apostle Paul went from persecuting early believers to propagating their faith.

Once Paul embraced Christianity, he traveled as an itinerant messenger—the first missionary, if you will. He was often imprisoned, and sometimes he remained in a place for a time, helping churches get established. While in one place, he often wrote letters to other places he'd been, to encourage believers, correct any wrong notions, and instruct in matters about which they inquired. His letters include Romans through Philemon (13 books), and some scholars attribute Hebrews to him, though the author of that book is not identified.

Paul's letters are followed by another section of letters. This seven-book section is relatively brief compared with Paul's writings. The books—James through Jude—carry the names of their authors (while Paul's letters bear the names of their recipients). These messages were (for the most part) written to the church in general, not to a specific audience, thus the designation "general" letters.

The book of Revelation closes out the Bible. This book stands alone in its own section for a reason. It uniquely describes the final outcome of God's redemptive plan and final judgment of evil. At the beginning of the Bible, Genesis describes a God-initiated beginning to the world. Here at the end, Revelation describes its consummation and a re-creation, in which there will be no pain, suffering, or sorrow. Evil will be a thing of the past. God's goodness will overcome and rule for eternity. It's called the Christian's "blessed hope" when Christ returns to establish his eternal kingdom of peace.

OK, so that's the basic outline, and reading just one book or section at a time can be less daunting than trying to tackle the whole Bible at once. However, there *is* good news for fans of a more linear approach. You can find Bibles on the market now that orchestrate biblical content so that it flows in a chronological sense wherever possible. This approach places the writings of the prophets and poets alongside the places where they show up in the historical books. It synchronizes Paul's letter writing with his missionary journeys, and so on. It's a great way to read the Good Book.

A Devilish Dictionary

Today's veteran journalists have seen it all, metaphorically speaking, and it's not uncommon for them to become jaded and cynical. And online bloggers are even worse—without an editor to rein them in (or perhaps with an editor to egg them on!), their posts may become filled with sarcasm and cynicism.

✳   ✳   ✳   ✳

IMAGINE WHAT RENOWNED journalist Ambrose Bierce (1842–1913), writer of 1911's *The Devil's Dictionary*, a satirical lexicon that "redefines" more than 1,000 words, would have to say today. Here is a sampling of some of the dark and sardonical entries in *The Devil's Dictionary*.

* **ABSURDITY,** *n.* A statement or belief manifestly inconsistent with one's own opinion.

* **ACADEMY,** *n.* A modern school where football is taught.

* **ALONE,** *adj.* In bad company.

* **AMNESTY,** *n.* The state's magnanimity to those offenders whom it would be too expensive to punish.

* **APOLOGIZE,** *v.i.* To lay the foundation for a future offence.

* **BRAIN,** *n.* An apparatus with which we think what we think. That which distinguishes the man who is content to be something from the man who wishes to do something.

* **BRIDE,** *n.* A woman with a fine prospect of happiness behind her.

* **CONGRATULATION,** *n.* The civility of envy.

* **CONGRESS,** *n.* A body of men who meet to repeal laws.

* **CONNOISSEUR,** *n.* A specialist who knows everything about something and nothing about anything else.

* **CONSULT,** *v.i.* To seek another's approval of a course already decided on.

* **DESTINY,** *n.* A tyrant's authority for crime and a fool's excuse for failure.

* **EDIBLE,** *n.* Good to eat, and wholesome to digest, as a worm to a toad, a toad to a snake, a snake to a pig, a pig to a man, and a man to a worm.

* **FAMOUS,** *adj.* Conspicuously miserable.

* **FUTURE,** *n.* That period of time in which our affairs prosper, our friends are true, and our happiness is assured.

✳ **GRAVE,** *n.* A place in which the dead are laid to await the coming of the medical student.

✳ **LOGIC,** *n.* The art of thinking and reasoning in strict accordance with the limitations and incapacities of human misunderstanding.

✳ **MONEY,** *n.* A blessing that is of no advantage to us excepting when we part with it.

✳ **MONKEY,** *n.* An arboreal animal which makes itself at home in genealogical trees.

✳ **PHILOSOPHY,** *n.* A route of many roads leading from nowhere to nothing.

✳ **PLAN,** *v.t..* To bother about the best method of accomplishing an accidental result.

✳ **POLITENESS,** *n.* The most acceptable hypocrisy.

✳ **POLITICS,** *n.* A strife of interests masquerading as a contest of principles. The conduct of public affairs for private advantage.

✳ **QUOTATION,** *n.* The act of repeating erroneously the words of another. The words erroneously repeated.

✳ **RECREATION,** *n.* A particular kind of dejection to relieve a general fatigue.

✳ **RESPONSIBILITY,** *n.* A detachable burden easily shifted to the shoulders of God, Fate, Fortune, Luck or one's neighbor. In the days of astrology it was customary to unload it upon a star.

✳ **SELF-EVIDENT,** *adj.* Evident to one's self and to nobody else.

✳ **YEAR,** *n.* A period of three hundred and sixty-five disappointments.

Snack Attack

Are you hungry for word origins? Thank goodness you don't have to pay royalties to say "cheeseburger."

✳ ✳ ✳ ✳

✳ **Bock beer:** From the German word for a male goat, because the beer's strength was said to make its drinkers behave just like the wild animal.

✳ **Butter:** Creamy spread; from Old English *butere*, a derivation of Greek *boutyron*, from *bous* (cow) + *tyros* (cheese).

✳ **Cheeseburger:** Although you might think it has been around forever, the cheeseburger first became part of American culture in 1935, when Louis Ballast of the Humpty Dumpty Barrel Drive-In in St. Louis, Missouri, applied for a patent on the concept. (Although other places in California and Kentucky also claimed credit for the first cheeseburger, Ballast was the only one to finish the paperwork.) Alas for Ballast, the word *cheeseburger* remains in the public domain. No one can own it, and everyone can use it.

✳ **Coconut:** Of course, the coconut is not a nut at all, but it looked like one to the early Portuguese explorers as they sailed around Africa. They saw the fruit hanging from trees and thought they looked like small heads, grinning. *Coconut* resulted from a combination of *nut* and the Portuguese word *coco*, which means "a grinning face."

✳ **Ketchup:** This condiment would have been unrecognizable in its earlier incarnations, especially as a fish-based sauce. But as a matter of fact, that's how it got its name. Back in 1711, the Malay name for this sauce was *kichap*, from the Chinese Amoy dialect's *koechiap*, or "brine of fish." Early English versions of the condiment included mushrooms, walnuts, cucumbers, and oysters. The first modern form of ketchup began when New Englanders added tomatoes.

Catsup (earlier, *catchup*) is a failed attempt at Anglicization but is still in use in some portions of the United States.

* **Lager beer:** Because it is aged in a storehouse before it is ready for consumption, this beer derives its name from the German word for "resting place."

* **Mushroom:** This name doesn't describe the fungus but probably resulted from the mispronunciation of the French word *mousseron*. Before the French word became popular, the mushroom was often known by its more descriptive name: toad's hat.

* **Mustard:** A food condiment; originated in 1190 from Old French *moustarde*, derived from *moust* (must) and the Latin *mustum* (new wine), so called because it was originally prepared by adding the substance must to the ground seeds of the plant to make a paste.

* **Nachos:** The favorite midgame snack of millions—sturdy corn chips slathered in melted cheese and an assortment of toppings—was (at least according to the *Dallas Morning News*) named for the man who invented it in 1943. Ignacio Anaya was a cook in Piedras Negras, a Mexican town near the U.S. border.

* **Pretzel:** Though some have compared the twisted shape of these snacks to the arms of praying children, nobody knows for sure why pretzels are twisted—though the term itself is from the German word for "branch."

* **Sandwich:** Although John Montagu, consummate gambler, hasty eater, and the fourth Earl of Sandwich (1718–1792), is responsible for the name for this meal, people had eaten sandwiches long before the Earl made them trendy.

* **Sauce:** A condiment for food, usually a dressing or topping; from the Latin *salsa*, feminine of *salsus* (salted), past participle of *sallere* (to salt).

* **Snacks:** The tasty treats have been consumed since the 1600s, when the word was first used to describe small portions of food hastily snatched between meals.

* **Vermicelli:** Derives from the Latin *vermis*, or worm. Literally translated from Italian, it means "little worms."

Behind the Scenes: Publishing

For every published author there are dozens of hopeful writers. The industry doesn't work the way most laypeople think.

Q: What are galleys?

A: A galley is a printed version of a work in the process of publication. Publishers print galleys to assist in editing and proofreading, or as advance copies for reviewers. This is the intermediate step between a manuscript and a book. From the publisher's viewpoint, galleys are where editors fix authors' errors, edit boring or outrageous parts, and make the work the best it can be. From the author's vantage, galleys enable editors to insert new errors and cut out all their most brilliant stuff.

Q: How does a writer get "agented"?

A: Getting published is like borrowing money: Just as it's easy to borrow money if you don't need any, it's easier to get published if you've been published. If you haven't been published and want to use an agent, first you get a list of agents who represent the kind of thing you write (there are books listing them). Next, you send a query letter or book proposal that complies with the agent's guidelines. You want to seem enthusiastic but realistic, and don't come off as high maintenance. Agents hate high maintenance, and writers hoping to be published require higher maintenance than old Corvairs.

Q: What is a query letter?

A: These days, no one sends or wants a three-inch-thick paper manuscript as the first approach. A query letter is a one-pager introducing the author, describing the work, and attempting to sell it. It needs to be targeted and personal, explaining why you chose that agent or publisher. Even though you know damn well you are mass-producing 30 of them because your last 30 were rejected or ignored, you can't let on.

A little sucking up is fine. Yes, the agent will know you're sucking up, but if you can do so with muted artistry, it will imply significant writing talent. Or maybe don't risk it.

Q: What's a book proposal?

A: Ever seen a business plan? A book proposal is a book's business plan, most commonly used for nonfiction work. It tells about the book, introduces the author, outlines marketing strategies and target audiences, and attempts to convince the agent or publisher that this will make them big money with little effort. It should glow with enthusiasm, but it shouldn't sound like the author's overly enthusiastic. There is no point projecting sales of 20 million copies of a deep study of the ecology of the echidna—publishers know that won't happen.

Q: What are the reasons writers never become published authors?

A: In many cases, they just aren't as good as they imagine they are. Some are taken hard aback by the business end of the literary life; they hold the naive misconception that if they write a great book, they'll succeed. In reality, the right time and place matter as much as quality. Some get sick of rejection; some are so difficult to work with that agents and publishers throw up their hands.

Most published authors developed a strategy, implemented it, refined it, adjusted with the buffets and pitfalls, and persevered anyway. They also lucked out a little. They succeeded because they kept marching while others gave up due to the mud, or stepped in dog poop and got disgusted, or got sore feet.

14 Best-Selling Books Repeatedly Rejected by Publishers

Novelists spend years developing their craft, editing and reediting their work, agonizing over the smallest word, often to be rejected by publisher after publisher. The following famous books and authors were turned down by publishers at least 15 times before they became household names.

✴ ✴ ✴ ✴

1. *Auntie Mame* **by Patrick Dennis:** Based on his party-throwing, out-of-control aunt, Patrick Dennis's story defined in 1955 what Americans now know as "camp." However, before Vanguard Press picked it up, 15 other publishers rejected it. Within years, *Auntie Mame* would not only become a hit on Broadway, but a popular film as well. Dennis became a millionaire and, in 1956, was the first author in history to have three books simultaneously ranked on *The New York Times* best seller list.

2. ***Jonathan Livingston Seagull* by Richard Bach:** Richard Bach has always said that this story, told from the point of view of a young seagull, wasn't written but channeled. When he sent out the story, Bach received 18 rejection letters. Nobody thought a story about a seagull that flew not for survival but for the joy of flying itself would have an audience. Boy, were they wrong! Macmillan Publishers finally picked up *Jonathan Livingston Seagull* in 1972, and that year the book sold more than a million copies. A movie followed in 1973, with a sound track by Neil Diamond

3. ***Chicken Soup for the Soul* by Jack Canfield and Mark Victor Hansen:** Within a month of submitting the first manuscript to publishing houses, the creative team behind this multimillion dollar series got turned down 33 consecutive times. Publishers claimed that "anthologies don't sell" and the book was "too positive." Total number of rejections? 140. Then, in 1993, the president of Health Communications took a chance on the collection of poems, stories, and tidbits of encouragement. Today, the 65-title series has sold more than 80 million copies in 37 languages.

4. ***Kon-Tiki* by Thor Heyerdahl:** With a name like Thor, adventure on the high seas is sort of a given, isn't it? In 1947, Heyerdahl took a crew of six men on a 4,300-mile journey across the Pacific Ocean. But not on a cruise ship—their vessel was a reproduction of a prehistoric balsawood raft, and the only modern equipment they carried was a radio. Heyerdahl wrote the true story of his journey from Peru to Polynesia, but when he tried to get it published, he couldn't. One publisher asked him if anyone had drowned. When Heyerdahl said no, they rejected him on the grounds that the story wouldn't be very interesting. In 1953, after 20 rejections, *Kon-Tiki* finally found a publisher—and an audience. The book is now available in 66 languages.

5. **The Peter Principle by Laurence Peter:** In 1969, after 16 reported rejections, Canadian professor Laurence Peter's business book about bad management finally got a green light from Bantam Books. Within one year, the hardcover version of *The Peter Principle* was in its 15th reprint. Peter went on to write *The Peter Prescription, The Peter Plan,* and the unintentionally amusing *The Peter Pyramid: Will We Ever Get to the Point?* None of Peter's follow-up books did as well as the original, but no one can deny the book's impact on business publishing.

6. **Dubliners by James Joyce:** It took 22 rejections before a publisher took a chance on a young James Joyce in 1914. They didn't take too big of a chance—only 1,250 copies of *Dubliners* were initially published. Joyce's popularity didn't hit right away; out of the 379 copies that sold in the first year, Joyce himself purchased 120 of them. Joyce would go on to be regarded as one of the most influential writers of the 20th century. *Dubliners,* a collection of short stories, is among the most popular of Joyce's titles, which include *A Portrait of the Artist as a Young Man, Finnegans Wake,* and *Ulysses.*

7. **Lorna Doone by Richard Doddridge Blackmore:** You know you've done well when you've got a cookie named after your novel's heroine. Not only does Nabisco's Lorna Doone cookie remind us of Blackmore's classic, there are nearly a dozen big-screen or TV versions of the story, as well. This Devonshire-set romance of rivalry and revenge was turned down 18 times before being published in 1889. Today, Blackmore is considered one of the greatest British authors of the 19th century, though his popularity has waned over time.

8. **Zen and the Art of Motorcycle Maintenance by Robert Pirsig:** Pirsig's manuscript attempts to understand the true meaning of life. By the time it was finally published

in 1974, the book had been turned down 121 times. The editor who finally published *Zen and the Art of Motorcycle Maintenance* said of Pirsig's book, "It forced me to decide what I was in publishing for." Indeed, *Zen* has given millions of readers an accessible, enjoyable book for seeking insight into their own lives.

9. *M*A*S*H* **by Richard Hooker:** Before the television series, there was the film. Before the film, there was the novel. Richard Hooker's unforgettable book about a medical unit serving in the Korean War was rejected by 21 publishers before eventually seeing the light of day. It remains a story of courage and friendship that connects with audiences around the world in times of war and peace.

10. *Carrie* **by Stephen King:** If it hadn't been for Stephen King's wife Tabitha, the iconic image of a young girl in a prom dress covered in pig's blood would not exist. King received 30 rejections for his story of a tormented girl with telekinetic powers, and then he threw it in the trash. Tabitha fished it out. King sent his story around again and, eventually, *Carrie* was published. The novel became a classic in the horror genre and has enjoyed film and TV adaptations as well. Sometimes all it takes is a little encouragement from someone who believes in you.

11. *Gone With the Wind* **by Margaret Mitchell:** The only book that Margaret Mitchell ever published, *Gone With the Wind* won her a Pulitzer Prize in 1937. The story of Scarlett O'Hara and Rhett Butler, set in the South during the Civil War, was rejected by 38 publishers before it was printed. The 1939 movie made of Mitchell's love story, which starred Clark Gable and Vivien Leigh, is the highest grossing Hollywood film of all time (adjusted for inflation).

12. *A Wrinkle in Time* **by Madeleine L'Engle:** The publishing house of Farrar, Straus and Giroux was smart enough to recognize the genius in L'Engle's tale for people of all ages.

Published in 1962, the story was awarded the prestigious Newbery Medal the following year. *Wrinkle* remains one of the best-selling children's books of all time, and the story of precocious children and the magical world they discover was adapted for television in 2001. Still, L'Engle amassed 26 rejections before this success came her way.

13. *Heaven Knows, Mr. Allison* by Charles Shaw: In 1952, Crown Publishing Group in New York took a chance on the story of a shipwreck in the South Pacific. Shaw, an Australian author, was rejected by dozens of publishers on his own continent, and by an estimated 20 British publishing firms, too. By 1957, this humorous tale was made into a movie starring Deborah Kerr and Robert Mitchum. The story and the movie are considered war classics and garnered several Academy Award nominations, including one for Best Writing.

14. *Dune* by Frank Herbert: This epic science-fiction story was rejected by 23 publishers before being accepted by Chilton, a small Philadelphia publisher. *Dune* quickly became a success, winning awards such as the Hugo Award for Best Novel in 1966. *Dune* was followed by five sequels, and though none did as well as the original, a film version of the book starring rock star Sting did quite well and remains a cult favorite.

Going Off Script

The mythically talented writer, an inborn natural whose stories flow freely as from a faucet, is an obstacle to the real and regular people who want to tell stories. Whether you write for fun or with ambitions to publish, having a realistic mental picture of the task ahead will help you feel confident and prepared. Let's debunk some writing myths.

✳ ✳ ✳ ✳

My first draft is perfect.

THE PHRASE "NOBODY'S perfect" is sort of a pointless tautology. Of course nobody is perfect, the same way literally nothing else is ever perfect. The word itself has no relation to reality, the same way the hypothetical circles you learn about in geometry class have no bearing on the shape of round things in reality.

So no draft is perfect, ever, and that isn't a reason to continue to pick at your draft until it's a lacy Swiss cheese of self critique. But no first draft is even proverbially perfect. Especially for short writing that's completed in one inspired burst, to suggest that the work just came out perfect is as good as assigning your talent to a mystical muse.

Writers are introverts.

It would be fun to interview a bunch of people who are married or partnered to writers and ask if this is really the case. Some writers are famously introverted, in the colloquial sense, like virtual recluse Emily Dickinson. But most prose writers, especially, understand that living in the world and being part of that world are how the font of ideas is renewed.

Writers listen to how other people talk, they research and interview people with the jobs they want their characters to believably do, and they understand the importance of a realistic voice. Writers who want to sell their work must be sociable networkers with scrappy self esteem that can take a beating. These are qualities we usually assign to extroverts.

There's something romantic and compelling about a figure like Emily Dickinson, whose work appeared after her death and cast an almost endless shadow. In a way, reclusive writers recognized only posthumously are a form of outsider artist, without the perceived taint of commercial concerns.

You have to sell out to write a bestselling book.

The idea of selling out is inherently kind of a scoldy thing. One lazy explanation for it is that writers who don't feel sufficiently recognized or rewarded can lash out at those who are given sweet publishing deals. In the best of all possible worlds, writers would be happy for each other, full stop, and feel the camaraderie of colleagues rather than the competitive spirit of a zero-sum game.

Individual publishing houses may have set numbers of books they publish per year, and there may be a natural equilibrium to the ebb and flow of the book market. That doesn't mean any writer is subtracting from another writer with their success. But what about other definitions of selling out?

James Patterson is the quintessential sellout by almost any definition. He hires writers to coauthor his books and churns out as many as possible. The interesting thing is that Patterson *had* a superstar career writing his own bestselling novels for many years before the Patterson novel factory opened for business.

Author David Lagercrantz has taken over the *Girl With the Dragon Tattoo* series, which lit the world on fire after the release of the first book in 2005. The original author, Stieg Larsson, had already died, and the manuscripts were found only after his death. Who could be less of a sellout than that? He apparently wrote them as a pure hobby with no steps toward seeking a publisher. The first novel has sold fifteen million copies in the United States alone.

Is David Lagercrantz a "sellout" for picking up the mantle of a beloved series whose author has died? Like Larsson, Lagercrantz is an accomplished journalist. He has published successful books of his own, and his installments in the world of Lisbeth Salander have won awards in addition to being massive bestsellers. He seems to have earned his invitation to the party, and he has even donated part of his profits to literacy organizations. What a sellout!

A real writer sticks with their great idea and doesn't worry about what others want to read.

The perfect artist working in a vacuum is one of the worst myths for any creative person. Anyone who writes is a writer, and there is no "real" writer. If the question is of authenticity, what is authentic, besides an ephemeral word to use to criticize someone's work?

There are great ideas that are never sold. There are mediocre ideas that sell millions of copies. None of it is objectively fair, because again, none of it happens in a vacuum. If a writer finds satisfaction in telling a great story that has no commercial potential at all, they could spend their life telling and retelling that same story and feel great every time they stood up from their desk to stretch.

But there is also nothing wrong with researching what others are reading, thinking about what is successful, and framing your own raw thoughts using those perspectives. Many writers have a list of ideas circulating at any given time, and the right one may pop up at the right time, like the last winning number in the Powerball lottery. A successful book may also kick another writer's incipient idea into becoming a fully developed concept.

Young people can't write good books.

Speculative fiction writer China Mieville's first novel, *King Rat*, was released shortly after he turned 26. In 2013, Mieville spoke with fellow novelist James Bradley about his early novels, making fun of himself: "I can barely empathize with that callow fool. I like the book and I'm proud of it, but to my eyes now, there's a certain slightly embarrassing...it's *very gritty*. I was really gritty."

The argument that young people can't write good books, with the implication being that they can't write good books *yet* because of their relative lack of life experience, precludes many of the world's favorite works. Stephen King published a number of short stories before he sold *Carrie* when he was just 26. *Carrie*, second novel *Salem's Lot*, and third novel *The Shining* form a bewildering three superhits by age 30, and King also found time to release a fourth novel under a pseudonym.

King is both a popular novelist and a genre writer, which critics might say means the rules of age don't apply. But that's exactly the point. If a twentysomething writer wants to publish a novel about the inner workings of an extended family, yes, that writer is probably out of their depth. On the other hand, there's no reason young writers inherently lack storytelling, craftsmanship, or dedication.

Marilynne Robinson's Pulitzer Prize-winning novel *Housekeeping* was published when she was 36. The popular discussion around Robinson usually involves how long she has waited between her relatively few novels. But *Housekeeping* is like a fever dream compared with Robinson's pragmatic later works. If this bewitching psychological quasi-fable is a product of Robinson's younger mind, we should be grateful to her for writing it when she did.

China Mieville's comment about his own early novels vibrates with harmonic resonance because we all know what it's like to feel a little embarrassed about our younger selves. They're more earnest, less damaged, and more vulnerable even without realizing it. And these qualities are valuable in writing itself, but also, as with Marilynne Robinson, as points by which to review a writer's whole career.

There's a profound difference between feeling *entitled* to be published at a young age and being the uncommonly polished and ready young writer. Remember that only children have ever demonstrated the ability we call "photographic memory," with evidence that their imaginations work in much more vivid visions than language can possibly recreate. And a little sublime imagination goes a long way.

Best Baseball Books

The shelf of great books written about the game is a long one, but some stand out even there.

✳ ✳ ✳ ✳

BASEBALL HAS STORIES, baseball has history, and baseball has stats. All three play important roles for every fan's enjoyment of the game. These books do the best job of connecting us to the game we love in one way or another. And we didn't have room to mention the absolutely critical statistical works, such as encyclopedias, that belong on every fan's bookshelf.

Book: *Babe*

Author: Robert Creamer

What's the story?: It's only fair that the greatest player should get one of the greatest biographies.

Why we like it: Ruth comes across as a talented, but largely undisciplined, lovable lug. Which is how we want to think of him.

Book: *Baseball: The Early Years; Baseball: The Golden Age; Baseball: The People's Game*

Author: Harold Seymour

What's the story?: Academic research comes to baseball, and the results are serious yet pleasurable.

Why we like it: The first two volumes, which track professional baseball from its beginnings through the late 1920s, are indispensable. The third, a history of nonprofessional baseball, is truly breathtaking.

Book: *Baseball Before We Knew It*

Author: David Block

What's the story?: Finally, an in-depth study of the question "Where did baseball come from?"

Why we like it: It goes everywhere in search of the answer, and what it delivers is very satisfying.

Book: *The New Bill James Historical Baseball Abstract*

Author: Bill James

What's the story?: Using Sabermetrics to discover the historically best players.

Why we like it: James knows his stuff, and his style is always engaging and appropriately light. He takes his place in the first rank of baseball historians.

Book: *The Boys of Summer*

Author: Roger Kahn

What's the story?: A bittersweet look at what happened to the adored Dodgers of the late 1940s and early '50s when they left baseball and glory to face the often harsh realities of the world.

Why we like it: They were our heroes, but we love and respect them even more when we see them as mere mortals.

Book: *The Glory of Their Times*

Author: Lawrence Ritter

What's the story?: The men who played for and against John McGraw, and with and against Honus Wagner and Christy

Mathewson, relate the tale of baseball life in the first decades of the 20th century.

Why we like it: Their voices leap off the page and draw us in.

Book: *The Hot Stove League*

Author: Lee Allen

What's the story?: Stories from baseball's golden age.

Why we like it: Lee Allen was one of the game's first true historians, and he's a writer with a fine, strong, yet mellow style.

Book: *The Long Season*

Author: Jim Brosnan

What's the story?: It's hard to understand today what a clamor this book set off in the early 1960s. It looked behind the puffery of the sports pages into the actual lives of the players.

Why we like it: It isn't always pretty, but it is fascinatingly honest.

Book: *The New Dickson Baseball Dictionary*

Author: Paul Dickson

What's the story?: The first edition, in 1990, had 5,000 citations; the second, in 1999, had 7,000. A third, underway, should have 10,000.

Why we like it: Baseball's language is as rich as its history, and the two are wedded beautifully under Dickson's talented hand. The definition of "Chinese home run" alone is worth the price of this book.

Book: *Nice Guys Finish Last*

Author: Leo Durocher and Ed Linn

What's the story?: For 50 years, whenever there was a battle going on in baseball, Durocher wasn't far from the middle of it. This is his autobiography—nasty, bristling, and full of the giants of the game, from Branch Rickey, Babe Ruth, and Rabbit Maranville to Jackie Robinson, Willie Mays, and Bobby Thomson.

Why we like it: It's a rare sports book that puts so much lively storytelling between two covers.

Great Civil War Books

What are some other favorite Civil War books? Here's a list of a few—both fiction and nonfiction—in no particular order.

✳   ✳   ✳   ✳

Fiction

***Gone With the Wind* (1936)**—Atlanta's Margaret Mitchell only wrote one book in her entire life—good thing that book was the best seller *Gone With the Wind*. Winning a Pulitzer Prize in 1937, the epic novel tells the story of Scarlett O'Hara and her romances during the Civil War. Mitchell didn't quite get everything right in the first draft, however. She originally wanted Scarlett's first name to be Pansy!

***The Killer Angels* (1974)**—Michael Shaara penned this stirring story of the Battle of Gettysburg, earning himself a Pulitzer Prize. Shaara describes the event through the eyes of Union soldiers and generals, including General John Buford and Colonel Joshua Lawrence Chamberlain, as well as Confederate leaders such as generals James Longstreet and Robert E. Lee. Although it is a work of fiction, many history professors use this in college history classes. The book was also the basis for the 1993 film *Gettysburg*.

***The Last Full Measure* (1998)**—Jeff Shaara picks up where his father left off, dramatizing the Confederate retreat after Gettysburg and the events through to the end of the war as seen by several key players in the conflict. This book rounds out a trilogy that includes Michael Shaara's *The Killer Angels* and Jeff Shaara's 1996 prequel, *Gods and Generals*.

Little Women (1868)—Louisa May Alcott's classic story tells of the lives of the March family and its four daughters—Meg, Jo, Beth, and Amy—during and after the Civil War. This story has been turned into countless movies, a musical, and even an opera. Alcott penned two sequels, *Little Men* and *Jo's Boys*.

The Red Badge of Courage (1895)—Written by Stephen Crane, this longtime best seller tells the story of young Union soldier Henry Fleming and his personal experiences around the time of the Battle of Chancellorsville. *The Red Badge of Courage* has become an indispensable work of literature for classrooms across the United States.

John Brown's Body (1928)—A narrative poem of epic proportions, this book was written by Stephen Vincent Benet and won the Pulitzer Prize in 1929. Benet covers the entire expanse of the war, from Harpers Ferry to Generals Grant and Lee at Appomattox Court House.

North and South (1982)—The first of a three-novel series by John Jakes, North and South relates the friendship of two young men—South Carolinian Orry Main and Pennsylvanian George Hazard—who meet on the way to West Point. When the Civil War splits the friends, the story follows the complex consequences through the rest of the trilogy, which includes *Love and War* and *Heaven and Hell*. The books became enormous hits as three TV miniseries in the 1980s and '90s.

March (2005)—Another look at Louisa May Alcott's March family, this book focuses on the absent father, gone to the war. Geraldine Brooks takes *Little Women* as a starting point to imagine what Meg, Jo, Beth, and Amy's father experienced as a Union chaplain. March is the fourth Pulitzer Prize winner on this list, snagging the award in 2006.

Nonfiction

Battle Cry of Freedom (1988)—Many regard *Battle Cry of Freedom*, written by noted historian James McPherson, as the finest single-volume work on the Civil War. As a professor of American history at Princeton University, McPherson brought life and vision to the American struggle from 1850 to Reconstruction. Many colleges and universities with classes focusing on the war use this book. And yes, it's another Pulitzer Prize winner.

The Civil War: A Narrative (1974)—Author Shelby Foote spent 20 years researching and writing this seminal series on the War Between the States. The 3,000-page, three-volume set was written entirely by hand with an old-fashioned dipped-ink pen. Foote's knowledge led to prominent appearances on Ken Burns's PBS series, *The Civil War*.

Chancellorsville (1996)—Historian Stephen W. Sears penned hundreds of pages on what many consider to be the greatest of Robert E. Lee's victories. But Sears takes a path less chosen, giving much of the credit for Lee's success to luck. Sears is also the author of *Landscape Turned Red: The Battle of Antietam* and *To the Gates of Richmond: The Peninsula Campaign*.

A Stillness at Appomattox (1953)—Aiming to explain the strategies and battles of General Ulysses S. Grant beginning in 1864 until the end of the war in 1865, this well-written book earned author Bruce Catton a Pulitzer Prize in 1954. It is the third in a three-volume series about the Army of the Potomac. The first two are entitled *Mr. Lincoln's Army* and *Glory Road*.

Lincoln at Gettysburg: The Words that Remade America (1992)—The Gettysburg Address is possibly the most famous speech ever given in America, and author Garry Wills takes an in-depth look at it piece by piece, examining Lincoln's influences in writing it and his intentions in delivering it. Wills helps readers gain a new appreciation and understanding of these few but immortal words.

The Life of Johnny Reb: The Common Soldier of the Confederacy (1943)—Bell Irvin Wiley wrote this book and its companion, 1952's *The Life of Billy Yank: The Common Soldier of the Union,* to present the experience of the regular trooper down among the rest of the rank and file. Through contemporary letters and diaries, Wiley portrays what everyday army life was like for all those people whose names we'll never know.

Chapter 12

History

A Real Head-Scratcher

Cutting off an enemy's head and keeping it dates to at least 600,000 years ago. What did headhunters do with those heads?

✳   ✳   ✳   ✳

Sacred Heads

AS BARBARIC AS headhunting might seem, the practitioners had good reasons for doing it. Aboriginal Australians and tribes such as the Dayak in Borneo believed that the head contained the victim's spirit or soul. Taking the head, they thought, took the essence of a person's soul as well as his strength. Chinese soldiers during the Qin Dynasty (221–206 BC) carried the heads of conquered enemies into battle to frighten foes. The heads also served as proof of kills, which enabled soldiers to be paid. Headhunting wasn't always associated with war. The ancient Celts, for example, incorporated it into fertility rites and other ritualistic practices.

Now What?

One problem for headhunters was that it doesn't take long for a severed head to begin to decompose. Some headhunters kept only the skull; they cleaned and boiled the head to remove all tissue and brain matter. Others cooked and ate parts of the head, literally consuming the essence of the conquered foe. Still others painstakingly preserved the heads, some of which are still with us.

In New Zealand, Maori headhunters removed the flesh from the skulls of their enemies, then smoked and dried it. This process preserved distinctive tribal tattoos, which meant that the deceased could be identified. Some of these heads were eventually sold to Europeans for private collections or museums, and Maori are today attempting to reclaim the dried heads of their ancestors. In New Guinea, tribes mummified the entire head and sometimes wore it as a mask.

Some of the best-preserved heads come from the Jivaro (or Shuar) tribe of South America. These are shrunken heads, known as *tsantsa*. They are unique among headhunting trophies because of the way the Jivaro preserved them.

There is evidence that some Allied soldiers took skulls as trophies and souvenirs during World War II, and there are indications of similar practices during the Vietnam War. As recently as 2001, the Borneo Dayaks practiced headhunting during conflicts with another ethnic group, the Madurese. Reports of headhunting still surface occasionally, so if you're visiting a remote locale, you are well advised to stay vigilant.

History's Lady Pirates

"Lady pirate" may not sound like a job description our great-great-grandmothers would have gone for, but according to historians, many women did indeed pursue lives of plunder on the high seas.

✳ ✳ ✳ ✳

The Roll Call

ONE OF THE earliest female pirates was Artemesia of Persia, whose fleet preyed upon the city-states of Greece during the fifth century BC. The Athenians put a price of 10,000 drachmas on her head, but there's no record of anyone ever collecting it. Teuta of Illyria (circa 230 BC) was a pirate queen who led raids against Roman ships. Another notable female marauder was Alfhild (circa the ninth century AD), a Viking princess who reportedly kept a viper for a pet and whose all-female longboat crew ravaged the Scandinavian coast. Prince Alf of Denmark captured Alfhild, but her beauty so overwhelmed him that he proposed marriage instead of beheading her, and they ruled together happily ever after. At least that's one story; there's a little blarney in every pirate yarn.

Legend has it that Grania O'Malley (1530–1603), who was captain of a pirate fleet based in Ireland, gave birth to her son Toby while at sea. The next day, blunderbuss in hand, she led her men to victory over a Turkish warship.

Madame Ching (circa 1785–1844), perhaps the most notorious of all the pirate queens, ruled her league of 2,000 ships and 70,000 men with an iron hand—anyone who was caught stealing loot for private use was executed immediately. But she was relatively kind to some of her prisoners: For example, she ordered that captive women and children *not* be hung by their hair over the sides of her ships.

Anne Bonny and Mary Read

Closer to home, Anne Bonny (1698–1782) and Mary Read (circa 1690–1721) dressed as men and served aboard pirate ships that sailed the Caribbean. They met when Mary, disguised as one James Morris, joined a crew that was commanded by Anne and her husband, Calico Jack Rackham.

One night while the men were sleeping off a rum binge below deck, Anne and Mary were left to face down a British man-of-war alone. Despite their bravery, their ship was quickly captured and the pirates were hauled off to prison. After learning that Calico Jack had received a death sentence, Anne's last words to him were: "I am sorry...but had you had fought like a man, you need not have been hanged like a dog."

Anne and Mary escaped death by "pleading their bellies," meaning they both were conveniently pregnant. Mary then died in childbirth a few months later; Anne dropped from historical view. She is said to have married again and become a respectable matron in the city of Charleston, South Carolina. But one rumor suggests that Mary only pretended to die, and that she and Anne escaped to New Orleans, where they raised their kids and occasionally plied their former trade—fast friends and pirates of the Caribbean to the very end.

Unlucky Friday the 13th

It's probably the most pervasive superstition in North America, Western Europe, and Australia.

✳ ✳ ✳ ✳

It Started With the Ancients

WHAT EXACTLY MAKES Friday the 13th more luckless than, say, Tuesday the fifth? The answer is deeply rooted in Biblical, mythological, and historical events.

Friday and the number 13 have been independently sinister since ancient times—maybe since the dawn of humans. For Christians, Friday and the number 13 are of the utmost significance. Christ was crucified on Friday, and 13 is the number of people who were present at the Last Supper. Judas, the disciple who betrayed Jesus, was the 13th member of the party to arrive.

Groups of 13 may be one of the earliest and most concrete taboos associated with the number. It's believed that both the ancient Vikings and Hindus thought it unpropitious to have 13 people gather together in one place. Up until recently, French socialites known as *quatorziens* (fourteeners) made themselves available as fourteenth guests to spare dinner parties from ominous ends.

Some trace the infamy of the number 13 back to ancient Norse culture. According to mythology, twelve gods had arrived to a banquet, when in walked an uninvited 13th guest—Loki, the god of mischief. Loki tricked the blind god Hother into throwing a spear of mistletoe at Balder, the beloved god of light. Balder fell dead, and the whole Earth turned dark.

In modern times, 13 continues to be a number to avoid. About 80 percent of high-rise buildings don't have a 13th floor, many airports skip gate number 13, and you won't find a room thirteen in some hospitals and hotels.

An Infamous Combination

How did Friday and 13 become forever linked as the most disquieting day on the calendar? It just may be that Friday was unlucky and 13 was unlucky, so a combination of the two was simply a double jinx. However, one theory holds that all this superstition came not as a result of convergent taboos, but of a single historical event.

On Friday, October 13, 1307, King Philip IV of France ordered the arrest of the revered Knights Templars. Tortured and forced to confess to false charges of heresy, blasphemy, and wrongdoing, hundreds of knights were burned at the stake. It's said that sympathizers of the Templars then condemned Friday the 13th as the most evil of days.

No one has been able to document if this eerie tale is indeed the origin of this superstition. And really, some scholars are convinced that it's nothing more than a phenomenon created by 20th-century media. So sufferers of paraskevidekatriaphobia (a pathological fear of Friday the 13th), take some comfort—or at least throw some salt over your shoulder.

Don't Mess With Her!

Universal gender equality may be a relatively new social concept, but history records plenty of women who went out and got respect anyway—by force, if necessary.

✳   ✳   ✳   ✳

Then-CPT Kim Campbell: Born in 1975, this Air Force Academy graduate became an A-10 Warthog (ground support) pilot. On April 7, 2003, Iraqi ground fire shot her Hog to Swiss cheese, knocking out her hydraulics. Refusing to eject over Baghdad, she managed to land the plane safely without hydraulics—an amazing feat that won her the Distinguished Flying Cross (Valor).

Phoolan Devi: Born into a low–ranking Indian caste in 1963, she became a *dacoit* (bandit) in her teens. After being captured and gang-raped by a rival gang from the Thakur (landowner) caste, she led an attack that massacred 21 of their number, including some of her rapists. She eventually surrendered, did prison time, and became a parliamentary champion of the Dalit ('untouchable') caste until her assassination in 2001.

Dahomey's *Mino*: From the early 1700s to the late 1800s, these women formed a fearsome regiment in the Dahomeyan king's military. Executing prisoners was part of their desensitization training. Superbly conditioned, and dedicated to winning or dying, they rarely met defeat until the French Foreign Legion arrived with machine guns in the 1890s.

'Stagecoach' Mary Fields: Born around 1832 into slavery in Tennessee, she went west some years after the Civil War. Fields wound up supervising construction work in Cascade, Montana. One roughneck resented taking orders from an African American woman, and hit her; Fields shot him dead. She drove the local mailcoach for years, and died a local legend in 1914.

Fredegund: Born a slave attendant around 550, she was a Merovingian Frankish queen with a ruthless rep. She seduced her way into the affections of King Chilperic I, arranging oft-sadistic assassinations to clear the way for his ambitions (which were often more hers than his). When Chilperic died, Fredegund maneuvered similarly to advance her son Chlothar's prospects. Many Frankish nobles breathed easier after her death in 597.

Tomoe Gozen: Born in 1157 in Japan, this samurai warrior was an expert rider, swordswoman, archer, and wielder of the naginata (a sort of halberd). In a culture and caste where honor and bravery were all, Tomoe was Lord Minamoto's preferred first captain in battle. Stories conflict; some say she retired from arms and died peacefully in 1247. Others say she sought and found death in battle grieving her liege's slaying.

Violette Morris: Born in 1893 in France, she believed she could do anything a man could do—and proved it as a boxer, wrestler, Olympic medalist, and race car driver. Morris actually had a double mastectomy just to better fit into cars! Sadly, during World War II, she went to work for the Gestapo occupiers. The Resistance gunned her down from ambush in 1944.

Jennifer Musa: Born into a large County Kerry Irish Catholic family in 1917, she fell in love with a young Afghan Baluchistani prince in college. Moving to his rugged homeland, then going into Pakistani exile with him, she defied gender restrictions and got away with it. After her husband's 1956 death, she became her adopted people's foremost advocate. Called 'The Irish Queen of Balochistan,' Musa passed away in 2008.

Sr. Lt. Anna Yegorova: Born in 1916, this Soviet pilot started out flying harassment bombing against the Nazi invaders, but unlike most Soviet female pilots, she flew with the men. She survived wartime captivity after her Il-2 Sturmovik was shot down, then survived the NKVD persecution common to all captured Soviet personnel. Named a Heroine of the Soviet Union, Yegorova died in 2009.

Scarlet Woman

The most-accused Salem "witch" was hung, not burned at the stake.

✳ ✳ ✳ ✳

Contrary to popular belief, not all so-called "witches" were burned at the stake. Just look at Bridget Bishop, the first person hanged during the Salem witchcraft trials of 1692. Bishop held the dubious honor of being accused by more individuals of witchcraft than any other defendant.

Bishop was a widow who remarried to Thomas Oliver in 1666. From the start, the match was abusive—Bishop's face would often be bruised, and many times the couple were publicly chastised for fighting. Her husband claimed that Bishop "sat up all night conversing with the Devil." Ultimately, after Oliver died, hysteria against Bishop (and the belief that she was a witch) grew, and a warrant was issued for Bishop's arrest on the charge of witchcraft.

A long list of detractors took the stand against her, including her brother-in-law. Within eight days, Bishop was charged, tried, and hung. As it was recorded, "Now the honest men of Salem could sleep in peace, sure that the Shape of Bridget would trouble them no more."

It's Over There—The Real Battle of Bunker Hill

In June 1775, two months after the start of the Revolutionary War, the Battle of Bunker Hill erupted across the Charles River from Boston. But where, exactly, did the fighting take place?

❋ ❋ ❋ ❋

THE LOGICAL ANSWER is, of course, on Bunker Hill. History books continue to cite that location more than 230 years after the fact—but they actually have it wrong.

Word had gotten around that British troops were planning an attack from Boston, Massachusetts, where they held complete control. On June 16, nearly 1,000 American militiamen led by Colonel William Prescott dug into the highest land in the area—a spot known as Bunker's Hill. But the commander thought better of the location and moved his troops a half mile closer to Boston, a lower elevation referred to as Breed's Hill. The soldiers quickly built a barrier of dirt that was 6 feet high, 80 feet across, and 160 feet long.

The next morning, British major general William Howe led more than 2,200 redcoats from Boston against the militiamen. But they were hampered by a lack of boats, lousy maps, and low tides. While cannons fired against the patriots across the Charles River, Howe struggled to reach Charlestown itself. By mid-afternoon, his soldiers were finally ready to make their assault on Breed's Hill.

As the British advanced, Prescott famously yelled, "Don't fire until you see the whites of their eyes—then shoot low!" It took the Brits three separate charges to eventually overtake the position and capture Charlestown. But they paid a high price, with more than a thousand deaths and injuries among the troops. The militia, which had grown to more than 2,500 soldiers, suffered close to 400 casualties. But the grit and determination of the Americans led Howe to never again fight a battle in Massachusetts.

Culture and History of the Cherokee

When 16th-century European explorers first began exploring what would later be called the United States, they found a land already inhabited by a variety of groups. Among these were a people living in the southeast corner of the continent who referred to themselves as the Aniyunwiya, or "the principal people." Their Creek Indian neighbors, however, called them the Tsalagi, and the white tongue morphed that word into Cherokee, the name generally used today.

✳ ✳ ✳ ✳

THE ORIGIN OF the Cherokee is uncertain at best. Tribal legend speaks of an ancient time of migration, which some historians have projected as far back as the time of a land bridge linking North America to Asia. Linguists report that the Cherokee language is linked to the Iroquois, who lived far to the north; others point out that traditional Cherokee crafts bear a resemblance to those of the people of the Amazon basin in South America. Regardless of their origin, the Cherokee held sway over a great deal of land when Spaniard Hernando de Soto made contact with the tribe in the 1540s.

De Soto did not find the gold he was looking for in Cherokee territory. What he did find was a people who had heard of his horrific treatment of other tribes and did everything they could to hasten his exit from their land. They quickly traded him some food and other supplies—including two buffalo skins, the first European contact with the animal, which at the time ranged as far east as the Atlantic coast—and suggested that he might be better off looking to the west. With that, de Soto headed off.

The total number de Soto found living in their traditional lands is a matter of speculation; the oldest reliable count dates from 130 years later, long after the smallpox the Spaniard left behind had wreaked havoc on the tribe. The disease left somewhere between 25,000 to 50,000 people alive after killing an estimated 75 percent of the natives.

Culture Shock

The Cherokee were quick to realize that white intruders were there to stay, and they did what they could to adapt to the changing world. On the arrival of the British, they became active trading partners, seeking to improve their situation through the acquisition of European goods and guns. They also became military allies—by many accounts, a trade at which they excelled—fighting with the British against the French and later against the Colonists in the American Revolution. The British, however, always viewed their Cherokee allies with suspicion, the effects of which ranged from the occasional massacre to the imposition of treaties demanding that the British be allowed to construct forts in Cherokee territory. This ceding of property was only the beginning of one of the biggest land-grabs in history, culminating in the 1838 Trail of Tears, in which 17,000 Cherokee were forcibly sent west, resulting in thousands of deaths along the way.

Part of the difficulty with the early treaties was that the Europeans were in the habit of making them with anyone who claimed they represented the tribe; in reality, nobody could speak for all of the Cherokee. Their system was one of local autonomous government, with each village being responsible for its own affairs. The individual villages even had two chiefs: a White Chief in charge of domestic decisions and a Red Chief in charge of war and general relations with outsiders. The society itself was matrilineal and focused on a spiritual balance that the Cherokee believed existed between lower and higher worlds, with the earth caught in the middle. Europeans were ill-suited to understanding such a culture. In turn, the Cherokee realized that their society was ill-suited to dealing with Europeans.

The Times, They Are A-Changin'

Cherokee society proved up to the challenge, however. Part of the advance was because of Sequoyah. Sequoyah was a silversmith who devised the first syllabary for the Cherokee language in 1821. Although he was illiterate, he had observed the white man's system of written communication. His Talking Leaves system, consisting of more than 80 symbols that each represented a syllable of Cherokee speech, was rapidly adopted and soon the Cherokee had a higher literacy rate than most of their white neighbors. One immediate result was the publication of a newspaper, *The Cherokee Phoenix*, in 1828; it was soon renamed the *Cherokee Phoenix and Indian Advocate* to indicate that its pages addressed issues faced by Native Americans of all tribes.

Along with the alphabet, the 1820s proved a time of change for Cherokee society as a whole. Realizing that they must deal with the white man on his terms, the Cherokee had unified their autonomous tribes by the close of the decade, adopting a constitution that provided for a formal judiciary and elected legislature, electing John Ross as principal chief, and declaring themselves to be an independent nation. They took the nearly unheard of step of sending Indian representatives to Washington, D.C., to persuade both the Congress and the Supreme Court that the United States ought to be held to both the spirit as well as the letter of various treaties that were signed over the years. However, despite favorably impressing many with the quality of their arguments, their efforts proved fruitless, and the Cherokee joined their Native American brothers—being treated as second-class citizens for decades to come.

The repercussions from the almost unimaginable changes imposed on the Cherokee as European settlers came to dominate the continent echo to the current day. However, Cherokee society has proved itself equal to the task, and today its people are the most numerous of any Native American population, and the leadership of various parts of the tribe continues to actively work to remedy past inequities.

Famous Figures in Ghost Research

These days, it seems as though you can't watch an hour of TV without running into people who tout themselves as ghost researchers. And while most of these folks have only been working in the field for a few years, ghost hunters have been chasing after things that go bump in the night for centuries. Here are a few pioneers in the field of paranormal research ... some of the names might surprise you.

✳   ✳   ✳   ✳

The Fox Sisters

OFTEN CREDITED WITH inadvertently starting the Spiritualism movement, the Fox Sisters—14-year-old Maggie and 11-year-old Kate—spoke to a ghost in their Hydesville, New York, home in 1848. The spirit, whom the girls referred to as Mr. Splitfoot, would communicate by knocking responses to the girls' questions.

By 1850, the sisters were traveling the country giving demonstrations on how to communicate with spirits. According to them, Mr. Splitfoot had revealed that he was the ghost of a man named Charles B. Rosma, a peddler who had been murdered and buried in the basement of the Fox home.

Word about the mysterious gifts of the Fox Sisters quickly spread, and before long, they were conducting séances in crowded theaters nationwide and privately for the wealthy members of society. Fame had its price, however. Skeptics and scientists alike attempted to debunk the sisters' claims by placing the two inside restrictive boxes or asking them to perform their séances in broad daylight. No confirmed sign of trickery was ever detected, and years later, the Fox Sisters retired with their reputations intact.

But in an 1888 interview published in a New York newspaper, Maggie stated that she and her sister had faked the whole enterprise and that the ghostly noises were nothing more than them popping their joints and knuckles. However, a year later, Maggie recanted her story, leaving everyone to wonder what the real truth was when she passed away in 1893. The previous year, Kate had passed away without ever confirming or denying her sister's claims.

A final twist to the story came in 1904, when a group of children who were playing in the abandoned Fox house discovered a false wall. Behind it, they found the skeletal remains of an adult male. Unfortunately, the remains could not be identified, but believers point to this as proof that there had indeed been a peddler murdered and buried in the Fox Sisters' basement.

Harry Houdini

While he will forever be remembered as a magician, Harry Houdini was also a passionate psychic investigator. When his mother died in 1913, he was so devastated that he started going to psychics to attempt to contact her spirit. Upon seeing that many of the psychics he visited were using the same sleight-of-hand tricks that magicians used, Houdini set out on a personal quest to expose those who were trying to deceive the public. He would often travel in disguise, lest the psychics recognize him. He also supposedly developed a series of devices that could restrain psychics from moving, thereby preventing them from faking paranormal activity after lights were extinguished. Forever the optimist, Houdini never abandoned his research or his belief that life continued after death, even promising his wife that if he could reach out to her after he died, he would. He even went so far as to create a secret code that only the two of them knew, so that if his wife was given a message from a psychic, she would know whether or not it was legit. Despite conducting several public séances after Houdini's death, she was unable to contact his spirit.

Harry Price

In 1920, Harry Price joined the Society for Psychical Research and almost immediately began to make a name for himself by exposing hoaxers. He began by showing how certain photographers—who claimed to capture photos of ghosts—were simply performing double exposures. He also found that the "ectoplasm" that a medium was supposedly spewing from her mouth was nothing more than cheesecloth.

In 1929, after spending most of the decade conducting experiments and researching ghosts, Price began the investigation that would make him famous: Borley Rectory, a building in Essex, England, that was long rumored to be haunted. In the late 1930s, after the last residents of the rectory moved out, Price rented the building for an entire year and conducted a series of investigations. The enormous amount of activity that Price encountered during his time there—including a psychic contacting two spirits that were inhabiting the building—turned this avowed skeptic into a believer.

Allegedly, one of the spirits—a ghostly nun who claimed to have been murdered on the property—went so far as to scribble messages to the researchers on the rectory's walls. The other spirit, which identified itself as Sunex Amures, claimed it would burn the rectory down that very evening. It didn't, but the rectory did catch fire and was destroyed a year later, in early 1939. When Price returned to the property after the fire, he excavated the cellar and discovered unidentifiable remains there. Price's research at Borley Rectory resulted in two books: *The Most Haunted House in England* (1940) and *The End of Borley Rectory* (1946).

Peter Underwood

As a boy, Peter Underwood became fascinated with ghosts and the paranormal because his grandparents lived in a haunted house. Underwood later spent several years compiling interviews with everyone who'd been involved with the original 1929 investigation of Borley Rectory, including Harry Price himself. Along the way, he joined the Society for Psychical Research and was also personally invited by Price to join his Ghost Club, for which he served as president from 1962 until 1993, when he left to serve as president of the Ghost Club Society.

When Price passed away in 1948, Underwood was one of only a handful of people entrusted with the privilege of reviewing all of Price's research. In addition, Underwood has been actively investigating hauntings for decades. His most famous case is his lengthy investigation of Queen's House in Greenwich, England, where perhaps the most famous ghost photograph of all time—a snapshot of a hunched-over figure in white pulling itself up a staircase—was obtained.

Hans Holzer

Perhaps no other individual is more responsible for bringing ghost research to the masses than Hans Holzer. Beginning in the 1960s, Holzer wrote more than 140 books about the paranormal, including many on cases that he investigated firsthand. When not writing books, Holzer taught parapsychology at the New York Institute of Technology and worked with some of the world's most famous psychics, including Sybil Leek and Ethel Johnson-Meyers. It was Johnson-Meyers who, in 1977, accompanied Holzer on his most well-known case: the investigation of the infamous "Amityville Horror" house located at

112 Ocean Avenue in Amityville, New York. The team's work resulted in the claims that the house was built on sacred Native American land (which may have included a burial ground), which caused angry Native American spirits to haunt the property.

Loyd Auerbach

Since receiving his master's degree in parapsychology from John F. Kennedy University in 1981, Loyd Auerbach has been a major player in the ghost-research community. In addition to conducting investigations across the United States, Auerbach also serves as the director of the Office of Paranormal Investigations.

While conducting his research—which has included many famous locations, such as Alcatraz—Auerbach constantly looks for ways to standardize ghost-hunting procedures and protocols. He has written several "how-to" books about investigations, including *A Paranormal Casebook: Ghost Hunting in the New Millennium*, which was published in 2005.

Auerbach believes that one visit to a location does not constitute an investigation. Rather, ghost hunters need to continually visit places and constantly gather data. For that reason, Auerbach has made numerous research trips to historic sites such as the USS *Hornet*—which is currently anchored in Alameda, California—and the Moss Beach Distillery in Moss Beach, California. In fact, Auerbach has been visiting the Distillery since 1991 and has reportedly had several encounters with its resident ghost, "the Blue Lady."

Who Cracked the Liberty Bell?

Aside from the Statue of Liberty, the Liberty Bell might be the most enduring symbol of America. It draws millions of tourists to its home in Philadelphia each year. Yet for all of its historical resonance, anybody who has been to Independence Hall will attest that it's not the most attractive bell in existence.

✳ ✳ ✳ ✳

IN FACT, IT looks kind of cruddy, due mostly to the enormous crack that runs down its side. Whom can we blame for the destruction of this national treasure? No one has come forth to take responsibility, though there is no shortage of theories regarding the crack's origin.

A quick survey of the Liberty Bell's rich history shows that it has been fraught with problems since it was struck. The original bell, which was constructed by British bell-founder Lester & Pack (which is still in business today as Whitechapel Bell Foundry), arrived in Philadelphia in 1752. Unfortunately, it cracked upon its very first tolling—an inauspicious beginning for a future national monument.

Disgruntled Philadelphians called upon two local foundry workers, John Pass and John Stow, to recast the bell, with firm instructions to make it less brittle. The artisans did as they were told, but the new bell was so thick and heavy that the sound of it tolling resembled that of an axe hitting a tree. Pass and Stow were told to try again, and finally, in June 1753, the bell that we see today was hung in the State House.

Of course, in those days, it wasn't known as the Liberty Bell. It got that nickname about seventy-five years later, when abolitionists adopted its inscription—PROCLAIM LIBERTY THROUGHOUT ALL THE LAND UNTO ALL THE INHABITANTS THEREOF—as a rallying cry for the anti-slavery movement. By that time, the bell was already an important part of the

American mythos, having allegedly been rung in alarm to announce the onset of the Revolutionary War after the skirmishes at Lexington and Concord, and in celebration when independence was proclaimed in 1776.

Exactly when the crack happened is a matter of debate amongst historians, though experts have been able to narrow it down to between 1817 and 1846. There are, in fact, several possible dates that are offered by the National Park Service, which is charged with caring for the bell well after the fact. The bell may have been cracked:

* in 1824, when it tolled to celebrate French Revolutionary War hero Marquis de Lafayette's visit to Philadelphia,

* in 1828, while ringing to honor the passage of the Catholic Emancipation Act in England, or

* in 1835, while ringing during the funeral procession of statesman and justice John Marshall.

All of these theories, however, are discounted by numerous contemporary documents—such as newspaper reports and town-hall meeting minutes—that discuss the bell without mentioning the crack. In fact, the first actual reference to the Liberty Bell being cracked occurred in 1846, when the Philadelphia newspaper *Public Ledger* noted that in order for the bell to be rung in honor of George Washington's birthday that year, a crack had to first be repaired. The newspaper states that the bell had cracked "long before," though in an article published several years later, "long before" is specified as having been during the autumn of 1845, a matter of a few months.

Unfortunately, the paper gives no explanation as to how the bell cracked or who did it. Nor does it explain something that, when confronted by the crack in the bell, many viewers ignore: Not only were the bell-makers fairly shoddy craftsmen, they were also terrible spellers. In the inscription, the name of the state in which the bell resides is spelled "Pensylvania."

Will the Real Buccaneers Please Stand Up?

Don't rely on Edith Wharton's novel The Buccaneers *for a glimpse into a gilded age. Its heroines had real-life counterparts: Women who crossed an ocean to rule the social world.*

✳ ✳ ✳ ✳

A Sense of Entitlement

IN THE LATE 19th century, many English aristocrats found themselves in the uncomfortable position of being "land rich and cash poor." Their lofty titles and grand estates couldn't save them from impending financial doom, but marriages to wealthy young American women sure could. And there were many, many "nouveau riche" American parents who were more than happy to facilitate these marriages of convenience—as long as it meant securing their social status on both sides of the Atlantic.

The girls who willingly (or unwillingly) traded their families' money for titles and breeding are sometimes referred to as "buccaneers," after Edith Wharton's unfinished novel *The Buccaneers*. (Wharton died during the writing process in 1937, and the novel was published unfinished in 1938.) Wharton, born Edith Newbold Jones, intimately knew the privileged world she wrote about. Indeed, her blood was so blue that some historians believe the phrase "Keeping up with the Joneses" began as a reference to her family. *The Buccaneers* followed five rich American girls as they traveled to London and made their debuts during "The Season," that lovely time of year when aristocrats left their country homes to search for suitable brides while living it up in the city.

For Love? No, Mostly Money

But while Wharton's book was filled with glamour and drama, its stories were just that: fictional stories. Want the real scoop?

Turn to the true "buccaneers" of the 1870s, '80s, and '90s—the accounts of these women are just as exciting, not to mention true. Perhaps the most famous was Consuelo Vanderbilt. Born in 1877 to a socially ambitious mother and a father who had made millions in the railroad, Consuelo knew from an early age that her most important duty—her only duty, really—was to marry as well as she possibly could. She was even named after a friend of her mother's who had "overcome" a part-Hispanic background to marry an English viscount.

Consuelo was a raving beauty and succeeded beyond her mother's wildest dreams—she attracted the attention of many European and English aristocrats. Unfortunately, however, Consuelo was in love with a respectable but relatively undistinguished American, Winthrop Rutherfurd. Her mother would hear nothing of it and went to great lengths—even faking serious illness—to get her daughter to agree to marry Charles Spencer-Churchill, the ninth Duke of Marlborough. Eventually, Consuelo gave in—and spent three miserable decades in the marriage before it was annulled.

A Brazen Buccaneer

Consuelo had followed another "buccaneer" who had also married into the Churchill family: Jennie Jerome. The daughter of wealthy New York banker Leonard Jerome and his wife, Clara, Jennie grew into such an unconventional beauty that rumors flew about her true parentage and ethnic heritage (one observer noted that there was "more of the panther than of the woman in her look"), however no evidence was ever presented to validate the speculations.

Jennie was a passionate woman with a wild side, and her first marriage to Lord Randolph Churchill, third son (second surviving) of the seventh Duke of Marlborough, didn't slow her down. Soon after giving birth to their son Winston (Britain's future prime minister), she was back on the scene in London. Jennie's second son, John, is believed to have been squired by

Evelyn Boscawen, the seventh Viscount Falmouth. And her third and last marriage was to Montague Phippen Porch, a man three years younger than Winston!

The Democratic-Republican Party

The name of the Democratic-Republican Party, which held the presidency from 1801 to 1829, now sounds like a contradiction in terms. It was the party of Thomas Jefferson and James Madison, founded in the early 1790s to oppose Alexander Hamilton's Federalist Party. Members of the party first called themselves "Republicans" to stress their antimonarchical stance. Federalists began to call their opponents "Democratic-Republicans" to stress their sympathies with the French Revolution, and the Republicans eventually came to refer to themselves the same way.

Neither modern major party really encompasses the core issues of the Democratic-Republican Party. Its members believed in literal constitutional interpretation and states' rights (as opposed to a strong federal government). The party favored the interests of workers and farmers, was unfriendly to banking and mercantile interests, and abhorred national debt. Its foreign policy generally took the side of the French in the on going Franco-British squabbles. During the John Quincy Adams administration (1825–29), the Democratic-Republican Party gradually split into National Republican and Democratic factions. John Quincy Adams, the last Democratic-Republican president, ran on the National Republican ticket when he lost his 1828 reelection bid.

Early Settlers Use First Nation Tribes as Scapegoat

In an early instance of flock mentality, Mormons in Utah in 1857 ran across a wagon train of families on their way to California. No one is exactly sure why, but for some reason the church members felt threatened by the travelers, banded together, and decided to attack them.

But they didn't want to be blamed for the attack, so they disguised themselves as Native Americans, and recruited some Paiute Indians to help them out. The ambushed travelers defended themselves for five days, after which the so-called "Mormon Militia" approached with white flags to signal a truce. The travelers accepted, hoping for basic provisions as they were taken into Mormon protection. But as soon as they surrendered, the mob once again turned on them and murdered the last of them.

The incident has been a source of shame within the Mormon community, who initially denied their role in the massacre, blaming the Paiute Indians. But eventually, Mormon leaders admitted that the Mormon Militia participated, although they emphasized that Brigham Young, the church's prophet and president at the time, was not involved. Today, the church maintains a monument in the meadow where the massacre occurred to honor those who were murdered.

Exposing the Sundance Kid

Butch Cassidy and the Sundance Kid, *released in 1969, is considered one of the most charming and entertaining Westerns ever made. The movie depicts Sundance as a ruthless, though charismatic, gunfighter. But was he a good shot?*

✳   ✳   ✳   ✳

THE FILM, OF course, features Paul Newman and Robert Redford in the title roles, and as the Sundance Kid, Redford displayed exceptional skill in handling six-guns. William Goldman's screenplay describes the outlaw's pistol prowess during the climax of the movie this way: "[He is] firing with both guns, turning around and around, firing as he spins, and maybe he wasn't the greatest gunman that ever lived but then again, maybe he was…"

A Relatively Sedate Sundance

The immensely popular motion picture established the Sundance Kid as a deadly fast-draw shooter to be hailed alongside Wild Bill Hickok, Billy the Kid, and Wyatt Earp. But facts reveal that during his career of outlawry, the Sundance Kid rarely fired his guns and never killed anyone.

From August 1887 to February 1889, young Harry Longabaugh was incarcerated for horse theft in the county jail at Sundance, Wyoming, an experience that produced his famous nickname. The Sundance Kid became a member of Butch Cassidy's Wild Bunch, but most of the gang's bank and train robberies were pulled off without bloodshed.

Following a train robbery in 1899, the Sundance Kid and three other gang members had to shoot their way past a posse, but the only casualty was Sheriff Joe Hazen, who was killed by Harvey Logan. Sundance and Butch then fled to South America.

Hot Shot...Not!

The next year, Butch and Sundance were jumped by Bolivian soldiers, and the Kid apparently was killed in the first volley. It seems that screenwriter Goldman was right about one thing: "Maybe he wasn't the greatest gunman that ever lived..."

Remember the Alamo, Correctly

A mistaken legend holds that no one survived the Alamo.

✳   ✳   ✳   ✳

A Desperate Situation

THE SIEGE OF the Alamo began on February 23, 1836, when the army of General Antonio Lopez de Santa Anna surrounded the San Antonio mission. It proved to be a key event in the Texas struggle for independence from Mexico. Fewer than 200 volunteers defended the Alamo for 13 days against Santa Anna's estimated 6,100 troops. They were led by William B. Travis and included such famous names as knife man Jim Bowie and adventurer and former congressman Davy Crockett. By sunrise on March 6, 1836, the Alamo had fallen, and virtually all the Texans bearing arms lay dead or dying.

The Survivors

Although the exact number of survivors is not entirely clear, documents indicate that as many as 20 women, children, and slaves survived the famous battle. Some of the defenders had brought family members into the Alamo, and a number of them were spared by the conquering Mexican army.

Several slaves owned by members of the volunteer army also survived the siege—pointedly, two were owned by the aforementioned leaders William Travis and Jim Bowie. One member of the Alamo rebels, a former Mexican soldier, survived the battle by claiming to have been a prisoner of the Texan volunteers.

With a Whistle in His Hand

"The Ballad of Casey Jones" was first sung in 1900, and more than 40 versions of the catchy tune have been recorded in the years since. Despite his folkloric status, however, Casey Jones was a real person.

* * * *

JOHN LUTHER JONES was born in 1863 and grew up in Cayce, Kentucky. While working as a railroad engineer on the Illinois Central Railroad, known as the IC, his fellow railroad men dubbed him Cayce Jones after his hometown. His wife mistakenly spelled it Casey in her letters to him, and the name stuck. Without the popular folk song, however, it's unlikely anyone would remember Casey Jones today.

The ballad tells of Jones's heroic death in April 1900, when he gave his life to save the passengers on the train he was driving. After his death, Jones's friend Wallace Saunders, an engine wiper for the IC, coined the lyrics and set them to the tune of a popular song at the time called "Jimmie Jones." Soon it was sung all along the IC. In 1909, vaudeville performers T. Lawrence Seibert and Eddie Newton had the song published under the title "Casey Jones: The Brave Engineer."

Although the ballad celebrates Jones's heroism, an investigation concluded that he was responsible for the train accident that took his life. In the early morning hours of April 30, Jones drove engine 382 toward the town of Vaughn, Mississippi. A disabled freight train on the same track could not clear the way, and Jones slammed on the airbrakes to slow his train. He was unable to avoid a collision, but because of his quick actions, only the caboose suffered impact. Jones's body was discovered in the wreckage with one hand on the brake lever and the other, as the song correctly suggests, on the whistle chord.

A Real Bag Lady

Brown paper bags are so ubiquitous that we take them for granted. It's time to give some props to the person who made them possible: a 19th-century inventor named Margaret Knight.

✳ ✳ ✳ ✳

A Can-Do Attitude

CONSIDER THE FAMILIAR, flat-bottom brown paper bag: It's useful and utterly simple. Now get a sheet of brown paper, a pair of scissors, and some glue, and try to make one yourself. Not so simple, huh?

In 1870, Margaret Knight of the Columbia Paper Bag Company in Springfield, Massachusetts, was doing the same kind of puzzling over paper bags. Back then, the only paper bags that were being manufactured by machine were the narrow, envelope kind, with a single seam at the bottom. Flimsy and easily broken, they were despised by merchants and shoppers alike. The paper bag business was not booming. So Maggie Knight set out to build a better bag.

Not Her First Invention

Born in 1838, Knight had been tinkering with tools since childhood; while other girls played with dolls, she excelled at making sleds and kites. She was especially fascinated by heavy machinery. At the age of 12, Knight invented a stop-motion safety device for automatic looms after witnessing an accident in a textile mill that nearly cost a worker his finger. Though never patented, her invention was widely employed throughout the industry.

During her 20s and early 30s, Knight tried her hand at several occupations before finally landing at Columbia Paper Bag. Working alone at night in her boarding house, she designed a machine that could cut, fold, and glue sheets of paper into sturdy, flat-bottom bags. This time, she applied for a patent. On July 11, 1871, Patent No. 116842 was issued to Margaret E. Knight for a "Bag Machine."

Her employer was eager to implement her design, but the male workers that were hired to build and install the new machines refused to take direction from a woman, until they were convinced that Maggie was indeed the "mother" of this particular invention.

Beyond Bags

Knight also had to fend off a challenge to her patent by a rival inventor, who had spied on the construction of Knight's first prototype. The court decided in Knight's favor, and she persisted in her career.

After leaving Columbia, she co-founded the Eastern Paper Bag Company in Hartford, Connecticut, and supervised her own machine shop in Boston. Between 1871 and 1911, she received 26 patents in her own name and is thought to have contributed to more than fifty inventions patented by others; she also built scores of unpatented devices. Upon her death in 1914, the press lauded her as America's "female Edison."

Among her most successful inventions were an easy-to-install window frame, a number-stamping machine, and a mechanical roasting spit. The humble paper bag, however, remains her greatest contribution to civilization. Even today, bag manufacturers rely on her basic concept.

So the next time you decide to brown-bag your lunch, stop and give thanks to Maggie Knight.

The Genuine Cowgirl Lifestyle

What did cowgirls do in the Old West?

✳ ✳ ✳ ✳

HERE'S ONE THING they didn't do: spend a lot of time chatting with biographers. Although it's generally acknowledged that there were plenty of women whose work was indispensable on the ranches of the American frontier—just like their more glorified male counterparts—their travails are not well documented. It wasn't until the late nineteenth century that cowgirls came into their own, and by then the Old West was fading into history.

The cowgirls who achieved fame in the 1890s did just about everything that the cowboys of the day did: They competed and performed in public, demonstrating their riding, roping, and trick-shooting skills. And that's it. Gone were the days of driving herds across the dusty plains; cowboys and cowgirls had become rough-and-tumble entertainers.

The genuine cowboy lifestyle flourished for only about twenty-five years, from the end of the Civil War in 1865 until around 1890. This is when cattle ranching on the Western frontier was extremely lucrative—it's when small groups of men rounded up herds, watched over them in the open country, and drove them hundreds of miles to railroads so that they could be shipped to cities for butchering. But it didn't last. Farms took over the range; barbed-wire fences enclosed the herds; and ranches were built close to railroads. Consequently, long drives became unnecessary.

Even as the lifestyle was disappearing, the Old West was being romanticized and cowboys were becoming larger-than-life heroes. Their independence and freedom inspired a nation that felt more and more constrained by city life and industrial drudgery. Wild West shows like Buffalo Bill Cody's began to appear—they were hugely popular events in which large casts of performers entertained crowds with trick riding, roping, and other cowboy feats that evoked the rugged freedom of the plains.

And this is where cowgirls first appeared. Although women had carried much of the burden of ranch work in the Old West, they weren't doing the glamorized jobs of the cowboys. But once cowboys became entertainers rather than laborers, talented women could join in the fun.

The most famous cowgirl of her day was Lucille Mulhall. Born in 1885, Mulhall honed her skills while growing up on her family's ranch in Oklahoma. On her way to becoming the women's world champion in roping and tying wild steers, she appeared frequently in her father's Wild West show and was, for a time, the featured performer from an all-star cast in the Miller Brothers' 101 Ranch Real Wild West Show. Will Rogers dubbed her the "world's first cowgirl," which probably came as news to women like Annie Oakley, who had been performing in Wild West shows for years.

Then there was Fannie Sperry Steele, who was born in 1887 in Montana. Steele was a world champion bronc rider and also handled firearms with aplomb. After establishing herself as a rodeo star, she and her husband put together their own touring Wild West show. Steele remained active past age seventy, running a guest ranch in Montana.

Steele lived long enough to see herself immortalized. In 1978, she was inducted into the National Cowgirl Museum and Hall of Fame in Fort Worth, Texas, where what little history there is of cowgirls is lovingly collected and preserved.

King Henry VIII's Children

How many children did he have?

✳   ✳   ✳   ✳

ALTHOUGH HE IS reputed to have had at least one illegitimate child, Henry VIII had only three legitimate ones: Mary, with first wife Catherine of Aragon; Elizabeth, with second wife Anne Boleyn; and Edward, with third wife Jane Seymour. Mary and Elizabeth both had their legitimacy called into question after Henry issued legal proclamations annulling his marriages to their mothers (with the marriages declared invalid, the girls were illegitimate according to law). Elizabeth was legally declared a bastard three times, once even by the pope himself!

Edward became King Edward VI upon Henry's death and ruled for six years (1547–53), until his own death from tuberculosis. Mary became queen in 1553 and ruled until her death five years later. Elizabeth succeeded Mary, remained queen for more than 44 years, and was the last living legitimate child of Henry VIII. It is ironic that the most well known event of Henry's life, his divorce of Catherine and marriage to Anne Boleyn, was partly due to his belief that a woman could not rule England. His two daughters did just that, and the latter was one of the most powerful monarchs in history.

We Know Them...Or Do We?

Q: Why did Lady Godiva become an exhibitionist?

A: Sadly, she didn't—it's a myth. There was a real woman named Godgifu, wife of a powerful Briton in the 11th century, but she had nothing to do with the story about the naked tax protester. Lady Godiva was dreamed up a couple of centuries after Godgifu's death.

Q: How could someone as rich, dashing, and successful as Howard Hughes die a paranoid, disheveled hermit?

A: He started out quite differently—as a young playboy and businessman. Hughes's germ phobia came from his overprotective mother; in those days of deadly epidemics (Hughes was a teen during the flu pandemic of late World War I), it wasn't inherently weird to flee from disease. As he grew older, Hughes became the squire of many popular Hollywood actresses before his social phobia forced him into isolation. He died in 1976 with broken needles embedded in his arms, and at six-foot-four, he weighed only 90 pounds.

Q: If Abner Doubleday didn't invent baseball, who was he?

A: Mainly a distinguished warrior who served in the Mexican War and the Seminole campaign and commanded a division at Gettysburg. Doubleday's obituary didn't even mention baseball. Team owners invented the connection with the national game to discredit baseball's origin in the similar English game of rounders—they wanted people to believe it was 100 percent American.

Q: Was Caligula a depraved monster or not?

A: Not for most of his life, though the last three years (A.D. 38–41) pretty well spoiled his legacy. As a child, he went on military campaigns with his famous father, Germanicus; in his little legionary's uniform, he was the army's beloved mascot. In his first year as emperor (A.D. 37–38), he did some good things for Rome, though he did just about break the treasury. After that, much of what you've heard about his excesses and insanity is credible.

"Lady" Loch Ness

What do Loch Ness and Lake Erie have in common? No, not castles, sheep, or even kilted Highlanders (although Lake Erie has those, too). They are each supposedly a perfect home for sea monsters.

✳ ✳ ✳ ✳

KNOWN OCCASIONALLY AS Lake Erie Larry or the Lake Erie Chomper, the monster in the Great Lake is most often—and affectionately—known as Bessie, short for South Bay Bessie, although no witnesses have ever been able to report definitively about its sex. Bessie has been a regular figure in the lake's mythology for centuries. Even before Europeans settled the area, the Seneca nation told of a "huge water serpent" that patrolled the waters of Lake Erie and the Niagara River.

The Early Sightings

The first recorded sighting occurred on Put-In-Bay's Middle Bass Island in 1793, when a ship's captain described seeing a 16-foot-long serpent in the grass along the shore. Throughout the 19th and 20th centuries, reports of the monster became more common as Lake Erie became an important waterway for trade, transportation, and leisure. During the 1970s (perhaps due to the lake's reputation for pollution), the legends became more widespread, although sightings were less frequent.

Bessie is most often described as a 30- to 40-foot long serpent, with a body circumference of two feet and slippery gray-black skin. One account from 1887 included the detail that the monster had long arms and shed scales the size of silver dollars. Some witnesses claim to have seen humps above the waterline; still others maintain that the monster sports bony plates (like a reptile) rather than fishlike scales. Its eyes are usually described as extremely large (approximately the size of softballs) and placed on the sides of its head, rather than in front.

Believers maintain that Bessie is a prehistoric creature similar to a plesiosaur, but scientists think it is more likely to be a large lake fish. The normally bottom-dwelling sturgeon can grow to be more than seven feet long and weigh more than 300 pounds, but they lack Bessie's distinctive neck. Yet others suggest the phenomenon is not one creature at all, but a school of catfish.

Although many have tried to apprehend the beast, Bessie has managed to evade capture. In 1873, the combination of strange tracks near the Lake Erie shoreline and the disappearance of livestock spurred townspeople to form a posse and search for Bessie, but to no avail. In 1931, a pair of anglers claimed it attacked their boat. After clubbing the beast with their oars, they dragged its body to shore, where it attracted a lot of attention. A scientist from the Cleveland Museum of Natural History finally identified it as the carcass of an Indian python, and the fishers were discovered to be show people from a traveling circus. Even now, a Huron businessman has offered $100,000 to anyone who can bring Bessie in alive. As of this book's publication, the reward remains unclaimed.

Bessie at Large

Although the *Weekly World News* reported in 1993 that the monster attacked a sailboat and killed three people (more reputable sources failed to report on the incident, for whatever reason), encounters with Bessie have been mostly benign. In 2001, three separate swimmers near Port Dover, Ontario, reported being bitten by something while in the water. All three incidents occurred within a day of each other and at the same beach. Doctors who treated the victims couldn't come up with a logical explanation for the identical, six-inch bites, dismissing turtles, lamprey, and other sorts of fish.

The creature was captured once on film, swimming about a mile offshore, and was spotted by a sonar-style "fish finder" as a 35-foot-long snakelike creature, swimming at a depth of 30 feet. The author of a popular cryptozoology Web site, monstertracker.com, has placed web cameras at several of Bessie's favorite haunts and encouraged readers to do the same. Although Bessie has been seen everywhere from Detroit and Windsor in the west to Buffalo and Niagara in the east, sightings are most common along the Ohio shoreline and the nearby islands of Put-in-Bay. Visitors to the shore should keep binoculars and a video recorder handy—just in case Bessie says hello.

Revolutionary Leader Loses His Head

Marie Antoinette may be one of the most famous victims of mob mentality, but during the French Revolution, she was only one of about fifty thousand people who were executed for supposed treason and counter-revolutionary plotting.

❈ ❈ ❈ ❈

ONCE THE DOWNTRODDEN citizens of France were worked into a frenzy about social injustice, the executions committed by the revolutionists became a regular event, with not even women or children spared from witnessing the violence. It was a struggle between the exploited proletariat and the complacent bourgeoisie that erupted into the beheading of oppressors and all of those who spoke out against the revolution.

And the guillotine wasn't the only method used: victims were beaten, faced firing squads, and were thrown from boats with weights tied to them, just to name a few of the other terrors unleashed on counter-revolutionists. Although aristocrats were frequently targeted, they weren't the only victims.

The revolutionists used any arbitrary reason to round up those they felt weren't loyal to their cause. Few of the victims were given fair trials—if any at all. After almost a year of fear and executions, the people started to realize that their revolutionary leader had turned into a murderous fanatic, and in true mob fashion, they solved the problem with one last beheading.

King Henry VIII's Wives

In his quest for a male heir, King Henry VIII married six times. His fourth marriage, to Anne of Cleves (1515–57) in 1540, was primarily for political reasons. Henry was urged to marry Anne to strengthen England's ties with Germany and increase the king's power over Holy Roman Emperor Charles V.

Anne was never actually crowned queen of England, and the marriage was annulled after six months because Henry greatly disliked Anne. She was granted land and continued to live in England as "the King's sister"; she even socialized with the king and his next wife, Catherine Howard. Anne died in 1557, the last of Henry's six wives. She outlived him by ten years.

The following were Henry VIII's other wives:

* Catherine of Aragon, married 1509–33; divorced by Henry

* Anne Boleyn, married 1533–36; executed by Henry

* Jane Seymour, married 1536–37; died after childbirth

* Catherine Howard, married 1540–42; executed by Henry

* Catherine Parr, married 1543–47; widowed by Henry

Maiden Voyage

The spiked sarcophagus of the Iron Maiden was never built to use for torture.

* * * *

COMPETING THEORIES POSIT that the Iron Maiden was originally a simple barrel or sarcophagus without spikes, and that the spikes were added later to increase the spectacle when the Iron Maiden was displayed in traveling shows or museums. It was first invented in the 1300s, a time when there were plenty of other practical ways to torture someone, so the Iron Maiden's use as an *objet d'art* was not any kind of political commentary. If indeed it was just a human-shaped box to imitate the feeling of being buried alive, that was torture enough for anyone placed inside.

But the Iron Maiden has a centuries-long career as a setpiece for villains. It appears in the village detective show *Midsomer Murders* as the weapon of an eccentric rural killer. On *The Great British Bakeoff*, the hosts call any device to punch holes in a cookie a "biscuit Iron Maiden." In America, we probably associate the term with the band Iron Maiden more than the contrived torture device.

The Men Behind the Beheadings

One of the great ironies in history is that Dr. Joseph-Ignace Guillotin was an opponent of capital punishment. But despite the fact that he was the guillotine's namesake, he did not invent it.

✳ ✳ ✳ ✳

How the Guillotine Came to Be

THE INFAMOUS DEATH machine's true creators were Antoine Louis, the French doctor who drew up the initial design around 1792, and Tobias Schmidt, the German piano maker who executed it. (Pun intended.)

Joseph-Ignace Guillotin's contribution came a bit earlier. As a delegate to France's National Assembly of 1789, he proposed the novel idea that if executions could not be banned entirely, the condemned should at least be entitled to a swift and relatively merciful death. What's more, he argued that all criminals, regardless of whether they were rich or poor, should be executed by the same method. This last point may seem obvious, but prior to the French Revolution, wealthy miscreants who were up to be offed could slip executioners a few coins to guarantee speedy dispatches. Poorer ones often went "coach class"— they got to be the coach while horses tied to their arms and legs pulled them in four different directions. What a way to go!

In April 1792, the Assembly used its new guillotine for the first time on a platform in Paris' Place de Grève. Two vertical wooden beams served as runners for the slanted steel blade and stood about fifteen feet high. At the bottom, two boards with a round hole, called the *lunette*, locked the victim's head in place. The blade was hoisted to the top with pulleys and released with a lever. After a few grisly mishaps, executioners learned to grease the grooves on the beams with tallow in order to ensure that no one was left with half a head, which in this case was definitely not better than having none at all.

The Reign of Terror

The first head to roll was that of Nicolas Jacques-Pelletier, a common thief. During the Reign of Terror, from January 1793 to July 1794, more than ten thousand people had an exit interview with "Madame Guillotine," including King Louis XVI and his wife, Marie Antoinette. The daily parade of victims drew crowds of gawkers. Journalists printed programs, vendors sold refreshments, and nearby merchants rented out seats with unobstructed views. This bloody period ended with the execution of Robespierre, one of the Revolution's leaders and an early advocate of the guillotine. France continued to use the guillotine in cases of capital punishment throughout the nineteenth and twentieth centuries. The last official guillotine execution took place on September 10, 1977.

Because they were embarrassed by their association with this instrument of terror, the descendants of Joseph Guillotin petitioned the government to change the name of the machine. The government declined to comply, so the family changed its name instead and passed into obscurity. Not so for the guillotine itself: Though it is now relegated to museums, it remains a grim symbol of power, punishment, and sudden death.

Pride and…Ööps!

Ask the Swedes: For wounded national dignity, it's hard to surpass having your state-of-the-art warship sink in sight of shore—on its maiden voyage!

✳   ✳   ✳   ✳

From Kingdom to Empire

SWEDEN WASN'T ALWAYS famous for neutrality. The early 1600s saw the rise of Sweden, under the leadership of King Gustav II Adolf Vasa, as the strongest Baltic power, with Poland as the primary challenger. In 1625, deploring recent storm losses and damage to the Royal Swedish Navy, His Majesty ordered four new ships of the line. Shipwrights began work on the first, HMS *Vasa*, in late 1625.

Pride and Joy

Vasa took nearly two years to build. No expense was spared. Over a thousand mature oaks went into her construction, with sixty-four bronze cannon. Her masts rose over fifty yards high. Six of the cannon were 'assault guns' meant to fire lethal blasts of scrap metal and grapeshot at close range. She could throw one of the heaviest broadsides of her day.

Vasa was designed not only to usher in a new era of Swedish maritime power, but as an artistic showcase. Her figurehead and stern were intricately carven artworks, painted in bright colors and trimmed with gold leaf. While the royal ego played a part, the baroque display was also intended to awe the opposition with evidence of wealth and power, while inspiring Swedes to patriotic pride.

The King meddled with the design, demanding mid-project changes to the original keel size and armament, all the while badgering the builders to hurry up and finish *Vasa*. The Swedish crown's powers are very limited today, but in 1627 Gustav's word was law. The shipwrights obeyed. But His Majesty should have let his shipwrights do the job their way.

Physics Always Wins

On August 10, 1628, HMS *Vasa* was finally ready to move from the shipyard to its naval base. Only 100 sailors and soldiers were aboard, roughly one quarter of the wartime complement. Some had brought families aboard for the adventure. Crowds lined the docks of Stockholm to watch this symbol of Swedish imperial might make her maiden voyage.

All was fine as the shore crews towed *Vasa* to her sailing point. Guns roared in salute, crowds cheered, and the crew made sail. The costly new battleship caught her first gust of wind, rocked uneasily to port, and then steadied. The second gust heeled her over far enough to submerge her gunports. *Vasa* swiftly sank in only 100 feet of water, settling with her maintop visible barely a hundred yards offshore. Her maiden voyage spanned less than a mile. Those who could do so took to boats or flotsam, and numerous boats rushed out to rescue the passengers and crew, but some forty people drowned.

We Are Not Amused

Luckily, King Gustav wasn't in attendance. When he heard the news, he was understandably furious and demanded an inquest, jailing the captain. Of course, everyone blamed someone else. In the end, the inquest attributed the sinking to God, who received no punishment.

We now know that *Vasa* didn't have enough ballast in the hold to keep her stable, given her high upper gun deck (a mid-construction modification by Gustav). The captain had run a stability test before sailing, showing that rapid weight shifts might capsize her. The shipwright supervising the latter phase of construction had lacked experience with warship design, and the King, no naval architect, had of course altered the original plans.

In 1961, a team of experts succeeded in raising *Vasa*. Thanks to diligent modern restoration work, she has been preserved for future generations. Since 1990, *Vasa* has resided in her own museum in Stockholm, open to the public.

A Day in the Life

Hip, Happening Florence

The wealthy merchants of Renaissance Florence actively cultivated the monumental cultural and intellectual movement that originated in their city. The following fictionalized account offers a glimpse into a day in Renaissance life.

✳   ✳   ✳   ✳

NICOLO PEERS FROM the fifth-story bedroom window of his townhouse overlooking the streets of mid-15th century Florence. It's early morning, and Europe's most vibrant city is jumping. Florence is the epicenter of the Renaissance, the great cultural and intellectual reawakening sweeping Europe. The city-state of 60,000 people is thriving as it sets the tone for Europe commercially, politically, and artistically. And Nicolo, a wealthy Florentine merchant, embarks on another day as the quintessential man of his times.

At Work at Home

Nicolo's home also accommodates his prosperous cloth manufacturing business. Nicolo is a leading member of Florence's influential textile guild, and the goods he produces are among the finest in a city that dominates Europe's cloth industry.

Nicolo spends the morning in the ground-floor store, arranging displays and tending to customers. At mid-morning, he retreats to the fourth floor for the first of the two daily meals Florentines typically eat. He, along with his wife, Leonarda, and their two children eat fruit, salad, cheese, and pasta—a new culinary delight that's all the rage in Florence.

Hanging with the Movers and Shakers

After, Nicolo changes into an outfit befitting a man of his stature. Overtop his green long-sleeve collarless shirt, he wears a burgundy velvet doublet, a long vest belted at the waist to create a skirt effect. White hose leggings and brown leather boots round out the ensemble. He also dons his cioppa, a red, full-length, fur-lined velvet gown worn by influential Florentine men.

Nicolo hires a horse-drawn carriage to take him to the Palazzo Vecchio, where 12 powerful merchant guilds conduct the business of Florence. Here, Nicolo makes his real money as he haggles with other textile merchants, arranging for the purchase of 300 wool bales from England and Spain and sales of finished cloth for export all over Europe.

Later, Nicolo and members of other guilds transform into political powerbrokers. In Florence, those who create the city's wealth also run it, and the 5,000 guild members, led by the powerful de Medici banking clan, provide Florence with an enlightened form of government unseen in Europe since the ancient Greeks—one that emphasizes republicanism, democracy, and the welfare of the city over despotic rule.

Nicolo Gets Cultured

With the day's business done, Nicolo returns home for dinner. As on most days, Nicolo and Leonarda are entertaining. They serve up the usual guest-impressing cuisine: fruit and cake appetizers, a main course featuring roast lamb (only the well-to-do serve meat), a cheese plate, and dessert pastries. After, Nicolo proudly shows off a recently purchased painting by a young emerging local artist named Botticelli. He, like many wealthy Florentines with the money and time to explore the arts, is a devoted patron of the city's flourishing arts scene.

Later, Nicolo reads aloud from Plato's Republic, reflecting on Europe's rediscovery of classic Greek and Latin writings triggered by the humanist movement, the intellectual driving force of the Renaissance. He is enthralled by the humanist philosophy that stresses man's interaction with his world and the idea of determining one's own destiny.

Peace Churches: Anabaptists and Quakers

The Protestant Reformation of the 1500s sent chunks of Christianity, such as Lutherans and Calvinists, flying in all directions. The Anabaptists and Friends represented some of the more radical trends in late medieval Christian thought. Both branches have nourished their core faiths into modern times.

✾ ✾ ✾ ✾

Anabaptists

"ANABAPTIST" MEANS "REBAP- TIZER." In January 1525, a group of young Swiss Christians agreed that Christian faith should be an informed adult decision, not something imposed upon an infant. Anabaptists baptized one another and planned not to baptize their children until they were of age.

Anabaptism spread swiftly throughout German-speaking Europe and the Netherlands, and many of its adherents paid the ultimate price for their "heresy." Amid gruesome persecution and martyrdom, they began to scatter, forming the sects described as follows.

Mennonites

Father Menno Simons, a Dutch Catholic priest, became an Anabaptist in 1536. Soon, his followers began to call themselves Mennonites, and most eventually moved to Prussia and Russia. In the 1870s, they joined the great waves of immigration to the United States. Today, there are some

350,000 Mennonites in the world, two-thirds of them in the United States. They range from communal groups (who practice with varying degrees of strictness) to mainstream urban dwellers who simply happen to attend a Mennonite church.

Amish

By 1693, some Mennonites in Alsace (modern France) felt the movement had lost its way. Under the leadership of Jakob Ammann, they separated to form their own communities removed from worldly influence and corruption. During the following century, Amish groups (along with a few Mennonites and Brethren) started migrating to the Americas. Nearly all of  today's approximately 100,000 Amish live in the United States. Their strict communities are the most conservative of all Anabaptist groups.

Brethren

The story of the German Baptist Brethren begins (not surprisingly) in Germany in 1708 with Alexander Mack. Sr. Mack's congregants embraced many Anabaptist beliefs and found themselves mockingly called "Dunkers" by the general public for their pratice of adult baptism by immersion. By 1740, nearly all had moved to what would soon become the United States; today, there are some 215,000 North American Brethren, mostly in the United States. Some Brethren subgroups are very conservative, others less so.

Hutterites

In 1528, one group of Anabaptists fled to Moravia, taking their name from leader Jakob Hutter. Their efforts to live in communal peace came to naught in Moravia; Hutter himself was burned alive in 1535. In 1770, the small Hutterite remnant fled to Russia. One hundred years after that, the group began a migration to North America, particularly to Canada. Today, they number approximately 24,000. About 70 percent live in Canada's western provinces, pursuing a communal farming lifestyle. As dedicated pacifists, they refuse to fight in any war.

Most Anabaptists today live in North America. Anabaptist diversity is nearly as great as the general diversity of Christianity itself. Less conservative Anabaptists accept government benefits and serve in the military; members of stricter groups do neither (though all pay taxes). Although some use technology in business and agriculture, the conservative Swartzentruber Amish have gone to jail rather than affix modern reflectors to their buggies.

Friends

In the early 1650s, some 60 independent-thinking English Puritans reached a radical conclusion for the day: direct experience of the light of Christ was universally possible regardless of clergy, sacrament, or church. Founded by George Fox, they soon organized as the Religious Society of Friends. Their worship was centered on the Meeting (congregation), where silent prayer was combined with preaching and testimony. Outsiders began calling them Quakers due to their emotional way of trembling when giving their testimony of faith. They believed in pacifism, which they practiced by refusing to cooperate with warlike actions or with leaders who encouraged them.

While the Friends were originally mocked as "Quakers," most today have embraced the term. Oliver Cromwell's Puritans, not known for their warm tolerance or rollicking sense of fun, threw many Friends in jail. From that prison experience stems the longtime Quaker sympathy with inhumane jail conditions—a tradition of social activism that would become, after worship, a second *raison d'être* of the Quaker faith.

By 1656, Friends had begun moving to North America. Unfortunately for them, the Massachusetts Bay Colony, like England, was in Puritan hands. Many Friends were jailed and abused. Most moved to less hostile Colonial areas: Rhode Island, New Jersey, Delaware, Maryland, and especially Pennsylvania. It didn't take long for the plight of the slaves to trouble the collec-

tive Quaker conscience, and Friends were early rejectors of the "peculiar institution." They wouldn't have countenanced war to free slaves, but from the Quaker standpoint, if ever a wrong spawned a right, it was the Civil War, which led to the abolition of slavery.

Most of today's 350,000 Quakers live in the United States and England. Unlike many Anabaptists, Quakers don't live apart from society. You'll find them active in all professions and volunteering in numerous organizations that promote peace and human rights.

A Day in the Life

Working For The Man
In Olde England

An average day for a serf in medieval England involved working land allotted to him by his master, the manor lord. But although his lord giveth, his lord also taketh away, thus relegating him to a life of servitude and poverty. In the following account, we take a look at what a "day in the life" may have been like.

✳   ✳   ✳   ✳

I T'S NOT YET daybreak, but Thomas is getting ready for the workday. Flickering rush-lights illuminate his tiny wood-frame, mud-walled cottage, which is topped with a straw thatched roof—much like the other dwellings in the small, mid-14th century English village Thomas calls home.

Thomas has a bit of oatmeal porridge and his usual breakfast drink—tepid ale poured from an earthenware jug. The same brew will quench Thomas's thirst throughout the day.

At sun up, Thomas, along with his wife and children, trudge to the plots of land allotted to him by the lord of the manor on which Thomas's village is located. Ostensibly, Thomas works the land for himself, but in reality most of the fruits of his labor go to his lord. It's medieval England's version of working for The Man.

Thomas, like more than half of his fellow citizens, is a serf. He is socially and legally indentured to his lord for life, unless he can buy his freedom or his lord grants it.

Slogging Away in Fields of Dreams

The latter isn't likely to happen. So Thomas works his own fields of dreams hoping that his toiling will earn him a ticket to freedom.

Thomas dresses for the hard work ahead: a tattered shirt tucked into well-worn wool breeches; a ragged knee-length hooded coat; thick-soled leather shoes. It is standard serf garb, and Thomas wears it pretty much every day.

First task is weeding and watering the onions, cabbages, beans, leeks, and herbs sprouting in the gardens near the cottage. The two hogs in the cottage-side sty are thrown scraps and waste. The rooster, hens, and geese are fed while eggs are collected.

Next it's off to scratch out a living from the ten half-acre strips of land Thomas holds outside the village. Today, wheat and rye are harvested from the first strip. Thomas cuts the sheaves by hand with a sickle while his wife and children gather them onto an ox-pulled wooden cart that carries the crop home.

Sticking It to The Man

After harvesting, Thomas uses the little remaining daylight to surreptitiously find some necessities at the expense of his lord.

First, he forages for dung, an activity done on the sly since all droppings on manor grounds are the exclusive property of his lord. Then he treks to the woods to poach his lord's forests and streams. Poaching usually involves late-night fishing for eels or salmon, but today Thomas goes to a well-hidden rabbit snare where tonight's dinner struggles vainly to get free. It's his lucky day—meat at supper is an infrequent treat.

Refuge at the Ale House

After dinner, Thomas walks to the village alehouse to escape the monotony of his dreary daily existence. There he spends the evening quaffing ales, socializing, singing, and gambling.

Thomas chats with a mate about the prospect, however bleak, of buying his freedom. What Thomas doesn't know is that freedom will come shortly, but at a terrible cost. The approaching scourge of the Black Plague will quickly wipe out a third of England's population and suddenly make Thomas's labor an extremely valuable commodity. Thomas will soon have the economic leverage he needs to get out from under his lord's thumb.

Julius Caesar: Rome's Greatest Emperor?

The question assumes that Caesar was an emperor. He was powerful, illustrious, famous, and Roman to the core, but he was never an emperor. He couldn't have been, because Rome became an empire after his death, and then only gradually.

✳   ✳   ✳   ✳

GAIUS JULIUS CAESAR was born around 102 B.C. to one of the Roman Republic's noblest patrician families, and he rose swiftly through the military and political ranks:

75 B.C.: Cilician pirates kidnap Caesar for ransom. Their demand of only 20 talents of gold offends Caesar's colossal ego, so he orders the pirates to increase their demand to a more fitting 50 talents.

60: Caesar joins Pompey and Crassus in the First Triumvirate, which dominates Rome for seven years.

51: He completes his conquest of Gaul (modern France and Belgium) for Rome—and his popularity makes the senate nervous.

46: After pummeling Pompey in civil war and fighting his way back to Rome from Egypt, Caesar is elected dictator. Apparently, the senate didn't feel it had much choice.

45–44: The senate votes Caesar frequent and random honors and powers, fawning over him and making him dictator-for-life.

44: Senators rescind the "life" portion of dictator-for-life, using sharp knives. Messy but effective.

Caesar held great power, of course, including privileges that actual emperors would one day hold—all voted to him by the republican senate. The point is that these powers were the senate's to grant. Rome was in transition from republic to empire, and few historians would call Rome of 44 B.C. an empire. Most consider Caesar's great-nephew and adopted heir, Augustus, the first leader whose powers became imperial—and those powers far exceeded Caesar's former offices.

Ghost Towns of The Ancients

It's hard to think of great cities like New York or London ever becoming the ghost towns of future centuries. But many New Yorks and Londons of the ancient world did just that—then kept archeologists and scientists busy for hundreds of years looking for them.

✳ ✳ ✳ ✳

A Wall, a Horse, and a Mystery

MOST PEOPLE HAVE heard of the siege of Troy, that epic battle over a stolen princess that the blind poet Homer immortalized in the Iliad. The image of a "Trojan Horse" has made its way into film, literature, and even computer lingo. But the city that gave us the famed wooden horse faded into legend around 700 B.C. For the next 25 centuries, the city of Troy was dismissed as a fable—an elusive ghost for archeologists and historians.

Details of the real Troy are fragmentary, handed down mostly through Greek myths and Homer's poetry. The city, on the Aegean coast of modern-day Turkey, lay along major trade routes from the Mediterranean to the Black Sea, and it steadily prospered since its Bronze Age founding around 3000 B.C.

As Troy grew wealthy and powerful, its inhabitants protected themselves with massive stone walls. Homer's Troy boasted towers nearly 30 feet high and probably contained around 10,000 inhabitants at the time of the Trojan War. The city rose and fell several times (the last around the end of the 8th century B.C.), and it was rebuilt as a Roman outpost around the time of Christ. The "Roman Troy" remained an important trading center until Constantinople became the capital of the Eastern Roman Empire and traders began to bypass the ancient town. Troy then began its final journey into decline and ruin. By the time Europe emerged from the Dark Ages, the city had been lost to the ages.

But in the 1870s, an eccentric German businessman named Heinrich Schliemann, who had been schooled on the Iliad as a boy, built a small fortune and began searching for the lost city. Over a 19-year period, Schliemann completed several amateur digs around a city that, in due course, yielded nine sites to bear the name "Troy." The seventh "Troy," a city (or succession of cities) from around 1200–1000 B.C., appears to have been destroyed by fire and is the most likely candidate for the Troy of Homer's epic.

Go Tell the Whom?

Today we think of the ancient Greek city of Sparta as the "Spartan" (austere, militant, and culturally empty) counterpart to the more enlightened, democratic Athenian society. But in ancient times, Sparta lay at the "cutting edge" of political and military arts.

Sparta, the capital of the Lacedaemon kingdom on Greece's Ionic coast, inaugurated many idealistic traditions for which the Greek world became famous. It established a democratic assembly years before the Athenians adopted the practice; it allowed women broad rights to own property and attend schools; and it took its religion and art seriously.

After the Greek city-states combined to defeat the Persian invasion of 480 B.C., a rivalry between Sparta and Athens led to the bitter Peloponnesian War (431–403 B.C.). The war ended in Spartan victory, but Sparta's defeat by Thebes 30 years later sent the city into a period of decline. It fell under Roman rule and succumbed to barbarian invasions, ultimately vanishing into ruin before A.D. 400.

In a passage from Thucydides's ancient work *The History of the Peloponnesian War,* the old chronicler muses: "Suppose the city of Sparta to be deserted, and nothing left but the temples and the ground-plan, distant ages would be very unwilling to believe that the power of the Lacodaemonians was at all equal to their fame."

Sure enough, the city left little of its original grandeur for later generations. It was not until some 1,500 years later that serious efforts were made to recover the home of the Spartans. In 1906, the British School at Athens did serious archeological work, discovering a theater, temples, and beautiful examples of early Spartan art, and opening the world's eyes to the cultural world that was Sparta.

Rome: Total War

One of the ancient world's greatest cities had the misfortune of bumping up against the most powerful military force of its time. Set on the North African coast near modern Tunisia's capital city, Tunis, the great city of Carthage was the hub of a Mediterranean trading empire that rivaled that of the later Italian upstarts. This rivalry with Rome produced three great wars of antiquity, called the Punic Wars.

By virtue of its location—south of Sicily on Africa's Mediterranean coast—Carthage, a trading empire founded by the seagoing Phoenician people around 814 B.C., held a dominant position in Mediterranean trade from the 3rd and 2nd centuries B.C. In 264 B.C., Rome and Carthage got dragged by their allies into a war over Sicily. Round One went to the Romans. Two decades later, the Carthaginian general Hannibal led his elephants over the Alps into Italy on a legend-ary campaign of destruction, but the Romans eventually won that one, too.

A half century later, Rome goaded the Carthaginians into a third war. This time, the Roman general Scipio Africanus led a three-year siege of Carthage. After storming the walls and capturing the city, he burned the metropolis to the ground, destroyed Carthaginian ships in the harbor, and sold the populace into slavery. By 146 B.C., the destruction of Carthage was complete.

In the 1st century A.D., the Romans rebuilt the city as a shipping hub, and the "new" Carthage became a major food supplier for the Roman Empire. It remained a center of Roman Christianity until the end of the 7th century, when Arab invaders toppled the city and replicated Scipio's "complete destruction" formula. The city was supplanted by nearby Tunis, and today the ancient capital is a series of ruins in Tunis's suburbs, where archeologists are digging up statues, tombs, and other relics of one of the ancient world's lost empires.

Were Roman Gladiators Condemned by Their Audiences?

Luckily (or unluckily) for the gladiators, their fate was not always left up to the crowd. Such games were often fixed, or the emperor or another powerful figure had the final say in matters of life and death.

Fatal gladiatorial games were actually not as common as is now perceived. Gladiators were expensive to train, so a dead gladiator was usually not in the best interest of anyone. The most gruesome gladiatorial games involved the mass killing of criminals who had already been sentenced to death. In these cases the gladiators were sure to die, regardless of the direction of the crowd's thumbs.

Neanderthal Man

Daily life for Neanderthal man was no picnic, but it wasn't all about clubbing and bludgeoning thy neighbor either. Europe's Ice Age residents were social creatures by nature, which helped make their stark existence tolerable until their disappearance 30,000 years ago. The following depicts what was likely a typical day in the life of a Neanderthal.

✳ ✳ ✳ ✳

DAWN BREAKS, AND a cave on the edge of a forest in prehistoric Europe begins to stir with life. Inside the dark chamber, Neanderthal man rises along with his family and the rest of the communal group of cave dwellers that form the basis of his world. Shucking aside the animal skins that kept him warm during the night, Neanderthal man readies himself for the one everyday activity most critical for the group's survival—the hunt for food.

Bringing Home the Bacon

Neanderthal man gathers with other men and women from the group to embark on the day's hunt. If it's a cold day or if inclement weather looms, he will clad himself in animal skins—being no more hairy than humans are today, he needs to protect himself from the elements. If it's hot and sunny, he'll go completely naked. Modesty is not one of his strong suits.

The hunting party heads into the woods in search of their daily bread, or more accurately, meat. A voracious carnivore, Neanderthal man will eat almost nothing but meat, and in a typical day he'll devour twice the amount of food that his present-day counterpart normally consumes.

Neanderthal man brings with him a short wooden thrusting spear tipped with a sharp-edge stone. As he and his colleagues stalk bears, wolves, deer, wild horses, or cattle, he keeps an eye open for obsidian stones suitable for making highly effective cutting tools. Neanderthal man is an expert tool maker, though not a very innovative one: The stone and wooden tools he has forged will remain basically unchanged throughout 250,000 years of existence.

Taking One for the Team

Today the hunt goes well for Neanderthal man. He and the others have strategically trapped a small herd of deer in a natural enclosure. Together they carry out an ambush-style attack against their quarry, thrusting their spears into the animals' flesh at close range.

Ideally, they would have driven the herd over a cliff or steep embankment to lessen the risk of injury. But Neanderthal man has to get his food while the getting is good, so he braces himself for the blows often accompanying close-quarter hunting—a stiff kick of a hoof, a painful bite, or an unpleasant goring from a pointed antler.

After a brief but frenzied flurry, the animals are subdued. Neanderthal man emerges from the kill bloodied, but the pain from his wounds is tempered by the thrill of a successful hunt and the promise of a full belly tonight.

An Evening of Frivolity

Tired and sore but happy nonetheless, Neanderthal man returns with the hunting party to the communal caves with the evening meal for the group.

The fresh meat is cooked over an open fire, and Neanderthal man and the group dig in. Later, his hunger sated and his spirits soaring, he joins the group in an evening of frivolity and social bonding that includes singing, clapping, dancing, body slapping, and stick banging. The songs mimic birdsongs or other sounds of nature. The melody is nothing like anything we know today, but it's music to his ears.

Before finally falling asleep, Neanderthal man contemplates a way of life that is often harsh, but considerably less brutish than modern stereotypes suggest.

Day in the Life

I, Claudia, Trophy Wife

Upper-class women in ancient Rome weren't expected to do much during the course of an average day—just manage the house, oversee the slaves, educate their daughters, and allow themselves to be put on public display. The following is a fictionalized firsthand account of what a day in the life of an ancient Roman might have been like.

✳   ✳   ✳   ✳

IT IS EARLY morning in ancient Rome. Claudia, matron of her aristocratic household, finishes her breakfast: bread, cheese, dried fruit, and honey. Her husband, a Roman senator, has left for the day. She now assumes her daily role as the consummate 2nd century B.C. Roman wife.

Only 27, Claudia possesses the virtues esteemed Roman men most want in a wife—fertility, impeccable housewifery skills, and loyalty to her man and family. In 12 years of marriage, she has produced five children, and most importantly, three sons. She excels in household management, including supervising the slaves. And as a woman in a staunchly patriarchal society, she accepts her husband's legal and social control of her private life and obligingly dons her public persona as adoring trophy wife.

Developing Future Claudias

During the day, Claudia manages the house and cares for the kids—being a working mom is forbidden for women of Republican Rome's elite. After checking on things and instructing the slaves, she summons her two young daughters. It's time to school the girls in the fine art of being Claudia.

Claudia's sons attend schools outside the home where they learn the classics and martial arts in preparation for political or military careers. The girls are trained at home in how to be the ideal housewife. Today, Claudia teaches them wool working—spinning, sewing, and weaving—skills necessary for every Roman woman.

Claudia takes her daughters' education very seriously. Their performance as wives will be one of the standards by which her success in life will be measured.

Keeping up Appearances

After lessons and a light lunch—generally leftovers—Claudia readies herself for some personal time outside the home.

Even a casual stroll requires getting all dolled up. Claudia puts on an immaculate white stolla, the female version of the ubiquitous toga, which is usually cloaked by a palla. A slave styles her hair, elaborately raised, layered, and accented with cascading ringlets. She bedecks herself in ornate jewelry and accessories. She slips into her calcei, standard leather shoes that typically accompany the stolla.

Claudia leaves escorted by a slave who carries a parasol to shade her from the sun. Her first stop is the luxury goods market for a little shopping. Her slave then totes her purchases home as Claudia makes her way to visit a friend. From there, Claudia stops at the public baths to relax and gossip before heading home.

Claudia on Display

The baths reinvigorate Claudia for tonight's engagement—attendance with her husband at a grand banquet. As with any outing with her husband, Claudia will be on display as the perfect wife. The banquet lasts for hours and becomes a gluttonous affair. A first course of eggs, salads, vegetables, and shellfish is followed by a main course featuring meat ranging from beef, lamb, and pork to wild goat, porpoise, and ostrich. Fruit, cake, and pudding are offered as dessert.

During dinner, Claudia's husband reclines on his left elbow while picking food off the table with his fingers. She remains upright. He downs goblets of wine. She abstains altogether. She is careful not to upstage him in any way.

Her acquiescence earns her the life reward she desires most—a place of reverence in ancient Roman society.

Lords of the Rising Sun

For nearly 800 years, they held the power of life and death in the Heavenly Kingdom. The supreme lords of the samurai, they were called shogun.

✳   ✳   ✳   ✳

The Rise of the Shogun

SINCE ANCIENT TIMES, the title *sei-i taishogun*, or "great general who subdues barbarians," had been awarded to the highest military officers recognized by Japan's imperial court at Kyoto. But in A.D. 1184, the title took on a new, more powerful meaning. That year, General Minamoto Yoritomo wrested power from the emperor during a brutal civil war. Thus was born the shogunate, a period in which the emperor retained formal power—as mandated by heaven—but where the real power lay with the shogun (the short form of *sei-i taishogun*) and his administrators.

Two great houses nominally ruled a patchwork of warring feudal provinces from 1192 to 1600, when one climactic battle settled Japan's affairs for the next two and a half centuries. At the Battle of Sekigahara, nearly 150,000 samurai, retainers, musketeers, and men-at-arms viciously fought against one another in two rival factions. In a bloody day of fighting, General Tokugawa Ieyasu destroyed his rivals and emerged as master of Japan.

Tokugawa established the Tokugawa shogunate at Edo (now called Tokyo) and began his reign by redistributing lands and political power among his most loyal vassals. Two years after taking office, he abdicated, putting into practice the Japanese custom of officially retiring, but sharing the governing of the country with his son, Hidetada. Hidetada and his successors consolidated the shogun's authority, and the Tokugawa dynasty survived as the dominant Japanese government until 1868.

Rule by the Sword

The Tokugawa ruled Japan with an iron fist. Its early governors banned Christianity along with other Western influences. They established a formal caste system that placed samurai, the warrior class akin to Western knights, at the top of the hierarchy, followed by farmers, artisans, and merchants. The great han, or provinces (akin to European duchies), were ruled by the daimyo, powerful nobles who were required to live at the Edo court every other year and keep their family members in Edo when they spent their alternating years at home.

In the late 1630s to early 1640s, the Tokugawa imposed sharp limitations on foreign business and immigration that created an insular kingdom, little known to the outside world until the turbulent 19th century. As a result of this strict control, Japan grew up in isolation, creating new forms of philosophy, poetry, and literature within its borders and promoting trade almost exclusively within the kingdom.

The shogunate system was efficient but inflexible and fostered a groundswell of local dissent that percolated under the surface during its 264-year reign. Lower classes chafed at the impossibi-lity of advancement on merit, while the business class became frustrated by the shogun's monopoly on foreign trade.

Breaking the Sword

In the mid-1800s, foreign powers pushed Japan into accepting the outside world. In 1853, Commodore Matthew Perry led a U.S. naval squadron into Tokyo Bay in a dramatic display of American military might, and the following year coerced the shogun into opening diplomatic relations with the United States. As foreign powers forced the shogunate to open its borders, Japanese liberals began pressing for a restoration of the emperor's powers. The last Tokugawa shogun abdicated his throne in November 1867, and civil war broke out between forces backing Emperor Meiji and those of the former shogun. The Boshin War, or "War of the Year of the Dragon," ended in early 1869 with the destruction of the emperor's foes, many of whom met their ends in the ancient suicide ritual of seppuku.

The age of the mighty shogun had ended.

Brains and Brawn

The Olympic Games haven't always featured athletics alone. Relive the era when pens carried as much weight as the pentathlon and a gold-medal performance was measured in both breaststrokes and brushstrokes.

✳ ✳ ✳ ✳

TODAY'S OLYMPIC GAMES feature sports exclusively, but there was a time when artists competed for gold medals alongside runners, swimmers, and discus throwers. Cultural events ran side-by-side with athletics during both the ancient and modern Olympics. But because the most recent edition of these "brain" games took place just prior to the television era, knowledge of them is limited.

Herodotus the Hurtler?

Records are scarce, but it appears that the first competitor in this artistic free-for-all was the writer Herodotus. Competing in 444 B.C. at Olympia, Greece, the athlete participated in both writing and sporting contests. His pairing of brains and brawn would represent the ideal throughout much of the ancient era.

After a 1,500-plus-year hiatus, the Olympics made a comeback in 1896. International Olympic Committee founder Pierre de Coubertin lobbied to reinstate the cultural element into the modern games. His wish became reality at the 1912 Stockholm Olympics.

A Slow Start

The roster of events at that meet included architecture, painting, sculpture, music, and literature. Despite its historic nature, turnout was disappointing—only 35 artists entered the competition.

The 1928 Amsterdam Olympics represented the height of artistic participation. More than 1,000 works were entered, and organizers permitted artists to sell them at the competition's end. This move, though well intended, violated the IOC's stance on amateurism. Following the 1948 games, an IOC report concluded that most artistic contestants were receiving money for their works and recommended that such competition be abolished.

Wisconsin's Federal Fearmonger

Wisconsin has produced many notable U.S. senators, but the state also claims one very infamous senator, Joseph Raymond McCarthy, best known for his sensational communist witch hunt.

✳ ✳ ✳ ✳

A Promising Youth

BORN TO A farming family in rural Grand Chute on November 15, 1908, McCarthy was a bright but restless youngster. He dropped out of school after graduating from eighth grade and started his own chicken farm. Unfortunately, his birds fell victim to disease, and at the age of 20, McCarthy went back to school.

Somehow, he crammed an entire high school education into nine months, while also managing a grocery store in Manawa. He earned such stellar grades that Marquette University accepted him as a law student. At Marquette, he was known as "Smiling Joe" for his good humor and became a champion middleweight boxer, often felling larger opponents with his high-energy fighting style. McCarthy was so good that he even considered making a career in the ring, but a local boxing instructor talked him into getting his degree instead.

Throwing his energy into school, McCarthy dove into campus debate clubs where he proved he could be as much of a pit bull with his words as he was with boxing. After graduating in 1935, he became a lawyer in the small towns of Waupaca and Shawano and, by age 30, was elected judge in Wisconsin's Tenth Judicial Circuit.

Serving His Country

McCarthy put his legal practice on hold to join the Marines in 1942 and serve in World War II. He was an intelligence officer in the South Pacific and saw action as part of a bombing raid crew, which earned him a second nickname, "Tailgunner Joe."

McCarthy would later falsely say he carried ten pounds of shrapnel in his leg, but in truth, he returned to Wisconsin unscathed and determined to regain his circuit judgeship. In 1946, he dared to run for the Republican candidacy for the U.S. Senate against the popular 21-year incumbent, Robert M. LaFollette Jr. McCarthy barely squeaked through to win the nomination and became the youngest U.S. Senator at that time at age 38.

The Beginning of the End

The 1950 Senate election may have spurred McCarthy's monumental decline. Perhaps grasping for a campaign issue, McCarthy made the shocking claim that he had a list of 205 government officials who were communists. The government's House Un-American Activities Committee had already paved the way for such suspicion with its investigations of the Hollywood entertainment industry starting in 1947. The Senate opened hearings on McCarthy's allegations in March 1950, but McCarthy never proved his case. In 1952, the Senate turned the tables and began investigating McCarthy.

Although the committee found him guilty of unethical actions, his loyal base still reelected him in 1952. Ironically, McCarthy was made Chairman of the Committee on Government Operations and Investigations. "Tailgunner Joe" kept looking for communists, even going so far as to accuse the U.S. Army and the Eisenhower presidential administration. However, hearings broadcast via the new medium of television in 1954 helped discredit McCarthy. By December of that year, he was officially condemned by the Senate for abuse of power. He finished the two and a half years of his term, largely powerless and unpopular. At the same time, McCarthy began to drink heavily and suffered various physical ailments.

McCarthy succumbed to hepatitis on May 2, 1957. His grave in Appleton's St. Mary's Cemetery is marked by a gray granite headstone that simply reads "United States Senator." He left behind a wife, Jean, an adopted daughter, Tierney, and a new word that's still in use: "McCarthyism." Thanks to this term, Joseph McCarthy's name will forever be associated with the act of aggressively hunting for certain people based on unsubstantiated charges.

A Day in the Life

Rural 1920s America

The mechanization of American agriculture during the Roaring Twenties created a good news-bad news scenario for small farmers. The following account explores what "a day in the life" might have been like.

✳ ✳ ✳ ✳

IT'S SHORTLY AFTER sunrise on a July day in Nebraska. Hollis stands by the roadside watching a billowing dust cloud rumble its way toward his 30-acre family farm.

It's 1925, and the cloud is bringing another dose of modernity to Hollis's farm in the form of a big, noisy, steam-driven threshing machine.

Modernity first arrived last year when Hollis partnered with four fellow farmers to buy a gasoline-powered tractor. The tractor was a godsend. It plows an acre three times faster than his five horses did. Now the ten acres of land he previously used to grow horse feed yield cash crops instead. The tractor pulls the seeder, manure spreader, and binder (which cuts and bundles wheat stalks)—other machines that have reduced Hollis's dependence on paid labor.

Today, the thresher will separate wheat kernels from their stalks in a fraction of the time it takes a gang of workers to do it by hand.

A Social Gathering Hard at Work

Threshing season is as much a social gathering as it is work. Area farmers band together to work each other's farms using the same thresher. Meanwhile, the women prepare home-cooked feasts.

Hollis and the men gravitate to the thresher as it chugs into the field. Clad in ubiquitous denim overalls, short-sleeved shirts, and wide-brimmed hats, they feed bundles of dried wheat into the thresher. The machine spits out straw collected for livestock bedding and shoots grain through a spout into a wagon hitched to Hollis's tractor.

Meanwhile, the women butcher chickens, cook, and set up tables and chairs. Kids tote sandwiches and cold well water to the men.

The women will lay out gigantic spreads at mid-morning, noon, and late afternoon. Platters of fried chicken, ham, home-made bread and biscuits, butter, jams and preserves, mashed potatoes, vegetables, pies, cakes, iced tea, and lemonade are gobbled up.

At 7 P.M. the works stops, and everyone heads home. The pattern will be repeated on Hollis's farm over the next several days.

More Signs of the Times

Exhausted, Hollis leans against another machine transforming American rural life: his 1920 Ford Model T pickup truck. The vehicle enables his family to make daily visits to town, whether it's to sell produce at the market, visit friends, attend a baseball game or church social, or see a movie at the brand-new movie house. The pickup truck has ended their isolation from the outside world.

Tonight, however, Hollis is too tired for any of that, choosing to stay home and listen to his battery-powered radio. Sandwiched between music programs is a broadcast from the U.S. Department of Agriculture offering weather and market reports.

Hollis grimaces as the crackling radio voice warns of lower wheat, oat, and corn prices this fall.

Earning Less for More

Although technology is helping Hollis produce more than ever, he's finding this is not necessarily a good thing.

Food production in the United States is now outpacing demand, causing steadily declining commodity prices. Hollis is producing more but earning less. He's swimming in debt from buying new machines. He's hoping to eke out a profit this year—hoping.

Many small farmers have already succumbed to this cruel irony and have sold their farms, joining the exodus of people leaving rural America for the cities during the 1920s. But Hollis doesn't want to leave. As upbeat ragtime music blares from the radio, he somberly wonders how much longer he can hold out.

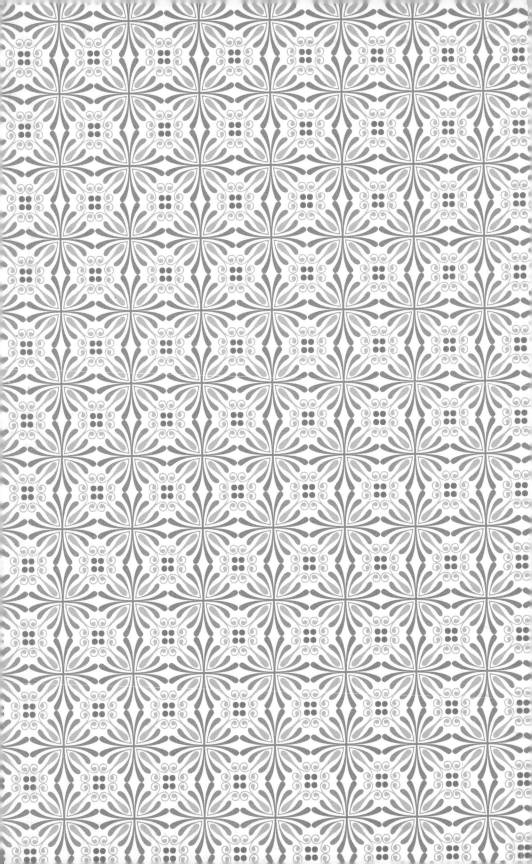